FAST GUYS, RICH GUYS AND IDIOTS

SEPTEMBER PRESS

September Press, Inc.
P.O. Box 584
Jamestown, RI 02835

Library of Congress Cataloging-in-Publication Data

Moses, Sam, 1947-

Fast guys, rich guys, and idiots.
1. Automobile racing.   II. Title.

GV1029 M6175   1986   796.7'2   86-60155

ISBN   0-937159-09-3

FIRST EDITION

10   9   8   7   6   5   4   3   2   1

For my parents

My deepest appreciation to Gil Rogin for his faith and indulgence; to Jerry Tax, my unfair advantage, for his wisdom, experience and generosity; and to Bob Brown for his idea, and for covering for me.

Special thanks to Frances, Alex, David, Andrew and Anna Gray, for moral support when I needed it most. And to John and Jean Cole, for accommodations, advice, proofreading, catering and warmth.

FAST GUYS, RICH GUYS AND IDIOTS

Sam Moses

Contents

Mark Yeager

PART I

Chapter One

George Tiedemann

Chasing Rabbits

I might have known what I was in for, when I finished my first race sliding backward. And I should have realized that things would be complicated, from the strange range and combination of the day's emotions. But my feet were off the ground. And they would stay there, sweeping me away, until long after the last race.

It was spring in the lush hills of the Deep South: Dateline May 23, Flowery Branch, Georgia. I was behind the wheel of a Volkswagen Rabbit on the lovely and rolling Road Atlanta circuit, a "driver's course," it's said. There were 30 other Rabbits in the race, but their drivers were anonymous to me since I allowed them no identity, for fear such familiarity might slow me down. On the first ethereal lap the cars ahead of me were a whipping ribbon in my windshield, like a rainbow stunt-kite darting against the sky. By the second lap I was swerving into the dirt to pass people. On the third lap my heart pounced on my throat when a yellow Rabbit suddenly appeared sideways in my path at the bottom of the downhill esses; I missed it by inches. I became the tail of a seven-car draft, and speeding down the long backstraight, which was capped by an acrobatic roll — dip, twist, climb, turn and dive — my Rabbit was the crack of a big steel whip. A dark brown Rabbit in the center of the draft, the weak one, was being ruthlessly nipped at by the others, and I wanted my turn. A red Rabbit crept up on my tailgate, bound for revenge since it was he whom I'd passed in the dirt, after he'd braked to avoid a spinning white Rabbit which I'd passed in the same dusty stroke. When I heard red Rabbit's thump on my rear fender, I knew I was going into a spin. A few laps later it began to rain, and now I knew I was in trouble since I'd started the race with bald tires, gambling on a dry track. I was washed away in a turn called the Caroussel, and slid dreamily to the right, at full lock; the left, at full lock; back to center and over the edge, glissading in slick grass down, down, down to the woods. Near the end of the race I passed a white Rabbit with delicate black striping, scrunched on its roof at the end of a messy trail of red clay. On the first turn of the last lap I had a collision with a black-and-mustard Rabbit, knocking it off the track. Its driver, who had been in second place and lapping me, owned the very Rabbit I was in — #1 no less, with a black hood that made it feel all black. In the final turn, a 70-mph sweep right, lurking at the bottom of the rollercoaster backstraight and shooting the cars at the finish line, my car began its final slide. It went gently, even gracefully, in cahoots with the smooth tires on the slimy track. The flagman, perched in a box over the finish line, drifted across my windshield as the car rotated 90 degrees and showed its trunk to the drizzly stands. Staking its claim to infamy, my Rabbit performed another quarter-twist, and its rear bumper took the checkered flag.

The first race was like the next two years, and now it seems as if it had been some cosmic message.

* * *

The race was the second of nine in the Rabbit/Bilstein Cup, a series sponsored by Volkswagen of America and the Bilstein shock absorber company. The Rabbits were the opening act at Sports Car Club of America (SCCA) events featuring more powerful cars, and they often stole the show. Many of the drivers were veterans and few modifications were permitted, which made competition skintight; one year, the cumulative margin between first and second for the entire season was only 4.2 seconds. The fast guys fought for inches as if they were emeralds, and they knew all the tricks. They drafted at 110 miles an hour on the straights, lightly whumping each other's bumpers to go faster, and banged fenders for position in the curves, where the cars' front-wheel-drive raised the inside rear wheel, as if the Rabbit were a dog. Spectators at the Road Atlanta hairpin watched colorful rows of them slide by on three wheels, then steam away down the backstraight like trains.

Two months earlier I'd attended the British School of Motor Racing in Riverside, California, and the week before the Rabbit race I'd taken the Road Atlanta Driving School. I liked my instructor there, Doc Bundy, a lot. He was a professional race-driver who couldn't make a living at it yet, so he taught at Road Atlanta, a position which was a perfect hub for his career operations. Doc was smart, and had been around. The things he said about racing made sense. The secret to fast driving is to let the car do what it wants, he said.

By the end of the rainy three-day course I'd adopted him as my mentor. I never informed him of this, but he didn't shoo me away. I stayed for two more days, and he let me race around Road Atlanta in my Hertz Rabbit until I'd frazzled the tires and his nerves. He tried not to watch the lifting of the rental car's rear wheel through the final turn at 70 miles an hour.

My #1 racing Rabbit was also a rental car, of sorts. It was owned by the Hacker brothers, Paul and Karl, who had finished one-two in the series the previous year as well as one-two in the opening race this season at Charlotte. Paul was the team's manager and Karl was the crew chief. They squeezed a profit out of their operation, a divine rarity in racing, by working hard and cutting corners. Back at the shop in upstate New York it was usually just the two of them, and if they took a mechanic to a race he'd have to be willing to sleep in the truck. For $1,000 plus the prize money, they sometimes prepared and rented out a third — and occasionally a fourth — Rabbit. When I was introduced to Paul at Road Atlanta, he said that #1 had been towed down from New York by #15, which was also rented. I chuckled, assuming he was joking. But there they were, the two racecars, parked outside the Road Atlanta office, tethered by a towbar. Number 1 was crammed with tools, oil and spare tires, and a rusty old exhaust pipe snaked across the pile of things.

The Hackers had been regulars in the series for four years, and were its bad boys. They called themselves the "Hacker Express," and their own cars were #0 and #00. They drove as a team against the field when necessary, towing each other with drafts and running interference for each other. They reminded me of the goony brothers in "Slap Shot," a perception invited by Paul's pugnacity and his bald, egg-shaped head, ornamented with eyeglasses. Paul was known for his unorthodox lines through the turns, as well as the speed he could squeeze out of them, and for his perpetual claim to right of way. Mini-feuds with fellow drivers and debates with officials drafted him from track to track. His latest complaint — a valid one — was with the SCCA for their failure to fully appreciate the show that the Rabbits (especially the Hacker Express) put on.

All the cars in the series used Goodyear Eagle NCT radials, which were shaved of half their tread since a smooth tire puts more rubber on the road, which improves traction and cornering as long as the road is dry. The Hackers had provided #1 with a new set of Eagles, which needed a routine scuffing of about 50 miles, but I'd already missed most of Friday's practice because a new clutch was being installed, and by qualifying on Saturday afternoon I still hadn't gotten enough laps on the track to rub the tires dull. I qualified 17th at 1:56.4, while the pole sitter, Gary Benson, three-time champion of the series, set a track record 1:53.2. I figured the tires cost me a second or more. I grumbled to Paul, but somebody had to have the new tires and it wasn't going to be him or Karl.

I wasn't particularly pleased with 17th, but another driver had told me that I was "the talk of the paddock" — so quick and aggressive for a first-timer. I liked hearing that, but still denied my competitors any identity. During qualifying a driver had stuffed his steel-gray Rabbit under mine in a turn, and when I gave him room I discovered I didn't have enough for myself and ran off the road. He apologized afterward, approaching as I sat on the rail of a fence next to my car. He seemed nice enough, although I don't know whether the apology was genuine; he might have been testing me both on the track and now. "Did I screw up?" he asked. "Don't worry about it," I replied. "I'm glad it happened. I learned a lesson. It was my mistake for giving you the room. It won't happen again." He seemed somewhat stunned.

I'd been counting on the five days with Doc Bundy to be my secret weapon, but now, after so little practice, they looked as if they would be my only experience. The last thing I needed was a disadvantage such as tires. So early Sunday morning, I picked through the team's spares and found four bald rejects. Paul said I could use them...if I really wanted to. On the grid before the start I checked everybody's tires and mine were the only bald ones, which made me feel better.

It was hot, loud and tinny in the car. For six or eight of the 20 laps

I held my own and gained some. There was never any space around me — Rabbits in my way, Rabbits down my neck — and I was swept along by the train. There was an occasional whack on a fender or smack from behind, and the harassment was taking my breath away. I moved up to 13th, passing a light blue Rabbit leaving the track in a cloud of red dust. I was beyond the fringe of the fast guys — I could see about eight cars ahead, but the leaders were long gone. Most of the time I was on the tail of the white Rabbit with the delicate black striping, whose driver's name was Spider. Then that opportunistic red Rabbit punted me out of the way, and the next time I saw Spider, he was crawling through the web in his upside-down window.

My spin had cost four or five positions, and I'd worked back up to about 15th when a light rain began falling. The dark clouds had swept in from behind the Caroussel, a banked and looping turn at the top far corner of the circuit. I nearly lost control there on the second or third wet lap, and the slide impressed me with the hopelessness of my tires. Unfortunately, it wasn't a lasting impression; on the next lap, I sped toward the Caroussel even faster. I had forgotten it was raining.

It came to me about 40 yards too late. I pounced on the brakes and the dreaded and predictable occurred: The car hydroplaned, as my bald tires floated on their own thin layer of water. I see why they call the turn the Caroussel, now. The Rabbit skated in slow motion, perpendicular to the track one way and then the other, as if it were waving goodbye to the fans. They gleefully watched it disappear over a grassy slope, where it gathered speed as it slithered toward the woods. It stopped where the grass ended, the front bumper nudging a tree. At first I couldn't get away from the tree as the tires whirred in reverse, but I made the Rabbit squirm and got turned around. Then I couldn't get back up to the track, until I traversed the hill. As I emerged, some stragglers who had lost the train were passing.

After three spins (I haven't mentioned the third because I couldn't squeeze it in; it was in the downhill esses on the first rainy lap, and left me briefly facing slithering traffic and holding my breath), and with the rain falling harder now, I was merely trying to survive the final few laps. I could hear Doc's voice saying that it was important not to blow the first race. On the next-to-last lap, the big "0" on Paul Hacker's mustard hood appeared in my mirror. The leader, Gary Benson, had just lapped me, and Hacker was chasing him. Hacker was in my draft as we began the final lap, speeding down the front straight toward the first turn, a third-gear right-hander bending up a hill that rolled out of sight. I wanted to help my teammate so I backed off early, giving him time to pass and expecting him to. When he didn't, I cut for the apex. I suppose I could have tried to stay wide in the turn, but I never considered it. I was trying to let the car do what it wanted, and it wanted to use every inch of the track.

Hacker dive-bombed the turn, squeezing down the inside and heading me off at the apex, filling my windshield so suddenly that it startled me. Our trajectories were different: I was pointed toward the apex, and he was pointed only he knows where (he had suggested that I use his line there, and when I tried it I'd thought it was crazy). I stabbed my brakes, but still hit the back of his car; he says it was the quarter-panel and I thought it was the tailgate, but who's to quibble. I didn't think the contact was that hard, but his car shot straight off the track as if it were a cue ball and I was the stick. I accelerated up the hill and away from the scene, carrying the image of his skidding Rabbit and thinking, "Better him than me."

On the 20th lap the track looked like a combat zone; Rabbits were spinning and spun all over the place. As I was ejected by Turn 12 for the final time, and the car kept sweeping right when it was supposed to go straight, I couldn't believe it — *not again*. But as I slid down the front straight sideways — "Just like the 'Dukes of Hazzard,'" a spectator would say — I was aware of what a grandstand finish I was in the middle of. I was a promoter's dream. The chief steward would tell me that I did a great job of controlling the slide. "Thank you," I said.

I returned to the paddock and parked, elated over finishing — and it had been so *thrilling*. Cascading adrenaline carried me away, flitting and jabbering. Soon Hacker came ka-thumping in on a flat tire and with a bashed rear end; after I'd left him, he looped in the mud and whacked the guardrail tail-first. He got going again and finished third, but he was mad. He pulled up to me, glared through the nylon net in his window, and queried sarcastically, "What *happened*, Sam?" I didn't know how to answer. I wanted to ask him the same thing.

He got out and stormed away, but came back a few minutes later and said that between the damage to #0 and the lost prize money, I had cost him $1,000. He added that I had choked, couldn't handle it, should never get in a racecar again, was a tight-ass, drove like an asshole...things like that. His outburst wasn't very convincing, but I still wanted to punch him. I think the only thing that stopped me was that I could already hear the anecdote; the circumstantial evidence was not in my favor. But I'm not used to being called such names at close quarters, and I do have some pride, so I had to will my fist to stay at my side. I turned away, took about five paces and a deep breath, told myself, "Don't hit him, don't hit him," walked back, gritted my teeth and glared in his face, called him a dirty name back, and said that I was willing to talk about it if he wanted to, but not take any more abuse. I pointed out that he knew it was my first race, knew my line in the turn, knew that my tires were bald, and had nothing to gain by passing in that tight spot anyhow, since he couldn't have caught Benson. I might also have reminded him of the unwritten rule that says it's a passer's responsibility to avoid a collision. I told him that if I were him, I'd be cursing myself.

He was no more convinced of my arguments than I was of his, of course, but at least I was able to walk away. I thanked his two mechanics and gave the one who had worked on my car $20 and went off looking for Doc, who had driven in the Trans-Am race and had crashed his Porsche 924 Turbo on the second lap when his brakes had failed.

I believed in my relative innocence in the fender-bender, but Hacker's tirade was shocking enough to make me wonder. Had the incident uncovered something important about driving that I was ignorant of? Maybe a driver is supposed to be able to watch his mirror as he steers into a turn. Or maybe I hadn't given him as much time to pass as I thought I had, and then took my eyes off the mirror too soon. Maybe I shouldn't even have tried to make it easy for him to pass; had he not been my teammate, I wouldn't have.

The whole incident had been witnessed by the driver following Hacker, Don Knowles. Knowles was known for being particularly rational — he was an EPA scientist — and was generally considered the best front-wheel-drive racer in the country. Doc suggested that I ask Knowles how he had seen it. Knowles stopped to talk to someone as he was pulling away from the paddock — I recognized him by his name on the door of the Rabbit on his trailer — and I could have asked him then. But I didn't want to risk finding out I was wrong, and didn't want to allow myself the doubt anyhow. I watched him drive away.

I never spoke to Hacker again, and no one else said I'd blundered, so I didn't worry much more about it. But I still wondered — for a year. Then, at another race, I met Knowles and asked him. He said he'd seen the collision coming. "I couldn't believe Hacker made that move," he said. "I said to myself, 'Don't tell me that stupid twit is going to try to pass there.'"

After the race was over, after everyone else had gone home, I didn't know where to go or what to do. So I continued speeding, south to the Atlanta airport, around anything on the interstate that got in my way; it was a post-race dash that would become familiar. I flew to New York City, which wasn't home but on the way. On the plane the realization that I'd finished 23rd out of 31 washed over me like a wave — a 20-foot tube, wiping me out. *Twenty-third.* My failure depressed me horribly. I'd committed brain-fade, the worst of all lapses behind the wheel. Forgot it was raining! The other spins were less costly; it was the wayward ride in the Caroussel that had caused the 23rd-place finish. I remained fiercely glum all the way to New York.

The adrenaline rushed back in the LaGuardia terminal, as if the plane had landed without me. I went straight to my office and fiddled at my desk, wired, thinking at 90 miles an hour. Disappointment began to creep back — I imagined it a monster outside the door, lurking in the dark Time-Life Building in the middle of the night — but I talked myself out of it, into the tape recorder that would be my diary and therapist on this odyssey. Just before I submitted to good sense and checked into a hotel, I decided to give myself a break and recognize the achievement, even it if wasn't good enough for me. It had been a professional race in a hard-contested series, on a circuit known for its demands. I'd never driven a racecar in traffic before qualifying, and had gained ground in the race until I was bumped off by a driver who recognized my vulnerability. I had skimmed the watery surface and survived. Twenty-third place remained an unimpressive statistic —the hard part was knowing I'd have to reply, "Twenty-third," when asked how I'd done — and the brain fade made me sick, but all things considered, it had been some debut. Then I slept, and woke up four hours later as wired as I'd been the night before, and stayed that way for two more days. The rush would only lull and taper, for the next two years.

They were merely colors to me.

Karl and Paul, the Hacker Express.

The last time I saw Spider, he was crawling out of the web in his upside-down Rabbit — safely.

Chapter Two

John Gacioch

In the Dark

My mother once told me that she would never try marijuana because she was afraid she might like it too much. I know how she feels. For 25 years I'd been around motor racing, from the day my father took me to his own first race through seven years of writing about it for *Sports Illustrated*. And although I'd raced karts and motorcycles, I had always resisted getting behind the wheel of a racecar. It drew me too well.

Speed must have always been in my blood. It started to stir when I was nine, when Dad carried me away to the Giant's Despair Hillclimb in Wilkes-Barre, Pennsylvania, where he had entered his silver AC Bristol, which he called the "Ace." We drove there at night and I curled up on the floor, resting my head on the edge of the leather bucket seat. Light from the instrument panel gave the interior a dim glow, and the heater warmed my cozy cubicle. It felt secure there, even though I knew we were speeding. I could feel the hum and vibration of the engine, and I loved the way it revved as my father shifted through the gears. He used to say that the Ace was the sweetest car he'd ever owned.

I raced karts when I was 13 and 14. Dad bought the black Yazoo chassis and I bought the yellow McCulloch engine (skipping lunch to save 30 cents on the way to $100 was agonizing). It was a fast kart, but it never ran long enough for me to learn how to drive it fast. I was a clumsy mechanic; impatient and lacking guidance (my father was "guilty of golf," to use a Mencken expression), I spent countless frustrating hours fixing something simple that would inevitably break again. Because of the kart's record, the glib young teenager named it "Never on Sunday," after the movie that was popular at the time.

When I was 15 I began hanging out with the hot-rodders, whose company was more exciting than that of the in-crowd. I was the youngest member of a loose band we called "Revvin' Four-Eleven" (4.11 was a rear-axle gear ratio), whose uniform was a black corduroy jacket, across the back of which was a slingshot dragster belching orange flames. The jacket was the badge of an outlaw, which I aspired to be in high school, most of which I cut. My hero was Bill McCloskey, who was about 35 and the leader of the pack. The toughest and fastest, he drove a black 426 Dodge Hemi. He liked me because I never said much, but was always there. I'd hitchhike to the custard stand where we gathered on summer nights, and when it closed at 11 p.m. we'd go racing on back roads. A couple of times the police broke up our action; cars split from the scene as we scattered into the woods. If my parents ever knew where I'd been — I suspect they might have — they never said anything because they trusted my instincts. That fall I got my driver's license, and a couple of Sundays later sneaked Mom's Jeep Wagoneer to the dragstrip at Hagerstown, Maryland. The next day my father heard about it in the barber shop — word of my four-wheel-drive holeshots, which was carried back by my buddies, had travelled fast around our small town. But Dad never said anything about that, either; he was probably secretly tickled. Chip off the old block.

The summer after high school I began racing motorcycles. My first race was on an 80cc Yamaha at Watkins Glen, which was like racing a beetle around a golf course. By the time I was 23, a swabbie stationed in San Diego, I'd moved up to a 750cc BSA, which could do 155 miles an hour. I raced it at Daytona in 1971; the chain, which was the last thing I had adjusted before the race, fell off on the 10th lap.

Four years later I was hired by *Sports Illustrated*. I got occasional offers to sample the racing cars I wrote about, but rejected them. I couldn't see the point in driving a racecar — not even on a demo run —if you couldn't drive it well. And I'd learned a few things about racing since that night in the Ace, in particular how much time and money it demanded. Speed may have infected my blood, but racing seemed like a fruitless pursuit for anyone who wasn't either very rich or prepared to devote his life to it. And, as with my mother and marijuana, I was afraid to find out what I was missing.

Until duty called. Bob Brown, my editor at *SI*, suggested I get a license, "compete some," and write about whatever happened. If he'd only known. He sent me off to the Jim Russell British School of Motor Racing, at Riverside Raceway in California. My athletic style has never been very relaxed, but when I was strapped deep into the cockpit of the open-wheeled Formula Ford, bending through Riverside's bumpy esses at more than 100 miles an hour, I was so loose that I had to remind myself to grip the steering wheel. And when the instructor had told the students to get in the cars for each session, I was usually already there. Harness cinched and helmet buckled, I was enclosed in a world of my own eager anticipation. It felt as secure as the floor of the Ace.

* * *

The details of the Road Atlanta race were fuzzy the moment they were past, which troubled me. I worried that I'd been seduced or stimulated into a daze, which would have been an unwelcome sign that my concentration wasn't up to the task. But Doc said that the same thing sometimes happened to him. He liked to think it wasn't a lack of concentration, but an abundance of it. He called it a "cavern of concentration" — sometimes he talks like that. He said that it might explain how I could have forgotten it was raining.

Doc's real name was Harry, but his grandfather hadn't liked that so he called the baby "Doc Henry," half of which stuck. He was 5'11½" and lean, and had a moustache that he'd recently been offered $300 to shave for a role as an extra in a commercial, but he told them no way. "A spontaneous and effervescent sort, the 37-year-old Bundy is sometimes perceived as being a bit relaxed for a fellow who regularly drives at speeds of 200mph," said an interview with him in *On Track*, the excellent racing magazine. It was the experience. Doc was experienced at breaking-in. Although they hadn't robbed him of much energy or enthusiasm, the years of unkept promises, collapsed deals and uncertainty over the next ride had made him wise to ups and downs. His emotional stride was hard to break; he was neither seduced by success nor burdened by setbacks. His approach could easily be perceived as being "a bit relaxed." When he told *On Track* that he considered himself a conservative driver, one who waits for opportunities on the track, he might well have been telling the story of his career.

In 1971 some friends had taken Doc to a race at the Mid-Ohio Sports Car Course, and he didn't want to leave, ever. He had little doubt in his mind that he had what it took to be a racedriver — even a world-beater — despite the fact that he'd never driven a racing car. He figured that what it took was talent and determination, and he was right, although he highly overestimated the value of the first, which caused him to seriously misjudge the required amount of the second. He bought a Formula C car, an open-wheeled racer with a small engine, and he enrolled in an SCCA weekend school at Watkins Glen. On the first day he spun out, and while his car was sitting in the grass another car spun in the same turn and stopped in the same spot. Doc's car was wiped out. And he had neither the money nor the know-how to repair the damage.

Although this first taste of racing had knocked his legs out from under him, it was a blow that could be dismissed as simple misfortune — maybe serious enough to recognize that it might not be so easy, but nothing to lose optimism over. However, he had definitely lost momentum, not to mention a lot of money and Plan A. So he retired to regroup. This time he asked for advice from racing people, most of whom pointed out his best, if not his only, option: Get a job on a race team. He had no specific skills that any team might need, but he called Peter Gregg, an owner/driver whose endurance-racing operation could be either the best or the worst place to start — certainly the most demanding. Gregg was talented, temperamental, and a champion. His crew called him "Peter Perfect" because of the standard that drove him, one which sometimes only he could grasp, let alone meet. When Doc called, Gregg asked, "Why should I hire you?" Doc said, "Because I have a lot of enthusiasm," which was a pretty good thing to say, "and someday I'm going to be a racedriver," which was exactly the wrong thing to say. "I don't hire guys who want to be racedrivers," said Gregg. "I'm the only racedriver around here." When he asked what Doc could do, Doc replied, "I can work longer and harder than anyone you've got."

Well, that was certainly the right thing to say, so Doc was hired. At 27, he quit his well-paying job as an airline agent and began drawing $75 a week, over his friends' cries that he was nuts. For two years he swept floors and scurried for hamburgers, and was promoted from gofer to apprentice mechanic by the end. He says he was the best wheel polisher the team ever had. But never once did he get to drive one of Gregg's Porsches, not even around the paddock.

In 1974 he tried again. This time he knew that a sponsor was the ticket. What he didn't know was that guys like him, guys with determination and dreams but no experience, didn't get sponsors. His second attempt got him no closer to driving than the first one had.

Gregg's strongest rival was Al Holbert. Each was a Porsche dealer — Gregg from Florida, Holbert from Pennsylvania — each an owner/driver, and each a winner. Being such keen competitors, they also noticed changes in each other's pit, and Holbert had observed the industry of Gregg's new gofer. After he got to know Doc, he coveted him. So when Doc's second stab at racing failed, Holbert offered him a job as his team's road manager — and, maybe, test driver. Doc became responsible for what the crew called "sparkle and glitter" — he was the team's publicist as well —and he kept his driving suit in Holbert's trailer, waiting for opportunities, which began coming. He started test driving for Holbert Racing, whose Chevy Monza won the 1976 and '77 International Motor Sports Association championships, and codrove with Holbert in six or seven other IMSA endurance races. He also tested Holbert's NASCAR Monte Carlo in '79. But that was it, the total amount of racing he had to show after eight years.

Then, in 1980, Holbert Racing entered a Porsche 924 in the D Production class of the SCCA national amateur series. In ten races, Doc won six, was second in the other four, and set five pole positions and four track records. He took the championship, needless to say. The next year he won three of four. He'd taken the job teaching at Road Atlanta that year, as Holbert paid him to also campaign the new 924 Turbo in the professional Trans-Am series, and they finished seventh while developing the car. After eleven years Doc was actually getting paid for driving, although he still needed the Road Atlanta job to make a living. "If it hadn't been for Al standing there, I don't know if I could have continued," he said. "Even this year, with the Trans-Am ride. If something happened to him, I might be out of luck."

His Holbert Racing press kit bio put it succinctly. "Success did not come overnight for the native of little Scio, Ohio. Behind the aura of his stardom as a roadracing ace are years of hard work and experience."

* * *

I had already been looking for a sponsor in order to take the next step in my own project — call it a furthering of research — but I was nearly as naive about that game as Doc had been. I thought that my *Sports Illustrated* assignment would swing open sponsors' doors, and I was ready to walk through them. But it didn't. A few doors opened wide enough to get my foot in, but it seemed as if I might have to pass my body through them one piece at a time. This didn't bother Doc. As I had appointed him my mentor, he had seen me as his medium. In *On Track,* addressing the low moment of his career, apparently one of those nights when you're ready to jump off a building, he'd said, "I vowed to myself that if I could make it, I would live my life as an example for others, to try and prove that the sport doesn't have to be structured so it's strictly for rich boys." The only problem was that by being the exception, he might have mostly confirmed what he was trying to disprove. Maybe a talented, poor driver could still make it, but he would need a dozen years and the exceptional spirit — among other qualities — of a Doc Bundy. The sport is still structured for rich boys.

Doc could see my fate more clearly than I. He knew there would be trouble out there, but he couldn't always tell me where it lurked.

I'm tempted to say that my next race was in the middle of nowhere, but with the feelings of the people of the town of Nelson Ledges in mind, call it the middle of Ohio. This was only the third year for the race, but it had already acquired a cult following, if not a certifiable claim to infamy. It was called the Longest Day, which is what it felt like to most of its participants and sometimes literally was, to the stars. It lasted 24 hours, and began on the Saturday closest to the summer solstice. The race was amateur, and its spirit was make-believe. This year it was held on the same day as Le Mans ("24 Heures du Mans," the French say), Europe's most famous motor race, and Longest Day entrants figured that Ohio, not France, was the place to be; T-shirts wryly proclaimed "24 Heures du Nelson Ledges." The Longest Day's distinction, dubious though it may have been, was its field: SCCA Showroom Stock cars, with soft suspensions, squishy brakes, catalytic conver-ters, warning buzzers and all. It was great fun, and as tales from the Longest Day travelled around the country each year, the entry list grew.

The ambiance of the circuit contributed to the event's reputation. It was equivalent to a minor-league ballpark, located on an old farm that was mostly cow pasture. (It had also been the site of my honeymoon, 15 years earlier. My bride and I eloped one Friday night — we were both 19 — and drove there in her Triumph TR-4, to be flagpersons at the motorcycle races.) There were a few shaky structures around the paddock, which was vaguely defined by falling fences. It wasn't used enough for anyone to bother with the weeds, and the mud was so accepted that people barely even griped about it.

But the circuit's layout was terrific. It was very fast for being only two miles long. It had a long, looping turn at its far end — called the Caroussel, no less — which led onto a backstraight where the fastest cars hit 130 before they took a kink at nearly that speed. The track was narrow, however, and didn't require many cars to create a traffic jam, so there was a lot of weaving, dodging, fist-shaking and fender-bending. The weeds grew right up to the edge of the road, and the tarmac surface was so dark that at night it was hard to tell where the road ended and the wilderness began. Talk about your cavern of concentration. The surface was also decrepit, and holes left by long-departed chunks of pavement behaved like small land mines. The Caroussel had two full-fledged potholes, as if some saboteur had put them there after giving their positioning careful thought. The first pothole was smack in the middle of the line through the turn, and the second pothole was in the middle of the second-best line. There was no reasonable third-best line, which left only the route the potholes dictated, calling for a 90-mph swerve at a moment your car might already be drifting.

I drove a four-speed V-8 Mustang, a model called the Cobra. Back in the muscle-car days of the '60s it was called the Boss. (I once owned a '69 Boss myself, and drove it in the final Cannonball Baker Sea-to-Shining-Sea Memorial Trophy Dash with George Willig, the "Human Fly" who had scaled Manhattan's World Trade Center. We ruptured a brake line in St. Louis, and drove the rest of the way to L.A. with almost no brakes, finishing mid-field with a time of 39 hours and 39 minutes. But that's another story.)

Now, after a decade of hibernation — when it came to high performance, Detroit retreated from the energy crisis like a bear from a blizzard — the hot Mustang had been reborn. The Cobra used the Boss 302 cubic-inch engine, a mill respected by hot rodders for its stoutness, although it was now detuned for the times. Ironically, the writing was already on the wall for the new Cobra — directions to Dinosaurland to join the Boss. The quick and nimble four-cylinder Mustang turbos looked like the future.

My team's maroon Cobra may not have been as hot as a Boss, but it was still awfully warm, and it stopped and cornered a whole lot better. It was owned by the Ford Motor Co. and had been prepared by Ron Smaldone, a Ford engineer, but it was not a factory entry. Smaldone, an SCCA champion in his own Mustang, had talked the promotion department into lending him the car for the Longest Day. I was glad that a corporation owned it, for the same reason Smaldone was happy to have gotten it: A crash wouldn't cost him anything. Altogether there were five drivers on his team, which was one more than most teams had. I was the fifth, only there because the promo department had asked him to take me on. Like Smaldone, the other three drivers — Larry Campbell, Dale Fazekas and Ron Kersey — had SCCA championships under their belts, so considering the car's power and the fast guys in the lineup, we were a solid contender for first place.

The race started on a drizzly Saturday afternoon. Smaldone had qualified the car fourth, and his plan must have been to jump into the lead and disappear from the pack for the next day. He was very competitive and a good, aggressive driver, but probably not cut out for endurance racing because he was also excitable and not so good at holding himself back. Which is how he managed to slide off the slippery Caroussel and get passed by about 20 cars on the first lap. The drizzle soon stopped, which was a relief to us four drivers watching from the roof of Kersey's motor home — not only for our own sakes, but because we worried less about Smaldone's charge now. He drove his 65-lap shift as if the race were two hours long instead of 24. When he pitted for gas, we were leading.

The Ford factory had its own entries. Their two white-and-blue Turbos had qualified third and fifth, which, with our Cobra fourth, made the three Mustangs a snake sandwich. Ford's performance division, Special Vehicle Operations, had entered the race in order to test the SVO prototype, designed to supplement the V-8. Most racing cars are far removed from even the sportiest street machines, so Showroom Stock endurance races were the best kind of proving ground. We should all thank the factories for participating; the cars we drive are better and safer for it. Ford took the Longest Day seriously, as a significant exercise in the development of the Mustang SVO, which was released to raves about a year later.

There was an in-house rivalry between our crew and the SVO people. SVO had come to the race full tilt, as factories will, bringing the enormous Ford Motorsports transporter, jammed with resources and technology; there were spare parts galore, and stacks of tires surrounded their pit as if to ward off raiding Indians. There were uniformed mechanics, and compressors and tarps and fluorescent lights and food and plywood on the ground to keep them above the mud. Ours was a volunteer crew, and, pitted next to SVO, we looked like poor relatives. On the roof of the SVO trailer — about six stories up, it seemed — was a perch that looked down on us, and that might have been a little bit how Smaldone felt. He hadn't forgotten that he'd had to persuade Ford that he was worthy of the car. The promo boys had relented as much as consented, and only because the Cobra was a dinosaur and there wasn't much else they could do with it. Smaldone's feisty spirit hardly needed the fuel.

When he stopped for gas, we fell to third. Pit stops were our handicap, since the Cobra had a small gas tank and dinosaurs are heavy drinkers. They eat a lot of rubber too, so we had to stop for tires a lot. My shift followed Smaldone's, who was understandably dubious about me. The leading SVO Turbo was in fourth place, and I could see it in my mirrors. I was determined to stay ahead; like any rookie, I wanted to please the coach. So I, too, drove as if the marathon were a sprint. I could gain on the Turbo when the track was clear, but usually lost ground in traffic, where I respected my inexperience by slipping through the spaces conservatively, and sometimes tentatively. But for more than 90 minutes I held off the factory car, and was rewarded by compliments from the crew.

At about 2 a.m. we were still third, and both SVO Mustangs were in trouble — one was sputtering around the track with a fuel-feed problem, and the other was in the garage with most of its engine on the floor. I drove 62 more laps on that dark cavern of a circuit, weaving through traffic that never ended since there were only two cars that could match the Cobra's speed and 45 that couldn't. I suffered no concentration lapses, which almost relieved me of the brain-fade burden I'd carried like baggage from Road Atlanta. And there remains one indelible vision from the shift: speeding down the narrow backstraight in the middle of the night at 120 miles an hour. A sensation comes with the mental image, even now. The Cobra felt like a space ship. It cut so swiftly through the night that I felt invisible. In the afternoon, the car had felt as if it were bashing through some force; in the night, it was as if it were being drawn by that force — like the difference between a headwind and a tailwind. Maybe it was simply because you can't ever go too fast in the security of daylight, but in the dark you're more likely to cry "enough."

The kink at the end of the backstraight was a righthand dogleg taken at nearly top speed — maybe it could be taken at absolute, pedal-to-the-metal top speed, which was 125-130 miles an hour, but not by me, and certainly not at night. You knew the kink was coming when you saw a short white post at the left edge of the road; every lap, the instant before the post appeared, the anticipation and doubt — *Did I miss it?* — made the final heartbeat a bouncy one. It was always a relief to see the post pop into the headlights' yellow swath: It was okay to back off, now. When the Cobra did, the exhaust rumbled and the suspension settled together, sensually.

To take the kink well you needed all the road, and that meant finding it. The white post also marked the turning point; when the car's left front fender reached the post, you peeled off. That was an act of faith, since at 120 miles an hour the headlights — all six of them — were overdriven. After you were committed, the only reference point was a small green reflector on the apex. Because of the Cobra's speed, if you missed the reflector you were likely to run off the track and bounce into the weeds. It happened to Larry Campbell once, and a few other drivers during the night, after which there were no more weeds. Until I saw the reflector in my line, to be clipped by the right front tire, I was never sure that the thrilling ordeal of the kink, which came every 90 seconds, was over.

It was a good thing that brakes weren't needed for the kink — although many drivers used them for security — because, at the start of my shift, the crew chief had told me to avoid them because the pads were nearly worn out. Keeping my foot off the brake pedal required self-discipline, and it was valuable training in smooth and rhythmic driving. I discovered that it wasn't necessary to brake for two turns where I'd been braking that afternoon, and the lap times didn't suffer. When I finished the shift the pads were worn to the rivets; I think they had been more worn than the crew chief had noticed in his brief and shadowy inspection. Taking the kink quickly may have been so stimulating that I heard bugles, but sparing the car without slowing down was more rewarding, and much more important to learn.

During the long night — or short night, as the case may be — a tremendous three-car race for first place had been going on. It must have been one of the closest 24-hour races in history. A Porsche 944, Camaro Z-28 and our Mustang were never separated by more than a few minutes, and the positions changed nearly every hour. The Camaro was superbly prepared by Guldstrand Engineering in California — with quiet and substantial support from Chevrolet — and was a clever rule-bender, as its conspicuously stiff suspension and cornering stability revealed. It led far into the night, until one of its three drivers planted the racy red car into a tire wall, deeply enough so that the wrecker had to haul it out. For the rest of the night they raced to regain lost minutes. The Porsche, which enjoyed the advantage of a long range between gas stops, slipped into the lead, although it was being driven gingerly because of a racket in the front end which the team feared was a crumbling wheel bearing. The Cobra was running like a locomotive, its 302 engine living up to its reputation; it actually felt stronger with the miles. We had to drive harder to stay up front because of the time lost refuelling, which meant that the Cobra was usually the fastest car on the track. During the night, both Dale "Fuzzy" Fazekas — he was a tiger after dark — and Tom Kersey, who had been racing since the '50s, took excursions into the boonies and we lost a couple of laps. By daybreak, the three cars were still only minutes apart.

Late in the morning, when we were on the same lap as the Camaro and two laps behind the Porsche, Smaldone, ever-aggressive, decided our only chance for victory was to run flat-out for the final four hours. That meant I would be benched; Larry Campbell would run two shifts in a row. He was two seconds per lap quicker than I, and capable of running still faster, so the arithmetic made it simple: 65 laps per shift multiplied by three seconds equalled more than three minutes, which was two laps. I understood, and, although I resisted the emotion because I didn't approve of it, I was even relieved. I would have had to race the clock under heavy pressure, and I didn't have the confidence for that. I had done well so far, and wasn't eager to push my luck. Blowing it in your own race is bad enough, but to make a mistake that costs four teammates a victory would be enough to make you want to go down with the car. Still, I wouldn't let myself back out, so when I saw that Campbell, Fazekas and Kersey had changed into their street clothes while Smaldone drove the final shift, I stayed suited up, just in case. As I sat in the pit, all dressed up with nowhere to go, I realized I wasn't relieved at all. I wanted Smaldone to get sick so I could get back in the car.

The Porsche won, the Camaro regained its lost minutes for second place, and we finished third after a flat tire in the 23rd hour. Smaldone ran out of gas on the final lap, and sputtered across the finish. As congratulations flowed around the team, I slipped away; I hadn't driven badly, but was suddenly so disappointed at missing the final shift that I didn't feel as if I had contributed enough to take part. I couldn't help wanting more. There was no high as I drove to the Cleveland airport.

I was thinking of Doc. One week earlier he had won his second straight Trans-Am race, and he now led the series. The two victories would be memorable to him because they were his first professional wins, and the second one was especially satisfying because he had done it right. His Porsche 924 Turbo, with a two-liter four-cylinder engine, had less horsepower than most of the competition, V-8 Firebirds, Corvettes and Mustangs. And many of the other drivers were as quick as Doc. So he had to be smarter. He had hung back, while the powerful V-8s raced each other to their graves. The victories gave his career a big boost. Afterwards, an *On Track* reporter had asked Doc why he didn't seem very excited. "I've got a long way to go, still," he said. "I'm about five years behind schedule."

That was how I felt after two races: five years behind schedule.

In the darkness it was like steering a space ship.

Doc Bundy drove the Holbert Racing Porsche 924 Turbo to his first pro victory, and won again the next week.

Hal Crocker.

Doc was "...sometimes perceived as being a bit relaxed for someone who regularly drives at speeds of 200mph."

Chapter Three

Steve Schiff

Michael Zimicki

Fast Guys

M y rides at Road Atlanta and Nelson Ledges had been excellent, and the races had seemed extraordinarily exciting — an adventuresome beginning for the story. But I knew there was more. Ideas, for where to raise money and how to spend it, came and went. After Gordon Smiley had been killed at Indianapolis, I'd thought his sponsorship might be available; with it, I could codrive a Holbert Porsche 924 with Doc in seven professional endurance races on the IMSA circuit. That would have cost as much as $120,000. Too hungry to care that I was being vulturous, I inquired about the money that Smiley wouldn't be claiming, and was told it would remain unspent. None of my other plans were getting any closer to action either, yet I thought sponsorship would come any day; surely some corporation would recognize the value of exposure in *Sports Illustrated*. So while I waited to be discovered, I entered the Skip Barber Series.

Skip Barber was a former professional road racer who had been a star in the early '70s. He was a three-time SCCA Formula Ford champion and had even run a Formula 1 season for the world driving championship, backed by a Philadelphia lawyer. When he retired from driving in 1975, he started the Skip Barber Racing School, which, along with the Jim Russell British School of Motor Racing was the best thing to happen to American road racing since Dan Gurney. The schools amounted to a farm system, which had never before existed. They carried their instruction beyond gradua-tion, by offering their students cars and somewhere to race them. Their series consisted of about 15 races, which were like seminars since instructors ran them. The cars were prepared as equally as possible, and that was the system's foundation: Skill, not money, got you to Victory Circle. You had to pay to enter, of course, but that was all you had to do. No other investment was required — such as of your time, working on a car all week. The economic risk wasn't even the entrant's; if the engine blew it was the school's problem, and if you crashed your financial responsibility was reasonably limited. Major crashes were rare, since erratic driving guaranteed expulsion; Barber's safety record was one broken leg in seven years. A Barber Series weekend cost $800, which was as cheap as racing gets.

Barber ran his show like a travelling circus. He owned about two dozen Formula Fords, half of them stored at the home base in Connecticut and half in the Midwest. But they were usually on the road, moving between engagements at circuits from Connecticut to Florida to Oklahoma. The mechanics, who drove the rigs and set up the tents, so to speak, were mostly young, would-be racedrivers motivated by the test driving, not the wages. And they were kept busy, since 60 drivers sometimes showed up for a race, to share maybe 12 cars.

Formula Fords were an ideal choice for a school series. They were full-fledged, open-wheeled racecars using 1600cc, four-cylin-der Ford engines modified to produce 115 horsepower. They weighed only 900 pounds, so they cornered, braked and accelerated exceptionally quickly. They were simple, reliable and cheap — you could get a new one for $20,000. But the best things about them — for driver, instructor and promoter alike — were their precision and reliability. Teaching and driving were both easier when the car was predictable.

Ironically, the fact that extra horsepower couldn't be bought was the Barber Series' weakness as well as its virtue. The experience was unreal, because the series couldn't help being a cocoon. It wasn't like the outside racing world, which might or might not be waiting for a student. Many of the Barber racers were good enough for bigger-time places, but they settled for the series because they didn't have the fare for those places. They were young lions who marked time without knowing it, carrying their dreams and illusions like matched luggage for the trip they thought they were on.

The series champion was a fast guy named Michael Zimicki. He seemed an unlikely type to be a racedriver. He was 22 and a student at Hampshire College, an exclusive and progressive New England school; he was preppy from his tortoise-shell glasses to his seersucker Bermuda shorts. At 5'10" and 140 pounds, he was wiry to the bone. He was a rock climber, and seemed to carry a climber's air toward risk — so accepting he didn't appear to recognize it. It was as if he was casually sitting on a bomb, and he lit the fuse when he got in the car. His driving was spectacular. He broke all the rules. He locked the brakes going into turns and slid the car with acrobatic abandon. His control was so good that he rose above the classic technique. He was a terrible example. Though Skip Barber was fond of Zimicki and tried to help him further his career, Zimicki's speed must have driven Barber batty. Zimicki was aware that he was gifted, but he played down his style. Maybe Barber had made him an offer he couldn't refuse, such as: You can race here as long as you disown yourself.

Zimicki took a crack at the SCCA National Formula Ford circuit that year. He raised some money by selling his Saab, and three of his wealthier fellow Barber racers expanded his kitty to $20,000. He entered four Nationals in a new red Crossle owned by Barber, and qualified for the championship race at Road Atlanta that November. In his heat race another driver ran into him, so he had to start near the back of the grid in the main event, which was the most competitive single amateur race in the country. He drove brilliantly up to fifth place before his motor began misfiring; he dropped to 12th, where he finished. That was the end of the money. The next year he was mostly just another college student.

* * *

Five days after Nelson Ledges, I was practicing for my first Barber race, at Pocono Raceway in Pennsylvania. I hadn't been in a Formula Ford since my British School of Motor Racing course three months earlier, and it felt odd — strapped down and reclining in a cramped compartment that was open to the world, with the pavement about six inches under my buttocks. It was strange to be able to see the front wheels, which seemed close enough to reach out and touch, if I could have moved. It reminded me of a peach-crate racer built by the "Our Gang" kids, and how they always flew down the steepest street in the neighborhood, out of control at breakneck speed until they hit a full clothesline. The car's rear wheels seemed to wrap around my ears, and the engine was between my shoulder blades. My elbows were squeezed against my sides, and my feet were in a little box. All that day I had trouble with my footwork; when I downshifted, pressing the brake with the ball of my right foot while blipping the throttle with the heel, I was klutzy — either too much throttle, which screwed up the shift, or too much brake, which upset the car and murdered lap times. And what little physical driving sense I'd so far acquired was confused, since I'd gone from a front-wheel-drive Rabbit to the heavy and powerful stock Mustang to this precise little crate. I needed every one of the day's 50 practice laps.

In Saturday's heat race I spun out on the first lap. The car neither left the track nor stalled, but the spin put me dead last. For the remaining nine laps I madly chased the field, and caught three stragglers to finish sixth. The leaders were cutting laps in the low 1:11s while my fastest time was 1:13.2, and two seconds was a big difference for equal cars on a track with few turns. I went to bed that night dissatisfied, and annoyed at my light foot in the narrow 70-mph esses.

In the warmup before Sunday's race, I forced my foot to stay on the floor through the esses. It was easy the second time through, which was inspiring but also infuriating, because it shouldn't have taken 50 practice laps and a heat race to find that out. In the race a rhythm came to me early, making it easier to follow a racing axiom: "Race the road, not the other cars." Starting ninth in the 12-car field, I began picking people off, on the heels of a white car that had passed me at the start. A few laps from the finish I drafted him onto the Pocono triangular oval, which surrounded the serpentine infield section of the circuit. Halfway up the oval's backstraight was a wide kink that flowed back into the twisty part, and the white car approached a straggler there. He went high to pass so I went low, and when the three of us canted toward the bend virtually abreast at 120 miles an hour, it was a new rush — flying so low and exposed, and feeling so much of the sky and earth. I came out ahead, in fourth place; when the second-place car spun one lap later, I inherited third. I finished with the second-place car in my sights, although I wasn't gaining on it. The winner, Zimicki, was about 100 more yards ahead.

My lap times were better than I'd thought I was capable of. Sixteen of the 20 laps had been under 1:12, and the best was 1:11 flat, which was .2 under the old lap record, although a new lap record had been set that day at 1:09.9 — by Herb Means, who had been a playmate at the races when our fathers raced each other. I was pleased — for once — more with the times and their consistency than the finishing position. My father was there since my parents lived just 200 miles away, and he was all revved up, puffed and proud as fathers will be. And his juices got stirred; he wanted to drive one of the Formula Fords.

As I drove through the Poconos to my house in upstate New York, I was thinking about Doc again. The same refrain, too: A long way to go, still. I didn't feel any elation over my run from ninth to third, nor even the 1:11. It had been too easy, and too soon. I may have wanted to believe that I was a natural, but I knew better. It would have actually been optimistic to consider the pace a fluke; if it weren't, I had an imposing standard to meet in the races ahead. I knew the car had been good — quicker than the one I'd drawn the day before — but not that good. But no matter how much I complicated things in my mind, I could see one thing clearly: I had kept my foot on the gas. That might not be all there is to racing, but without it, you might as well stay home and have fun.

There had been an incident during the race which meant more than the 1:11, and was more satisfying. A car that was about 60 yards ahead of me had begun to spin as I came out of the hard right-hander that led onto the oval, which was the worst possible spot to back off because any momentum lost there would stay lost for nearly a mile. The car spun 270 degrees and began rolling forward toward the wall on my left. I knew that I could miss him by braking and veering right, and I suppose the fact that I recognized it means that I considered it, but I didn't really. I mashed my foot to the floor and steered for the narrowing hole between the wall and the car's blue nose. I passed through cleanly at about 60 miles an hour, with less than two feet between my left front tire and the wall and another three feet from his nose. As racing goes, the call wasn't that close; but if I had hesitated, it would have been. My eyes immediately returned to the tachometer, to make the upshift into third gear at 6,000 rpm. From that moment until I was 50 miles from the track, I forgot all about it. That seemed to be a very good sign.

In the days following the Pocono race, I began inventing conundrums. They were like Catch-22s rattling around in my head, which was the only place they existed. It was a classic trap: thinking too much about the execution, making it more difficult to complete. I believed I should have been a fast guy already — a standard I recognized as a conceit — but I couldn't think of any convincing reason why I should be. After Pocono, where I appeared to be, I questioned it. It wasn't a reservation like "a-long-way-to-go-still," which was healthy and optimistic; this was merely confused. Even if I were as fast as I felt I should be, what was it relative to? It was difficult to tell, since the clock seemed to tick differently at each race, and the fast guys I measured myself against were basically still students, which I tended to overlook. Did I deserve to be satisfied? If so, should I allow myself to be, so soon? Ever? I didn't know where to ease off, or when to give myself a break. There was Tommy Tune on television, saying that Martha Graham, the great choreographer, preached dissatisfaction: It's what keeps you dancing. But it couldn't be much fun, and it certainly hadn't kept Peter Gregg dancing.

Three years earlier, I'd written a story about Gregg which my editor had prophetically titled "The Price of Perfection." Gregg had won nine of ten IMSA races that season, and was the best sports car driver in the country. But he was having trouble staying inspired, he said, because now all he could do was not lose. It seemed a sad way to look at life, and I hoped he hadn't meant it quite that way, but it suggested otherwise when he committed suicide. He had suffered a head injury six months earlier — ironically in a highway crash, while he was in France for Le Mans — and Doc says Gregg wasn't the same after that, but he never did seem happy.

I called Doc, who was still on a roll. He'd just returned from Le Mans himself, where he'd won the GT class in a Porsche 924, although he wasn't celebrating because the car had been slow and troubled. All the fast guys had broken down, including the hot Camaro driven by two more Americans, Billy Hagan and Gene

Felton, and prepared by Tex Enterprises out of Ether, North Carolina.

I told Doc what was troubling me. He sounded like Martha Graham. He said, "Good. In fact, I should hope you're not satisfied. You'd be in trouble if you were driving as well as you could. There's always something more — there's got to be. I hope you never find out you couldn't have done better. That's what's thrilling, to feel like you can do better all the time." He said I was confusing improving with winning.

I was also wondering about the space between the top of my potential and the top of my head — how I might find that space in order to drive within it. My potential was what I was chasing; it may have been *all* that I was chasing. If I were near it, then it might be okay to be satisfied; if not, I should give more. But what could be more elusive than potential? It was harder to define than "fast," and impossible to pin to a line as fine as I wanted — and needed, to be a fast guy. What was I capable of right now? A 1:10 at Pocono?

My friends were already beginning to tell me that I was pushing myself too fast, if not too far, which was becoming hard on me and boring to them. I was perpetually hyper, and aggressive with people. Since I was constantly thinking about racing, I was constantly filled with adrenaline and wanted to accomplish everything at 90 miles an hour. It wasn't a unique problem for a racedriver. On the track, that was what it was all about; impatience to speed you up, self-control to calm you down.

I wondered if I could find more speed by thinking — and worrying — about it less. By any reasonable standard I was doing fine, and to sit around and wonder why you're doing fine seemed counterproductive, if not downright dumb.

I was now wondering if the things I wondered were worth wondering about. I felt like a Jules Feiffer character. It also reminded me of a story about Henry Aaron. Aaron came to the plate for the Milwaukee Braves in the 1957 World Series and was told by Yogi Berra, the Yankee catcher, that the label on the bat was facing the wrong way. "I ain't up here to read," said Aaron, "I'm up here to hit." I had remembered that story for 25 years because of its very message, and I didn't want to start reading labels now.

Stan Crilly

*Skip Barber
believed that talent
should prevail, and
did something about it.*

Stan Crilly

Precise little crates, rolling through the Pennsylvania countryside.

Chapter Four

Klaus A. Schnitzer

The Learning Curve

"The Unfair Advantage" was a book by Mark Donohue, a driver whose word was gospel around the Barber school. Some believed that Donohue, an engineer, had thought too much, but if it were true he'd been awfully good anyhow; he won the 1972 Indy 500, and a number of road racing championships. He retired in 1973 but was miserable without driving, and came back in 1975 to set the closed-course speed record of 221 miles an hour, which still stands. Two weeks later he was killed at the Austrian Grand Prix. His book suggested that because there was little that was fair about motor racing, any advantage a driver could finagle was also unfair, which was fair. The game was shuffling fair, from unfair, to your advantage, while avoiding downright cheating.

Every few years a well-known driver will get caught cheating, and it looks sleazy in the newspapers. But it's more roguish than that. A racer's code is a straight-shooting one; it's just that cheating has a place in it. Richard Petty, with a good-ol'-boy wink, calls it "Jes' tryin' to get an edge," and his edge and Donohue's unfair advantage are the same.

In what other sport is success so affected by equipment? Imagine the opportunities and temptations to cheat: A racecar consists of hundreds of pieces that might be altered against the rules, and many of them, such as engine components, are already concealed. And think of the traps: In effect, a rule comes with every piece. Racers — drivers and mechanics alike — are often unaware when their car violates them. They have to interpret many of the rules, since the book can't cover every millimeter, let alone every unrealized inspiration in a creative tinkerer's mind. And as long as the car can be made to go faster, a racer will try, because that's his nature; expecting a racer not to soup up his car is like expecting a dog not to bark. Trying too hard not to cheat is like reading labels — a good racer ain't there to worry about rules, he's there to go fast. Racers know that if they try to figure out all the rules, let alone follow them to a "T," they'll be beaten by someone who's not so encumbered. Cheating is surviving. Some rulebooks indirectly but wittingly provide room for cheating, which increases officials' power. When Bobby Unser won the 1981 Indy 500, the victory was taken away from him the next day because he'd passed a row of eight cars under the yellow light. But he'd known the rule was vague, and then its post-race enforcement was wrong and arrogant; he fought back, and a special court eventually gave him the victory he deserved. But for ten weeks he looked like a cheater to the world, which gave him an ulcer and caused him to retire the next year.

The challenge for a racer is to get more out of the car than you're supposed to be able to. There's enough of the outlaw in him that he gets a kick out of outsmarting authority. When racers cheat, they're often trying to beat the system as much as each other. After making a questionable modification to the car, any good mechanic will assume he's innocent until a technical inspector proves him guilty, and he's quite willing to hide the modification in order to spare the inspector the bother. Fellow racers may be each other's victims, and there may be a lot of money at stake, but they're forgiving. When the unfair advantage is ingeniously gained and its cover clever, it might even be admired by other racers, who might also complain but they know they'd do the same thing. The racers' code views the lodging of official protests with disdain; it's whining, inviting authority in, and a rotten way to win a race. Even when he knows he's been cheated against, a racer might say nothing, but simply be smarter — maybe cheat better, himself —

the next time. And the code will keep him available to lend a needed hand to a competitor he may be cheating with the other one.

Sometimes, of course, cheating is clearcut and calculated. And for every incident that's exposed, there are scores — hundreds — of times the racers get away with it. No matter how much room the rules provide, it won't be enough. There have been gas tanks having legal dimensions but extra-legal capacities after expanding like accordions upon filling; chassis tubes carrying buckshot to give the car its required weight until the first pit stop, at which time a plug is pulled so the buckshot trickles out around the track; fuel additives and tire softeners; and hidden canisters containing nitrous oxide — a dentist's laughing gas — sprayed into the carburetor when the driver presses a secret button, giving the car a rocket-like boost at an appropriate time. And there was the infamous "banana car," which was built to seven-eighths scale and ran two or three races before officials figured out what was funny about it. They called it the "banana car" because it was so slick.

Racers have always been mavericks, often notorious ones; it's in their roots. Stock car racing evolved from the war between moonshiners and the revenuers. Superspeedways, giant purses and zillions of fans have replaced the midnight backroad chases of 40 years ago, but between racers and officials, it's the same game: Catch me if you can.

* * *

The Thursday after Pocono I flew from New York to Milwaukee, to race at Road America in Elkhart Lake, Wisconsin. The town was an hour's drive north of Milwaukee, and it was beautiful in June. Road America was the best-managed of circuits; it was maintained like a park, boasted a positive ledger sheet — its calendar was perpetually booked — and offered the best racetrack food in the country. During big summer race weeks, a nearby college rented dormitory rooms since the few local motels were always full, and a church offered a cheap all-you-can-eat breakfast. The Barber Series used just two of Road America's four miles in order to eliminate two long straights, but even half the circuit was a joy to race on.

There was a rule in the Barber Series against revving an engine over 6,000 rpm. It was enforced by the reading of the telltale needle on the tachometer. Most racing tachs have two needles; the main one, usually white on a black face, pushes a thin red one. The red needle has no return spring, which makes "telltale" an apt name. It tells mechanics how the car is being used, information which may reveal as much about the driver as the state of the engine. If a driver misses a shift, the telltale will be sky-high when he comes in. Or, if it's low, the mechanic will know his driver isn't using all the power — the only reason for which, in a mechanic's mind, is that his car is too hot to handle. For months, I thought the needle was called "tattletale," because that's what it more truly seemed to do.

The series used a rev limit for two reasons: to prevent abuse of engines that Skip Barber had to pay for, and to teach drivers mental awareness and self-discipline. After each race the telltale would be read and recorded by a staff mechanic, who would reset it for the next race. Drivers who exceeded 6,000 rpm were penalized on the clock, and the formula was rigid enough so that any overrev was almost certain to cost at least one finishing position. If a driver won a race but missed a shift and overreved along the way, he got no official recognition or congratulations. The drivers themselves mostly recognized their positions on the track, not the results sheet, but still, overrevs tainted success and cost points toward the season championship.

But there were two problems to the rev limit. First, it sometimes affected lap times, although this was a running debate, as Barber argued that the engines' power peaked at about 5,800 rpm anyhow. And at Elkhart, at least, because of the long backstraight, the rev limit could become a speed limit, especially since every car was fresh from the crate — Barber had just gotten a shipment of 12 slippery Crossle chassis from North Ireland. In a good draft, the new cars could exceed 6,000 rpm in fourth gear on the backstraight. So in order to stay within the rules, you had to back off the throttle — and maybe lose the draft. You couldn't count on the guy in front of you overrevving, because his engine or tach might be different. In this situation the rev limit could even be dangerous, because it was a terrible time to have to watch the tach: You were going 120, the track was bending, and the exhaust pipe of the car you were drafting was in your face.

The second problem to the rev limit was that it sometimes created an artificial driving technique. On one particular stretch, a short uphill straight connecting second-gear turns, the engine could reach 6,000 if you didn't shift into third. But if you did, the downshift back to second would be right on top of the upshift. And if you feathered the throttle in second, you were backing off again. Feathering wouldn't have cost much time — a few tenths, maybe

— but I couldn't bring myself to slow down for the sake of a training rule.

In Friday's practice my best time was 1:37.2, while the quickest that day was 1:36. When Michael Zimicki showed up on Saturday morning, having never before seen the circuit, he clocked 1:33.5 on his fifth lap. I tried not to measure myself against this natural, but I couldn't help feeling that I should be three seconds faster than I was, which would have made me fourth or fifth fastest among the 40 or 50 drivers there. It wasn't that I thought I was better than the others, it was just that I was in a hurry and didn't care how long it took them. I told this to an instructor, Bill Proutt, who sat me down in his rental car and warned me that my impatience could get me in trouble. He said that when he started racing he was in a hurry too, and he made a lot of mistakes because of it. But when he decided that he was in the sport for the long run he eased off, and suddenly got smoother and faster. He added, "If you respect the craft at all, you can't expect to be a fast guy after only two races. And if you do, then you don't know what it takes." I listened to him and believed him, and it was consoling, but I still had a unique problem: I was in it for a story, not the long run, and didn't have much time. Proutt's little talk didn't stop me from going straight back to the paddock to check out the competition. Just eight days earlier in practice at Pocono, my goal had been decent footwork; now, after one good race, I wasn't interested in anything less than first place.

As acutely competitive as my antisocial behavior at Road Atlanta should have proven me to be, the evidence went right by me because it was a foreign drive. I had somehow gotten through 34 years repressing or otherwise failing to discover my competitiveness. Dale Earnhardt had once told me that he thought I could be a racedriver, and I replied, "Nah, I don't care enough about winning." I'd apparently forgotten about the time when I was 11 and we neighborhood kids invented bicycle motocross. We raced against a stopwatch over a course we had laid out in the street and through yards, and I wasn't satisfied with anything less than the lap record. My dad raced sports cars, after all.

I wish I could say that the technical problems with the rev-limit rule were my sole motivation for devising a method to break it, to beat the system, to cheat. But they were mostly a justification. I can't even claim that I was simply surviving, since I doubt very much that any other driver was so devious and premeditating.

I knew the reset button for the telltale needle was located

somewhere behind the instrument panel. In order for the mechanics to locate it, they had to squat beside the car and reach between the driver's knees, under the panel and upward. It wasn't possible for a driver to get his arm up there, which I found out Saturday while I was sitting in the car waiting to practice for the heat race (which would be rained out). After checking over each shoulder to make sure there were no witnesses, I'd reached under the instrument panel and groped around behind it, feeling only the rounded bottom of the tach. Later I waited until a mechanic removed the fiberglass cowling from a car, exposing the tach. My peering was as guilty and stealthy as my groping had been; like a nervous shoplifter trying not to eye the necklace he was about to snatch, I tried not to get too close or appear too interested. But there it was, a tiny chrome button, tucked away at midnight on the rim of the tachometer body.

It came to me the morning of the race, while I was shaving. Wondering how I could reach the button, and wishing my middle finger were six inches longer, the answer appeared before my eyes: my razor. It was a long and slender Gillette Trac II, and it looked as if it might close the distance between my finger and the button. I could use it like a little hammer (and, running with the theft now, I figured if that didn't work I would try my toothbrush). I would be able to run the entire race inhibited by neither the rev limit nor the fear of missing a shift; I could rev to 6500 if I felt like it. On the cooloff lap I would loosen my shoulder straps, remove my right glove, take the razor from the breast pocket of my driving suit, wait until I was on the backstraight where no corner workers could see me, lean forward and hook the razor over the button, reset the tach, then rev it back up to 6,000.

I examined my eyes — my conscience — in the mirror, and a sneaky grin appeared. I felt almost smug, for having figured out how to beat the system. I was doing what a racer would do, and it felt good. It would be my Unfair Advantage.

The spanking new Crossle was bright red, and its chrome suspension arms gleamed; its sharp nose sliced the wind, and everything about it felt crisp. For the first three laps I stayed on the tail of the leaders; we were a tidy three-car draft, turning high 1:34s. On the backstraight, winding through the trees at nearly 120 and into the section called Kettle Bottoms, I looked into the black tailpipe of the second-place car. It made me feel giddy: I'm a fast guy! I glanced beyond the leader, wondered what it was like up there, and realized that it was almost literally within my reach. But at the end of that lap my excitement got the best of me, and I fumbled for first gear while downshifting directly from third for the last turn, an awkward and artificial hard right that was used only for the Barber Series. That bobble with the gearshift was all it took to lose the draft, and for 17 laps I watched the leaders slip away and race each other for the victory. At the finish my telltale needle read 6200, and the readjustment on the cooloff lap went without a hitch. I was third. By the rules, I had finished sixth.

Road America had a lovely right-hand kink, isolated at the back of the circuit where a kink belongs, since it's the high-speed bend, more than any other, that is the driver's private challenge. (The Indy 500 is a race of 800 kinks taken at 200 miles an hour, with millions watching.) The Elkhart kink was bent like a boomerang, on dark, smooth pavement with a neat white ribbon of guardrail behind haybales around the outside edge. Behind the guardrail, a row of trees threw long afternoon shadows onto the exit of the turn, which rushed into the backstraight. It was a graceful curve that could be taken at full throttle, 110 miles an hour, if you used all the road.

On the last lap there had been a slower car ahead of me as I approached the kink. I wasn't sure if there was enough room before the kink to pass him. I knew I could ease off the throttle and follow him through, but my problem with easing off in general was in the way — and I could see the fourth-place car in my mirrors. So I swung out and made the pass, but found myself in the middle of the road when I reached the turn, which is what I'd been afraid of. I gave the car a quick swerve to get back some of the road, but still entered the kink four or five feet tight. Near the apex the car began to slide. I could feel myself countersteering and see the guardrail looming at eye level. I thought, "If I'm going into that guardrail, I'm going in with my foot on the floor."

I know how outrageous that sounds, and I'm aware that it appears to be the kind of pointless bravery people think race-drivers are stupid or crazy for having. But it wasn't — and usually isn't — bravery and/or stupidity; it was a commitment to a technical decision. If I had thought that backing off would have corrected the slide, my foot would have flown off the throttle. But it was a delicate situation. Backing off might have shifted the car's balance and caused a spin. I'd bitten it off, and now I had to swallow it.

The moment made quite an impression on the seat of my pants. Because I got away with it, the decision to stay on the gas was probably right. And I never would have been satisfied had I backed off, which may be the strongest, if not the best reason for not doing so. I took the corner as fast as a Formula Ford can take it, which is what you're supposed to do, and the fourth-place guy didn't catch me, although he wouldn't have anyhow. My prize was an everlasting thrill: a ride in a wonderful open-wheeled racecar that I controlled through a beautiful bend, crossed-up and flat-out at more than 100 miles an hour. I can feel it now; I want more. As I sped away through the trees, I whooped in exhilaration.

Keeping it floored had been instinctive, which was good, but it was also the problem: I'd been over my head and didn't know it. It took the next kink for me to see the light, so to speak.

* * *

Lime Rock Park, a circuit in Connecticut and the Barber home base, was stuffed in a woodsy pocket of the Berkshire Mountain foothills. It was short, fast and narrow. It took less than a minute to get around its 1.5 miles, and the difference between a good lap and a hot one was only a few tenths, which were hard to find. It was renowned for its subtle seductiveness; it was easy to memorize, but difficult to master. All but one of the six turns swept right, making it like a distorted oval, so acceleration and top speed weren't as important as momentum. It was unique — a fast course where the Barber Formula Fords were as quick as many 500-horsepower cars. That was its trouble: It was faster than it looked. And that led drivers to believe it was faster than it was.

In a Formula Ford, the ultimate lap around Lime Rock was uncompromising: four-fifths of the track needed to be taken flat-out. A driver would have four consecutive turns to survive without lifting his foot — at 70, 90, 95 and 100 miles an hour. It was rarely driven that way — I doubted if even Michael Zimicki challenged the course like that — but it was possible, and after the first day of practice there, it was my goal. Racers sometimes call such blind ambition the "Red Mist."

The expression "flat-out" might be misleading. Flat-out, or simply "flat," merely means that the gas pedal is floored. Motorcycle racers call it WFO, for Wide Fucking Open, which refers to the position of the carburetor's mouth when an engine is at full throttle. It doesn't necessarily mean the car is moving at top speed, although it frequently does, which is flat-out at its most dramatic. But a 60-mph turn can be as flat-out as a 120-mph one, and what is flat for one car may not be flat for another. To take a turn flat is to take it without lifting, as in your foot off the throttle. And lifting can sometimes be like flinching — involuntary. Your foot often has less courage than your heart, and more sense than your head.

Lime Rock's kink was called West Bend, and it was the third and most difficult of the four flat-out turns. It had the arc of a sickle, and was actually more than a kink for more powerful and less precise racecars, which had to brake for it. It sat hard by the base of a hill, following a brief backstraight on which the Formula Fords reached 95 miles an hour, and a softly-rounded yellow curb lined its inner edge. At 95 mph every inch of the curb looked the same as the next, which was bad enough, but West Bend's radius also decreased just a pinch, enough to hide the apex, at least from the eye level of a Formula Ford. There were black scuff marks on the yellow curb at the apex, but there were also scuff marks on a false apex before it. If you turned too early or aimed for the wrong marks, you were likely to be carried to a point outside the curve where it was off-camber, which sucked a wheel off the track and onto sand that usually spun you out. Only a very confident and precise driver could get through West Bend without lifting.

Because it was a Wednesday, there were only about a dozen drivers for the first day of practice — also because each practice day cost $250. One of them was a ballet instructor from Nashville who said her Formula Ford footwork was not unlike her dancing. Another was Steve Pope, whose first driving years were in the Barber cocoon. He'd won a number of Barber races, but he still wondered how good he was because he wasn't sure it was "real racing." So he'd bought a car, hired a mechanic, and entered the Renault Cup, a support series at IMSA races and the bottom rung of professional road racing, contested in unmodified Renault Le Cars. The Renault Cup was relatively dirt cheap, so there were huge fields and the racing was back-biting. The tiny Le Cars smashed into each other and tipped over a lot.

In the series' premier, at Road Atlanta one month before my own debut there, Pope rolled his car on the third practice lap — no harm done. He qualified eighth and passed six cars on the first lap, which, on the spot, dispelled his doubts about the Barber level of driving, as well as his own ability. He led for three laps, and finished second by half a Le Car length. Now he was fresh from victory in the most recent Cup race and was leading the series, which was very important to him; winning the Renault Cup might enable him to get a sponsor and move up to bigger things. And the top three finishers in the series would earn trips to France — paid by Renault — to compete in the international championship race for Le Cars. During a break in that series, he had entered the Barber race at Lime Rock to stay sharp.

Pope was a compact 5'8" and 160 pounds, with a shock of sandy hair and untanned skin that made me wonder where he spent his summer days. He wore gold wire glasses that slid down his nose and vaguely suggested nerdness. He was an architect, a graduate of Rhode Island School of Design, and worked freelance, accepting only the jobs that didn't interfere with his pursuit of a racing career. He went to professional races hoping to make contacts that might be useful in getting rides, and he mailed countless letters and proposals to car owners and prospective sponsors, attempts to present his racedriving career as a good business investment for them. His general proposal was 30 pages, including photographs.

Pope had run more than 50 Barber races, many of them at Lime Rock, his own home track, so he knew its tricks; and he was generous with his experience. After practice, I asked him if he were taking West Bend flat, and he shook his head. "Are you?" he asked. I said no, but added that I thought it could be taken flat. He said, "Yes, it can, but it probably shouldn't. It's really a handful to get around there without a lift. It can be faster that way, but you can only get it right one time in 10. The chances to screw up are much greater, and they'll get to you. But if you lift, you can get through there more consistently, time after time. It's a whole lot easier on your nerves, and no one will ever get away from you because of it."

Steve employed what he called a "confidence lift;" as the bend approached, he eased off the throttle for barely a beat, then pressed his foot back to the floor just before the turning point. He didn't think the interruption of momentum was significant; in fact, he said, the move settled the car's suspension and transferred weight to the rear wheels, which improved traction through the turn. It was called a confidence lift because that's what it gave the driver in the turn.

The expression was new to me, and it seemed a misnomer; wasn't it really a lack-of-confidence lift? It only gave you confidence that you wouldn't spin out, which seemed negative and a misdirected ambition. To me, it was simple: If the turn could be taken flat-out, it should be. I didn't believe that the suspension needed to be settled as much as the throttle needed to be mashed. I believed that hundredths of seconds could be gained by taking West Bend flat, and that a confidence lift didn't reduce the chances of spinning out by enough to make it worth the time. It seemed like a security blanket, and I didn't want any bundling. Attempting West Bend flat-out might even have been symbolic to me, and I might have viewed the outcome as a portent; I could shape my future by going for it and pulling it off. I was after the perfect lap, which was invitingly finite at Lime Rock. If you're going 98 yards, why not 100? Chasing hundredths of seconds is what winners do. The less you lift, the faster you go. Hadn't that been the lesson at Pocono? And hadn't the fact that I survived the slide in the Elkhart kink — and felt so good about it — proven that WFO was the right approach?

I might have survived West Bend too, if it had been the only turn like a tightrope at Lime Rock. But two more turns, going back more than half a mile, preceded it. The first one was a quick right-hander that completed a stretched-out S bend, and was taken flat-out in second gear, about 70 mph. Then you sped onto No-Name Straight, whose curious tag fit because the stretch felt so remote. At the end of that straight was a bend called the Uphill, which was neither as tight nor as fast as West Bend, but many drivers found it dodgier because it was blind; in one of the heat races, there was a serious flip (without injury) there. The Uphill climbed from its apex for 50 pinched yards, where it levelled and hurled the car onto the backstraight. You knew you had taken the Uphill right when your rear wheels lifted and the tach twitched as you shot onto the backstraight.

It was about 95 degrees on the second day of practice, Thursday, July 13. Temperature records were being broken all over the East. By mid-morning the woods around the circuit sagged in the muggy air, and the locusts buzzed madly. The sun softened the grease and rubber in the track, which got slicker by the hour. In the early practice session I'd begun taking the Uphill flat-out and it felt good; now, in the second session, I was passing other drivers as if they were senior citizens on the freeway. I was flat everywhere I wanted to be, except West Bend. I was hot, and ready for it. The Red Mist floated over my visor.

I waited until I got a clear lap. I sped down the empty

backstraight watching West Bend coming and knowing my foot was committed: No flinches. I held my breath. Until then, I'd always figured "held my breath" was merely a figure of speech — Mario Andretti even used it, describing how he went through Turn 3 at Indy that year.

I might as well have closed my eyes, too. The fact that I got through West Bend that lap, and the next two after that, is mostly evidence that dumb luck is also more than a figure of speech. The car didn't even slide. I heard myself whooping again, and at the time I would have said the whoops were excited expressions of self-congratulation for such stunning execution, but they were more likely outbursts of relief. Or should have been. You know what they say about pride before the fall. Or as Bruce MacInnes, Barber's chief instructor, said, "Basic rule of racing: If it feels good, watch out."

The problem went back to the right-hander entering No-Name Straight. That was where the breakthrough came. By accident, I found that if I just threw the car around the turn — shades of Michael Zimicki — it would come out faster than if I used all the road. A broadside was quicker because the track was so greasy; the line probably only works during a heat wave. I could hear the difference in the engine; the car seemed to lunge onto No-Name, and it felt fantastic.

Carrying that burst along No-Name and taking the Uphill flat, I was now approaching West Bend two or three miles an hour faster than I had been the previous day, when the track was cooler and I was lifting. I was taking three steps at once, but was too excited for anything to register that took that much thinking. Doc said that Al Holbert always told him that when you have a breakthrough like that, stop and think about it that very lap; because on the next lap, you crash. Of course, Doc's telling me that three days later didn't do much good at the moment.

I think I must have turned in too early; or maybe it was too late, or maybe right on time but imprecise, or maybe — though this is unlikely — I had everything right but the decision to try it, and my speed into West Bend was more than Dan Gurney himself could have handled this day. For whatever reason, the car got loose this time, and I kept my foot in it because it seemed like the right thing to do.

West Bend was not the Elkhart kink, however; this was not the same day, nor was this the same car — it wasn't even the same model. The slide continued into a tidy 180, and I was suddenly merely along for a backward ride down the track at 70 or 80 miles an hour, the half-twist having scrubbed off speed. The car angled off into the dirt, making awful noises as stones battered its belly, and as it slid along backward I worried about dirt getting in everything. I couldn't believe this was happening. And I never dreamed I would actually come in contact with anything.

I was stunned out of my delusions by a thud against a dirt embankment around the foundation of a wooden bridge over the track, which I'd assaulted with my blind side. It could have been worse. I had slid for about 150 yards which slowed the car down, and it landed at a 45-degree angle, the left rear wheel striking first, then the left front. A layer of old tires padded the embankment, and one of them popped down and bounced off my head. I switched off the ignition and sat for a moment in the hot dust cloud, still disbelieving, then climbed out. The car wasn't seriously damaged; the oil cooler was smashed, but there were no wheels hanging like broken limbs. That was a big relief: The embarrassment would be smaller. Then I looked back at the track, and couldn't remember ever seeing it before.

Bill Proutt, the instructor whose words at Elkhart had just become prophetic, and Tristan Lewis, an instructor who had raced Formula Fords in his native England, screeched up in the school's van. The dust had settled, the car and I were both intact, and they see this sort of thing all the time, so there was no real alarm. "Do me a favor and drive me around the track right now," I answered when they asked if I was all right; "I might have a little problem." Before we got to the next turn — the track's final bend, a 100-mph sweeper at the bottom of a hill and flat-out for the brave yet again — I knew I was in Wonderland. It was perfectly clear who I was, where I was, and why I was there, but the track was like a road I'd never driven before.

They sat me down on a folding chair in a little air-conditioned room under the scoring stand, with instructions to remain still for a while. I had a vision of the day I learned to ride a bicycle. I was seven or eight, about two agonizing and embarrassing years overdue, and the breakthrough had come one afternoon during the summer's first heat wave, on the oiled-dirt infield of the local ballpark. I sped home on the bike feeling as if I were hang gliding, and ran inside to announce to my mother that I had finally gotten it. She made me lie down in a cool room with ice on my forehead, genuinely alarmed that I was near sunstroke.

Sitting in that little room at Lime Rock was like *deja vu*, except for one thing: I couldn't remember the breakthrough. The crash didn't concern me at the moment; it was past, and I didn't care about any postmortem so soon. But the breakthrough was important because it was the future; it meant a big chunk of speed. That was all that mattered. There would be no easing off, no remaining still, until I remembered it. I could *feel* the surge from the breakthrough, but I couldn't place it. It was enormously frustrating to think that I might not be able to recreate it.

Predictably, however, the memory blank didn't last. When my recollection of tossing the car around the right-hander returned, I ran outside and announced to Tristan Lewis that I had gotten it; I remembered the breakthrough! He said, "Maybe we better run you in to the hospital, for a little check." So we drove into the village of Sharon, and waited in the emergency room with the summer morning's assorted victims — lawnmower casualties and such. After the doctor was satisfied that I didn't have a concussion, we returned to the track in time for the final two sessions of the day.

I felt strangely feisty now, and wondered if this were how Jimmy Connors felt before a tennis match. My racing shoes felt like boxer's, and I walked on my toes. I leaped up to a beam over pit road and hung by my fingertips, then climbed to the starter's box. When Tristan asked me how I felt, I told him to let me in, coach, I'm ready, and I guess he believed in climbing back up before you lose your courage, but he didn't know that I was too dumb to lose mine. So I started the afternoon's final session. The car was an awful lime color. On the first turn of the second lap I spun despite being about 20 miles an hour below racing speed, so I motored back to the pits. Tristan asked what had happened, and I told him that something besides the car might be loose, so maybe I should sleep on it. He agreed that it was a good idea, and pointed out that supposedly your head doesn't have to hit anything for you to get a concussion, that merely the impact of your brain sloshing against your skull after a sudden stop can do it. The stop had certainly been sudden, and there was also the gong from the tire. Tristan added that it was a good thing we'd gone to the hospital, because (he said) Mark Donohue had seemed fine the day after his crash in Austria — a headache was all — but the day after that he dropped dead.

Back at the cool Sharon Motor Lodge, I took a swim in the small, shaded pool. That night I tried not to wonder if I were dingy. I had a headache, but that was common for racedrivers at the end of a day. I knocked a duffel bag off a table and gear dumped on the floor, but that was common for me. And the next morning I forgot my gloves, but did that really mean I was too goofy to drive? I held fourth place for a few laps in my heat race, but spun out in West Bend again. I hadn't been taking it flat-out, of course; in fact, I probably spun because I was being tentative. It was a much quicker and less threatening spin than the previous day's, and there was no thought of here-we-go-again. I was actually relieved, even before the car stopped sliding. As I pulled away, I was glad it had happened: It was over with, out of my system, I could get back to business now.

I was optimistic about the main event on Saturday. (They don't race on Sunday at Lime Rock, because there's a big old stone church next door, overlooking the front straight.) But I was out of the hunt from the start, which I fouled up, and finished seventh. I didn't feel slow, and my reflexes seemed okay, but the difference between mediocre laps and good ones escaped me. The day was so hot that the race was shortened from 30 to 20 laps. The track was as slick as anyone could remember; the racing line actually glistened black on the gray pavement. Only 11 cars started, so my ego was nicked by seventh-place — it was the mark of a fast guy to do well at Lime Rock — but I had a decent excuse if I wanted to give myself a break. Which I did, without hesitation; I wasn't going to worry about this race. I had already thought too much about the wrong things and not enough about the right ones. I'd been thinking about my psyche when I should have been thinking about my ass — literally, for my biggest mistake was forgetting to feel the seat of my pants in West Bend. That's where you feel a slide first, because that's where you're closest to the car. Doc even taught his students to hold the steering wheel at 3 and 9 o'clock and shuffle it in the turns, in order to keep your shoulders against the seat.

Tackling West Bend flat-out had been dumb because I wasn't good enough yet, but it wasn't necessarily wrong — even though it might have killed me, remote as that possibility was. At least it showed — as cheating at Elkhart had — a racer's heart. So what, if I still didn't know when to ease off? This time I would. I wrote off the seventh-place finish to a physical impairment beyond my control, and tried to forget it.

Steve Pope won his race, after dicing for 20 laps with two other drivers and taking the lead on the final lap. He drove a racer's race and a thinker's race. He would go back to the Renault Cup and finish fourth, missing his trip to France in the final race when a

wheel bearing burned out. The next year he would race five times —
two IMSA endurance races for which he bought rides, the cars
finishing neither, and three Barber events. He went to six or seven
other IMSA races, however, trying to pry open the door. I would see
him there, wandering around, looking and hoping for a ride.

Even two of Road America's four miles were a joy to race on.

Lime Rock Park was deceptive and seductive.

Chapter Five

David Darby

More Kinks

T he West Coast counterpart to Skip Barber was a thin, sandy-bearded Montreal native named Jacques Couture. It was Couture who had introduced the idea of a Formula Ford school/series to North America, bringing it from England in 1968, where he had pursued his own driving career. He borrowed the format and name of the Jim Russell British School of Motor Racing and set up shop at Le Circuit Mont Tremblant in Quebec. Jim Russell himself was uninvolved, so the acronym BSMR, awkward as it was, became the school's operating title. After eight years at Mont Tremblant the school had expanded to California, where I was headed for two BSMR races.

Couture believed that there was no such thing as a "born" driver, and that it took *five years* to recognize if a driver had what it took to be a champion. During his own racing career he'd been known as a technician; he rarely set a wheel wrong, and never took an unnecessary chance. He still burned with a fire so contained it seemed cool, which was how he perceived driving: The object was control. Speed was merely the result. He preached precision the way he had practiced it, and he absolutely badgered people about mental awareness. That was the key to Victory Circle, if not the secret to success. Forget about bravery, forget about natural ability; without the proper decisions first, those traits were merely dangerous and expensive trouble. Throw emotion and ego out the window. Race the road, not the other drivers. Mental qualities were the thing. Good judgment. At BSMR races he often stood amidst the cars on the grid, sending them off on the pace lap one-by-one, looking squarely at each driver and tapping his head in order to deliver one last message: *Use it.*

When he was in his early twenties, Couture had been Quebec's Great White Hope. The French-Canadians, who can be as fervent as Italians over their racedriving heroes, had never had a Formula 1 grand prix driver, and young Jacques excited their desire. When the famous drivers came to Mont Tremblant — Stirling Moss, Phil Hill, Pedro Rodriguez and others — he held them off. Some supporters sent him to Modena, Italy, to the racedriving school of Piero Taruffi, who had literally written the book on technique, in 1953. The itinerary — pilgrimage — included dinner with Enzo Ferrari himself, *il commendatore*, the silver-haired godfather of European racing. Couture returned to Montreal and continued racing, scraping up financing as he went...for the next nine years. He won the Canadian Road Racing Championship in 1971 and the next year tried to crack Formula 2 in Europe, just one step from the grand prix circuit. But the price of a Formula 2 season was $165,000, and he could raise only 80.

His racing career tapered off after that, and the experience inspired his teaching career. He burned to make motor racing "less of an auction," a desire not unlike Skip Barber's, but more than providing shelter from the cruel world, Couture wanted to change it. The revolution would be manned by the aspiring racedrivers he would turn into good ones. Now, after 15 years, he had influenced thousands of drivers, most of them young. The sport's structure was unmoved.

The first time I saw Jacques, he was chewing out a roomful of drivers on a BSMR practice day. I'd entered the room late and didn't know who he was, nor could I fathom what he could have to bitch about, since no one had even been on the track yet. Displayed on a slide-projector screen was a page of the BSMR orientation book, a diagram of a decreasing-radius turn. Couture was jabbing it as he spoke, emphasizing the turn's proper line by indicating where not to be on the asphalt, which he pronounced "ashphalt," as if that were the one English word he had yet to get right. The corner on the screen was unlike any on the track which the drivers had yet to see, but he was growling at them as if they had just spent the day driving through it backward. But he wasn't really angry, merely passionate. This was his mission.

Despite my vow not to let it, the seventh-place finish at Lime Rock had gotten to me. I was detuned when I went to California for races at Riverside, east of Los Angeles, and Laguna Seca, south of San Francisco in Monterey. My ego wasn't convinced that there had been extenuating circumstances; you're only as good as your last race, which made me a seventh-place driver. But it wasn't just that; in one week I'd been turned down by STP, Gatorade and Warner Hodgdon, an industrialist and heavy racing investor, for a sponsorship I'd thought would come easy: $5,000 to do five stock car races on short ovals around New England — a small slice of the NASCAR North tour. That was to be the story's next leg. Its final leg would be the IMSA ride with Doc Bundy in the Holbert Porsche.

A much-needed rebound came with practice at Riverside. I drove well, and rediscovered someone from my past: Eddie Wirth, a true-grit racer I hadn't seen in 10 years. Long before I'd met him, I coveted Eddie's life. I was 19 and California Dreaming, reading *Cycle World* magazine in my bedroom; he was a professional motorcycle racer from Southern California who hit the county-fair circuit each summer, travelling with his mechanic in a van carrying four bikes built by his father. There he was in a photo, carrying his surfboard over the seawall between his porch and the beach. And in another with his Harley flat-tracker. He was tall, lean and handsome, with wispy hair which I knew could only grow that white in California. The Harley and the county fairs seemed sensationally romantic. Such a life was out of my reach, I was sure, but not beyond my imagination.

A year later I'd made my way to California — although I had to join the Navy to do it — and a few years after that I met Eddie. I was working for the tabloid *MotorCycle Weekly*, spending Friday nights at Ascot Speedway, the famous half-mile dirt oval near L.A., the track "where the Harbor Freeway meets the San Diego," an earthy intersection that was the hot heart of motorcycle racing in America. Wirth was one of the fast guys there. The rest of the racers all looked the way flat-trackers are supposed to — 5'7", 135, wiry and bowlegged — while Eddie was 6'3" and 190, which didn't help him on the track. But the Ascot fans loved him, largely because he was faithful to the place. His allegiance wasn't completely by choice, however; he never got the deal that would have put him on the full national circuit. When the BSA factory brought some gravy to motorcycle racing in 1971, Wirth was 27, and it was offered to younger riders.

I got to know him that summer. In September, at the AMA National in Ascot, I sat in the dark and rowdy stands along the first turn, where the cops sometimes looked the other way when the fans smoked grass, and cheered for Eddie with his friends.

I moved back East, and lost touch. A few seasons later, Wirth crashed while leading the Semi one Saturday night in Oklahoma City, and badly burned his leg against the Harley's exhaust pipe. He left for another race that night — racers travelled together, and the show keeps rolling. He kept racing on the unhealed leg, and tore it open later that summer in a crash at Dayton. The two-week stay in the hospital there wiped out his bank account, and exhausted his enthusiasm for competing against fearless 19-year-olds with rubber bones. He stayed away from racetracks for a while, working on Hollywood transportation crews and socking away the good wages. "The trouble was, I took the money and went out and bought a sprint car, and was right back where I started," he says.

Now he was in his fourth year on the California Racing Association circuit. Most of the CRA races were at Ascot, and Eddie was again a fast guy there. He'd been racing 20 years, grinding out countless gritty Friday and Saturday nights under the lights of Ascot Speedway and the Harbor Freeway, and things hadn't changed much. The CRA was not the major sprint car circuit; that was the World of Outlaws, which was national and paid rich purses. The Outlaws was a young league but it had gotten a head start on Wirth, and he couldn't catch it. His timing still wasn't right.

He was currently fourth in CRA points, and had been driving confidently and getting faster by the week at Ascot, pushing for his first win in a main event. And here he was at Riverside, entered in the BSMR race — as rangy as ever, though some of the fine white hair was gone. The school and this race had been a birthday present from his girlfriend, who was also his partner, their business being his career. Although Formula Fords were a far cry from 650-horsepower sprint cars, and Riverside was hardly a dirt oval, he thought that driving the delicate-handling machines might make him smoother in the dirt.

BSMR had two classes, Novice and Experienced, and Eddie and I were Novices because we had run less than four BSMR races. I was glad to be a Novice — it would greatly improve my chances of winning — and it didn't really matter to Eddie, but the irony of his status was inescapable. And since he was as low-key as ever, nobody but me knew who he was. All that the others knew was that this old Novice was mysteriously quick for his first race. I wanted to tell them, "Hey, this is *Eddie Wirth.*"

By now I had driven hundreds of laps in Formula Fords, and could run with him. We were on the front row for the heat race, with me on the pole by .4 seconds. I led the field snaking through the esses and into Turn 6 where I missed a downshift, gnashing the gears as I got a piece of reverse in my clumsy and frantic search for second. Wirth nearly rammed me, but since I was right on the line he couldn't get by. On the backstraight a bright red car blew past us both. The BSMR Van Diemens were exceptionally clean, tight and reliable, but sometimes a rocket — such as this red #27 — would slip into the field. It led the first lap and into Turn 2, a kink sprawled in the desert and opening the long and legendary four-turn esses. The leader wasn't very good through there, so Wirth and I jammed up on him. As the three of us approached the chicane, a left-right jog at the end of the long backstraight, #27 braked so hard it caught me by surprise; I locked my brakes to keep from smashing him, but the nose of my car poked his gearbox behind his engine. Wirth nearly made it a chain reaction. As we exited the chicane #27 accelerated away, until we caught him again in the esses.

As we entered the chicane on the third lap, I was thinking about how to avoid him; Wirth, the racer, was thinking about how to pass him. I obligingly kept my distance behind #27, overbraking with him, and Eddie swung out and dove beneath us both, hugging the inside of the turn and taking the lead. The instant he began going by I realized how misplaced — stupid — my conservatism had been, and on the next lap I passed 27 there.

Eddie and I had a terrific race the rest of the way. If there had been any spectators — it was about 105 degrees, and even the lizards were under the rocks — they would have been on their feet. I was rarely more than two car lengths behind him, less when I could be, and was loving every minute. It felt as if we had taken over the place. I was using a confidence lift in Turn 2 that was apparently briefer than his, and as we flew into the esses I had to feather the throttle to keep from nudging him, since the line was too narrow to pass (a problem I once saw Parnelli Jones solve by cutting straight through the dirt in a big Mercury stock car, gobbling up about 10 cars on the first lap). I was glued to his gearbox, almost close enough to read his tach over his shoulder, and lap after lap we flicked through the esses: right, left, right, left at 110 miles an hour. I couldn't see much of the road but was still comfortable, secure that he wouldn't steer me astray; Hey, this was *Eddie Wirth*. He never gave me an opportunity to pass, and I couldn't find a place to take one. As we left the chicane on the last lap I gave it my best shot, drafting him around banked Turn 9 and swinging out to try a slingshot pass at the finish line, but the nose of my car got no farther than his rear tire. He had outdriven me according to the Jacques Couture book.

Except for one thing: I'd pushed him to 6300 rpm, 500 over the limit — which wasn't too bad for him, considering his sprint car didn't even *have* a tach. But I was drawn to 6200 myself — and then received a 30-second penalty for contact with #27, who was declared the winner. Wirth was third and I was fifth. He hardly cared — he was incredulous over the rule anyhow — and suddenly I didn't care either, and we sneaked away from the track. The drivers were supposed to stay and work as flag persons, but when we saw the driver of #27 leave in his Lincoln Continental, we split and found a dark and cool bar on the highway. We drank icy long-necked bottles of Budweiser until we both had a light buzz, the first time I'd allowed myself any alcohol since I'd begun racing. The day was the most fun I had all that summer.

That evening it cooled down to about 95. Streaked clouds in the smoggy sky glowed orange like oven coils over the parking lot of the Holiday Inn. I paused there, on my way to Wendy's for dinner, and wished to the spectacular heavens that Wirth and I might have a rematch the next day, and that #27 would be in another race — or that I would draw it.

In order to reduce luck's influence, there was supposedly a BSMR rule preventing a driver from getting the same car both days. But in the main event, #27 ended up in the same hands. Its driver,

Charles Nameless, had been chummy with one of the instructors, French-Canadian Richard Spenard, who had been my own excellent teacher that March. Couture was absent this day; I suspect that Spenard let the rule slide for Charles — an Unfair Advantage. I wouldn't have cared, except that Charles not only drew #27 again, but my race, too. Wirth was in another.

Charles had brought a few of his fans along in the Lincoln. They might have been valets, judging from the way Charles carried himself. He had his strut *down*; his quilted red driving suit was snugly tailored to his six-foot, 190-pound frame, and he had a macho-man moustache that was probably trimmed by the same stylist who shaped his thick black hair. He sat buckled in his car on the grid before the start, shaded by an umbrella held by one of his attendants, and wore a padded neck support. A horse collar! For a 30-minute race! It was hilarious. For 20 years Bobby Unser raced Indy cars, whose G forces whip your head as if you'd been socked in the jaw, without a horse collar. And he has a skinny neck.

There was a fast and hungry kid in the race. I did a doubletake when I saw the name "Johnny Rutherford" sewn over the breast pocket of his driving suit, and wondered if he were JR's son, if one existed. He might as well have been; his father was Hap Sharp and his stepfather was Ronnie Hissom, both successful Texas road racers in the '60s. His name was Robert Hissom, he was 19, and the uniform was a hand-me-down from his friend "Lone Star JR," who, after A.J. Foyt, is the most famous Texas racedriver. Hissom had learned to drive on Rattlesnake Raceway, the test track in Midland owned by Jim Hall, who, after A.J. Foyt, is the most famous Texas car owner.

On the first lap I moved from fifth on the grid to second behind Hissom, outbraking Charles into Turn 7, a sinking loop. As we accelerated onto the backstraight the red car sped by me, and I knew this would be a rerun. For another 1½ laps he held me off, and up; I pushed him through the esses and slipped under him in either Turn 7 or the chicane, but on the straights he would fly past. On the third lap he began a long, slow fishtail in Turn 2, his gearbox swinging like a pendulum before me, and he flew headlong off the track at 90 miles an hour. Since there was a rule requiring a driver to pit for a checkup (and possible lecture) if he bit the dirt, I backed off and gave him room for his re-entry, preparing for it to be sideways. Had it not been for the rule, I might have kept my foot flat and my fingers crossed, because Hissom was getting away.

Such a decision would have been questionable; it's always brain-fade to get wiped out by a squirrel. Charles came back on the track with his tail twitching, and when I passed him in Turn 6 I figured, "So long and good riddance." At the end of the lap, I watched in my mirror as he pitted.

Hissom was about 200 yards ahead now, and it took me two laps to settle down for the chase, leaving me nine or 10 laps to catch him. If I could gain half a second per lap I'd be there, and maybe I could pass him before the finish. As I sailed down the front straight watching him in Turn 1, I saw #27 speeding up pit road...and settling right in front of me, as if the track were a roulette wheel and Charles the little ball, landing on my unlucky number. I outbraked him into 7, and when he repassed me on the back-straight I couldn't believe it. I outbraked him into 7 again, and when he passed me on the backstraight I gestured at him — it wasn't even a shaking fist or flipped bird — but he ignored my protest. On the front straight, I pointed an accusatory finger at him for Richard Spenard's benefit. Charles got the black flag on the next lap, but he never saw it.

So I continued to try to put him behind me, before Hissom got completely out of reach. I had outbraked him enough times into Turn 7 that he wised up and began blocking me. My frustration drove me to a quick outburst of teeth-clenching, steering wheel-tugging and shouting. It was not an unfamiliar reaction — it's how I generally respond to traffic jams, my refusal to slow down for the world at its most unpleasant then — but this was the first time that such loss of control had reared its head in a racecar, and it alarmed me. I caught myself and snapped calm again, knowing I needed to slam the door on this weakness early.

As we began the last lap, the odds against catching Hissom now hopeless, Charles was in my draft. He moved alongside me one last time, and we approached Turn 2 abreast, at about 100. I sensed that there was no way he was going to back off; and there was no way I was *not* going to. The only race was for ego; it was a dangerous race, and it wasn't mine. I slowed down as if I'd just crossed the finish line, and followed him at a safe distance through the esses, watching as he took Turns 6 and 7 wildly; he thought I was on his tail, still racing him! He was probably rendered so stupid by his macho ego that — besides forgetting that his car had mirrors — he assumed racing meant the same thing to everyone that it must have meant to him.

Back in the pits, I walked over to him before he got out of his car — he was probably waiting for his umbrella. As he was climbing out, I said, evenly, "You had no business pulling a stunt like that. You were out of the race, you had blown your chance, you were a couple of laps behind. A lapped car isn't supposed to get in the way of a race for the lead. The only reason you could keep up with me in the first place is because the Goddamn car is a rocket ship, and you know it." He responded by throwing his $250 helmet against pit wall. He shouted, "I had the right to unlap myself! I had as much right to race out there as you did!" I knew then that his ignorance nearly equalled his affectedness, and I told him that he was sorely mistaken — "That's horseshit" were probably the words — and if he didn't believe me he could ask Richard, whom I grabbed for him and said, "Go ahead, Ree-shar, tell him." Which he did, and he also calmed him down, and for the rest of the afternoon Charles and I ignored each other.

I watched Eddie Wirth handily win the other Novice race. He would go back to Ascot the next Saturday and win his first main event, and would take two more that season, finishing fourth in CRA points. At 40, he was the latest young lion at Ascot Speedway.

I thought about my race as I drove north the next day. I regretted that I hadn't been more ruthless. I wished that instead of having repeatedly tried to pass Charles, I had tricked him into spinning out or running off the track, which probably wouldn't have been that difficult. It might have meant a crash for him; but too bad. This was the mean streak that Dan Gurney once said every good racedriver has. I was glad it was there.

I was headed for Sears Point, a circuit in the wine country just north of San Francisco. Rick Mears, the Indy car champion, was entered in an IMSA endurance race there, and I was beginning a story on him. I also wanted to meet with IMSA's president, John Bishop, to explain *Sports Illustrated*'s intention and my hope. But I didn't come away with much. Mears' factory Mustang broke on the first lap, and Bishop's response to my outline of the project was, "So? Everyone wants to drive." So much for influence.

With little choice, I climbed back into the BSMR cocoon.

* * *

Laguna Seca Raceway is the West Coast's answer to Lime Rock Park. It has a rich heritage dating to the early '50s, when tweed-cap types raced their box-nosed MGs over the old Pebble Beach road course, which wound through the pines of Monterey Peninsula's private Del Monte Forest. It's a short, fast, rolling driver's circuit, with two consecutive bends that can be taken flat-out in a Formula Ford if you hold your breath for the first and swallow your heart for the second. It contains an infamous corner called the Corkscrew, which is slow but easy to spin out on. A twisting left drops onto a twisting right, and for a moment between the two, all you can see is sky and treetops, while the pit of your stomach plops on the floorboard. Laguna was the BSMR base, and its challenging nature made it an ideal camp for Jacques Couture's revolution.

Couture didn't take the same pains as Skip Barber to keep his cars equal because he was more interested in improving his drivers than pleasing them; the student's satisfaction would have to come from learning. It was fine to standardize the equipment so the best driver won, but the best driver also needed to know how to make a slower car win. I finished fifth in the heat race that Saturday, dragging a dog and my attitude toward it. My lap times had been nearly four seconds slower than they'd been in practice the day before. Couture had been watching me, and when I protested that the car was at fault he whipped out a scrap of paper on which all my lap times were scribbled, as well as those of a driver who had raced the day earlier. My numbers were unsteady 1:25s and 1:26s, while the other fellow had clocked consistent 1:23s to finish third. It was humbling, and I got the point: I'd fought the car instead of dealing with it. Couture added that the idea was to improve as much as to win; I'd heard that before. The next morning I mentioned to the other driver that the car seemed way down on power, and he responded blithely that he hadn't noticed, which made Couture's point no less true but somewhat ironic; the guy drove it better because he was less sensitive to it. He simply drove the thing as fast as it could go, and didn't argue with it.

It all became moot when I drew a fast car for the main event. I took the pole with 1:20.5, and watched the second-place car grow steadily smaller in my mirror to the finish. It was clear that my car was superior, which added to my confidence but detracted from my satisfaction, although I would hardly have traded with the guy in my mirrors; if he'd had my car, he would have won. I turned consistent 1:21s, although another missed shift from excitement on the first lap caused an overrev that erased the official victory. Couture let me run that afternoon in another car and I finished the Experienced race third, with Robert Hissom winning.

I was booked on the redeye flight that night from San Francisco to New York; with a few spare hours, I wandered toward the beach. I struck Half Moon Bay, parked off the Pacific Coast Highway, and sat in the rental car watching the sunset over the ocean. It was not a particularly happy moment. Something was missing. My premature pursuit of the perfect lap had gotten me confused after Pocono, gonged at Lime Rock, and now it was getting me down. I'd felt no elation at the sight of the checkered flag that afternoon. And those sensational adrenaline rushes that had occurred in the beginning were absent. Was that normal, a good sign, or a bad sign? All I knew was that I missed them. And I was still worrying that I wasn't trying hard enough, mostly because I hadn't scared myself once that day. Was I backing off for security? I wasn't gaining on the fast guys. Had I plateaued? So I'd won the Novice race: Big deal, luck of the draw, and technically I hadn't won it anyhow. There had been so many drivers there who were faster than I.

That wasn't the only thing that caused this untimely funk, however. I was facing no next step, a blank racing future. No hot prospects for sponsorship loomed, no warm ones even existed. The darkening horizon held only more pitching and proposing, which seemed too much like begging for me to easily stomach. I was sapped of enthusiasm because of the rejections. I couldn't get enough of the driving, but hated the hassles of pursuing the money. Whenever I weighed myself to see if I could have been a professional racedriver — which wasn't all that often — that was the weakness I figured would have affected me most. Sensitivity — or call it lack of determination. The Doc Bundys can't afford such self-indulgence. I'd been hustling just six months, with opportunities that other drivers didn't have, and I was flagging. And the prospect of failing in the assignment depressed me at least as much as the thought of a racing career dying.

I guess it was ironic that, parked there at Half Moon Bay, I would think of the night I made up with a female co-worker after a long feud. We buried the hatchet after the *SI* Christmas party, at one of those Irish pubs in New York called O'Grady's or O'Malley's, and we closed the joint; the bartender was stacking the chairs on the tables around us. My co-worker asked me if I knew what my problem was. I said, "No, what's my problem?" She said, "Your problem is that you want the moon." I laughed; I knew she was dead right. I liked its ring as an epitaph: *His problem was he wanted the moon (and cursed the earth because it wasn't).* I really did have it all; I was getting paid for an exciting chase which nearly everyone around me was making heavy payments on. I hadn't known Peter Gregg very well, but his suicide nagged me. Not so much the actual shot in the head on a lonely Jacksonville beach one morning, but his managing to be somehow unsatisfied with his life. He had a Harvard education and three successful car dealerships — Porsche-Audi, BMW and Mercedes, nothing but the finest — not to mention the best IMSA record in history. It didn't escape me that Peter Perfect's problem was he wanted the moon.

I hadn't driven badly at all. My lap times were quick and consistent. It was still only my seventh race ever, not counting heats, and I had just won the damn thing, for heaven's sake. What more could I do? Would another second off my lap times have made me happy?

Probably. I was sure of one thing, and it was the thing that depressed me most: I should have gone *faster*.

BSMR

It felt as if Eddie and I had taken over the place.

Steve Giberson

*Eddie Wirth, a fast
guy from the old school
and buoy for the spirit.*

Owen and Judith Richards

Eddie Wirth's sprint car.

David Darby

*Jacques Couture's
passion was
driving integrity.*

*The Laguna
corkscrew, where
the bottom drops out.*

David Darby

Chapter Six

David Darby

Swept Away

F or the rest of the summer, which continued to be a hot one, I wrote about champion drivers. I brought a new perspective to my job now, and there were new questions to ask. I caught up with Bobby Allison at the Talladega 500 at Alabama International Motor Speedway, the world's fastest track, a 2.6-mile oval whose turns are banked so steeply they look like walls. Allison, 44, had been racing stock cars since he was 16, and was still hungry after all these years. He believed that he had run more races than anyone on earth; he'd covered about 160,000 miles in NASCAR Grand National alone, and between those races he flew around the country in his hopped-up airplane for smaller-time events when they paid well. What made Bobby run seemed simple: He couldn't get enough of driving around in circles. I spent a sizzling week in New York writing the story, and, later, five baking days in Las Vegas for the Caesars Palace Grand Prix, a race around the Caesars parking lot that was created — why else in Vegas? — to attract high-rolling gamblers. At the end of August I went back to California to rejoin Rick Mears. He lived in Bakersfield, and would be racing his Indy car in the CART Riverside 500 that week.

The assignment was an opportunity to break my California wheels out of storage. Sitting under a blanket in a garage in San Juan Capistrano was a 1,000cc, six-cylinder, candy-apple-red Honda CBX motorcycle. Its purchase had been inspired by a memory lingering for 15 years. I was standing in a fall drizzle at the Mosport circuit in Quebec, watching Mike (The Bike) Hailwood shriek down the front straight on a 250cc six-cylinder Honda in the Canadian Grand Prix. When he shifted through the gears at 18,000 rpm — into fifth, sixth, seventh and eighth — it was the most exciting sound I'd ever heard. But the six-cylinder wasn't for sale until the CBX came along. Honda had instructed the designer of Hailwood's engine to create one for the street — with everything four times as big. My CBX had 103 horsepower, which was nearly as much as a Formula Ford. It could do the quarter-mile in 11.36 seconds. There wasn't a production car in the world that could touch it. Ninety thousand dollars for a Lamborghini Countach, and the CBX would smoke it. I paid $3200 for the bike off the showroom floor; acceleration per dollar, it was a world's record. I kept it in a friend's garage, next to his 1948 Hudson Commodore. It was a wonder he allowed it. He was so queer for his Hudson that he posed his lovely family in its rear window for their Christmas card one year.

That week I covered Mears by motorcycle, along the freeway triangle from Los Angeles to Bakersfield to Riverside to L.A. again, and I held the bike's throttle WFO whenever I could. Out of L.A. on the Golden State Freeway one afternoon, weaving through traffic at 70 and 80 for the art of it. (Billy Joel supposedly calls such riding "terror chess," a clever metaphor but the wrong picture.) Up the backside of the Grapevine at 90, and on the downside pegging it just for the rush of seeing the speedometer needle nudging 130, as high as it goes. I spent the evening at the Mears residence, arriving late for a barbecue because I'd run out of gas just below Bakersfield — the bike had six carburetors, too — and I'd had to push about three miles over a stretch so desolate that the sunset looked like sundown on the prairie. The next day Rick, his then-wife Dina, two of their friends and I tubed down the Kern River, which was one of his favorite summer pastimes. He guided his craft with a mere occasional flick of one dangling hand, with a can of Bud Light between his knees at even keel, while those about him flapped like crazy to miss the eddies. It was how he drove. Mears won the Indianapolis 500 before he ever spun out in an Indy car, a statistic that boggled my mind.

For the three days I'd been in California, I'd been nursing an urge to speed through the baking heat. It felt strangely instinctual; on the plane from New York it felt as if that were my main mission. The brief pass over the Grapevine hadn't been nearly enough. I left for Riverside the next morning — Rick would drive their motor home down, Dina their Ferrari. I took a route through the Mojave Desert, leaving cowboy and oil country by way of Tehachapi Pass, was a red blur through the town of Mojave, flew past Edwards Air Force Base feeling like Chuck Yeager, then took a hard right at Four Corners and dodged-em on the freeway to Riverside. I averaged about 80 miles an hour including gas stops, which were frequent, the memory painfully fresh of what it feels like to push 550 pounds by its handlebars. At daybreak on the morning after the race, which Mears won handily, I rode over the twisty Ortega Highway and returned the CBX to its spot beside my friend's immortalized Hudson. I got back to New York with some nasty cobwebs blown out, courtesy of that little Japanese engineer who knew the way to my soul.

Inspired by the freedom of the saddle — and by long-distance pep talks from Doc — I had decided to try harder. Take a deep breath, chase sponsors with more effort (but less heart), and bear down on the assignment. I thought that would require more mobility than I currently had, living in the mountains — especially in winter, which was coming. I was bored with frozen pipes and wayward woodstove fires anyhow, as well as reclusiveness, having lived seven years either on the road or in the woods. And as long as I was racing, having a home, not even one I was quite attached to, didn't matter very much. In the four months that I'd been driving I'd been home just 23 total days anyhow, so it seemed as if moving could only simplify my life.

I owned a Florida condo which had just become vacant. So I loaded my pickup truck and a U-Haul trailer, kissed Cooper Hollow goodbye, and rolled south one September evening with a bunch of diet pills and a box of highway tapes. For most of the night the truck's cab was filled by Dire Straits — the same tape, playing over and over and over, with the truck's rumbling glass-packs backing up the after-dark rhythm of the music. The next day, through the South, I shifted to the clear, bluesy rock 'n' roll of Bob Seger, Joe Cocker and the Allman Brothers, with some Joe Ely rockabilly to replace the pills. I threw in Pat Benatar and then Rickie Lee Jones, just to hear a female voice. The final leg began at the second nightfall. Rolling down the Overseas Highway, which slices the ocean until the road dead-ends 90 miles from Havana, I slipped in some Texas swing from Asleep at the Wheel, a tape I'd found at a Carolina truck stop. After 28 hours and 1,504 miles, the truck's stout 350 Chevy motor still pulling hard, I reached the end of the continent. It was midnight, and about 90 muggy degrees. I wheeled up to the elevator beneath my condominium in Key West, a town they call the Last Resort. In the neighborhood were Southernmost Motel, Southernmost Pharmacy, Southernmost Texaco and more, so I dubbed my new home Southernmost Condo and settled in, looking forward to sunrises, sunsets, and maybe even a hurricane from my balcony facing the ocean.

* * *

Septembers have changed my life. In September, I was born (under a full moon); first fell in love (at 17); left home (18); got married (19, same girl); separated (after seven years); divorced (the next year); was hired by *Sports Illustrated* and moved to New York City, a town that drove me to the woods after 12 months. Now, after seven more Septembers, here I was on a small island that, so they say, hangs on the edge of desperation. That may be a melodramatic description, but I know what they mean, now.

This September was a world beater. It not only took me to a foreign land, it brought me DD. Talk about cosmic messages. Simplifying my life by moving. Ha-Ha.

I loved her unalterably; she loved me obsessively. Once, while watching a TV movie about a heart transplant she burst into tears the moment the heart was transferred. That was how she clutched the people she loved, as if it were her heartstrings attaching her. Love was her overpowering and frequently unguided instinct. My own unguided instinct may be survival, which is what made the romance all but tragic. It was some kind of dirty trick: It took us forever to find each other, and when we did, we didn't have the slightest idea how to handle each other, except when we made love. "All my life I've been waiting for someone, and when I find her she's a fish," said the guy who falls in love with a mermaid. "Nobody said love was perfect," he's told.

She had so many qualities — eight or ten, at least — both physical and emotional, that were stronger than any I'd ever known. I never imagined anyone could have so many "mosts." Half of them were good. Some could go either way. I don't like to think about the rest.

Volatility controlled the affair. It seemed as if our relationship would be our purgatory: a perpetual knife fight. Once, merely walking down the street, DD was approached by a psychic who was awed by her aura, it was so full of sparks (if only I'd had his vision). They flew off her when I touched her, as if she were a big battery and I was crossing the cables. The relationship was a cruel conundrum: She wanted to change me and I wanted her to stop trying. "Helping someone who needs me is the only thing in my life that can make me happy," she once said, and boy, did that scare me, even before I realized how much she meant it. Her idealism was so hopeless it was irrational. She disapproved of reality and fought it with her passion.

When we were separated, I read a "Personals" ad in which a woman billed herself as a "Classic Underachiever of Dubious Sanity," and I thought for sure DD had placed it. Friends said we clashed so hard because our temperaments were so much alike, and that may have been true, but the reason we clashed at all is because we were so different. We couldn't change the chemistry, or the odds. We'll never live together (again), but we'll always want to; our love might follow us like a curse. Our best shot, a very long one, is to meet again years from now, when we're older and wiser, and lonelier.

It may be stretching credibility when I say I can't remember what the arguments with DD were about, not even the worst of them — fights I'll spare you the details of, involving police and leaving bloody palmprints on the walls. I never discussed them with my therapist the tape recorder, and now I can't remember what started them, if I ever knew. Things were usually fine between us the next day anyhow; it's easy to make up when you don't know why you're fighting. And when you wonder — as you will — why I let myself live with this, especially while I was trying to drive racecars, I won't be able to answer because I didn't know then, and I don't ask myself the question any more. After 18 brutal months I only know this: I loved her. And the way I know I loved her is that I put up with her.

On a hunch, I once consulted an astrologer about DD — the hunch had struck when I learned that Cancer, the claw, DD's sign, represented clinging. The astrologer, a Texan named Mary Orser, was 60, looked 40, and wore her pigtails well. She said the universe was just a big tuning fork and we were all merely vibrations, a metaphor I found lovely, and easy to live with. I'd given her DD's time and place of birth — nothing more — and she told me DD's past so specifically and accurately that it made me tremble. Then she got into DD's "mosts." She used the same words to describe DD that I'd used at times. She said DD was a little girl looking in the window of a wonderful doll shop she couldn't get into, and told me things about the woman I loved that had taken me tormented months to discover. She had made a chart, and planets were floating on the coffee table. There it was, she said, fingering a tight cluster of five of DD's stars. She'd never seen an arrangement quite like it. Once a week DD's moon passed through the five stars, hovering to gang up on it, an ambush repeated for infinity. The astrologer said it was like turning on all the electricity in the house at once.

I used to kid DD that it was in-breeding that made her crazy. She was a fifth-generation Conch, as Key West natives are called. She believes she's different — she concedes no more than that — because of the cat-scratch fever she had when she was five. She says her mother told her that her temperature hit 106. Later that summer she ran into the corner of the house, and the soft, lovely dent in her forehead gently reminded me of her uniqueness. (And how many times did I think of the lyric in the song "Vincent" — "...the world was never meant for one so beautiful as you" — to keep from hating her when she drove me toward it.) She knows she's not crazy. She once admitted herself to a mental hospital on one of those electric days, then demanded to be released when she discovered that people were crazy in there. But it's the only place that makes her feel sane, she says. She knows it's the rest of the world that's crazy; her problem — her own tragedy — is that she doesn't realize it's bigger than her.

She grew up next door to Tennessee Williams, the dramatist of lost souls. It's been said that he never created a character who had recovered from the wounds and desolation of childhood, and there were times when I thought he must have been watching DD. "I never lied to you in my heart," Blanche said, and how many times did DD justify the destructive things she did by saying she didn't mean it. But to Tennessee she was only a no-neck monster, and it was she who was watching him, as he lounged around the pool with young men he called his "secretaries," although she had no idea what it all meant. Sometimes he would see her and chase her away — DD and her giggling girlfriends running down Duncan Street.

Her grades were always sky-high — she has a photographic memory, a weapon I had no counter for — but her report cards carried notes home, things like, "DD is so bright, but she won't pay attention. She's doing better at staying in her seat, but she is such a stubborn little girl, and she refuses to listen." When she was 10, her mother left the family and moved into the window of the doll shop. That's really what has made her different, she says. But she was always a troubled child. There is a haunting photograph of her at 15, and she looks no more than 11. Pale, reed-thin, with eyes expressing fear and wariness, she seems to be hiding — or wanting to — behind the corner of her house. She was pale because she was so skinny. "Everybody would make fun of me so I stayed inside all the time," she says. "I lived in the tropics and never had a tan." When her bangs were cut short she looked like a little boy. She thought you had to be shaped like the Cuban ladies to be sexy, and she's still blind to her beauty, of course. She usually carried a day-old sandwich in her purse, at the ready, to nibble at the slightest hunger pang since they came so infrequently.

She was nearly 5'8" and weighed 116 pounds now, and she didn't look frail any more. She had nice muscles, a body that was half ballerina and half high-jumper; there was probably a natural athlete buried and going to waste somewhere in those lazy bones. But she was self-conscious of her long legs. Despite the heat of the tropics, she didn't wear shorts very often; usually she wore loose cotton pants that she liked to make go whoosh when she walked. And she always wore those little canvas Chinese shoes — she bought them by the bunch, in different colors at three dollars a pair, and wore them until a toe popped through. That was one reason she never seemed tall; another was because she walked so fast, moving like water along steps. People always remembered that, along with her voice. They constantly told her how sexy it was, and she wouldn't have known how to affect it if she'd wanted to. She was briefly a disc jockey once, until she quit because it was boring to work all alone in a little room, and the radio station wanted her back pretty badly. Her words came out low and smooth and husky — also at random and highly original, as if Casey Stengel was her syntax coach. She said the most remarkably genuine things, half of them disarming and the other half defiant.

Her resistance to being tampered·with, however creative it may have been, got her in trouble a lot. Her college boyfriend called her "Dangerous Darlene" (the D's are a coincidence). Late one night they had a fight at her house and he drove off furious. DD chased him down, they made up at a gas station, and each headed home. On her way back a policeman tried to pull her over, and she ignored him — it was 2 a.m. and she was in her pajamas and hadn't been speeding anyhow. As his red light flashed and siren wailed, she continued to cruise along at 35 miles an hour, staring straight ahead. The cop radioed for reinforcements, and when DD saw the other police car speeding toward her with his high beams on her like a spotlight, she swerved onto the sidewalk and the cop cars collided. The case was dismissed because they had nothing on her. The policeman said he'd tried to stop her because her pajamas made her suspicious. The judge asked her why she didn't stop. "Because I was in my pajamas," she said.

People also remembered her smile. But it's her eyes that I remember. I would say they haunt me, but they're more subtle than that. Maybe that's why I didn't notice them for so long. Or maybe because it was dark where I met her, in a cocktail lounge one steamy afternoon during the World Series. Her eyes are green, but they seemed much darker. In every picture I've seen of her, including baby pictures, they retreat and draw you along. They're pushed up exotically by her cheeks, tight rising bundles of flesh like her breasts, and make her look as if she's been crying even when she hasn't. What baby cheeks they must have been. I imagined baby DD in her carriage punching anyone who reached in to pinch a cheek. My favorite photo of her was taken on a frozen lake in Wisconsin, where I would be racing four months later; she's wearing a beige scarf wrapped over the tip of her nose just below the peaks of those cheeks, and her brown bangs fall to her brows. All that's left are beautiful, mesmerizing slits and a memory.

Until four months before we'd met, DD was an occupational therapist in Jacksonville. Her patients loved her because she was more real than they might have hoped for, and because she was an ally against the house — the hospital system. She befriended and fought for everyone from the little old lady who wanted to die comfortably more than she wanted to do exercises, to the bitter Vietnam vet who had paid for his freedom with his legs. The career had sounded good in college, where she stayed seven years because she loved the escape offered by books, but she quickly became disillusioned by the reality of administered therapy. Her fast tongue and irreverence, qualities that endeared her to her patients, made life difficult for her supervisors, and for DD too. Her perceptions were too sharp and her style too original for the book. She couldn't follow orders she didn't understand or agree with (the two are the same to her), and she believed she couldn't help her patients enough — "I can feel guilty helping the handicapped," she says with an irony she usually lacks. So, after 18 months in the profession she had trained seven years for, she left one day and moved back to Key West to think about it. She was a cocktail waitress in that dark lounge where we met, and, as she says, she was a flower in that dive.

* * *

I hadn't made much progress in the chase for rides, until an invitation arrived from the British School of Motor Racing to compete in a special event at Riverside as part of their North American Formula Ford Festival, a tournament of races in which the winner would be declared season champion and awarded $10,000 by BSMR to further his career. Jacques Couture attracted and edified the press by staging a support race called the Media Challenge, in which all the drivers were reporters. A couple of them had no racing experience, but most were decent drivers since skill behind the wheel was requisite for fair and credible road testing in the car magazines they worked for, and a few of them had been racing for years.

The trouble with DD started on the airplane, I guess, although it might have started when I invited her to Riverside and, in the same breath, cautioned her that I might be preoccupied while we were there. She wanted to talk on the plane, and I wanted to read. My "race face" was already on. She couldn't understand why anyone would invite her along on a trip and then not want to "relax" with her. I see it less simply now, but I still don't know if it was that basic, or if it was as complicated as "change." Who's trying to change whom in such a situation? Now, after all these grievous months, I can see her point of view — there's no difference between asking me to talk and her not to talk. But I still don't really get it. I wasn't asking her to *do* anything. The fact that she needed my participation was merely her misfortune.

So it was a skirmish of stubborn wills from the runway in Miami — she won because we sure were "talking" — to the runway in Houston, where the plane made a stop. We stayed in our seats and made up, and as the plane was about to take off again we took a blood oath of fidelity. We didn't have anything sharp to prick our fingers, so DD jumped up and asked along the aisle — chased by the stewardess to sit back down — until she found a lady with a needle. We started fighting again in the rental car leaving Los Angeles — the same debate, talking/not-talking, which I'd thought was five hours and 2500 miles behind us. By the time we got lost that night in downtown Riverside, driving in what seemed like concentric squares to find the romantic old Mission Inn, I wanted to scream for help. We made love ferociously — her word, a year later — and I went to the track the next day reeling.

Either I was capable of enough concentration to block out my personal problems, or the three-month layoff had improved me, or the track was fast because it was cool. I certainly wasn't prepared to believe that the previous 24 hours had somehow helped chop nearly two seconds off my best lap time from the race there in July. And I was surprised that I only spun once in the daze. Still, I felt fairly fast, and my timing seemed all there. On Saturday I qualified at 1:45.2, which was two more seconds faster, 2.5 seconds faster than anyone else in the field, and only one second off the lap times of the contenders for the festival championship. I suspected the time was an error — although BSMR's expensive electronic timer was foolproof — but I took it, and accepted the sheepish feeling that came with the congratulations at a reception at Jacques Couture's house that night. One of the "writer/racers," as our ilk was known, wondered if racing had changed my life yet. "Has it made you a slave?" he asked.

"Not me," I said.

"It will," he replied.

DD was nervous and got tipsy and charmed everyone who came near her with her deep voice and genuine manner, and as we drove back to the hotel, with her head on my shoulder, I loved her all over again. I knew we were over the hump. Our trouble had been merely a kink in the beginning of the relationship. The next morning we had a fight because I thought she was taking too long to get ready. She had promised to be ready by nine, my adrenaline had been rushing like whitewater since about six, and at 8:55 I couldn't stand it any longer. I burst into the bathroom where she was drying her hair, and told her how rotten she was for breaking her word. In the course of the brief fight that followed I reached over the open suitcase between our feet and tried to slap her. I missed. It was the first time in my life that striking someone had been a reflex action. She had jabbed a nerve that I didn't know existed. As we drove to the track I was stunned, shocked and disbelieving. As if I were viewing my own bad dream in the windshield, I saw my hand lashing out at her face, connected to my shoulder but free of my control. DD was sitting cheerfully beside me, as if it were no big thing. She says she would have been ready by nine, and I believe her, I guess.

In the heat race, from which five would transfer into the 10-car Media Challenge, I stayed in the draft of the leader, Jim Gandy, for eight of the 10 laps, knowing that all I had to do to make the main was stay there. But I wanted to pass him, simply because I thought I could. It wasn't a particularly bright thing to try, but it was the kind of thing a racer would do. The only place I had any chance to pass him and hold it — his car was faster, he admitted — was out of the chicane at the end of the backstraight. It should have been a last-lap move, if at all, but I got eager and forgot to care. When I flew into the chicane attempting and intending to charge out of it, the car went around in a little semi-circle and three guys passed. I finished sixth, missing the transfer.

For the next couple of hours I was so hangdog it was probably comical — intense moping. I wouldn't remove my driving suit. There were more than 10 cars at the track, so Couture could add one or two to the main event if he wanted to. He posted a 10-car grid, but I wasn't going to stop hoping until the race began. The moping became tense, now.

When it was time to grid the cars, he announced a 12-car field. I leaped over the pit wall toward the track. It was actually a leap for joy; the wall merely saved me from looking silly. I would start last, in a car that was a backup because it was down on power, but I didn't care. I worked up to fifth, the top four running in a draft in my sight. I might have been able to catch them if I hadn't made mistakes, but I made them. I was giving the throttle the respect that my car from the heat race had needed — taking Turn 2 with a confidence lift — but this car wasn't fast enough to warrant it, and I didn't adjust quickly enough. Forgetting the seat of my pants again. As the leaders drifted out of reach, I figured my only chance was the redline. I drove with one eye glued to the tach, carefully keeping the needle at the 5500 rpm limit, and the leading four overrevved from racing each other. After the time penalties were assessed I was pronounced second, behind the winner, Gary Witzenburg, and, because of the publicity, the official position at this race was the important one.

The victory podium ceremony felt as unreal as it was stretched. It was virtually an enactment. Most of the spectators had gone home, and slightly bewildered, I looked down from the podium to 30 or 40 people cheering as if they had been cued, with the empty gray grandstands behind them. This is what making a commercial must be like, I thought. I was standing up there under photographers' strobes, holding a bouquet and drinking from a bottle of champagne for being fifth among a group of reporters, and when the trophy queen came over it felt as if I were stealing the kiss. After the pictures were all taken I climbed down and gave DD the flowers and we walked off hand-in-hand, just like in the movies. We leaned against the front fender of the rental car with our arms wrapped around each other, watching a spectacular orange sunset — probably smog again. We vowed never to forget the moment. She would later tell me, long after the fights, "I knew then that I loved you more than anyone I've ever loved in my life — and it scared me." But I wasn't scared. I was thinking about Half Moon Bay, about what had been missing, and why the victory at Laguna Seca had been empty. Now I knew.

It had been a lucky weekend all around. I was lucky to have been invited, lucky to have been fast qualifier, lucky to get in the main event, lucky to finish second — in fact, lucky not to have overrevved, because my tach had read 5,550 rpm and an instructor had given me a break. And I was lucky to have in my arms the most beautiful creature I'd ever known.

PART II

Chapter Seven

Bob Costanza

Piracy on the High Banks

B ack home in Key West, DD quit her job — I convinced her that a dive was no place for a flower like her (maybe the only thing I ever convinced her of) — and moved into Southernmost Condo with me. We had a fight on her porch on moving day, over a difference in our packing techniques. It flared so fast that one minute we were carrying things to my truck, and the next minute — literally — I was halfway down the block on my way home, leaving a trail of boxes in her yard. Twenty minutes later I sped back, and there she was, gliding head-down along Simonton Street toward the drugstore luncheonette for soup to calm her never-calm stomach, a trip she'd been taking since she was a girl, from all parts of town. I stopped in the street and swept her off the sidewalk somehow feeling gallant, my truck a faded silver steed. So we became roommates, along with Moon, a kitten who had been thrown at our feet on our first date. We named him Moon because that's where he seemed to fall from, and because we were leaving the Full Moon Saloon when he was lobbed like a hook shot out of a passing convertible.

I spent hours on the telephone, trying to get a ride for the last race of the IMSA season, the Daytona Finale over Thanksgiving weekend. It was a three-hour race, and the rules required two drivers per car. Depending upon the value and speed of the car, as well as the whims and wealth of a car owner, a 90-minute shift could be purchased for any amount from $2,000 to $15,000. Three classes raced together: GTO, for sports cars having engines "over" 2.5 liters; GTU, "under" 2.5 liters; and GTP, the "prototypes," which were fast, exotic and outrageously expensive. What I offered was vague: no money and little experience, just my winning personality and the possibility — no guarantee — of eventual exposure in a major magazine. To a car owner I was basically a carrot; I might pay off later by attracting a sponsor for him.

There were better drivers around willing to pay for rides; but I had connections. About 10 days before the race, Ron Meade, who handled publicity at Daytona, suggested I call an owner named Gordy Oftedahl, who had two GTO-class Firebirds entered for the Finale but only three drivers named. Since Oftedahl was known to be a dealmaker, Meade said, maybe I could work something out with him. I knew that Oftedahl was from somewhere in the Midwest and had a reputation for building fast cars, but I couldn't recall his name from Victory Circle anywhere — not that his past mattered. All he knew about me was whatever Meade may have told him. When I called, after asking if I had $4,000, he asked what kind of driving I'd done. "Mostly Formula Fords," I said, which was true enough, although I didn't volunteer that it was with Barber and BSMR, not the SCCA national circuit. That was all he asked. He said he'd been negotiating with another driver but it didn't look as if the guy had the $4,000, so I could drive the Firebird if I provided tires for the race. A set of Goodyear racing slicks cost $600; he needed six but would settle for four. I'd already made a general proposal to Goodyear knowing that I would ultimately need their support, and was confident of getting the tires — Goodyear gives thousands to racing teams all over the world. I hung up the phone, whooped, and jumped around the apartment a lot that afternoon while DD watched, curiously. But Oftedahl's accepting me so easily made me wonder, too.

DD and I argued a lot in the two weeks we lived together before Daytona, and I left for the race without her; it was undecided when, or if, she would come. The first day of activity at the track was Tuesday, "Press Day," an unofficial and free practice for select teams which were asked to cooperate with the media — and they were happy to, because publicity pleased their sponsors and lured potential ones. And it was an important unfair advantage to have a full day's practice in advance. Ron Meade had invited Oftedahl as a favor to me; since Oftedahl had never been to a Daytona Press Day before, and since all the other cars were prototypes, he might have been impressed by what connections can do. And I was trying to do all I could for him, to compensate for my empty pockets.

Gordy Oftedahl was a large Minnesota Swede with a shock of silver hair that made him look older than his 44. He was six-foot-three with a barrel chest and belly, and was so excitable he seemed to be a heart attack trying to happen. Before he became a professional car owner he was an independent trucker, and he'd also been a racing mechanic for 15 years. His racing transporter was an old semi-rig with over a million miles on it, most of them from carrying his racecars around the country. He kept it parked outside his small and cluttered shop, which was next to his house in a rural area north of Minneapolis. Oftedahl Racing was a resourceful operation, without cash, perpetually clutching survival. Oftedahl was known not only for his small-time wheeling-dealing, but for his ability to breathe horsepower into engines — or rather, squeeze it out of them. His engines weren't always reliable since he could rarely afford the best parts or even new ones, but everyone knew his cars could fly.

Oftedahl had entered every SCCA Trans-Am for the last five years, despite never having a major sponsor. He managed by scavenging parts and selling rides, but he was growing disparaging of the types of drivers that used him. Renta-drivers were rarely winners and were hard on equipment — sometimes even irresponsible with it — so he often lost money on them. Even when selling rides paid off, it was a hassle. He was tired of it, and said he needed a sponsor to continue racing. Each race appeared to be his own finale. So I was his latest Last Best Hope.

When I got to the track his two Firebirds were on pit row, being tinkered with by the mechanics. I watched anonymously for a while; #15 was apparently my car, because there was only one name — Chip Mead — painted on the door. Since Goodyear hadn't delivered the tires yet, my status was tentative. The car was gorgeous. It was low, sleek and a rich, deep Pontiac red. Its long, bulging hood raked toward the pointed nose, which hung over a black spoiler that nearly nudged the ground. Fat slicks were mounted on chrome-and-gold wheels, and the fiberglass fenders swelled to contain them. A black exhaust pipe ran like a bazooka beneath each door, and when the 350 Chevy engine — the same block as in my truck — was fired up it went *brappa-brappa-voom*. Oftedahl had poked the motor out to 366 cubic inches and stuffed in nearly 600 horsepower (the Rabbit had had 75). The car weighed just 2600 pounds, and its sharp contour sliced the wind — Firebirds are among the aerodynamically cleanest cars in the world. With the right gearing, the Oftedahl Firebirds could hum down the Daytona backstraight at 205 miles an hour. I introduced myself to Oftedahl. "Okay, go do it," he said.

Daytona is the most famous track in the world, but its 3.8-mile road racing circuit is no driver's course. There were just five turns, mostly easy, before you climbed from the infield onto Turn 1 of the speedway tri-oval, and stayed there for 2.4 of its 2.5 miles. Even if you drove the infield brilliantly you could only gain a little bit, but full seconds might be lost on the oval if you lacked horsepower. The track was famous for its 31-degree banking, which the fastest prototypes could take at nearly 220 miles an hour.

I got dressed and climbed in the car, realizing what an absurdly large step this was but too eager to have self-doubt. On the first lap, looking out over the long hood and wide fenders, I felt as if I were in a pit. I couldn't see the ground around the car; the view seemed to be mostly of sky sailing over my head. I weaved around, hunting for apexes hidden by the Firebird's fenders. On the second lap, coming out of the aptly-named Horseshoe onto the short infield straight, I put my foot down far enough to make me gulp. My God — the *power*. I wondered what it would feel like to use it all, all the time, and how long it would take to get that good.

I got about ten laps in three sessions on the track; the car was in the pits for repairs and corrections a lot. It was sure no Formula Ford, reliability or otherwise. There was so much power that the tail squirted loose in the turns. It had power steering, which made it feel boat-like, and a stock steering wheel, not unlike the one in my truck. The interior was an echo chamber of sheetmetal and thick rollcage bars, integral with the chassis; it boomed inside, and vibrated a lot. The brakes smelled, and faded when you used them hard. The textbook lines through the turns didn't work, but then it didn't feel as if they should.

But 10 laps was enough to relieve one big apprehension: the banking. The Firebird handled beautifully up there, as if it were locked in a groove. I didn't go much faster than 175 miles an hour around Turns 3 and 4, 20 mph below the car's capability, but I could see myself going around there flat-out. Soon. If you could forget the banking's reputation and not be intimidated, it was easier than a good kink; the hardest part was convincing yourself you wouldn't fly into the wall as you shot down the backstraight toward it. Because it was a big bowl you had to look up through the top left corner of the windshield to see ahead, and that was strange; but basically you just got up there and kept your foot as far down as you dared, until the road straightened and flattened again.

This wasn't my first time on the Daytona oval, however. I'd faced it twice before, on two wheels. First on the 750 BSA at about 150 mph, so high on the bank I felt as if I were crouching on the wing of an airplane. And in 1977 I'd been on an 11-man, one-woman Kawasaki factory team that set 18 world records in four days on the oval. The big enchilada was the 24-hour record, which I shared with four other riders. We ran a 130-mph pace on a 650cc Kawasaki, averaging 116.9 mph after pit stops. The bike's engine was all heart, but the stock chassis wasn't up to the banking. It had a horrific wobble there; at night the headlight beam undulated on the white wall, a reminder that you were half out of control.

On Wednesday there was a seminar conducted by the Road Racing Drivers Club, an organization pioneered by the late Mark Donohue. There were two classroom sessions in the morning, but the afternoon was reserved for the track — five tutored sessions of five laps each, followed by half an hour of open practice. To many, including me, the practice period alone made it worth the $200 fee. And since there was still no word from Goodyear, for all I knew the school would be my last chance to drive that weekend.

I missed most of the first session because the brakes were fading, and all of the next while the crew changed the pads, which needed to be bedded-in during the third session. In the fourth I turned 1:59 and 2:00 on the last two laps. It was very promising. And encouraging, since my lines were still wrong, I was still tentative with the throttle in the infield, and I was lifting on the banking. Also, the car was "pushing," which means it was plowing in the turns from lack of traction at the front wheels. I ran off the track once, sideways in the grass around the outside of a turn like a sprint car up in the cushion, and a film clip of the earth-moving slide made the sports on the Orlando TV station that evening.

In the fifth session I knew Oftedahl again had the stop watch on me, because he'd been excited about the 1:59. So I went for a hot last lap. So far I'd remembered to check the gauges regularly, in particular the water and oil temperatures — usually twice a lap, on the backstraight and short infield straight. But this time I had other things to think about. The lap itself went okay — it might have been a 1:58 — but when I got on the banking between Turns 3 and 4 and the geometry of the bowl raised the instrument panel to my eyes, I saw the needles on the faces of the water and oil temp gauges: pegged.

The guy behind me probably ran over my heart, the way it fell through the floorboards. Panicked, for a futile instant I hoped the gauges had snapped, and this was some quick nasty nightmare. My foot jumped off the gas, and I cruised past the start-finish line and around the first turn. The red oil-pressure light came on, as if it were signalling my last ride in a racing car. I coasted to a stop on the escape road at the Horseshoe, believing that it had been.

The Firebird had also overheated the day before, when it was being wrung to a 1:55 by Hurley Haywood, one of the IMSA aces. Gordy had wanted Haywood's opinion on the car's setup, as well as a fast time for the press. And Haywood naturally wanted to impress — he might have been thinking about driving the Oftedahl Firebird in the next year's Trans-Am Series. So he leadfooted it, and the centrifugal force on the banking mashed the spoiler against the track, bending it and blocking air to the radiator. Apparently I had reached the speed on the banking where the spoiler gets squashed. I should have remembered what happened to Haywood and been watching for it, but Oftedahl had said the problem was fixed.

Gordy drove up to the fence around the Horseshoe in a rental car with Arlen Schleif, his bright and lanky 23-year-old crew chief, whom everyone called "Elwood." When he asked what was wrong, I couldn't admit that I'd forgotten to watch the gauges. I said the water had reached 230 degrees — the gauge went to 270 — and that I'd stopped just to be safe. The telltale on the tach was at 8000 rpm, 800 over the redline — a weak throttle return spring had allowed the engine to rev during upshifts — and I didn't think such a relatively small overrev could blow an engine, but not realizing why it had overheated, I wondered if big racing engines could actually be that fragile.

Elwood poured water over and into the radiator, and the engine didn't make any clanking noises when we fired it up, so Gordy told me to drive it around to the pits. Elwood hadn't noticed the telltale, and although I'd already told Gordy about the overrev I thought he might forget, so I reset it (the button was exposed for the mechanics' convenience) and brought it back to 6800 on the backstraight.

Boiling the engine couldn't have helped it, but it probably did no major damage. The oil-pressure light had come on because the engine was idling, which is normal. And as lies between drivers and mechanics go, mine was a small one; that game is like the cheating one, with different players. It was good (for me) that it happened, because I never made that mistake again. It had been such a terrifying close call. Ironically but not surprisingly, gauge-watching was another thing Jacques Couture preached, for the very reason it had meant my almost-downfall: Watching the gauges keeps you from getting carried away.

The SCCA Trans-Am Series was over, and Doc Bundy had finished second. Now he was entered in the IMSA Finale in a Porsche 935 twin-turbo owned by Preston Henn, a Florida drive-in theater/flea market magnate. The 935 was a GTP car, though technically not a prototype since it was based on a street design. The 935s had ruled IMSA endurance racing for years, but their days were numbered by technology and updated rules. The new prototypes were changing the picture. The Finale was only Doc's second race in a GTP car and Preston Henn was paying him, which was no small distinction; there were only a few paid drivers among the couple hundred there. It was important for Doc to do well in the Finale; if he were to get a regular ride in a prototype, which is what he wanted, he needed a good result.

We walked the track on Thanksgiving morning, through an odd sea of seagulls on the Horseshoe, and Doc showed me some new lines. He explained something about the Firebird that I'd felt but hadn't figured out: You had to adjust to its power and imprecision by aiming it one place to get to another. That first sounded like a golfer compensating for a slice, but it was the definition of "drift." And you had to pitch the Firebird around. As we walked I took notes. Mostly they were steps: Back off at this fencepost, brake at that oil spot, turn toward this gouge in the pavement, point the car at that grandstand coming out of a turn. Plus where and when to check the mirrors and gauges. I created 35 such steps; my compulsions were sometimes as crazy as DD's impulses. The notebook should have had a title: "Driving Daytona by the Numbers" (and forgetting the seat of your pants). Doc knew I was getting carried away again, but I guess he also knew I'd figure it out myself.

We had Thanksgiving dinner at Valle's, a restaurant near the Speedway which offered an excellent all-you-can-eat turkey special for $7.95. It was Doc's traditional Thanksgiving dinner — his 10th in a row there, at least. Matter-of-factly, if not casually, he said that there would definitely be some crashes on the banking on Sunday. There were 74 cars entered in the Finale — a record — and they would be moving around up there at dangerously disparate speeds. Technically it was an endurance race, but it would be run at a sprint pace since one 90-minute shift was easy at the physically undemanding Daytona, and since it was the last race of the year and the teams wouldn't be afraid to use up their cars. The banking may have been a piece of cake so far, said Doc, but I hadn't seen everything that happens up there.

He said I had to be certain to do two things. As soon as I got into Turn 3, turn my head and look through the net in the window for trouble in Turn 4, where it often struck. Blowouts occurred there, since that's where the tires got hottest, and sometimes — too often — GTP cars got pinched against the wall by slower cars as they levelled off the banking. He also told me to check my mirror as I went down the backstraight, and stay in my lane unless I was passing. Unfortunately, my inside mirror was useless because the plexiglass rear window was scratched and vibrated, and would face the sun on the backstraight anyhow. "Well," said Doc, "make real slow moves, then."

Doc's credibility was almost impeccable to me, and here he was, chewing his Thanksgiving turkey and talking with certainty of 200-mph crashes. This was getting serious. Yet the fear was mostly of failure — of spinning out, damaging the car, hurting my chances for the next ride. The expense of a mistake was the most intimidating thing about driving. To a struggling driver a broken bone is only a temporary setback; wipe out somebody's car and that might be it for your career.

That evening I swam 36 lengths of the Howard Johnson's long pool; in my mind, each length was a lap of the track — gotta memorize those fenceposts and oil spots. I called DD, who had spent Thanksgiving with her family — a father, stepmother, brother and sister. We had talked every night that week. I loved listening to her low voice — her voice in general, most of the time — and she told me wonderful stories about Moon the cat. He was spending his days chasing the rainbow reflections that spun around the living room, created by the sun through the prisms hanging in the breezy window facing the ocean, and DD was spending hers in her rocking chair watching him. Sometimes her rocker seemed to power her, not vice-versa, as if it were her electric charger. She's been rocking for sanctuary since she was a girl — she shows off her hard tummy and gives the rocker credit. She also used it like a battlement from which to launch an attack. When our fights got physical she would run to it and clutch it as if it were her mother's skirt. Sometimes I pushed her over in it because I couldn't get her out of it.

DD and the Moon seemed so much alike. They both liked looking at the world upside down. They were both abandoned. They had both been knocked on the head at an early age. We figured Moon must have landed on his when he was thrown out of the car. Sometimes he would jump up from a nap, sprint across the room, leap on my office wall which was covered with straw matting, climb to the ceiling, and fling himself back down like a flying squirrel. Sometimes DD acted like that. They were both hopelessly tenacious, and their resiliency was as much a curse as a gift. DD bounced back from fights that floored us both, then did it all over again; and Moon...the Moon truly seemed to have nine lives. He was barely bigger than a mouse when we landed him, and in the next two weeks he lost half his tail to a kitchen cabinet door and half his voice to chest congestion. We think we caused the congestion by forcing his constipation medicine down his throat. And he had bald spots from ringworm. But he'd stop at nothing for cantaloupe, and attack when he felt inspired. He slept in a small linen closet in the bedroom. We'd hear him in the middle of the night, clawing his way up the louvered door, and in the morning he'd be on the top shelf.

Unfortunately, there were no Moon stories with the call this Thanksgiving night. It was a long argument over how, when and if DD should come. I tried to get her to reassure me that she wouldn't demand my attention — my hands were so full, already — but that only turned it into a debate.

Friday was the official opening of practice. I awoke at dawn and spread the drapes to reveal an ugly drizzle falling onto the HoJo's parking lot. The weather had been so beautiful that I hadn't considered rain; it was not what I needed. Stock car races are postponed when it rains, but sports cars just mount rain tires and keep blasting around. I was glad I wouldn't be driving until mid-afternoon; maybe it would stop by then.

With only three mechanics to prepare two cars, the Oftedahl team was perpetually behind. And with four drivers sharing just 90 minutes of practice per day, time in the cars was cherished and coveted. But it always is. This was the real world, outside the Barber/BSMR cocoon: You hardly ever get any practice. And you don't have the luxury of thinking very much about your driving; a real-world racecar, basically unreliable and rarely cooperative, needs all the attention. I got three laps Friday but you couldn't call them practice. I took one lap to warm up the car, another to warm up myself, and on the third the clutch began slipping. The other drivers got some good laps, though: Bob Raub, who earned his ride by doubling as a mechanic for Oftedahl — and was more valuable than Gordy ever realized — had a 1:57. His codriver in #14, Bob Lazier, a Colorado condo magnate, Gordy's Trans-Am driver back in '78, and CART's reigning Rookie of the Year — a rich guy/fast guy — had a 1:59. My codriver Chip Mead, who had also previously driven for Gordy, as well as a number of Indy car races, had 1:57. Mead was a 32-year-old real estate developer and venture capitalist, like his father. He told me he'd talked Gordy down to $2,000, arguing that he could expect less prize money teamed with a rookie.

Goodyear came through with the tires. I checked the yellow pages, called a sign painter to the track, and he painted my name on the door. I'm not sure what would have happened if some driver had showed up with $4,000 that afternoon.

DD called, at about 1 a.m. She was coming Saturday, she said; her plane would arrive at 7 p.m. I told her that if I wasn't at the airport to pick her up, it was because I was meeting with an owner about a ride for next year. It went downhill from there. She called again at 7 a.m. I needed this like I needed rain: demands, tears, questions about the relationship — psychological questions, philo-sophical ones, technical ones, emotional ones. Mostly to change the subject, I asked her if she was still smoking.

"Yes, I can't quit as long as you're racing and this stress exists in my life," she said. "Is that all right with you?"

"Yes," I said.

"Why did you say, 'Yes'?" she demanded. "It hasn't been all right before."

I said, "Because it's seven o'clock in the morning and today I have to drive 190 miles an hour in traffic, and for all I know in the rain, too, and I don't have the energy to resist you and I have more important things to think about."

She got real mad at that; it was always a mistake to tell DD there were more important things than her. "You always have more important things to think about," she said. "It's either seven o'clock in the morning or 11 o'clock at night, and....."

Just as I was about to pull out for practice Saturday morning, I looked in the mirror and saw a car coming up pit road streaming smoke. The driver stopped and jumped out, and flames spewed out behind him. "Good," I thought. It was the Datsun 280Z turbo of Don Devendorf, the quickest car in GTO. It could beat us. I wasn't particularly proud of my reaction, but the shame of it didn't strike until later. I walked by Devendorf's garage and there was the car, charred like toast. The crew was scraping off the burnt part. There were little pieces soaking in solvent everywhere, and mechanics from other crews were pitching in to rebuild it. Devendorf had gotten permission from IMSA to work all night; it would be a race to make the race. He was an engineer whose company, Electramotive, had designed and built the car, including the engine development, and it was one of the most sophisticated and best-crafted machines in IMSA. He was leading the GTO point standings but the championship wasn't clinched; he needed this race. Watching his team work, I came to my senses and realized that my newfound killer instinct, untempered by experience, had briefly run amuck. I was a closet Devendorf fan for the rest of the weekend.

Doc's report on Chip Mead was that he was fast but sometimes overdrove, which was hard on both the car and tires. When Chip pitted after his practice that afternoon he forgot to get the tire temperatures taken by the Goodyear technicians, a critical service. And he reported to Elwood that he'd locked the brakes and skidded on the tires. Elwood quickly checked them and sent me out. It was a big temptation to try again for some good laps, since the other three drivers were now down to 1:57 and I knew I could do it, too —

and that Gordy was hovering over his stopwatch. But the four laps I'd gotten that morning were the first time I'd driven with very many cars on the track, and I needed more time to feel the flow of traffic. And when I saw the checkered flag after just three laps, something told me not to drive hard on the cooloff lap for extra practice, as I normally did.

Apparently, Chip had overheated and blistered a tire, and Elwood had missed it. When I pitted there were two chunks the size of nickels missing from the left front tire. It was unlikely that my 2:04 pace caused them. I should have detected some vibration, but I was concentrating hard on traffic — thinking about the car instead of feeling it, again. Left-side problems are often hard to feel at Daytona anyhow, because the right side takes the load on the banking. But if I hadn't been driving conservatively, and if something hadn't stopped me from running another hard lap — I believe it's an instinct for survival — the tire might have blown.

The tire situation in general was not good. First, they had no inner-liners — tires within a tire to make blowouts less explosive. Stock cars, which are about as fast as GTO cars, have inner-liners; all those tires are the same size and Goodyear can tool up for that. But it was unrealistic for Goodyear to make inner-liner tires for all the various sports car sizes, especially since they would only be needed at Daytona; nobody could afford them if they did. Also, the Firebird used 10-inch wheels, although 12-inchers were legal in IMSA. That meant smaller tires, which slid around more and therefore ran hotter. But Oftedahl didn't have the money for new wheels for the cars, which he said cost nearly $1,000 each.

When I had spun for the TV camera on Wednesday, I'd thought it was my mistake; I thought all GTO cars must feel like 2,600-pound ice skates. But it was the tires. The fronts were worn, and wouldn't stick. That's what was making the car push. I was getting the picture now: Oftedahl knew more about horsepower than he did about preparation. And he was handicapped; three mechanics and one driver/mechanic for two cars is half a crew, at best. They were spread thin on top of starting out tired, having driven the transporter non-stop to the track from Minnesota. Things were frequently falling off the cars and going uncorrected, such as the front spoiler, which got mashed twice more. One time a duct hose fell off and dangled behind the brake pedal, and when I pushed on the pedal for the Horseshoe it pushed back, sending me down the escape road. Another time a long socket extension rolled out from under the seat and under my feet as I went up on the banking. And Chip had missed a shift and overrevved to 9,500; if my sizzling the engine hadn't done any damage, that could have. Oftedahl really chewed Chip out for that.

The team qualified well, although Raub's and Lazier's #14 didn't get the GTO track record that Gordy had been after — for the publicity, a nugget for his sponsorship pitch over the winter. He had built an especially potent motor for #14 and installed a set of soft qualifying tires, sticky and short-lived. Bob Raub turned 1:53.7, second-fastest, while the record went to a Corvette whose owner/driver, John Greenwood, had out-Gordied Gordy. He used a monster motor, 454 cubic inches, to blast to a 1:50.1, an average speed of 125.5 mph; the time-bomb engine would last six laps in the race. Chip qualified #15 at 1:55, fourth GTO and 21st overall. I got six laps after qualifying and ran 2:00s, still feathering on the banking, wary now because the race was so near, certain that 1:57s were right there if only things would go smoothly long enough to try.

I picked up DD at the airport that evening, and she was radiant as she glided toward me across the baggage-claim area, wearing whooshing white pants and a smile anyone would fall for. She had some crazy story about how they had held the small plane for her in Miami, since she was its only passenger. We had dinner at a Japanese restaurant that was so disorganized it was hilarious. The meal was hopeless, and we laughed all through it.

Doc had been right; up on the banking they were dropping like flies. In the first hour of the race there were three blowouts resulting in 2½ crashes. Doc was the half; when his left rear tire blew he wrestled the car away from the wall, but the exploding rubber smashed the transmission cooler and scattered pieces of the Porsche's bodywork all over the banking, so his car was out of the race.

Chip had started the Firebird, which had as much horsepower as many of the prototypes, and despite being heavier could stay in the draft of some of them around the oval — although they would scamper away on the infield, where they hugged the track. Attrition among the GTPs was high, so by clocking consistent strong 1:56s and :57s Chip was soon running seventh overall, first in GTO — better than any of us had expected. Gordy was in the signal pit, which was located inside the first infield turn; he was leaning over the guardrail with Chip's board, and when Chip came by he'd get so excited that I thought his own girth would flop him over the rail. Once Chip cut a 1:55, and Gordy cursed and shook his fist at him as the Firebird sped away toward the Horseshoe. That may give Chip a certain distinction: the only guy Gordy Oftedahl ever yelled at for going too fast. Number 14 was out; Lazier had spun and cut a tire, and as he limped back to the pits the flapping rubber broke the oil cooler and bent the suspension. Gordy's stakes were riding on #15.

Debris on the track kept bringing out yellow flags. Eager to capitalize on one of them, Gordy gave Chip the "PIT" sign, and radioed Elwood in the pit to have the crew ready. The Firebird got a quick refill, which would keep Chip going for 30 extra minutes. I looked up at the huge tower scoreboard and saw #15 in sixth now. It was obvious what my assignment in the final hour would be: Keep it in the GTO lead. The race was mine to lose. No experience, no practice — a damn *reporter* — and about 20 seconds ahead of Gene Felton, IMSA's heaviest-footed and hairiest-chested driver, behind the wheel of a Camaro that was a cannonball.

It might have been the wildest fantasy I had that year, to think that I could hold Felton off. But I was determined to, raging butterflies notwithstanding. Chip would be pitting in five more laps. I was just about to put on my helmet — allowing 10 minutes in case the D-rings got stuck or the visor wouldn't snap — when I looked down pit road. There, scurrying toward Oftedahl, was a funny-looking man with a scruffy rusty beard and granny glasses, wearing a red driving suit.

It was John Lee Paul, Senior. He was known around IMSA as "the old pirate," an image encouraged by the publicity people at R.J. Reynolds (Camel cigarettes was the series sponsor). His JLP Racing transporter was black, to match his normal mood. He was volatile, unpredictable, rarely made compromises, and generally anarchistic — he'd get what he wanted the way he saw fit. His official bio stated that he was born in the Netherlands on the eve of World War II and had learned to hustle on Nazi-occupied streets. When he was 15 his family moved to Indiana, and Paul attended Ball State and won a scholarship to Harvard, where he dishwashed his way to a Master's in business. By the time he was 32 he'd made millions in mutual funds. His wife left him and he bought a 56-foot sailboat and sailed twice across the Atlantic solo. After roaming in the Caribbean for a while, he emerged in Florida and added to his fortune through real estate.

The old pirate wasn't an especially fast driver, but he had an impressive endurance record, having twice won the World Endurance Championship and both the Daytona 24-Hour and Sebring 12-Hour in 1980 driving with his son, John Paul Junior, whose career Senior had nurtured with hundreds of thousands of dollars. Coming into the Finale, Senior was leading in points for the IMSA Endurance Championship, which consisted of the 10 longest races on the 19-race Camel GT circuit. The talented 23-year-old Junior had already clinched the overall championship.

Gordy was standing in the spot where the Firebird was supposed to be in four laps. Paul's red beard came up to Gordy's big chest, and he was talking to him as if he were yelling to someone on a balcony. Cars were roaring by in the background so I couldn't hear what was being said, and I couldn't read their lips. But I knew it wasn't good.

Here was the deal. There was no rule to disallow a driver from switching cars during a race; theoretically, one driver could finish first, second and third. But there was a rule that allowed him no points unless he drove in the same car for an hour. Paul had been entered in a 935, which had retired in the first hour. If he didn't get his points he might lose the endurance championship, which was worth $25,000. Second place paid $10,000. If Oftedahl would let Paul finish the race in the Firebird, and if Paul won the championship, Paul would split the $15,000 difference with him.

Gordy told him it was up to me. I could see through the butterflies to this one: If I said no, I would be standing in the way of (1) Paul and his championship; and (2) Gordy and 7,500 badly-needed dollars. Anything else hardly mattered — such as that I was also kissing goodbye the possibility of a GTO-class win, a gem whose value was incalculable to winter-time sponsor-hunting. Then, there was the specter of my crashing. A crash, or even a spinout, would spoil it for everybody. And it would be permanent: I would ache all my life. So I thanked Gordy for his honor in granting me veto power, and told Paul to take the Firebird away. His offer had been one I couldn't refuse. (I later learned that my fellow reporters in the press box across the track had been taking bets on whose seat Paul would commandeer, and mine had been heavily favored.)

Since there were no radios in the car — another $4,000 that Gordy didn't have — Chip didn't know what was going on. Chip thought some guy was so excited he was trying to get in the wrong car, and waved him away. But Paul insisted, so Chip climbed out, the stop was completed, and Paul tore off. Chip took off his helmet, looked at me, and said, "Who the hell was *that?*"

Our pit got pretty busy in the next 10 minutes. DD came back from the signal pit where she'd been timing for Chip; when #15 had passed, she'd asked the same thing Chip had. Steve Evans with Mizlou TV interviewed me, and I said I wasn't mad at anybody, Gordy had left it up to me, Paul was just after some championship of some kind, I don't even know which. As about three months' worth of adrenaline poured out, I babbled as if I'd just gotten out of the car instead of being shut out of it. Steve Potter from *AutoWeek* came over and said I'd feel the disappointment the next day.

He was wrong. I felt it about five minutes later. I sank in the grass against the chainlink fence behind the pit, and DD, attached to me by the hand, dropped too. She was incredulous. "You mean he just walked up, agreed to give Gordy a few thousand dollars, and drove off in your car?" she asked.

"Yep," I said.

"And it's *legal?*"

Gene Felton won GTO, codriving with the Camaro's owner, a tough Louisiana oil man named Billy Hagan. They were fifth overall. The Hagan Camaro had passed the Firebird while it was in the pits, and it hadn't made a second pit stop. Tex Powell, Hagan's crew chief, had been smarter than Gordy: He'd waited out the yellow flags and got farther on his gas. It was not uncommon for the race to be won in the pits like that. But who ever hears of the Tex Powells?

The #15 Firebird finished seventh; Paul ran conservative 2:03s to the finish, preserving his championship and 25 thou, minus Gordy's cut. He was third in GTO. Second GTO and sixth overall — coming from 72nd on the grid — was the Electramotive Datsun 280Z Turbo. The GTO championship was Devendorf's. I was very glad about that.

Doc's early blowout had only put his car out of the race, not him. Preston Henn had entered two 935s, with Al Holbert and himself in one car and Doc in the other with Preston's 21-year-old daughter Bonnie. Until that morning Doc and Al had been under the impression that the two of them would be teamed in one car, so all day they'd been scheming how to swing it. At the halfway point Holbert was leading and the car's throttle was sticking. Henn wisely sent Doc in.

Doc's reputation as a conservative driver took a big dive — call it a mid-career correction — in this race. He got on the tail of the new leader after the pit stop, Frenchman Bob Wollek, who was also driving a 935. But Doc got fooled; Wollek tapped his brakes as they entered the infield kink, and Doc's throttle stuck at the wrong time. He had to throw the Porsche off the track to keep from hitting Wollek. The $100,000 machine did three or four big donuts across the infield grass, ripping off the car's fiberglass front end. Doc pitted, the crew patched things up, and he went back out without the forward bodywork, in fourth place.

This is when he got inspired. Without the bodywork the car's aerodynamics were so disturbed that it darted on the back-straight, and it shuddered so badly that it blurred his vision. And on the banking it pushed toward the wall because there was little downforce. But it was colorful to watch, this once-sleek car with its front wheels and half its chassis now exposed...catching back up. The track announcer picked it up, and got another 935 driver in the booth. "That can't be done, what Bundy is doing," the driver said. "That car can't be driven like that!" But Doc drove it like that to the finish, nearly getting back third place. Maybe he'd blown the victory for the car owner — he was the only one who could have saved it anyhow — but he'd done it with such style. Until that race he hadn't proven that he was a GTP fast guy, so it was another big step for him.

DD and I went out for a quiet dinner alone that night, while the IMSA awards banquet was being held at the Plaza Hotel. When John Paul accepted his trophy and check, he announced his retirement from driving. He also thanked me. When we passed in the Daytona airport the next morning, he didn't recognize me.

"That car can't be driven like that!" said a fellow driver as Doc took the hoodless Porsche to fourth.

Gene Sweeney

If dreams were reality, Gordy
Oftedahl would have won big.

Peter Gloede

John Paul, Sr.,
the old pirate himself.

Bob Costanza

*In his two-hour stint, Chip Mead drove the Oftedahl Firebird to sixth
overall and first GTO in a field of 72.*

Chapter Eight

Bill Eppridge

Rich Guys

A l Holbert was the third-winningest GTP driver in IMSA history, after the late Peter Gregg and Hurley Haywood (he would later become number one). He had won the Camel GT championship in 1978 and '79, but he didn't like the way IMSA was headed: toward the rich guys. The GT schedule was heavy on long endurance races, which were doubly expensive to run because they wore out equipment. It was getting so that the only people who could afford it were rich guys, who were enticed by the relatively slow pace of an endurance race. Many of them — *too* many — owned and raced prototypes. What kind of man would spend $100,000 for such a toy, and then another $30,000 or $40,000 — which is what it might cost to run a prototype in the Daytona 24-Hour — to play with it for a few days? A rich guy with a big ego —not necessarily a bad guy, but not necessarily a good driver, either. Teams having little background and no apparent means of support were suddenly appearing, and some such operations appeared to be financed by drug money. It seemed as if John Bishop, IMSA's president, was selling out motor racing; he certainly knew what was happening as a result of IMSA's slanting toward "sportsmen." For all that the real pros had to put up with, the purses weren't worth it. So Holbert defected to the SCCA, IMSA's rival sanctioning body, where he ran the Can-Am Series for machines much like IMSA prototypes. In three seasons he won nine races, but not the championship.

While he was away, IMSA prospered. Maybe Bishop had had a master plan whose ends justified the means. Endurance races required more drivers — more rich guys — who brought friends and crews, so a lot of new people had been drawn to the sport. Their new money, tainted by invisible sources and squirrelly driving or not, had been buying better equipment. Better competition, driving, crowds and purses followed. Holbert had driven in the Daytona Finale to test the water for a return to the Camel Series, and now he was planning to build a GTP car over the winter.

He saw that one thing was the same, however. If you — yes, *you* — had enough money, plus a lot of courage and good coordination, but mostly the money, you too could be racing against him, wheel-to-wheel at 200 miles an hour at Daytona. It was not unlike being able to buy a Sunday on the mound in Yankee Stadium. The irony hadn't changed: A talented but poor driver couldn't get there, but a slow, rich one could. No experience necessary. Just attend the right driving school and get an IMSA license. There was no rule requiring you to start in the GTU class — "under" 2.5 liters was not so attractive to rich guys.

You couldn't blame the rich guys, though. It was a satisfying pursuit for them. It was about the hardest work a person could do, and still not make money. It was a demanding and thrilling job, offering grit and reality. It gave a rich guy respectability. The absurdly high odds against renumeration were immaterial since he could afford the chase. And some of the rich guys were good enough to become fast guys, too.

I might have felt victimized by the incident at Daytona with John Paul, but I wasn't mad about it; I was simply soured on IMSA. It seemed full of rich *strokers* — a stroker is someone who isn't serious about going fast — and I didn't want to get next to them for fear it would rub off, whatever "it" was. I was attracted by the special demands of endurance driving and all that track time, but I had to face the fact that the rich guys and I were there for at least two of the same reasons: We wouldn't be able to keep up with the fast guys in a sprint race, and we got our rides because of our connections to money, however gossamer mine might have been. I accepted it, but I wanted to be a better driver than that. I couldn't get rid of the ideal — the naive notion — that the ride should go to the best driver. My situation was an uncomfortable paradox of my own making.

There is a racing axiom: "When the green flag drops, the bullshit stops." But I was finding that it was ... bullshit. The stuff was built into the car with every expensive nut and bolt. The winner of a race was often merely the guy who could afford to win. Financing was not only part of the game, it was part of the race. The definition of "driver" was broadening before my eyes; money-raising was an actual driving skill. Now a driver was judged not only by his heavy foot and steady hand, but by his marketability, salesmanship and spokespersonship. Sometimes the order of importance got shuffled. Winning isn't everything, when you're trying to sell something. "Money talks, talent walks," goes another less optimistic axiom. But that one isn't quite right either. Getting the money is half the talent.

Christmas had come and gone. Since DD and I still weren't cohabiting very smoothly, and since an island wasn't the best place to hunt for sponsors, I flew up to New York, determined to stay at my office desk writing proposals and making phone calls until I got lucky. I tried to believe that it was just a matter of time, and thought that diligence would shorten that time. "I know that you're unhappy now, but I'm glad you're unhappy," Doc had said on the phone. He had ulterior motives; he wanted me to see the "real thing" about racedriving, the "torture." Then he told me that he knew I wasn't a quitter. His way of being encouraging.

Doc had a great idea for the next season. He would manage Preston Henn's racing team and be the number-one driver, and I would drive with him. But he couldn't pin Preston down; Henn would have a new brainstorm every day. I Federal-Expressed a proposal to Henn, volunteering to tackle one of his 935s for the upcoming Daytona 24-Hour. He politely turned me down, but offered me $1,000 to write a favorable freelance article about him, which he would have published somewhere.

It was probably an unrealistic standard, but I was convinced that the "real thing," the story I was after, had to be told from a fast guy's point of view, and that unless I became that fast guy I would miss it. But I was ready to wrap the project up, for practical reasons. The only problem was that it needed a happy ending. I thought a rousing and uplifting climax at the Daytona 24-Hour might be satisfactory.

I called Dan Gurney, who has been a friend since 1979, when I wrote an *SI* story about him. I'd been reading that his All American Racers team would enter three GTU-class Toyota Celicas at Daytona, which meant nine job openings. He said he was already committed to eight drivers, and was leaning toward Willy T. Ribbs for the final spot. Ribbs was a much better driver than I, but Toyota, which paid AAR to run the Celicas, would have loved to see a story in *Sports Illustrated* featuring their cars, and I thought that might sway Gurney. But a couple of days later he called me back and said he had chosen Ribbs, because Willy wanted to be a professional racedriver and had been struggling for five years, and this ride was important to his career. I respected Dan even more for that choice.

Almost from the beginning I'd felt like Groucho Marx, who said he would never belong to a country club that would have him. But I was convinced that I was a promotional bargain. *Sports Illustrated's* audience was enormous. Its advertising rate was something like $80,000 per color page, and the story, planned as a two-parter, stood a good chance of filling a lot of them. Big color pictures of a car with the sponsor's name on it. I tried not to measure it like that, and refrained from pointing out the economics to potential sponsors, but I couldn't help thinking that the corporations already spending millions in racing were blind for not grabbing me. But then, that's what every racer thinks.

Gordy Oftedahl was the only person other than Doc and my own magazine — the only person with a car or money, at least — who had a place for me, although I was aware that his faith was based on his desperation. But I liked his car and the fact that it was American, so most of my subsequent sponsorship proposals included Oftedahl, with the money to be paid to him. Recently I'd written three or four of them, for either the Daytona 24-Hour or the next season (take your pick) in the Firebird. Gordy called a lot, and asked the same thing every time: "Any word yet?" He had two telephones side-by-side in his house — one for wheeling and one for dealing, it seemed. Sometimes he'd use them together, and I found myself answering odd questions before I realized that Gordy was talking to whoever was on the third end.

Officially, General Motors didn't participate in racing, a policy that enabled them to be exclusive and secretive about whom they supported. The Gordy Oftedahls were not on GM's list. I called Pontiac and spoke to a man I think was the general manager, supposedly the man with the power (finding that man was always a problem). I explained all I could, and asked if there were anything Pontiac could do for Oftedahl if I drove his Firebird in the Daytona 24-Hour. He said, in effect: If you and Oftedahl do all the work and take all the risks and spend all the money and are successful, Pontiac would be happy to capitalize on it. I was quietly outraged, as much by the insult to my intelligence as by the exploitation of it. General Motors ripping off Gordy Oftedahl: what an ironic joke.

I called a top Chevrolet PR man, and wanted to know this: If Oftedahl changed his cars from Firebirds to Camaros (a switch of bodywork would do it), could Chevrolet help him? I spent an hour on the phone with the man, whose PRspeak was like a bramble-bush that wove into absolutely nothing — not even "no." In the end, he just benumbed me.

I went to Tavern On The Green, the restaurant in Central Park, for a splashy press brunch hosted by Pepsi-Cola to announce their sponsorship of the NASCAR Winston Cup Grand National team of Junior Johnson and Darrell Waltrip. The emcee, a Pepsi VP, bragged about the $1.5 million package — half for racing and half for promotion. There was Junior, the legendary car owner whose roots were as pure as the moonshine he had run for his daddy, ordained the "Last American Hero" by Tom Wolfe a decade earlier. He was up on the stage with a few of his mechanics, who stood at parade rest in spiffy new yellow-and-red uniforms that made them look like Pepsi delivery men. I thought of "The Electric Horseman," when the cereal company unveils the cowboy and his horse, both bedecked in blinking neon. I wondered where I fit into all this. At that very moment I had a proposal pending at Pepsi: $60,000 for Oftedahl for the "Florida Three" —The Daytona 24-Hour, which Pepsi sponsored, the Miami Grand Prix later in February, and the Sebring 12-Hour in March. The journalist in me squirmed at the professional compromise; the purist in me sadly shook his head at the commerical verity and vulgarity on the stage; the racer in me wanted to jump up from the table and say, "Hey! Over here!

Me! I'll whore for you!" It bit at me, like the cold air as I walked back to my office that January morning.

I picked up *National Speed Sport News*. There among the classifieds, was a bold-print bulletin headed, "TO ALL READERS AND RACE FANS." It was from a 45-year-old would-be NASCAR Grand National rookie. He had contacted almost 500 companies, he explained, and none of them was interested in sponsoring him. He had been racing since 1957 without a sponsor, but his hoped-for jump to Grand National was too expensive to make on his own, so he needed donations. In return, all he could promise was his best. "Thanks again," he said, "and if I get enough to get started, you will know my car as it will have, 'the Race Fan Special' painted on both the hood and trunk." My empathy for his desperation ran deep.

You might say I was saved by the bell when Steve Potter called. Potter was the most active writer/racer. He was entered that weekend in a 3-hour showroom stock ice race on Lake Superior in Duluth, Minnesota, and his codriver had just come down with the flu. Would I be interested in taking her place?

DD air-freighted my driving gear to NYC that afternoon — reluctantly, after resisting — and the next day I flew to Duluth. The race was called the Minnesota Cup, and Potter and I would be driving a Renault Le Car owned by Archer Import Motors, which promoted the race and had invited Potter in order to get some ink. Bobby and Tommy Archer were "Duluth's racing brothers," and local heroes. Tommy, 28, and Bobby, 30, were yin and yang: Tommy was the thinker, dark-haired and quiet; Bobby was the charger, light-haired and rowdy. They raced factory-backed Renaults in the Champion Spark Plug Challenge, an IMSA support series. Their Renaults were the smallest cars in the series, and it was exciting to watch the Archers make them the quickest. And they were legends on the "hard-water racing circuit," as it is called out on the ice. For the Minnesota Cup they had entered a new Renault Fuego turbo, which Renault's racing manager had asked them to test.

Potter's and my car was seven years old, the second Renault Le Car ever sold by Archer Motors. It had been traded for a new one after four years, and to call it "used" would be generous. It showed its 90,000 miles. The owner had hauled firewood with it, among other things, and made it suffer the indignities of neglect. How bad was it? "Too rough to sell," said Bobby. So Tommy had given it a valve job, patched the worst of the rust, painted it yellow and used it for trips around town for parts and pizza. But one winter it was all the Archers had to race in the Minnesota Cup — shades of Rudolph the red-nosed reindeer. After their victory they dubbed the car Old Reliable; when they won again the next year, the fans called it Ol' Yeller. It was a faded rustbox, but it was undefeated.

Tire studs were the tiny keys to success in ice racing. They were like rivets with carbide tips, shot into the tread with an air-driven "stud gun." They had to be seated through careful miles on the ice, so we went out to the track a day early. It was located on a sheltered bay in the southwest corner of icebound Lake Superior. We watched it being designed and constructed in one swoop. There, out on the snow-covered ice, was a highway department dump truck with a plow, its operator steering creatively, a six-pack at his side. The result snaked and looped for 1.5 miles, and had it all: sweepers, switchbacks, hairpins and a kink on the backstraight that was taken flat-out and crossed-up. It was a hard-water driver's course, with the advantage to the nimble (Old Reliable) not the powerful (Fuego).

I loved racing on the ice. Being sideways and still in control was a blast, as well as confidence-inspiring. Seldom was the car pointed straight; it went through the turns about three-fourths cocked, so you looked ahead through the side windows. The bend at the end of the backstraight was like a short-track turn; you'd go into it at about 80 and crank the steering wheel as hard as you could — just *pitch* the car, nearly perpendicular to the track, and wait till the corner came to you. If you did it just right the car seemed to glide through, steering itself. But if your timing was off you'd be frantically sawing at the steering wheel, trying to find the smooth spot or merely stay out of the snowbanks. Ice was the best possible place to break away from driving by markers, because the snow covered them; you stepped on the brakes when it felt right, and turned when it felt right. The lines were dictated less by geometry than by track conditions, which changed with the clouds. Pouncing on the gas pedal loosened the studs, so you had to squeeze the throttle — something that Doc preached. Your hands couldn't keep up with the steering wheel when you accelerated out of the tightest turns, so you let it whir wildly, like the helm of a yacht in a storm, and then tried to catch it — without breaking your thumbs — at the precise position to zoom away straight. The studs churned and the car shook, and, inside Old Reliable, snow squirted like geysers through the rusty floorboard.

The Minnesota Cup, first held in 1964, was the opening event in the modest International Ice Racing Association series. Weather for the event was usually frigid — the previous year it was 20 below and blowing — but this race day was fair. A few hundred rosy-cheeked Duluthians showed up, and their four-wheel-drives speckled the lake and ringed the bend that followed the backstraight. The turns were outlined by colored plastic pennants against the bright whiteness.

After the Le Mans start and first 90 minutes, Tommy Archer led Potter by about 30 seconds. We made a lightning-quick driver change — Steve was out of the car before it had even stopped — and the Archers pitted on the following lap, so for my first two laps I didn't know where the Fuego was. Then I got a pit signal that Bobby was 10 seconds back, which meant they must have had some trouble in the pit. On the next lap he was nine seconds back; then seven, then six, then I could see his headlights through my own cloudy roostertails in the mirror.

What I least wanted was to let myself by pressured into the face of a snowbank, or even into ripping out the studs with an excited right foot. Finishing second would be much better than that. Still, I wanted to beat Bobby a lot. He crept up for a couple more laps and got full in my mirrors going down the backstraight. But then he began falling back, and the numbers on the pit board started to climb back up.

I was having a wonderful time now, running off in the lead. Twenty-four cars had started — about half of them Le Cars sold by Archer Motors, with a smattering of Rabbits and Sciroccos and one ancient Corvair — and I was lapping them left and right. The transmission kept popping out of third gear so I had to hold it in, which meant taking the kink one-handed, but that just made it more fun. I was driving conservatively, but wasn't slowing down. That's when you know you've got it dialled.

After 76 of the 80 laps, in the far hairpin, I came up on the tail of the Fuego sticking out of a snowbank. The turbo's power had been too much for its studs, and Bobby had lost too many chasing me. Some spectators pushed him out — the rules allowed for such fan participation — but he'd lost a lap and finished fourth. As I took the checkered flag I shouted "Hot damn!" inside my helmet. It was nice to be that excited again. Potter and I had lapped the field.

We had run the race with illegal tires — we used 97 studs per tire, and 93 were allowed. Bobby had said not to worry — or maybe it was worry about it later — but when I got out of the car, the first thing I did was draw Steve aside, and, with my arm over his shoulder conspiratorially, suggest that we pull a few studs, fast, in case someone should count them.

Steve and I each got a little Minnesota cup that night at the banquet. Bobby wasn't crazy about being beaten by two carpet-bagging writer/ racers, especially since he had recruited them, but the promoter in him told him it was okay. And everybody had had a good time, which was what he figured mattered most. The next morning I caught a commuter flight in the frozen dark before dawn. There, in the *Duluth News-Tribune & Herald* sports section, was a headline across the page: "Sports Illustrated writer wins Minnesota Cup Race." I bought five copies: one for my parents and four for ammunition in the sponsor hunt.

Gordy Oftedahl and I had an appointment in Chicago with the Jensen stereo company, and I met him in the Minneapolis airport. He had recently gone to a big electronics convention in Las Vegas, looking for sponsors. I pictured him roaming around some arena full of booths manned by high-tech hustlers, trying to find his man. He believed he had. Our appointment was with the president of Jensen, with whom Oftedahl had apparently hit it off. He was calling the president by his first name.

We were asking for $250,000. The previous year Oftedahl had spent $160,000 of a northern California construction magnate's money to campaign a car in the Trans-Am for the man's quick but erratic 19-year-old son, and the team that won the Trans-Am supposedly spent $500,000, so we figured it was a fair figure, especially since Gordy would throw in his second Firebird.

"Here's what we'll do if we get the money," said Gordy, hopping up and down in his airplane seat. He knew of a Chevy Monza GTP car stashed in a garage somewhere, and he could get it cheap because nobody knew how great the car could be. He'd build a turbocharged motor for it. Twelve hundred horsepower! Two hundred and fifty miles an hour at Daytona! It would spin the tires at 190! He'd use Hurley Haywood and win the Miami Grand Prix! "We'll run the full IMSA series with it — and the Trans-Am with the two Firebirds. You and Hurley; we'll win both championships."

The good thing about getting a hot practice lap with Gordy was that by the end of the day, he'd chop off a second or two for you. Wishful thinking was his reality, and he believed in my driving ability the way he believed in everything he wanted. Unfortunately, his blind optimism was contagious — and I'm a sucker for the underdog. So I dismissed a lot of my reservations, in particular over his organization and temperament. Doc knew some things about Oftedahl's record that I didn't, but he neither wanted to taint my attitude nor inhibit my sometimes-fragile enthusiasm, and he knew that Gordy was all I had. So he left it at a general caution; he mentioned that Oftedahl had some burned bridges behind him, and suggested that he may be someone whose results would never improve no matter how much money he had. But I dismissed that, too. I thought that all Gordy needed was tempering, an occasional nudge toward reality. I might not have swallowed 250 miles an hour at Daytona, but I saw myself up there on the banking in this mysterious Monza, running with the fast guys.

We took a taxi from the Chicago airport to the Jensen offices, located in a nearby industrial park. The president was busy; so was the vice-president. We got as far as a marketing man who may have been number three or four. Gordy told the man his dreams, which he measured on the dyno. He would build a magical engine that would get us all we ever wanted. The Jensen man wanted to sell stereos. Gordy couldn't stretch stereos into his vision, and I suddenly saw why he'd never had a major sponsor. I tried to steer the conversation out of his toolbox without taking it into the pages of *Sports Ilustrated*, which left it hanging. We asked that Jensen let us know within 10 days because Daytona was fast approaching, and the man assured us they would. Three weeks later, Jensen would call Gordy and turn him down.

I'd been home for two days when Bobby Archer called. He and Tommy had entered Old Reliable in a two-hour ice race in Eau Claire, Wisconsin that Sunday, but Tommy's daughter had the flu and he wanted to stay home with her. Would I like to codrive with him?

DD came this time. While we were packing, we had a fight over old shoes. She didn't have any footwear suitable for a frozen lake; her Chinese shoes were about the only shoes she had with toes. I had a fine pair of L.L. Bean boots for her, but she thought she looked foolish in them because they were so big on her. I'll just wear my moccasins, thank you, she said.

I don't generally force people to wear the shoes I want them to. But I knew that DD's cold feet in Wisconsin would become my problem. I can't remember specifically saying, "Either you pack the boots or you're not coming," but I remember going down the elevator with my suitcase, alone. And going back, to find her standing in the living room next to her own half-packed suitcase, a little bit forlorn and funny-looking and endearing, with the big boots on her feet.

I said, "Okay, don't bring the damn boots if you don't want to," and she replied brightly, "Okay, I'll bring them," and things were fine until we changed planes in Tampa and I didn't want to have a drink at the bar with her, which started a fight that stretched into the rental car as we left Minneapolis for Eau Claire. It was over cigarette smoke now, and when I tried to snatch the cigarette out of her hand we started beating on each other's arms and shoulders. She climbed into the back seat and I opened both front windows and we drove along the beltway like that, shouting at each other as the icy night air blew over us at 60 miles an hour. Our shouts almost — almost — turned to laughter at the absurdity of it. Then the car started making horrible clanking sounds and the heater began blowing cold air, which meant the engine was freezing under our feet — Hertz forgot the anti-freeze — and the thought of being stranded with a dead car alongside the road in the Minnesota January night was enough of a crisis to bring us together. I raced impending doom back to the airport for a new rental car, and we got to Eau Claire only a couple of hours late that night.

Bobby Archer was the A.J. Foyt of the ice. His crew once made him start 30 seconds behind the field, then took bets on when he would take the lead. He was so confident he seemed complacent, and it drove me crazy; every time I'd worry aloud about something, such as loose studs, lack of practice or Old Reliable's rusty rear suspension, he'd say, "Hey, don't worry: I've been doing this for 12 years." He was so good it made me nervous that I'd let him down. Off the bat he and DD got along, which was standard for her with the genuine ones. She later told me that he told her that he sometimes throws up before races; that surprised me, but not that he confided in her. And he probably threw up on the morning of this race, he was so hung over. We had heard his bed being raised and dropped on the floor in the middle of the night, as if the Exorcist were in the next room with Bobby and his rowdy buddies.

Lake Altoona was a rustic place; the shore was dotted with cottages, some of which were frozen-in. Woodsmoke from a couple of stovepipes drifted into the gray sky. DD had seen snow only once before, and she had never stood on a lake. She was exhilarated, and taken by the friendliness of the Wisconsinites. We were fairly certain that we were the only people there who had traveled from the tropics for this afternoon. She was so beautiful behind the beige scarf, covering all but her eyes and cheeks. And she was glad she had the boots.

Bobby started on the front row beside a Rabbit, with a Scirocco and a Saab behind them. Our Le Car was the slowest of the four, so when the field approached the starter on the pace lap Bobby eased off the throttle, leaving the Rabbit hanging out there as if it were trying to jump the start. Its driver got nervous and backed off, and when he did, Bobby floored it. They took the green flag together, but Old Reliable was going about 10 miles an hour faster. After the first lap Bobby had a huge lead over the Saab and Scirocco, whose drivers had been stymied by the shifting front row; the Rabbit was a hapless fourth. Bobby passed the pits laughing, toot-tooting his horn to signal the success of his ruse.

He was turning sensational 2:14s and 2:15s, stretching the lead with every lap. I hoped he wouldn't ease up, because I wanted as big a cushion as I could get. The Saab, now nearly half a minute back, was about to be turned over to a ringer: Indy car driver Herm Johnson, who lived in Eau Claire. As I waited anxiously for Bobby to pit, I looked down pit road and saw Johnson standing there in his red quilted driving suit that had run the Indy 500, antsy for battle. The Saab pitted and he churned off past me; then Bobby arrived, and I jumped in the car and tore off with the belts tightened unevenly, canting me toward the door. My first lap was 2:17.5, more than two seconds faster than I'd gone in practice, but when I got the signal, our young crew chief, Donny Gorny — another genuine one DD clicked with — gave me a "get-going" sign with his hand. My next lap was 2:17.9, then 2:16.9, and Donny kept urging me to go faster. I was already going faster than I'd expected to — Bobby had said 2:18s would be plenty good — but it wasn't fast enough; our lead was being chopped away. Donny's chalkboard showed the decreasing distance between Old Reliable and the Saab, but I was so worked up over his spinning finger — *"faster, faster"* it said — that Johnson had erased about 10 seconds before the signals on the board even registered.

Suddenly I started doing 2:19s. The first turn was a big "U," and when I'd speed away from it I could see the Saab, black and malevolent-looking, coming the other way and closing ground. The tricky thing about ice racing is that you have to try to go slow in order to go fast; but how can you tell yourself to go slow when there's a Herm Johnson gaining on you? On the track it wasn't much different than when Bobby had chased me in the Minnesota Cup, but psychologically there was an enormous difference: This race was mine to lose *for* the king of the ice, not to him.

Donny's rotating digit drove me to try harder, which only spun my wheels. I was going into the turns too deep, and missing the groove on the way out. Bobby wrote "DRIVE SMOOTHLY" on the board and I waved an acknowledgement, but I didn't need him to remind me. Later, DD said that only inhibition had prevented her from telling Bobby to hold up some 2:16 signs to calm me down; it probably would have worked, and for some reason it surprised me that she understood me that well.

With about 10 laps remaining and Johnson eight seconds back, I was a dead duck. But suddenly, the board showed that I had a 40-second lead over #49, the Scirocco. The motor mounts in the Saab had broken, allowing the engine to tilt the fan into the radiator and chop it up. Johnson's drive ended in the pits with a humid hiss.

So Old Reliable won again. About seven of us took a victory lap — Bobby and DD and Donny and his girlfriend and Gary the mechanic, and somebody's dog, too, I think, and if that didn't snap the rusty suspension trailing arms, nothing would.

At the banquet that evening, my own celebration was reserved. I knew we had lucked out. My deficient driving could have lost the race. "Hey, wake up," Bobby said. "Cheer up. We won. You kept the car on the track and we won. What do you expect from your second ice race, to be as fast as me? Hey, I'm the best." It took DD to point out to me how unflattering my own standards were to Bobby.

Herm and his codriver, Steve Erickson, who owned the Saab, sat down for a glass of the champagne that Old Reliable (now four-for-four) had won. I admitted that I'd been rattled, and Johnson looked up from his glass and said, "Yeah, and I would have caught you and rattled you right off the track."

In his rookie year at Indy the previous May, Johnson had finished ninth in an old car. In October, his sponsor/car owner, an Eau Claire lumber magnate, dissatisfied with the results of the season and experiencing a business downturn, pulled out. It was the middle of winter now, and Johnson had no money and no prospects. "It got too depressing, so I've even stopped reading the racing publications," he said. "All these guys coming up with their money deals. It's just a money sport," he bitterly spit out. The best he could do now was wear his Indy 500 driving suit in a rinky-dink ice race, and lose to some writer/racer — who had an appointment in Milwaukee the next morning, to discuss sponsorship with the Miller Brewing Company. He glanced at me across the table with resentment in his eye, and envy in his gut.

Bill Eppridge

*Bobby Archer,
the A.J. Foyt of
the hard-water circuit.*

Bill Eppridge

Old Reliable was a faded rustbox, but undefeated.

Chapter Nine

Glen Gold

Dangerous Darlene Strikes Again or, Climaxing at the Daytona 24-Hour

DD and I went in different directions from the Minneapolis airport, she to Key West and I to Milwaukee for the appointment with Miller. That meeting didn't go much better than the one with Jensen had. There were just more people, and they sat at a round conference table that I seemed to be on the edge and in the center of. The same question was fired at me from all directions: How much publicity will we get? I couldn't connect my intangible vision —there's a *story*, out there — to theirs; maybe the two weren't connectable. I was sure they wouldn't be sorry if they sponsored me, but I couldn't tell them why. All I could promise was my best. Gordy didn't help our chances the next day, when he called Miller and told them that if they didn't have the $200,000 we were asking, $10,000 would do.

He had entered both Firebirds in the Daytona 24-Hour, with three drivers per car — though some teams used more, and two iron men could run the race themselves. That was six seats to sell for $10,000 per seat, and he had four buyers. Bob Raub, who was again paying his way with labor, would be the fifth driver. The sixth seat was vacant, and Oftedahl could have dropped his price and sold it, but I was still his carrot, his last best hope one more time. Goodyear offered five more sets of tires, which totalled nine since there were four on credit from the Finale. So I was in, on 36 tires and Gordy's hope that I was connected to some rich guy by an invisible thread.

It was more like an invisible rich guy. By now my pitch had branched toward sportsmen. A friend who deals with rich guys told me about a man named Mario Singh, a middle-class Italian boy from New Hampshire who had gone to India seeking truth and discovered capitalism. He'd adopted Sikkhism — from what I could figure, a religion in which you wore a turban, meditated to reach God, worked hard and got rich. Singh had made his fortune through real estate and landlording. "He's a self-made, insecure guy who needs a cachet to prove he's legitimate," said my friend. "He said he made two million dollars last year. It would be a great tax write-off for him." My friend cautioned that Singh also had a reputation for paying his bills late. But I mailed my proposal to him, feeling somehow better that with a sportsman sponsor, at least I wouldn't have to be an Electric Horseman.

On the Saturday night before I left Key West for Daytona, DD and I had a fight during which she screamed at me, "I hope you crash into the wall and kill yourself!" On Sunday night there was a silent, spectacular electrical storm over the ocean. We had a three-hour fight during which things flew off the sixth-floor balcony, and I smashed a louvred closet door (not Moon's) to smithereens, shouting with each blow like a karate exhibitionist as a neighbor yelled from his balcony to shut up. I slept on the couch from 3 a.m. until six, when I got up to catch the plane to Daytona. I had to be on the track that morning for Press Day.

Losing it with the louvred door was the most hysterical I'd been in my life. Now I was in the Miami airport, trying to find peace of mind as if it were a remote departure gate and I were late for the plane. The flight to Daytona was delayed indefinitely because of fog there. The man in line ahead of me said the fog would take hours to clear, and I jumped down his throat and called him a know-it-all. I'd told Gordy that I'd be at the track by 10:30, but the best I could now do was Orlando at 1:30, then rent a car and drive 70 miles to Daytona. I'd be in great shape by then.

But my late arrival after the 90-mph drive from Orlando didn't matter; the Firebird hadn't been running much anyhow. There was a problem with Gordy's secret weapon, a transmission he'd had specially designed to last 24 hours, eliminating an expected 45-minute pit stop to change trannies. That morning, on Bob Raub's second lap, the new transmission had popped out of gear. The crew had just finished putting the old one back in. Gordy wasn't even there; he'd taken the trick tranny to Smokey Yunick's shop, to sift for bugs lurking in the gears of his latest best hope.

I'd been trying to forget the previous night, but every time I opened my mouth my own hoarse voice reminded me of it. And I was exhausted. There were also the ghosts. I wished DD hadn't said what she had on Saturday night. Things like that shouldn't be thrown around. The possibilities for self-fulfillment are much too strong. I didn't even like repeating it for the tape recorder.

The worst part was that I'd brought it up. "If you don't give me some peace I won't be able to concentrate!" I'd shouted in desperation, "and I'll probably crash into the wall...," although I can't imagine not muffling that part. To me, it was a serious risk to utter those words. I'd been wondering for some time if she'd push me that far, into what I perceived as this ultimate threat, words with potential awful consequences for both of us. I'd tried to keep from creating a monster that might come to life and eat me. But I couldn't contain it; and the plea was true. Threats hardly scare DD, however. She only shouted, "I hope you do! I hope...." So, I'd invited it.

My codrivers were Bob Raub and Carl Shafer, a silver-haired Trans-Am veteran, and they got their laps first. The day was almost done before it was my turn to drive. All day, I'd been doing clumsy and absent-minded things: I backed the rental car into a chainlink fence, and walked the wrong way toward places I've been going for years. I considered telling Gordy that I didn't want to drive because I felt the flu coming on, which was true; instead, I told myself I'd be careful. But I intended to go as fast as I reasonably could.

I don't know if it was because I'd driven the car there before, because of the ice experience, or because this was #14, which had a racing steering wheel at least, but I was much more comfortable in the Firebird than I'd been two months earlier. It actually went where I pointed it. The lines came easy, and the thought of trying to drive by 35 markers seemed ridiculous. Since it was only Press Day there were no corner workers, and at quitting time Gordy was told to wave me off. But he was way down on the grass at the start-finish line and I was going 180 miles an hour into the sun, so I missed him twice. I roared around all alone for three laps, until an angry track worker stood in the first turn waving his arms. No one timed my laps, but they felt good.

The garages were open Tuesday but not the course, so crews registered and worked on their cars. Bob Raub was Gordy's hardest worker — and driver. He'd won the GTO class for Oftedahl at the Elkhart Lake 500-miler the previous August. He was from Denver, about 6'1", 200 pounds and bearded. Because he drove them, he knew the Firebirds better than Gordy himself, and at the races he worked on them more. He never took any time for himself — he never *had* any. He'd run a few laps, then work on both cars until the next session — all day, back and forth. He was often underneath one car or the other, in his driving suit. The team wouldn't have been much without him. He would have loved to do the whole IMSA season with Oftedahl, but he only drove when there were no buyers for his seat.

The tape recorder talks back:
Wednesday, February 2
Woke up to the sound of floods outside the motel room. A tornado watch is out.

I'm getting frustrated. Counting last November, I've been at Daytona for God knows how many days, trying to get one practice session in the car with everything right. Yesterday Gordy said, "Well, we don't need to practice much because you guys have all been in the car before, and I don't want to wear it out." Been in the car?! I barely drove the thing in November, and Monday I got five laps. Yesterday there was no practice and today there's a tornado watch. And tomorrow is qualifying. Amazing.

Elwood doesn't want to be a crew chief. "Enough of this crew chief shit, I want to drive," he says. He doesn't even like working for Gordy — he says Gordy vanishes when there's work to be done. But he likes being near the Firebird for the chance to drive it. Everyone wants to drive. Mechanics want to drive, rich guys want to drive, journal-

ists want to drive. Gordy said that IMSA told him they had a list of 25 guys who would pay $20,000 per race to drive a prototype. There's no room in this business for the pros. Maybe the Trans-Am is different, but that's the way IMSA is.

Later:

Gloomy, gloomy, gloomy. I'm at the track, it's still wet and drizzling, and the motor's out of the car. Gordy's latest killer motor. They found pieces of metal in an oil-line filter, so they're switching motors. Gordy had doubts about the motor Monday night because it was new, and they had all day yesterday to do something about it, but apparently no one checked the oil filters. It's lucky it's raining today — we're not losing practice time at least. But they didn't take the motor out until this morning. Gordy just doesn't have it together. So I'm feeling very gloomy. One more obstacle. One more day with no practice. I guess this is building character.

I haven't been concentrating all week. I don't know if it's the argument with DD or what, but I'm scrambled. I'm forgetting a million things everywhere. I'm losing things, forgetting things; I came to the track and left my sweater behind and I'm freezing; I lost my parking pass; I left my clothes behind when I switched motels. I just feel drifty, dizzy.

Carl Shafer didn't recognize me today. My codriver. We were just standing around talking with another guy, and he looked at me and said, "What are you driving?" I looked at him and said, "Carl, it's me, your codriver." He said I looked different without my driving suit on.

Friday, February 4. 4:20 a.m.

Gordy is so strange. He's just had a hernia operation, and he's lost weight and doesn't look well, but he's as hyper as ever. He's always ticking, his leg pumping, looking off over your head like he's trying to spy the next scheme. He invents things in his mind, pronounces and declares them. I didn't think he was serious, but he may have been: According to him, I blew the motor. When I started it in the pits on Monday it revved up high, and he says that caused the cam bearings to be shaved because there wasn't any oil pressure. He's decided that was the reason for the metal in the oil filter. He says my revving it up did it. I didn't "rev it up." It was ornery starting — because the float bowls weren't set right, Elwood said — and Gordy told me to put my foot on the gas to fire it up, which I did, and it may have gone up to maybe 6,000. Gordy seems to have conveniently forgotten that it revved up to 9,000 when his trick tranny popped out of gear.

He's decided that I didn't get him any tires, too. He says he would have gotten five free sets from Goodyear anyhow. So according to him, I not only haven't paid him for the ride, all I've done so far is blow a motor.

They spent most of Wednesday changing the motor and putting the killer tranny back in. That's another thing Gordy invented: that the transmission would work, without ever testing it, because he wanted it to. A smart car owner does not go to the Daytona 24-Hour with an experimental transmission. They got the car finished Wednesday afternoon and it stopped raining in time for the 3:30 session. Raub got out at 4:00, did a couple laps, came back in and said it was shifting great. He went back out and the rear wheels locked up when the transmission seized. Fortunately it seized in the infield, the kink. He did a whole bunch of loops across the grass and there was no permanent damage, but it could have seized on the banking and driven the car into the wall head-first. It's actually a wonder it didn't seize there.

The transmission had been rebuilt in the trailer. The designer himself did it, shaking his head the whole time, saying, "I hate to put transmissions together in the back of a truck. I don't have my tools, everything is so filthy." Gordy wants so much for this transmission to be a secret weapon that he brought it to Daytona believing in his mind it was.

They stayed late Wednesday night and put the first motor back in, after cleaning it out and deciding the bearings were okay. Gordy wanted to use it for qualifying. It was a killer motor, a 389, put out more horsepower on the dyno than any he'd ever built, he said. It died on Raub in qualifying yesterday. He lost 600 revs on the backstraight *right off, and ended up 13th, a 1:53.2, which was still pretty good. But Bob figured it cost at least a second.*

All week Gordy's been talking about how we would be in the top 10, set the GTO fast time; we would crack 1:50 and set a track record and make history and beat all those prototypes and show everybody up and get all the attention. It was a good idea, except for the fact that when the killer tranny popped out of gear, so much for the killer motor. Billy Hagan's Camaros got ninth and 10th, first and second GTO, exactly where Gordy wanted to be.

I've been calling Mario Singh, calling Mario Singh. The plan was for him to come down to Daytona and meet Gordy, watch the race, and hopefully like what he saw enough to back us to the tune of 150 thou. I talked to him on Monday. He said, "I'll call you on Tuesday morning, and if I don't, call me at this number, which is my lawyer's office, at 1:00." He didn't call me at the motel, so I called him at 1:00 from the track; he wasn't there. They said call back at 3; I did and he wasn't there. They said 5, then 5:30. I left a message to have him call me at the motel. He didn't call. All day I was running back and forth to the phone booth under the scorers' stand, and trying to remember what time I was supposed to call next.

I reached him Wednesday morning. He said call back at noon, if I'm not here call my lawyer's office. At noon it was busy. At 1:00 no answer. I called his home at 2:00, not there. I called the lawyer's office; they said he'd be there at 4:00. I finally reached him there at 4:00, and he said, "Call me back at home tonight, in Portsmouth. But I don't know the number there. Call my office in Boston, ask them for my home number. Call me at 9:30 tonight." I did; he wasn't there.

I actually reached him last night. He was very apologetic, said the problem was that he was closing this big million-dollar real estate deal, and was going crazy commuting between Portsmouth and Boston, etcetera etcetera.

After qualifying, I went out at about 4:30 — got a few laps, finally. Everybody told me I had a long face all day, which I did. I did about six laps, still didn't try to go fast, was just trying to feel comfortable. Had a couple of 2:00s, and wasn't at all pushing, so I'm not too worried. Then we had night practice. They adjusted the lights before the session. As it began, a bunch of cars came up pit road, and one of them had crosseyed headlights; I figured that must be ours, and it was. I'm afraid I'm beginning to get that feeling. I mean, everybody else's headlights were aimed pretty good. And our taillights didn't work; they hadn't checked them before they sent Bob out, so they had to call him back in on the radio to fix them.

I got about six night laps. Did some 2:12s, not as fast as I hoped they would be. But they'll get better in the race.

Gordy's decided I don't need any more practice. He says I'm going fast enough.

Saturday, February 5

Note that this is the second day in a row that you've gotten up at 4 a.m. to talk to yourself.

If you didn't make the top 10 on Thursday, you were allowed to requalify yesterday for 11th position on. Or you could stand on your time if you wanted to. What does Gordy do? He sends Bob out to try to better his time. He was already 13th, the best he could get was 11th. This was the price: Run the motor real hard. It was a ridiculous plan. I heard him tell Bob to rev it 7600 all the way around the banking, when the race redline will be 7,000; he even used a lower rear end.

A belt flew off the water pump and the engine over-heated, got to 265 degrees. That was our race motor. Now Gordy wants to save it, so practice is over.

I've lost track of where Mario Singh is supposed to be: the Portsmouth condo he didn't know the number of, his Boston home, the Boston lawyer's office, his Portsmouth office — or whatever it was. As of Friday afternoon, his secretary told me she had made Daytona plane reservations for Singh and his wife. He said call me late Friday night, I'll be home for sure; I started calling at 10:00 after I got back to the motel. I called every 10 minutes from 10 p.m. till 11, busy every time.

The telephone was at the top of DD's arsenal heap, and she'd been using it a lot during the week. When I'd left Key West I couldn't imagine her coming to the race, but somehow things

changed. It was so close to home, and she wanted to come so badly
— and I guess this was really it: She said she would come whether I
liked it or not, and I knew she meant it.

She came up Friday evening, and despite the fact that she tried
very hard to be pleasant — she was radiant again when she got off
the plane — I was leery, and couldn't pretend. We coexisted for 24
hours. It exploded Saturday night after my dad arrived. Because a
night practice was scheduled at the time his plane was due, I'd
asked DD to meet him at the airport so I could drive if I got a
chance. "I'd rather not," she said; she was too shy to meet my dad
for the first time without me. I got mad because she resisted. I'd
wanted Dad to have my Mustang rental car — I'd already rented a
station wagon to sleep in during the race — and, without DD to pick
him up, I had a new project forced on me that afternoon. I had to go
to the airport to leave the Mustang keys at the Hertz counter for
Dad, then call Pennsylvania and tell my mother to find him and
tell him there would only be an envelope to meet him. Oftedahl
didn't run the night practice so DD and I went to meet Dad
together, at which time we were two ticking time bombs. The three
of us didn't have dinner together that night. I told Dad I needed to
relax the night before the race. He went to a 7-Eleven for dinner,
which he ate in his room, alone.

DD and I fought until about 2:30 that morning. She bounced her
suitcase off the motel room window; finally, desperate for sleep, I
took a dramamine and curled up on the floor with a blanket and
pillow. In the morning we fought some more. She wouldn't go to the
track with either Dad or me, and insisted on having one of the cars.
If you knew her you'd understand: It's not that she was simply
childish, it was more that her emotions were as untethered and
exposed as a child's. And I was hardly blameless; if I were wiser
and less impatient — if I'd known how to handle her — it would
have been easy persuading her to pick up Dad that night.

We ended up driving to Dad's motel, where she took the
Mustang; Dad and I went to the track together, with me pouring
my frustrations on him, ranting about how much I hated DD the
whole way.

Here it is, race morning. I can't believe this. Oh, God.
Last night was hysterical. I got about four hours sleep, on
the floor. I'm fighting off the flu. I'm feeling really rotten.
It's a couple hours before the start of the race. DD is here

at the track. Dad is here. Mario Singh has jerked me off all week. Twenty calls to him, and I can't even corner him. I actually tried to call again last night, in the middle of everything with DD; no answer. All this horseshit. I'm feeling very cynical about this money aspect.

The SI *photographer has arrived. He wants me to be around to take smiling pictures of. I'm beginning to really feel what it's like to be a racedriver and have everyone want a piece of you. Mark Donohue supposedly said the reason he liked to drive so much was because it was the only time he could escape. I see what he means. I can't deal with everything. All this stuff. A few minutes ago Dad wanted me to solve the problem of somebody's car blocking somebody else in; it wasn't my car blocked in, it wasn't even my car blocking the other car. Why should I try to solve that? Why can't I just think about the racing? DD doesn't understand that. She thinks I'm egotistical and self-centered because all I want to think about is the racing. She thinks my idea of having a girlfriend at the races is to be a slave, and that she should come first, before the race, because it's just some car, a bunch of silly men going around in circles, and she's supposedly the woman I love. It will just never work.*

I just want to get this race over with. It's not the feeling one should have before a race. I haven't even had time to think about the driving — I haven't even done any driving to think about. I've been in the car 15 laps in a week. It's ridiculous. All week long the standard joke was, "You'll have plenty of time to practice during the race." I didn't know they meant it literally.

Later:

Here I am, alone with my tape recorder, sitting in the station wagon in the dark.

I crashed. Crashed on my first lap. First time around, crossed the start-finish line...and I drove it straight into the guardrail outside the first infield turn.

I went into the turn...too hot. Raub was talking about breathing it, backing off early and breathing it, and I backed off early all right, but I got on the brakes too slow, too casual. I just thought it would slow me right down and it didn't. I drove right off the edge of the track where it turned and I didn't. Got in the grass and the brakes locked and I slid head-on into this guardrail with an embankment behind it at about 40 or 50 miles an hour. The windshield shattered, hood buckled.

Took it all out on my dad. Just yelled at my dad. He tried to make a big deal out of my one lap. Said I went up on the banking high, looked great. He was smiling, talking about it, and when I saw him laughing and bragging about that, I turned on him. We were standing in the paddock by the station wagon; DD was watching, she had tears in her eyes. Of all people; yelling at my poor old Dad. My father. I said, "Don't you smile! Don't you laugh! I didn't do anything for you to be proud of! Don't be proud of me for that!"

Bob Raub walked by. I pointed at him and said, "You see that guy? You know how bad he wants to be a racedriver? You know how hard he's worked all week to get this car ready, and get a good result so he can be a racedriver? I ruined it for him. You see Carl Shafer? He paid $10,000 for this weekend, and I ruined it for him. Gordy's mortgaged his fucking house to be here, and I ruined it for him!"

The same time I was yelling at him I was holding my arm around him, telling him I didn't mean to be taking it out on him. I was bouncing back and forth between the outbursts, apologizing to him. But I didn't do anything for him to be proud of. Just because he got a kick out of seeing me go high on one lap. I didn't finish a lap.

DD. I hope she understands now. I kept trying to tell her, trying to tell her...without mentioning the unmentionable. I had to have some peace to have the concentration before I got in the car. We were in Gordy's motor home, alone, while I was dressing to go out, and she asked how I felt. Drained. I remember saying to her just before I got in the car, "I haven't been able to concentrate all week, there's no reason why I should be able to concentrate out there."

So I came here having broken up with her. So I got in the car with all those things. Completely without enthusiasm. And the fact that I haven't practiced. Gordy. Wants to save his car. Fifteen laps of practice all week. He told me to cool it, just go out there and cruise, every time.

It was my first good lap in the car. A total of two weeks at
Daytona, counting November, and I never had the chance
to do one hot lap. Every time I got in the car there was
something new why I couldn't go fast. I've been trying to
get experience, trying to get experience, couldn't get it. So I
went out there with a total of 15 laps practice all week.

All these other drivers were saying, "Well, that's all the
practice I've had." That's fine for those guys who are
experienced racedrivers. I've never been in anything that
went 200 miles an hour before, man.

My recollections of the day are hazy, like the dusk on the
backstraight the one time I went down it. After Dad and I got to the
track, I kept looking over my shoulder for DD and the Mustang,
with a mixture of hope and dread — and if I could explain the
ambivalence I might know why we couldn't break up. I took a
deep, apprehensive breath when I saw her gliding between the cars
in the paddock. She was very calm, even kind. She said she wanted
things to be normal. But it was too late; by then I was just trying to
survive the day.

The race started at 3:00 but I didn't drive until about 6:30. Just
before I took off, as the crew was changing tires under me, I looked
at DD standing a few feet away behind the short pit wall, and gave
her thumbs up. I didn't want her to worry.

Bob Raub had said that the brakes heat up during a pit stop. He
said a lot of guys tear onto the track and go into the Horseshoe with
hot brakes, and shoot down the escape road. I drove cautiously
through the infield, easy on the brakes, and climbed up the bank —
high, like my dad says — satisfied that the air rushing over them
on the backstraight would finish cooling them. A March prototype
passed as we both levelled off Turn 2. I followed its draft down the
backstraight, drawn into the twilight by its dark tail, and adrenaline caught up with me. For a moment, it was fun. It was probably
the fastest I'd ever taken the banking.

Bob had also said to back off early for the first turn, at the 300-
yard sign. That allowed the engine to breathe after its high-
revving haul around the oval. I'd been braking at 250 in practice
and had been saving 225 for the hot lap that never came, so 300
sounded easy. But maybe I should have used 350 on the first lap.
Maybe I was thinking more about breathing the engine than
braking, and took the 300 sign too lightly. Maybe the brakes were

still too hot; maybe they were too cold; maybe they were taxed by the weight of the full gas tank. Maybe I suckered myself into the turn, fixed on the tail of the March.

Most likely, I was too dazed to feel much urgency about anything, not even slowing from 190 miles an hour for a 40-mph turn.

If only someone had reminded me not to be in a hurry. Maybe I hadn't gotten enough guidance. I envied Steve Potter, who drove a GTU-class Mazda RX-7; his owner had gone over a long list of exigencies with him, things to do in case of 32 kinds of trouble. It seemed that everything I learned came from eavesdropping. Both my codrivers would have answered any question I had, but I didn't have much to ask because I didn't have much to go on. Doc was having his own problems — he would drive a Porsche called the Pink Panzer to 11th — and I didn't want to burden him with mine, so he didn't realize how lost I was.

When I saw the guardrail coming, my first concern was how hitting it was going to affect our position. After I did hit it, I thought, "Oh, I really blew this one." The shattered windshield was filled with a wall of dusk. A corner worker ran over and asked if I was all right, and I growled, "Yeah, I'm all right." I radioed the pit, and, as calmly as I could, said, "I just crashed into the guardrail. I'm going to try to drive the car around." I wanted to get out of there — that's where the embarrassment was — and to keep the car in the race. Simply crashing the car was no tragedy, but crashing it out of the race was an unbearable thought. As long as the car was rolling, some honor remained.

I didn't inspect the damage; if the car would run there was no point in it. I backed up, pulled onto the track and headed toward the Horseshoe. The hood blew up and covered the windshield like a red blanket. I swerved onto the grass, jumped out, yanked the pins, threw it aside and drove off, still having barely glanced at the damage.

I hadn't gotten a reply on the radio, because Gordy's wife Karen was wearing the headphones as she kept the lap chart on an elevated stand in the pit, and it took more time for her to relay my message to Gordy through the pit's perpetual noise, than it did for me to get going again. Then, when I'd jumped out to remove the hood, the radio's plug came out with me. I drove up the infield straight at 40 mph, with my eyes glued by dread to the water temperature gauge as cars roared by at 100. Like some astronaut, I began reading the climbing temperature to mission control, unaware that I was lost in space. It never occurred to me that I should be hearing Gordy's voice on the radio (not that I wanted to); it would have been the first time for it, since my helmet hadn't been wired until that morning. But it was just as well we weren't connected; he was back there yelling at me.

On the backstraight the needle shot past 270. I killed the motor and coasted around the banking on the apron, but ran out of momentum. I bump-started it, and chugged down pit road knowing everybody was looking. Through the smashed and steamy windshield I could see Gordy, in all his hugeness, hopping as if the pavement were on fire.

I climbed out and slumped in the same lawn chair I had so recently left, next to DD, who looked sad, not surprisingly. I didn't take my helmet off, because it covered my face. I just sat there, watching through the visor as Gordy ranted. He shouted, "Did you drive it around like that?" I thought, "How do you think it got here?" but simply answered, "Yes," without understanding the question or caring to figure it out. I think what he wanted to know was how long the gauge had been pegged. DD later told me he yelled, "You sonofabitch!" but I never heard him.

The crew pushed the car back to the paddock and began fixing it in the grass next to the transporter. It took about 90 minutes — maybe two hours, I wasn't counting — as Gordy paced and shouted orders. They hammered on the bent chassis tubes, and replaced the radiator, oil cooler, fiberglass nose and some lights, binding the ragged edges with silver duct tape. Floodlights glared on the car as they worked, and you could see their breath in the chilly, lit-up air. I stayed in the shadows, one of the watching crowd, wondering if it was conspicuous by my face that I'd been the driver. Bob Raub and Carl Shafer were good about it; Carl said, "Hey, I couldn't count all the cars I crashed when I was learning."

Raub took the battered Firebird back on the track at about 8:30, and after a couple of laps he came back and said it was as good as new. I hung around the pit for a few contrite hours, wondering when or whether Gordy would put me back in. I didn't say anything to him, not because I didn't think I owed him an apology and explanation, but because I figured he didn't want to hear anything from me. I didn't have any excuses anyhow. What could I say? I went into the first turn too hot on my first lap in a 24-hour-long race.

Bob and Elwood both told me they would work on Gordy when he cooled down, but it might be daylight before I could drive again. But suddenly it looked as if Gordy might need me sooner. Carl finished his shift weak and dizzy, his flu having struck that morning, and he didn't want to drive any more. And Bob had driven three hours between 8:30 and 12:30, so unless I drove, he was faced with an awfully long night.

I was sitting in the lawn chair, and Elwood came over and hunkered down on his long legs and said, "You're not gonna like this."

"Tell me," I said.

"Gordy's gonna put Craig Carter in the car."

Carter was champion of IMSA's Kelly Series, a sprint series for cars like the Firebird. When I saw him standing there with his helmet on, getting instructions from Gordy — the Firebird's engine was beginning to falter —I got mad. Bob pitted, and when Carter got in the car I walked out. I got about 50 paces, then turned on my heels and headed back, itching for a fight. I stood in the pit and fumed and glared at Gordy, but there was nothing on my tongue to start a fight over. I don't think he even noticed me. Then Carter came back and pronounced the car dead. Gordy blamed it on my overheating the motor. At that point, I didn't care.

So that was it. DD and I left. Dad was in the motel room we'd had the night before, so I checked us into a 20-dollar dive on Atlantic Boulevard, punishing myself with a seedy room. DD was actually very comforting. I sat on the floor against the bed, legs spread, shoulders slumped, in my racing suit. I looked down at it, and felt as if I didn't belong in it.

We slept until 10:00 the next morning. It was pouring when we went back to the track — doubtless one of the ugliest days on record in Daytona. The rain had begun at dawn, and since then the cars had spent much of their time cruising around under yellow because there was so much water on the track; the race had even been stopped for an hour. I parked the station wagon beside Oftedahl's motor home, facing the chainlink fence. Both gorgeous Firebirds were on the other side, broken, defeated, and left out in the rain — #13, driven by three rent-a-drivers, had blown its engine later in the night. I went into the motor home, where Gordy was sitting bleary-eyed and disconsolate on the edge of his bed. I extended my hand and said, "I'm sorry it turned out like this."

He shook it, and looked up at me. "Did you ever talk any more to that rich guy?" he asked.

"No," I said.

"Boy, we needed something out of this race. We're broke." Then he added, "We would have led the race. We were ahead of that Ferrari." It was a car that, for a while during the night, had been in second.

Preston Henn, millionaire racecar driver and veteran sportsman, won the SunBank 24 Hours in his Porsche 935. He'd started the race with Bob Wollek and another Frenchman, Claude Ballot-Lena, and had recruited A.J. Foyt at dawn (inciting Wollek to a small tirade and utterance of the "f"-word during the live TBS coverage, to which Foyt later responded by calling Wollek a "rum-dum"). Foyt was driving his first sports car race since he'd won Le Mans with Dan Gurney in 1967. His own car, a Nimrod Aston-Martin codriven by Darrell Waltrip and sponsored by Pepsi, had retired with engine problems after four hours. Henn drove one 90-minute shift.

Officially, we finished 47th overall, completing 165 laps, and won $200. Car #13 finished 26th, 411 laps, $250.

The Oftedahl Firebird looked great for the first few hours.

After the fall.

Gordy Oftedahl gave more than he got.

Bob Raub gave more than he should have had to, but would have anyhow.

Hal Crocker

Preston Henn, the veteran sportsman/millionaire racecar driver....and rich guy.

Stan Clinton

Bundy on the banking, behind the wheel of the Pink Panzer.

Chapter 10

Stan Clinton

Idiots

DD may have had her blind side, but she was perceptive about people she wasn't in love with. After Daytona, she said that most of the people she'd seen in racing seemed unhappy. She saw grown men and women spending millions of dollars to race around in circles. So much time and energy invested, the risking of lives and fortunes, for what? What did it prove when you won? And there were so few rewards to measure against the defeats. "I wonder how it feels to want to play that bad," she said.

Doc called one evening while I wasn't home, and he said to her, "I know what you think: You think we're all a bunch of idiots. We are.

"Racing takes away one's better judgement," he said. "That's really why it's dangerous. People get caught up in it and lose perspective, and reality gets away from them. I've seen it happen again and again, including to me. There have been periods when I couldn't get a ride, and I just about went bonkers."

"Don't worry," comforted DD. "We're all Bozos on this bus."

He told her about Peter Gregg. "His life was consumed by racing," Doc said. "He lost his factory Porsche ride and couldn't get a major sponsor that year. He had no real friends because he hadn't ever taken the time from racing to make any, and he thought he had nothing left to live for if he couldn't win races."

Anyone who watched me at a race might have thought I was having a miserable time, but when I was behind the wheel, it was the most fun I'd ever had in my life. But it was such a struggle, to have all that fun. That's what showed on people's faces. And it was impossible to have enough fun, because you could never go fast enough. An idiot was merely someone who couldn't stop trying. Sometimes the line between dedication and obsession was crossed; it *had* to be, because sometimes anything less isn't enough. You lose perspective, and reality gets away from you. DD, the idiot for love, should have understood that.

"The car is my relief," says Doc. "It's only when I get out of the car that problems come back. I can put things into perspective when I'm strapped in. It's the only place where you can deal with your true feelings. Nothing can hurt you in there, except your own mistakes. They can be minor — the loss of time — or major: crashes. But everything you do, you get some immediate reaction from. As much control as you can have in life, you have in that car, and you can never get enough of it. At least I haven't yet."

They don't call the drug "speed" for nothing. Speed is a sensation with a hard hook, and the people it grabs have about as much resistance as a worm on a line being cast toward sea. *Speed freaks*; the words sound right together. Those crazed characters in old movies, laughing hysterically behind the wheel as they speed toward a head-on crash ... racers, more or less. It's not the roar of the crowd that draws them, although it is the crack of the bat, which is akin to taking a kink flat-out. The most seductive thing about racing is the singular sensation of speed. The physical awareness may diminish with experience — after a while 150 miles an hour feels the same as 50 — but the sensation never stops, as long as you're in the car. The bat keeps cracking — or, even better (or maybe worse): It's one never-ending crack. Every moment on the track feeds the addiction. And the thrill never really goes; any idiot knows that. I said something in the brief *Sports Illustrated* article that started it all for me, describing my first drift, on the final day of my BSMR school at Riverside: "I can feel it now; I want more." The line would become a driving refrain in my mind.

Niki Lauda might say my "speed freaks" explanation is nonsense. "I get joy out of the fascination with perfection, not from the thrill of motor racing," he says in his book "My Years with Ferrari." "Imagine if you really felt a thrill racing; you'd get a centrifugal force orgasm on corners, a speed orgasm on the straight, you would go from one emotion to another and with so many thrills you wouldn't be able to drive at all. People whose 'needs are satisfied' are wankers, but not racing drivers."

I was at Nurburgring the day in 1976 that Lauda crashed and was nearly incinerated; after he recovered, he cursed the priest who had given him Last Rites. And I was at Watkins Glen when he returned to racing 10 weeks later and removed his Nomex hood to reveal a grotesquely scarred face, turning his back to the gawkers as he did. The very fact that he came back — let alone so quickly — says something he hasn't explained. Don't let him tell you that he doesn't have a need.

And don't confuse a racer's urge with a death wish. I've never seen a racedriver with a "death wish." I've seen a lot of crazy ones who were headed for the cemetery if they didn't slow down, and some whose death was not surprising, but it was because they wanted to go fast, not because they wanted to die. "The essence of life is to go as fast as you can without getting killed," says Dan Gurney, and motor racing idiots know what he means.

"I've always thought of racecar drivers as being clever or stupid," said Mario Andretti in *Time* magazine. "I'm still trying to figure out which we are." Smart racing promoters think they know. They're like the pushers: cool enough to avoid the affliction, clever enough to exploit the addiction. They know that racers are idiots. And that...Everyone wants to drive. They also know that racers will pay to perform. "Ah yes, the Great God Speed," goes the line in the movie "Silver Dream Racer." "It's the only show where the clowns pay to entertain the crowds." Even Steve Potter says, "Part of me, part of the time, says, 'No cost is too high.'" Like DD, I wonder how it feels to want to play that bad. My saving grace.

There are decent livings being made by racedrivers, of course, and it's getting better. There are the regional stars, rugged men who hammer out victories three or four nights a week, the Dick Trickles from the Midwest, Jack Ingrams from the South and the fast guys on the dangerous sprint car circuit. But they still pay, with all the hours of sleep they don't have time for, all the miles they endure in their trucks, and all the roadside hamburgers they swallow. Bobby Unser often bunked in the back seats of cars until he won his first Indy 500. Other major sports create prima donnas — if not spoiled punks — by throwing money and privileges at them, sometimes from adolescence; but for all that racing gives rich guys, it stomps on star attitudes. If John MacEnroe were a racer the other drivers would run him off the track. In fact, I doubt that your average pro ballplayer would have enough grit for the long haul of the racing circuit. But then anyone who would commit themselves to a sport where the odds against making it are enormous even if you're gifted, and where you can expect mostly disappointment, exhaustion, greasy knuckles and a low standard of living for years, is an idiot. The life of an idiot sure isn't boring, at least. Their own saving grace.

The dues are long if you're not rich — or born an Unser, Petty or Andretti, such as Little Al, Kyle and Michael. It's one reason the best stock car drivers are so old. "Only a handful of people are making money at racing," says Roger Penske, the most successful car owner. "Everyone else is in racing because they think they love it." Racers have to support their habit somehow. It's difficult to hold a regular job when racing requires so many days out of town and hours preparing the car, so racers are frequently self-employed, often in the racing industry. Financially, the job covers the racing; they combine the two and break even if they're lucky. Tax-wise and paint-job-wise, they are their own sponsor. Preston Henn's Porsche was the Swap Shop car, bought and campaigned largely with the profits from the Florida flea markets he owned. If the expense wasn't entirely justifiable as a sound investment in advertising, at least it was tax-deductible; he liked publicity not only because it stroked his ego as a veteran sportsman and millionaire and racecar driver, but also because it was evidence for the IRS. When he replaced himself with A.J. Foyt in the Daytona 24-Hour, it had been a smart business decision as well as a smart racing one (the two are inevitably inseparable). He had driven his one easy-paced daylight shift; if he puts A.J. in the car, he gets it all.

* * *

My strategy for the first few days after the Daytona crash was to blank it out. My mother had suggested I take Mark Twain's advice: "Drag your thoughts away from your troubles — it's the healthiest thing a body can do." Doc had read something about Mario

Andretti in *Road & Track*, and he told me to look it up. It said, "Mario Andretti made the big mistake of not getting enough practice with the car, and he crashed in the race." That helped. Doc also told me about a crash that he'd had under similar circumstances, and his was even worse. Al Holbert had qualified his Chevy Monza on the pole for a race at Talladega and had let Doc drive in the warmup —Doc wasn't even entered. He bounced off two guardrails and wiped the car out. "I was expecting Al to hit me in the head with a hammer," he said. "That was the only thing that would have made me feel better. But he just said, 'If you want to be a racedriver, you're going to have to learn how to handle it.'" Two weeks later Holbert made Doc his codriver in another car at another race. And even Holbert had had a crash like that very early in his career, driving over his head in the rain.

Doc's story was nice, but the only thing consoling about it was that it proved the possibility of coming back after a disaster if your owner were Al Holbert. At least he made me laugh, when he said that I had to somehow find a way to consider my crash a forward step.

I can't remember when I first began to think about quitting. It might have been in New York at the Pepsi brunch; that's when I began to get confused about my motives, at least. I might have been precisely on the course I'd set for myself in the beginning, but I didn't know it because I'd charted in the dark — "get the story" was my only direction. I'd carried this ambivalence to Daytona, but the crash had now cleared things up. No way was this story going to end smashed against a guardrail.

I didn't have a ride for the Miami Grand Prix, and although I didn't relish the idea — it hurt to watch, and I still wanted to cover my face — I went to the race, because I knew I couldn't find a ride in Southernmost Condo that weekend.

The Budweiser Grand Prix of Miami would be the richest sports car race in history. Eight years earlier, the Long Beach Grand Prix had re-started something: racing in the streets, which had ended in the U.S. with the death of a spectator at Watkins Glen in 1952. But in 1975 an expatriate Englishman named Christopher Simon Robin Pook talked the city council of Long Beach, California, into hosting a Formula 1 race. Long Beach was dying at the time, but it boomed on the heels of the new image created by the Grand Prix. Detroit had tried the same thing, and now Miami, another sinking city, was getting into the act — with full-bodied sports cars, rekindling a Latin-American tradition. And IMSA was pleased to deliver racing downtown, where the markets were. Technically, it was absurd to race 220-mph cars around the inevitable hopelessly tight and bumpy circuit, which included two railroad crossings, but that made it no less exciting.

Al Holbert brought his new prototype: a March that was owned by the factory in England, bearing his own 350 Chevy engine. He had secured a $100,000 season sponsorship with CRC Chemicals, makers of auto-care products. His codriver would be Jim Trueman, who owned Red Roof Inns, the motel chain. Trueman would pay Holbert $15,000 per race and receive 20% of the winnings. The distinguished Trueman was highly active and popular in racing; he also owned the Mid-Ohio Sports Car Course, an Indy car, and was patron to promising drivers. Had Holbert had a larger sponsorship, Doc would have been his codriver. Even at the top, the seat was for sale.

I'd first observed Al Holbert 25 years earlier, when I was nine and he was ten. We were with our fathers, who were racing in the Giant's Despair Hillclimb. Mr. Holbert was the country's best Porsche driver and had been quickest up the hill that day. I eyed Al across the hotel lobby; he was the fast guy in the sons-under-12 division.

He earned an engineering degree at Lehigh and was a Navy pilot before he thought seriously of taking over Holbert Racing, out of Holbert Porsche/Audi in Warrington, Pennsylvania. Speed might not have been a drug to him. He succeeded in racing by engineering, not flatfooting. No team was consistently better prepared. His entry in the Miami Grand Prix marked a full effort to regain the Camel GT Championship that he had left behind. It was ironic that John Paul, Jr. wouldn't be defending the title because he'd gotten an Indy car ride. Holbert had worked on that same ride all winter — the contract was even drawn. Then John Paul, Sr. offered $400,000 to the car owner, a Belgian count, and Junior got the ride. It wasn't that Junior didn't deserve it (he would win the Michigan 500, impressively); his dad's dough was merely his unfair advantage. He had gone from the Skip Barber School to Indianapolis in just five years.

Doc got a ride for Miami in the 11th hour — literally. At 11:00 on the Friday night before Sunday's race, he agreed to drive the Nimrod Aston-Martin that Foyt and Waltrip had driven at

Daytona. He'd been haggling with its English owner, Robin Hamilton, over who would get paid in the deal. (Supposedly it was a shocking, but not unheard-of, misunderstanding: A driver agrees with an owner on a price, and each shows up at the track expecting a check.) Hamilton could have dropped his $15,000 price and sold Doc's seat, but he needed a pro for a decent chance at a high finish and he valued Doc's technical input, since the Nimrod was undeveloped. So, after trying to do better right up to the 11th hour, Hamilton agreed to guarantee Doc $1,000 against a percentage of the purse.

DD and I drove up from Key West. We continued to quarrel — she said she was going to stay in Miami and move in with her cousin the policewoman (and her cousin's child) — but the arguing wasn't so bad. It bothered me more to be a long-faced racedriver out of a ride. He goes to races with little to do but wait for opportunities. He hangs out in the press box, feeling out of place but believing that's where to spread the word that he's available. He squirms under the weight of his street clothes, which are a stigma of his unemployment. "There's so-and-so. He can't get a ride." I used to watch them and think that; I never thought I'd be one.

It poured on the city's rebirth. Gene Felton won the separate GTO race in Billy Hagan's Camaro. His defroster was a clump of rags on a stick. Steve Potter quoted him in *AutoWeek*: "I can tell you where every street sign is at every corner," said Felton. "I'd just watch out the side window, and when I came to the right one I'd turn. I didn't know where I was. I didn't know I was leading. I just knew I was going like hell the whole time." Guess who else was there: Gordy Oftedahl, with both Firebirds. Number 13 retired on the second lap, #14 on the fifth; their defrosting system drew hot air from the exhaust headers, which channeled steam directly to the windshield. Other than that, the cars were running fine. I watched from the big window in the press room, about 15 stories high, on the top-floor ballroom of the Everglades Hotel on Biscayne Boulevard. Oftedahl's long, low cars chugged together through the paddock in the rain, to be parked. It looked like a two-car funeral procession.

Holbert won the big race, which ended by surprise. It was called off during a dark torrent that flooded the track. Fifty of the 310 miles had been completed, the final 14 of them a parade behind the pace car. The checkered flag fell on the cars as they sat in a long line on pit road, waiting for the rain to stop. Holbert got all of the $51,000 first-place money — by far the best payday of his 13-year career. DD was incredulous again. "That's it? That's how it works? That's *fair*?" Holbert was asked in the press box if the victory were tainted to him. "No, not at all," he said. *That's racing*, goes the cliché. The winner is the guy who's leading when the checkered flag falls on the free-for-all. The opportunities and pitfalls are the same for everyone. Holbert admitted — *volunteered* — that he had been prepared to cheat, because his throttle had been sticking. (*Think of it*: 600 horsepower with no reins in a downpour on city streets with a $51,000 reward for not backing off.) While the cars were parked and waiting for the rain to stop, he'd considered hooking a wire to the gas pedal, to be yanked by hand. It would have been for safety's sake, but it also would have been illegal since no repairs were allowed under the red flag. But since the race wasn't resumed he was clean. Jim Trueman was also in the press box for interviews; he was pleased, but seemed slightly embarrassed at having won the race without getting in the car.

Doc had arrived at the track in the middle of the first practice session on Saturday; since he lived in north Georgia, near Road Atlanta, he'd had to get up at 4:00 that morning to catch the first Atlanta-Miami flight. He carried his suitcase straight to the track, suited up, practiced, and qualified 16th in the 32-car field.

The Nimrod's V-8 Aston-Martin engine produced 530 horses and the car weighed 180 pounds over the GTP minimum of 1900, which was not a competitive power-to-weight ratio for a short race on a tight circuit. In other words, Doc's car was a sled. But in the rain that was good. He drove it well despite being unfamiliar with it, and moved up to sixth by the time the yellow flag came out on the 20th lap. But he'd been fumbling around to operate the windshield wipers — the switches were under the forward edge of the seat — and he'd turned on the headlights without knowing it. The crew held out a sign that said "LIGHTS OFF," but Doc didn't know which switch it was — nor that the lights would drain the battery at low speeds. The car died on the straight behind the pits, and his codriver, Lyn St. James, ran to the fence with a fresh battery for Doc to install. It took two laps, and they finished 20th. Robin Hamilton said that Doc had been guilty of brain fade; Doc conceded that he should have known what all the switches did, but rush jobs have a way of ending up like that, he added. And he still doubts that the battery died simply because the lights were on.

As I watched the race from the depressing but dry press room, I decided to quit, as soon as I could do so gracefully. The crash had

had more effect on my morale than my confidence. I wanted to keep driving, but didn't want to keep hustling. My ethical reservations were growing; how much more would I have to request from people, from Sikhs to breweries? And I felt guilty because of the time it was consuming. There has to be some point at which the story is more trouble than it's worth. My motives seemed more important than ever now, and more murky. I didn't know if I was obsessed with speed or the story. Was I a committed journalist or an idiot? Steve Potter had asked me, "If you weren't a writer, would you quit?" and I'd replied, "In a minute." It was comforting to know it was true. But I also knew this: When I'd walked the circuit during Saturday's GTO qualifying, I longed to drive the Hagan Camaro so much it made my knees weak, each time Felton blasted by. The car made the sidewalk vibrate, and I wanted to mash my tingling throttle foot through it.

* * *

Actually, I had discovered Nimrod Racing before Doc. Robin Hamilton had travelled from England to the Daytona Finale to check out IMSA and find sponsorship for the upcoming "Florida Three," and we'd had a straight talk in the press box. The possibilities had sounded appealing to us both. When I was in New York in January we'd met for lunch at his hotel, the expensive Parker Meridien. He brought his PR woman and I brought Steve Goldberg, who worked for a sports marketing firm in Manhattan and was the closest thing I had to an agent. It was a conference full of hope: a $200,000 sponsor would have bought me a spot on the Nimrod team and Hamilton somewhere to take it. His projected itinerary consisted of the "Florda Three," then European endurance races at Silverstone, Nurburgring, Le Mans and Hockenhiem, and back to the States for the final four or five IMSA races. I carried Hamilton's thick proposal — bound, and full of eight-by-ten color photos — away from the meeting and gazed at the Nimrod a lot. It was intriguingly handsome. Silver with subtle British racing green and light jade trim, it had a snub nose, wide mouth, and big glassy headlights that slanted up and back, deep in the contour of the rounded fenders. The big rear wing was supported by silver fins growing from the car's long tail. It looked like a stubby barracuda. Driving it was an alluring prospect. Doc believed I was ready for a prototype — at least the Nimrod, which handled well but was no rocket. I was happy to defer to his judgement — it freed me to fantasize about driving at Le Mans, at least — but the thought was too heady to take seriously. It was also $200,000 away from reality.

Nimrod Racing Automobiles was based in the hamlet of Fauld in the Midlands; Hamilton's business, an Aston-Martin agency that specialized in restoration of that classic British marque, was located there. Hamilton couldn't have been less like Gordy Oftedahl — he was small, calm and wore a necktie with his racing jacket — but they had a lot in common. The Nimrod was his idea, and he'd supervised the construction. He commissioned Eric Broadley, designer of the Lola, to construct a monocoque chassis for the Aston-Martin V-8, whose factory provided nearly a quarter million dollars worth of engines — six of them. Pace Petroleum Company invested about that much more in Nimrod, and Hamilton built two cars. He believed that Nimrod Racing could topple Porsche, which had dominated endurance racing for two decades, and become the greatest endurance racing team on earth. But his primary ambition was to win Le Mans. The name "Nimrod" came from the Book of Genesis; Nimrod was a descendant of Noah, and, said Hamilton, a "long-distance warrior." The team's logo was long-distance warrior's helmet, and sometimes Hamilton referred to the car as simply "Nimrod."

In his first race, at Le Mans the previous June, one car was all but destroyed by a crash from a blowout in the kink on the Mulsanne Straight, taken at over 200 in a prototype. The driver walked away without injury, which proved how strong the chassis was, said Hamilton the optimist. The second Nimrod finished seventh and was the only British car to see the checkered flag. In three more races the cars did well enough for Nimrod Aston-Martin to finish third in the manufacturers' standings of the World Endurance Championship. That encouraged Hamilton to ship two cars, a giant transporter and a five-man crew to America, land of opportunity. With a strong showing or two, he was certain he could land a sponsor.

Pepsi had sponsored one car at Daytona, and Waltrip and Foyt had gotten Nimrod some attention; they were running fifth when the engine had failed. The other Nimrod's engine blew in a big way — a broken crankshaft. By Miami, Nimrod Racing was already living week-to-week and selling rides. Hamilton had rented the second Nimrod to Seahawk Racing, a team better known for its offshore powerboat racing. The Seahawk company, based in South

Florida, also sold offshore powerboats, vessels often used for marijuana smuggling. Seahawk's driver, a young Latin-American karting champion who was quick but reckless, had crashed Nimrod in practice and finished 13th in the race.

Monday morning after the race I met with Robin Hamilton in his hotel, the Miami Hilton. This time the discussion was subdued, as if we were just going through the motions now. We were both near defeat, if for no other reason than we had run out of time — already. And Hamilton's impending failure could mean bankruptcy for his business. Looking for that graceful way out, I proposed that Doc and I drive the Nimrod at Sebring. Making the assumption — and taking the gamble — that I would drive well and the car would perform respectably, I would redeem myself, retire and go write already. Hamilton set the price at $30,000 for two seats, mine and Doc's. Fine, I said; it would have been a steal for a sponsor, exposure-wise. Hamilton said he needed to know in a week, because he couldn't afford to keep the team in America any longer than that. As I was walking toward the door he said, "You know, there's something about this sport that turns the most reasonable people into idiots."

I never made a call to try to raise the money. I didn't know where or how to start. That week, it was easier not to quit. Instead, I signed up for the Buck Baker School of Stock Car Driving.

* * *

The Stroh's Tour was a NASCAR oval-track series run mostly in New England. It was a AA league, two notches below Grand National, but when the Winston Cup drivers made appearances there, they often got beaten because the regulars were tough. Darrell Waltrip had run a Stroh's race the previous year and finished seventh; "There was just six guys faster than me that night," he said. The cars were Late Model stock cars, but Well Used would have been a more appropriate name for the class. It was not a series for rich guys. The rules were designed to keep costs down, and the tracks were blue-collar venues (Thunder Road Speedbowl in Vermont was my favorite, for its name). A $30,000 sponsorship could have bought a decent ride for most of the season, with the owner keeping all the prize money. Ken Squier, the excellent CBS and TBS racing announcer, who lives in Vermont and was a consultant for the circuit — his involvement in racing runs deep, sincere and long — had located a car for me; the owner/crew chief was apparently a colorful and irascible character to boot. If it would have saved the story, I would have gladly moved to New England for the next six months — said, "So long, DD, I've got to go to work now." But I had one big reservation: How many ways can you describe driving around in a circle? I went off to the Buck Baker School at the North Carolina Motor Speedway — the Rockingham Mile — to find out.

Elzie Wylie "Buck" Baker was the NASCAR Grand National champion in 1956 and '57. He was a heavyweight leadfoot rogue back in the days when they drove with hangovers — men such as Lee Petty, Junior Johnson, Curtis Turner and Fireball Roberts. He'd been known for his especially hard living and racetrack surprises; the windows in his Charlotte shop were blacked out so that the competition — and NASCAR — wouldn't know what he was up to. More recently he'd been working overtime to promote his latest idea, the National Pickup Truck Racing Association — stock cars with pickup sheetmetal. Baker was 64 and silver-haired now, but looked a decade younger and two decades stronger. He had two sons and a seven-year-old daughter from three marriages. The eldest son was Winston Cup star Buddy (Elzie Wylie, Jr.) Baker, whose right foot seemed to carry all his 6'5" and 220 pounds; then came Randy, 21 and ready to take his shot at Grand National (his mother had been Miss Southern 500); and now there was Susie, borne by Buck's third pretty, young wife.

The chief instructor of the three-day course, an affable and straight-forward fellow named Ed Sutton, had been the captain of a SWAT team in a Washington, D.C. suburb and was a former Figure-Eight World Champion. A figure-eight track is what you think: There's an intersection in the middle of it. The classroom was the infield infirmary, a cinderblock structure the size of a large woodshed. I arrived in the middle of Sutton's bit on crashes, and the importance of a properly-anchored seat harness and quality "fire suit." He said that when you're upside down, you can slip out of the harness because your organs get rearranged. "All that flab gets to movin' around, and the straps come loose," he said. Then he passed around a poster made from magazine pictures of famous crashes: cut-out stock cars cartwheeling and smashing into walls, bursting into flames and crunching into balls. There was Dale Earnhardt squeezing out the window of his upside-down and flattened Wrangler T-Bird at Pocono; the rollcage of Bobby Allison's Mercury, which was all that remained after he barrel-rolled into the Rockingham wall; Terry Labonte's compacted Chevy from his crash in Riverside's Turn 9 the previous November. "Just a few little visuals," Sutton said as the poster made its way around the room.

We five students were a strange crew. There were young twin brothers who hung on Buck's every breath; if he had told them, "Go drive into that wall, boys," they would have raced to it. There was a guy from upstate New York who brought along his wife to be his admiring audience; and there was the Red Baron. That's what Buck called him. He arrived in his airplane, which he landed on the dragstrip across the street. He wore a red "fire suit" that flapped in the breeze because he was so skinny, a yellow helmet that was so big it didn't always turn when his head did, patent-leather loafers that flashed when he walked because his ankles seemed loose, and a glass eye that fit like a cheap toupée. He was a lawyer, and said he specialized in Hell's Angels. He took it good-naturedly when Buck told him that he was just about the weirdest-looking sumbitch he'd ever seen.

Rockingham was a "superspeedway" since it was one mile long — anything shorter is a "short track." It was renowned for the effects of its narrow groove. Only the bottom 1 ½ lanes were fast, so the cars fought for that line, and the squeezing and shoving was thrilling stuff. If a car got out of the groove it would be caught in the "bear grease" — Rockingham's slippery track sealant. Actually, "bear grease" was a euphemism, cleaned up for image; in the '60s, Joe Weatherly originally called the surface "owl shit." There was also a more peculiar hazard. The concession stands sold a lot of fried chicken, and after the races gulls would fly off with the leftovers and drop the bones onto the track; rain would wash them down to the apron where they collected and stuck like little spears in the soft tires, causing flats. That's what Sutton said, at least.

Stock car racing is continually underestimated by road racers. Because it's simple — heavy, unsophisticated cars on one-dimensional tracks —road racers think it must be easy. Meanwhile, stock car drivers think road racers are pansies, and that their racing is soft. When road racers try stock cars they often get blown off; it happened to Al Holbert. When stock car drivers try road courses they usually do well; they're often wild at first, but they catch on fast. It must prove something.

There were three school cars: two Camaros and a monstrous 1979 Monte Carlo that Terry Labonte had driven on Grand

National short tracks. I looked at the Monte Carlo with a tinge of dismay; it looked like a tank. I was dreaming of prototypes, and facing three pigs. I already missed kinks and esses and chicanes and shifting gears.

After about two laps I thought, "If this is a superspeedway, I'd hate to see a short track." The brief straights seemed to blend into the turns, making it feel like a big circle. Once or twice I almost forgot which turn I was in; concentrating was tricky because everything seemed the same. I wondered when stock car drivers rested their arms, neck and back. When did they give their concentration a quick breather? And I hadn't even been in traffic.

There's no downshifting for the turns on ovals, which frees the left foot; and since there's not enough time to move your right foot from the gas pedal to the brake, left-foot braking is the technique. You lift your right foot off the gas and brake with your left, as you dive down into the groove from the top lane on the straight; then you ease off the brake and squeeze the throttle as you accelerate out of the turn toward the wall. One thing seemed unchanged: The trick was to be smooth. My Camaro droned around and around; the rhythm was so distinct in my ear that I thought it might actually be possible for some stunt driver to drive the course blindfolded.

After the 15-lap session I said to Buck, "I can see how this takes five or six years to master," and he said, "Nah, by tomorrow afternoon you'll be going fast enough to qualify for a Grand National. I can tell by the way you're going you'll be ready for 'the bear'" — whatever that was. It was flattering, but I didn't believe it. Grand National races were 500 laps! Imagine, 500 laps man-handling a 3700-pound car on a deep South summer afternoon, with three dozen others fighting you for every inch. No wonder stock car drivers think road racers are pansies.

Not much happened in the next two days. We had some mock three-car races; I got smoother and faster (the Monte Carlo was more like a cruiser than a tank), and by the final session was cutting laps in the 27s — the track record was 25.6, an average speed of 143 mph. Considering that the school's cars were hardly equal to Grand National cars, Buck said that I should be able to make a Grand National field with no sweat.

I stayed in Rockingham for the Carolina 500 that Sunday. Richard Petty, age 45, won; it was the 197th win of his 25-year career. He raced for four hours and 25 minutes, and gained half a length on the second-place driver, Bill Elliott, after 500 miles. I left

Rockingham believing that a strong case could be made for stock car racing being more difficult, demanding and generally tougher than road racing — because of all those "boring" circles. But I still didn't see how I could write about a season of thousands of them. And despite Buck Baker's generous assessment of my capabilities, I didn't believe I could do well enough on the Stroh's Tour to risk turning the story in that direction.

Buck Baker was a heavyweight leadfoot rogue, back in the days when they drove with hangovers.

Peter Gloede

Al Holbert came back when IMSA's ends justified the means.

Nimrod, an American Dream lost in the translation.

Chapter 11

Stan Clinton

Crimes of Passion

For Christmas the year I was 10, my parents got me the double-record album "Sounds of Sebring, 1957." It was a vivid and suspenseful documentary of that year's 12-hour race. There were interviews with the drivers, and the singing of engines. The narrator would say, "The 4.5-liter Maserati of Juan Manuel Fangio..." and you would hear it go *waaannhh,* and see the blood red car speeding down the front straight. We usually awoke at daybreak on Christmas — I started the family custom, eager for the booty — and that morning, as a spectacular sunrise threw orange beams into the living room, Ferraris and Porsches and Aston-Martins raced through the house. That's what my mother said she thought of when I told her I had a ride for Sebring.

I hadn't known it until the final day, but the Buck Baker School had a silent partner in Billy Hagan, who owned the Camaro that made my knees weak. Buck said that Hagan was one of the three people he'd set his watch by.

That Monday, the day after Rockingham, I called Bill Brodrick, Supervisor of Automotive Public Relations at Union Oil Co., and someone I'd liked and worked with for years. He said he'd call Hagan and feel him out. The next day Brodrick called back; apparently, Buck Baker had told Hagan that I was one of the smoothest student drivers he'd ever had. Brodrick said Hagan had suggested that I call him in Louisiana that evening. I did, and Hagan told me to call Tex Powell, his crew chief, whose shop was in North Carolina. I liked Tex's soft drawl and open mind. I told him that although I was a rookie driver, I'd been around racing as a professional for 13 years and had been picking the brains and observing the operations of the best of them. I'd seen what it took to win, and given an opportunity I would do my best to duplicate it. Tex said he'd call Billy back, and that I should call Hagan again that night. When I did, Hagan said that if I went to Sebring on Thursday, Press Day, Tex would try to give me a few laps in the Camaro. After that, no promises.

It sounded as good as the moon to me.

DD and I left Key West Tuesday evening in a Hertz Mustang convertible — they were on special in Florida in March — and stayed in Key Largo that night. We got to the track the next afternoon before the Camaro, which was due shortly. I wanted to wait for it so I could look at it and think about it that evening, and I wanted to make a good impression on Tex. DD wanted to leave. I offered her the car keys and directions to the house where we would be staying, but she wouldn't budge without me and demanded that I leave with her. She stayed on my heels even when I tried to walk away from her — first slowly, then faster. I led her to the paddock parking lot, not knowing whether my shadow (clutching my heart) and I were coming or going; we took a couple of checked swings at each other there. I finally left with her, feeling like her prisoner. The Camaro arrived later that afternoon. I believed that my absence hurt my chances of getting in the car. If I'd been the crew chief and my supposedly eager and deserving rookie wasn't there when the car arrived, it would have.

Neither Hagan nor Gene Felton was at the track Thursday, so I had the car to myself. It rained. I got four laps to tour the course and practice hydroplaning. In the night session on a dry track I spun after one-fifth of a lap in the notorious esses, where blackness engulfs the road. I must have wrenched the car out of control looking for the line. The car drifted along backward and I was helpless, as if I were falling down a deep, dark hole. It slid off the road and luckily cut a tire, the flat providing an explanation for the lengthy lap and concealing the mistake I never admitted. Tex didn't send me back out; the ugly shredded rubber possibly reminded him of the evils lurking in the Sebring night.

Late that night, back at the house, I nearly strangled DD. She says it's not like on TV, where the victim's eyes close and they go clonk; in real life, you have to squeeze for a long time to murder the person. So maybe it wasn't really that close, since my hands left her throat when she fell limp. And she's such a good actress.

She had stayed at the house that day, which was fine with me. When I got back she was waiting in a slinky black silk nightgown cut like an evening dress. She wore it often, and with her fashion-model's figure she looked sensational in it. But it was never as seductive to me as it should have been; I know why, now. She'd been drinking vodka most of the afternoon and it usually made her fun, but this time she'd started mad, without me. If she was ever a black widow, it was that night.

I really do believe it might have been the planets. All of DD's electricity had been turned on at once, at the wrong time. She kept me near her that night by smashing something every time I turned away. At one point in the fight she knocked at the door of the neighboring house to be rescued (no one was home); I wanted to do the same thing. At another point we were sitting in the car in the driveway; drained and zombie-like, I agreed to chauffeur her anywhere she directed. She couldn't decide whether we should go the hospital for her neck (it had been broken in a car crash years earlier and often got twisted when we fought) or the police station, for me to turn myself in. We went back inside.

Our physical fights were merely tussles. That's what DD said, anyhow, and she had me believing it, I guess. But if that were true, why did they take all my strength? And she said that the awful things we called each other during the fights were just words, and words could be taken back and later laughed about. But she never understood how much words meant to me.

Physically, it might have been an uneven fight, but it was no mismatch. I tried to fight only as hard as it took to contain her — a battle for self-control amidst a loss of it. Later, when the fights reached the ragged edge, I learned to make my hand slap my own jaw when I had the hateful impulse to slap her; it was the least destructive place a destined swing could go. I tried to hit myself harder than I hit DD; once I hit myself so hard I twisted my neck. It set her back the first time I did it, and I realized I had a good thing.

She always melted when I showed signs of cracking, but rarely was I clever enough to fake it. Hitting myself became a deliberate act of desperation. I would have used a club if it would have ended the arguments.

If this page were DD's, she might be able to convince you that I'm a lot more rotten than I think I am, or that I treated her more rotten than it sounds like here. (Rick Mears once said he never knew anyone who could convince you that black was white better than Bobby Unser, but he'd never met DD.) But if it's true I still wouldn't be able to see it, or wouldn't agree. I know I'm not easy, but I loved a woman for 10 years and lived with her for seven without having one argument of the magnitude of the seeming dozens that DD and I had had in six months. But I was in my teens and early twenties, then; I needed my wife a lot. And I wasn't an idiot racedriver.

I'm tempted to be flip and say the whole damn deal was simply a case of a woman going crazy because she was jealous of a car. The direction of my devotion was too hard on DD, and she wouldn't settle for second place.

She used her emotions ahead of her like a battering ram, and sometimes it hurt to watch since they were like crystal. And tenacity was one of her "mosts." She'd shatter herself and go back for more. If only she'd known how to back off, how to let things go at a difference of opinion. She never learned that not fighting isn't the same as giving in. She always won the debates she created with people she loved because she kept fighting after the rewards turned to spoils. Her drive to win was so strong that she felt no remorse over grieving me for half the night before I had to risk my life at 180 miles an hour. Yet she was desperately afraid that I would crash. It was her impossible irony. That night's small irony was that I would have loved nothing more than a quiet dinner alone with her.

DD didn't deny that she was afflicted with irrational spells. "I *do* do bad things sometimes," is how she once put it, pleading for tolerance. Sometimes, theatrically and breathlessly, she would say she was a victim of vapors. She wanted to clone herself, to clear her conscience: If her clone came out crazy she could blame it on genes. But the only thing she was irrational about was the way she wanted to be loved. I kept telling her she could be the moon if only she'd work on these spells, but she said it wasn't that easy. She took a stab at therapy, but there wasn't a therapist around who could handle her. And the problem was in her heart more than her head. Besides, she argued, she's always been this way. So who was trying to change who in this deal? Her logic left me speechless. My own tenacity was more like patience; I'd never known anyone like DD, and couldn't believe her craziness wasn't something that would pass.

I once complained to her that she was unpredictable, and she replied that she was predictably unpredictable. Not to me. As she was blind to my motivation and rarely understood my intentions — she thought they were so dark, sometimes — I was blind to her next move. Sometimes I didn't know whether to run toward her or away from her. It was her unpredictability that interfered with my racing because I had to consider all the ways I thought she might react to whatever I did. Paranoia takes a lot of concentration because of the possibilities.

I would have said or done almost anything to protect myself from another Daytona. I would have left her in Key West if I'd thought I could have. But I didn't *want* to, and after what had happened at Daytona I couldn't imagine her not being shocked straight. She was so easy to give repeated chances to anyhow; maybe the next chance would make her the moon. I don't really want to talk about the sex, but it's too hard not to. DD was a sexual diamond; the passion between us didn't stop at parking-lot fights. How can two people communicate so beautifully in bed and so wretchedly out of it? (I know I asked that before.) And it's not that I was blinded by my desire, unless now I'm being blinded by a flashback. I didn't love DD because she was a wonder in bed, I loved her for the purity of her heart, which made her a wonder in general. She could incite me to would-be strangulation and mostly she made me miserable, but I'm not sorry for my time with her. I would have changed it, but I'll never regret it.

I wore my clothes to bed that night, if you can call it bed. I was never sure whether it was bedtime or not — if the eruptions were over — and I didn't want to be in my underwear if it wasn't. I wore my jacket too, something I've done for emotional insulation — a security blanket — when I've been badly depressed, although it had been 15 years since the last time I'd done it. I would have left the house in a minute — I wasn't paralyzed — but I knew that that would ultimately worsen the scene, most likely move it to the racetrack the next day. (I recoiled from public scenes, which she turned into another debate: Why did I care more about strangers than her?) I stayed that night because I didn't underestimate the destructiveness of DD's love. Or maybe I was intimidated by the unpredictability of it.

Dan Gurney once called driving "controlled fury," which was the essence of the next day for me. You should hear the stuff that came out of the tape recorder, the stuff I put in, driving to the track that Friday morning. It's awful to listen to. DD's favorite picture of me would be taken that morning. I hadn't shaved for three days because I didn't care enough to. I was on the brink of quitting, and making the announcement to Billy Hagan — as soon as we were introduced. It seemed the sensible thing to do. I won't be able to get enough time in the car to feel comfortable, I would say; that was the truth. I couldn't see where I fit in the team's future, anyhow.

But I knew I wouldn't quit. Incipient idiocy kept me rational. I must have realized that I wasn't thinking straight, as I considered turning down an opportunity to drive the Hagan Camaro.

At the track I went into the press box, a rickety old room like a big enclosed porch on top of the pits. There was a press release of the previous day's soggy high points, and near the bottom it said, "The notable *Sports Illustrated* writer Sam Moses is now driving with Billy Hagan and Gene Felton." I guess that was the turning point. The release wasn't exactly inspiring, but it postponed my quitting at the lowest and most vulnerable moment. What would the next day's release say if I vanished?

I spotted Steve Potter talking to Gene Felton in the paddock. I greeted Potter and introduced myself to Felton. He asked me if I were driving anything. "Yea," I said. "Your car." He gulped. "Well, Tex doesn't always tell me all these things," he said. "I'm just the hired driver."

All I knew about Billy Hagan was that he was about 50 and in the oil business in Louisiana, but I liked what I saw of his style. He had two major ambitions in racing: Win the NASCAR Winston Cup as an owner — a goal he was approaching after eight years — and beat the Europeans at Le Mans with an American car. After two tries he was close to that, too. He didn't carry himself like a rich guy. He was 5'10½" but so stocky he seemed shorter, and his body looked as if it had a few oilfield brawls in its past. He looked like Dick Williams, the hard-nosed baseball manager. He wore a neatly-clipped gray moustache, tinted glasses, Western shirt and loose bluejeans.

Hagan was busier than I that morning, so we didn't talk until later. We had a chat in lawn chairs next to Tex's big Chevy pickup, which the crew called the "Doolie" because it had four — *dual* — rear wheels. The chat was intermittent because Hagan kept getting up and offering his seat to people.

He'd gotten started in the oil business with a partner in 1960, the same year he bought a Porsche Speedster. "But right away my partner fired me," he said, because of the time he was spending racing the Porsche at an abandoned-airport circuit near Galveston. So Hagan started his own oil-drilling company, Stratagraph, Inc. Then it consisted of Billy Joe Hagan; now it employed 300, with more than 100 rigs in the Louisiana Gulf, Oklahoma, New York and Pennsylvania. He said he'd once drilled a $15-million dry hole. It sounded a lot like motor racing to me.

He told a funny story about Gordy Oftedahl. At a race somewhere, Oftedahl had accused him of cheating because the Camaro was so low. Gordy approached the car with a tape measure, and Hagan chased him away. Gordy said, "Well, I can get this close. It's a free world." And Hagan drew a line with the pointy toe of one cowboy boot and said, "Well all right, but don't cross this line," and Gordy hollered, "You don't own the ground!" and it went on like that.

What I liked about Hagan was that he treated me the same as he might have treated any rookie he was giving a chance. He didn't need me to hook a sponsor, but he knew I wouldn't hurt. After recognizing *Sports Illustrated* once, and acknowledging that the prospect of publicity had gotten my foot in his door, he never brought it up again. He never even gave me the Stratagraph press booklet. I would stumble across one at a NASCAR race months later. It said that he had run 135 Grand National races as an owner before he won one.

I didn't expect to get much more time in the Camaro — if any — since the program was now a day behind schedule and I was third in line. I walked down to the first turn to watch qualifying. It was a left-hand sweeper, a bold 120 for a fast GTO car. It was a raw, wide, flat, exposed and wavy bend, defined by orange pylons since Sebring was an airport circuit. Beyond the turn's outside edge, spectators and vehicles lined a snowfence. It was a turn where an observer could easily tell the slow from the brave. I watched the cars from behind as they wiggled through it. Felton was drifting the Camaro in big, solid twitches, leaving behind the rumbling note of the stout Chevy engine as he sped toward the next turn. I probably shouldn't have gone down there; it was almost intimidating to watch. But I knew that watching is always scarier than driving. When you're behind the wheel, you feel more in control than you look.

I walked back to the pit and stared at the Camaro. Its paint was pearlescent white lacquer, with thick lines of metallic blue and candy-apple red swooping from the bottom of the doors upward to the tail — Hagan liked it red, white and blue. It had a 600-horsepower engine built by Junior Johnson. It looked low and powerful and beautiful and deadly. *Deadly.*

The previous night had everything to do with this dark and unhealthy impression, of course. It was a blatant break of my own taboo to think such a thing, but I didn't care. Or maybe I was just daring myself to think about it — *deadly* — pushing my luck because I was angry. DD had no idea that I was driven to this, even though I'd told her often enough by now; no more than I had any idea of what I was doing to make her so difficult, even when she told me. But I knew I was really driving myself to these scary thoughts. That might have been the biggest difference between us. I accepted responsibility for the moods that made my life difficult.

Felton qualified with a scorching 2:32.0, 111.9 mph, *six seconds* faster than the next GTO car. Hagan got to 2:46, which was below the race pace, and felt ready. By the end of the day there was time for me. After one lap a big piece of the front fender blew off and after another the brakes got mushy, but the crew quickly fixed those things. I got five decent laps, and didn't begin to get on the throttle until the last two; the best time was 2:58. It wasn't terribly impressive, but the race pace would be about 2:50 and I knew I could get down to it. Tex was satisfied with the tryout; I listened, did what I was told, and was in no hurry with the $60,000 racecar.

"GENE FELTON: FROM LIPSTICK TO AXLE GREASE," read the headline on the R.J. Reynolds press release. It said that Felton learned to drive while making beauty supply deliveries in the north Georgia mountains in a Mustang. He believed that driving a racecar might be less hazardous. "When you deal daily with women hairdressers with jealous husbands, it can be dangerous," he was quoted as saying.

Felton, 46, was about six feet and 190 pounds; he wore tinted plastic bubble goggles like the stock car drivers, and rarely wore fire-resistant underwear, so his hairy chest showed a lot. He had 37 IMSA victories in various classes, second only to the late Peter Gregg. He was consistently fast, and never did anything dumb on the track — he got the job done. He'd been driving for 20 years, building his own cars most of the time, usually Chevies. His career was roughly at the same stage as Doc's. His situation was more secure because of his paid ride with Hagan, but he had just quit the beauty business the year before, upon his first opportunity to make a decent living at racing.

My initial impression of Felton was that he boasted a lot, needlessly; he had just beaten the field by *six seconds.* That night DD suggested that Felton was probably threatened by me. (Things were almost okay between us now, the planets' cruel ambush evidently ended.) She had yet to even see Felton, but such perceptions of hers were rarely wrong. It seemed absurd; there were 26 seconds between Felton and me! But lately Felton had seen too many examples of ability weighing less than money, which was the danger I brought. This was his livelihood, said DD, and suddenly "some hotshot writer from *Sports Illustrated*" comes along who might jeopardize the hired driver's status by bringing a sponsor. Felton might have felt compelled to keep reminding people how good he was. Imagine, a power-hitting right fielder worried about his job because all he had going for him were booming homers and a .330 average.

Sebring, running since 1950, was the country's oldest sports car race, and this year there was a record 84 entries for the Coca-Cola 12 Hours. The circuit jogged around the Sebring Air Terminal, which was an airbase during World War II; situated in the thick of the peninsula, its locale had been ideal for patrolling the Atlantic Ocean and Gulf of Mexico. An old bomber sat beyond the first turn; you could see it from the track, although I never noticed it. The circuit was 4.75 miles long, nearly half of which was straight, and ran over broad runways with sprawling turns. The vastness stole definition, but it gave back character. The surface was rough and abrasive, and some teams wouldn't run Sebring because 12 hours there was so hard on a car.

The place was especially notorious for its perils at night. Strange things happened there after dark during the final four hours of the race, mostly on the desolate backstraight. It was 5,100 feet, longer than any other in the country, and four runways wide. Cows grazed on its outside edge, although I never noticed them either. Doc said that people have been lost out there at night.

On race day I got to the track before the mechanics, and everything was covered with dew. Warmup was scheduled for 8:15 and although I didn't expect to drive in it, I didn't want to miss an opportunity. The race would run from 11 a.m. to 11 p.m. Shortly before the start, I asked Hagan if he wanted me to suit up. "Just hang loose and stand by," he said. "'Round about the last shift before dark we'll try and get you in the car if everything is under control and it's a no-pressure situation."

Hagan started the race and ran strong — 10th overall, first GTO. On the 18th lap he drove the car into a concrete barrier. The track surface on one turn was fresh and crumbling in the heat already, creating "marbles" —grainy debris outside of the groove. Hagan had let the Camaro slip off the line and into the marbles, and that was all it took. Five or six more cars would bite that wall before the finish, painting it with colorful stripes and black tire streaks.

When the crash was announced over the PA system the announcer said the car was smashed but the driver was out and walking around. "That's it; it's over," I said to DD, almost relieved — of the suspense over driving, not the possibility of it. I went straight to Tex's trailer in a fast walk, leaving her to either move at my pace or not, grabbed my driving bag and put it in the trunk of the rental convertible. I was hiding it, the way one might hide a six-pack after a highway accident. "When Billy comes back, I don't want to be the first thing he sees," I said. "I don't want him to make any connection in his mind between the crash and me." The paranoid over-reaction sprang from my determination to allow nothing to endanger my chances of a future ride in the Camaro. My driving obsession took such strange twists; DD was right — more than I could see — when she said my personality had changed in the six months she'd known me.

The announcer said Felton had been driving, and I knew it was wrong but wished it weren't. I didn't have anything against him, but Hagan's crashing hurt my chances; Felton's might have helped them. A crash sets a program back and puts pressure on the crew, and rookie tryouts suddenly become a low priority. But if Felton were in the doghouse I would look better to Hagan.

Tex and two of the mechanics loaded some tools and parts in an El Camino and drove bouncing through the infield in search of the crash, but couldn't reach it. So Billy ran to a nearby hangar where some of the cars were garaged, and borrowed enough tools to get the Camaro running again, laboring in the hot sun for about 90 minutes. He brought it limping and overheating back to the pit and the crew attacked it with big mallets and a crowbar. Tex strapped a cable device across the hood and hooked it to each side of the chassis; like a torturer, he twisted a ratchet and the car's red skeleton creaked back into place.

Hagan sat on pit wall looking inscrutable. Tex had said Billy was impossible to read, and he did seem unperturbed. He was gracious to reporters — to anyone who asked what happened, in fact — despite having to repeatedly admit that he blew it. Sitting on the wall with his burly white upper body exposed, serenely explaining things to people as they came up to him, he looked like a yogi on a rock. He seemed so approachable I introduced him to DD. I stepped aside as she grilled him, disarmingly and inimitably.

Hagan had told me that when last year's race had ended spectators swarmed over the fence, across the front straight and into the pit. Things disappear during such familiarity between fans and equipment. He said he had grabbed a power bar out of a toolbox and swung it in an arc, yelling, "Out!" and threatened to take off the heads of those who didn't scram. Contained as he seemed on the wall, I suspected there was a power bar swinging around inside him. But he was man enough to keep his mouth shut. I took it as a lesson in after-crash behavior, and character.

I peeked at the clipboard with his lap times. In the three laps preceding the crash he'd clocked 2:48, 2:40 and 2:45; that was inconsistent, and the 2:40 was *flying*. Traffic might have affected the times, but not by eight seconds. It appeared that he had crashed because he was running strong and got carried away. Tex had said that the pace would be 2:55, and I'd taken that to mean that he would set that pace for the team, but apparently not.

It took an hour and 20 minutes to repair the car, although when it was done it hardly looked repaired. It had a new nose, but because the mounts were broken it was lopsided, as if one front tire were flat. There were holes where the headlights used to be. The front end couldn't be aligned properly, and the wheelbase had to be shortened one inch because the forward crossmember had been driven back by the engine. The standings after three hours showed #4 in 78th place out of 82 starters.

Felton drove off in the pearly wreck. He took a lap, came back, and said it was overheating and the hood was blowing off. Tex fiddled, and as Felton went out and came back three or four more times, silver duct tape piled up around the hood. Finally they removed it altogether, and the Camaro cooled down some.

Since nothing was wrong with the engine, the car could be driven nearly as fast as before if you were brave enough. Felton turned

2:45 to 2:48 for most of his shift. He got out and said the car was running at 240 degrees, handling rotten, weaving all over the place, and that he was taking the first turn almost flat-out on three wheels. I figured that was his way of saying, "I'm a hell of a driver for taking that piece of junk made by our rich-guy owner, and making it run like a racecar."

Hagan had said I could drive as long as everything was under control. What was this? The car was out of contention, which amounted to the same thing. During Hagan's shift Tex said, "You want to drive some?" and I snapped, "You bet." About half an hour before Billy was due in, DD and I were sitting behind the pit in lawn chairs and a mechanic suddenly said, "Okay, he's in, get ready." I jumped up and flipped off my hat so fast I yanked out some hair and never felt it. I tossed my sunglasses to DD in mid-backward stride, and scurried over the wall into the car. There was a film of clean pink oil on everything, from a leaking transmission breather that was mounted on a rollcage bar near my right elbow. I wiped oil off the mirror and plexiglass rear window just behind my head, as the crew hammered some more on the front end, mounting four fog lights that looked like frog's eyes on a makeshift bar above the radiator. Billy leaned in the window and said the handling was squirrelly and the radio was conked out. I tried to adjust the seat harness, but it wouldn't tighten enough. I liked to be cinched down so tight that I could hardly breathe; it gave me confidence to feel so much a part of the car that it hurt. Tex handed me a cushion covered with duct tape to take up the slack. I smiled to myself, thankful I didn't have much flab that could get to movin' around.

The problem in running without the hood was that oil sprayed on the windshield — it flew out the breathers of the hard-working engine like sweat off a marathon runner. And I would be driving into the setting sun. I wouldn't be able to see much in the mirror either, since both it and the rear window would soon be smeared with transmission oil. The handling would be dangerous, yet the car still had its 600 horses. I'd had 15 minutes practice. My big-time racing experience consisted of nine-tenths of a lap at Daytona. I still had strangulation on my mind. This would be the end of the line if I screwed up. The good news was that this was a no-pressure situation.

All I wanted was to be smooth, consistent, and conserve the car. The track was empty when I went out, a yellow flag waving at every turn, so I cruised until I caught up with the field behind the pace car. The engine immediately began overheating in this traffic jam, so I pulled back in when the parade reached the pits and Tex installed an aluminum cowl to direct more air toward the radiator.

The handling wasn't exactly squirrelly; actually, it lurched, especially under braking. Slowing from 130 for the 30-mph hairpin on the narrowest part of the track, it jumped about six feet sideways. You couldn't count on it jumping the same direction each time, so you had to run down the middle of the road. I tried to make sure there were no cars in my blind spots when I braked, but since virtually everything out of my peripheral vision was a blind spot I was rarely certain if anyone was around or not. Fortunately the hairpin was the only place it lurched badly. It tugged on the straights, roamed through the esses and resisted through the tighter turns, but I tried to drive only as hard as it took to contain it.

Redline was 7,000 rpm, but I was shifting at 6500. Seven thousand was too fast for my nerves, and it seemed unnecessary to run the engine that hard anyhow; that extra 500 rpm would hardly get us back into contention. After six or seven laps I was beginning to learn the course and was down to 2:55. I was startled by a scrape on my door as I bent into the first turn. The Racing Beat Mazda, a one-of-a-kind GTO-class RX-7 built like a tank for the longest races (it had finished third overall at Daytona), swept by on the inside. I hadn't seen it coming through the smeared rear window, but that wasn't the problem; my mistake was going too slow on the fast line through the turn. Whoever was driving the Mazda was letting me know. I knew it was either Pete Halsmer or Rick Knoop, both very good, so I tried to follow and learn something. My lap times dropped three seconds on the next lap; the Mazda pulled away as I settled into a groove and starting cutting low 2:50s. And I was a lot faster through Turn 1 now, having been shown how it should be done. I drafted one of Gordy Oftedahl's Firebirds down the front straight along the pits, and passed it by going deeper into the raw first turn. I hoped Oftedahl was watching; Elwood had told me that Gordy carrried hard feelings from Daytona.

The backstraight/runway was so wide that its parched concrete seemed to stretch like a dry lake bed, off to the edge of the world. You barely had to slow down for Warehouse Turn, a 90-degree right-hander that led onto the backstraight, because you could swing as wide as you wanted to; the fastest prototypes took the turn at nearly 150 and made an arc out of the straight. Near the end of the backstraight you were so far from the inside edge of the track that you had to turn your head to see the braking signs for the final corner. Half of the time I missed them, so I stopped looking. There were two big yellow X's on the runway, and if you were in position you passed over them. I would wait a couple of beats after hitting them, then pounce on the brakes, hoping I wasn't too late or too early for the turn, a meandering double apex right-hander that led onto the front straight. There were about 82 different lines being taken through the turn, and I never did find the right one. Doc said he still wasn't satisfied with his, after five years at Sebring.

The backstraight headed west, and the sun was huge and pink in my eyes, which made finding the final turn more difficult. But it was worth it. The Camaro's bucket seat was ringside for the spectacular sunset. I'd shoot around Warehouse Turn at about 130, the front of the Camaro lurching and the back twitching, and the sun would suddenly appear dead-ahead, hanging over the end of the long straight. Each time around I watched it drop three minutes worth. Its presence was comforting, something for me to greet each lap, something secure and tangible from the real world, which I was barely in contact with.

With twilight, the fast, narrow and darkly-paved esses dimmed. For too many laps I forgot that my helmet visor was tinted, and when it dawned on me I flipped it up and gained another few minutes of decent visibility. The other cars' lights were coming on, and I was waiting for a signal from the pits for mine, but Tex was leaving it up to me. I wasn't even sure they were working yet. Later, DD said I'd been the last car running without them. I was getting tired and was straining to see, so I backed off, and kept running until a chunk of the left front fender began flapping, possibly cracked by the Mazda. I considered continuing because it wasn't slowing the car down, but then I remembered that there were no more spare noses, and the piece of fiberglass might be needed. I was ready to come in anyhow.

I got out of the car covered with pink oil. It was streaming down my helmet and my suit was sprayed with it — my driving bag would smell of the sweet fresh oil for months afterward, and remind me of my successful Sebring. I didn't know how fast I'd gone, but was satisfied I'd driven fairly well, if cautiously. The times surprised me. The best was 2:47, and there were a few more under 2:50 and a bunch at 2:50-2:52; they rose to 2:55 after the sun went down.

My heart was still thumping — it picks up when you get out of the car — when Tex said, "You want to go out and drive some more?" At first I thought he meant immediately; I looked over my shoulder and was relieved to see Felton climbing in the car. I said, "I'd love to Tex, but I didn't practice at night." I didn't think I was ready; psychologically I wasn't, for sure. It would be faster and safer if Hagan and Felton handled the darkness, I said.

Hagan checked the clipboard with my lap times, and when I told him I'd been shifting at 6500 rpm he said, "That's good; your times would have been faster if you'd been using 7,000." DD later cornered and captivated Terry the redheaded mechanic with the Fu Manchu moustache, and he told her that when the mechanics had been informed that some reporter would be driving, they griped all the way from North Carolina. But they felt better, now; I hadn't been hard on the car, didn't try to prove I was hot, and wasn't slow, and sometimes that's all a mechanic wants from a driver he's stuck with. Felton had complained the loudest, Terry said. Afterward, Gene was the one who went out of his way to tell me I'd driven well.

DD and I walked over to the Racing Beat pit (I would have missed her now, if she hadn't been there) where I found Pete Halsmer, who had been driving the Mazda when we'd hit. I apologized for having been in his way and thanked him for picking up my pace. He asked me to tell his car owner about the incident, so that if a pearlescent scrape were discovered on the Mazda the owner wouldn't think him reckless.

When we got back, Felton had finished his shift and was in his street clothes; he was going home. He thought it was stupid to continue, that there was nothing to gain by nursing a battered racecar for three more hours. It was a hardcore pro attitude: What's the sense in stroking it? But to me Billy's choices after the crash had seemed clear: Race it or park it. Any man who would keep drilling into a $15-million hole wasn't likely to park it. The challenge for Hagan now was to finish. Felton didn't have one any more. Tex said that Billy didn't appreciate the desertion.

I didn't have much to gain by driving any more (not unlike Felton). I'd accomplished all I'd hoped for at Sebring — one good shift, a decent impression. And a mistake at night, very easy to make, could blow it all. But when I saw Felton put on his black cowboy hat and get in his black customized van and head home to Atlanta, I got motivated. I went back to the pit looking for Tex, to offer myself for a night shift.

Instead, I found Lloyd Frink. Frink had driven with Hagan and Felton at Daytona, and he and his wife Naomi had come to Sebring to help, however they could. And of course Lloyd's driving gear had been in his El Camino, just in case. He was now sitting in the corner of the sheltered part of the pit, suited up, his helmet in his lap.

A possessive streak hit me, *hard*. I found Tex and said, "I'm ready to drive if you need me. I didn't know Felton was going to leave when I said what I did about not driving at night." My wording was awkward to spare my saying, "turned you down."

"Well, you told me you didn't want to drive, and I already told Lloyd he could," said Tex.

Lloyd had night-time experience in the car, but he hadn't been around Sebring, ever; I was a leery prospect at night, but at least I knew the way around the track. I asked Lloyd how much he wanted to drive, and he said, "I want to drive, but I don't want to roll the car up in a ball." I dittoed that. We thought about flipping a coin, but our ambivalence would have made it difficult to decide what the winner would get.

Billy pitted. The fog lights and one headlight were working, but the other light was still missing; long-gone were the two pencil-beam lights, normally splayed toward the edge of the track to brighten apexes. There were ragged edges around the nose and chunks out of the fiberglass. A smoky, oily mist rose from the exposed engine, and streaked oil glistened on the windshield under the spotlights illuminating the pit. Hagan had cut a *2:45* during his stint; "I just got behind a good car with lights and followed him," he said.

I was standing at the back of the pit, helmet in hand. Lloyd was still sitting in the corner. Tex, lanky and bowlegged, walked around the car and spoke in the window to Hagan — Tex was so tall and the car so low he had to lean way down. He rose back up, looked straight at Lloyd, and pointed. His finger was like a stab in my heart, but I couldn't help thinking the scene was like some basketball game. I watched Lloyd drive off and disappear in the dark, in my seat. I had turned down an opportunity to drive and was sorry for it. I vowed never to do it again, under any circumstance.

Lloyd ran off the track on the first lap. He'd been following another car on the backstraight and it wandered off the runway, leading him into the spooky black boonies at 130 or 140 miles an hour as both cars ended up in the lumpy fringes of the cow pasture. He pitted and told Tex, "Get another driver; I can't see out there." Tex told him to go back out and try again. I didn't know that then, or else a twist might have been added to that stab in my heart.

The backstraight was littered with debris by now — exhaust pipes and bodywork and even gears and pieces of brake discs, as well as concrete chips kicked out of the runway by the unceasing pounding horsepower, as if the track's fillings were falling out. After a few more laps Lloyd spun in Turn 1, and the engine stalled and flooded. He got it restarted, but nobody in the pit knew where he was on that 15-minute lap; we watched closely for him but not a word was said about his being missing. By the end of the shift he had the course figured out enough to survive; following people when he could, he clocked 3:05 to 3:10.

"On the final lap, spectators were on the course," *On Track* would report. "The whole place seemed to be on fire; it was bedlam." Hagan drove the final half-hour and brought the Camaro home through the fire and bedlam 41st. As far as I was concerned, he had snatched moral victory from the jaws of defeat by not quitting.

As the crew was loading up the Doolie, Billy asked Lloyd how come he ended up driving; apparently he'd been surprised by it. Lloyd told him that it was because Tex couldn't find anyone else to do it. I was tempted to tell Billy that that wasn't true, but I let it go. DD said that generosity among drivers competing for rides was like one junkie giving another his leftover heroin.

Here's how Jerry Garrett began that *On Track* report:
"In the half-moon gloom of the Florida night, Wayne Baker saw an odd figure in front of him on the Sebring track. It looked like — it *was* — a man standing on the track. 'I almost hit him,' Baker said. 'He was standing right on the racing line. It was some spectator. Drunk, I guess. He had his thumb out, hitch-hiking.' "
Baker codrove the winning car, an ugly ochre GTO-class Porsche 934. It was the first time a GTO car had ever won an IMSA endurance race. The final hour was a scramble like so many memorable Sebrings, with positions and situations changing faster than anyone could keep up with. Halsmer had been leading when a front disc shattered in the hairpin; a nimble GRID-Cosworth prototype took over until a wheel bearing burned out; then the Porsche of Holbert and Haywood (Holbert preferred the

solid 935 for Sebring) led with a dying alternator, as Holbert drove largely without lights — *any* lights. They were in the pits when Baker took the lead, with 25 minutes to go and four of his five gears kaput. He didn't know he'd won until he was told over his radio on the cooloff lap. The Porsche had qualified seven seconds slower than our Camaro and had run a 2:48 pace, but it had endured. "It was a good Sebring for us," said Baker. "No problems. Six flat tires, two broken spoilers, a clutch adjustment. That's a light day here."

It wasn't such a light day for Robin Hamilton. He had again rented one Nimrod to Seahawk Racing, and had added a sponsor in *Gallery* magazine, although the deal involved more contingencies than cash. *Gallery* brought along the three finalists from its "Girl Next Door" contest. To enter, all a girl had to do was send in a naked or half-naked snapshot of herself to be published and judged.

Seahawk's driver, Victor Gonzalez, the young karting champion, had a shunt on Thursday night, breaking the nose off the car; when he spun again on Friday, Hamilton decided to cover his bases by entering the second Nimrod even though he'd told Seahawk he wouldn't. Until then, that car had been in the paddock bearing a "For Sale" sign. He called Lyn St. James at her home near Fort Lauderdale late Friday night — a girl sitting by the phone without a date for the weekend (so to speak) — and offered her the ride, mysteriously adding that he might have to withdraw the car before the finish.

The Seahawk Nimrod bent a valve and retired in the third hour; in the course of the week Gonzalez had added a few overrevs to the already-tired engine. At 9:30 p.m., after its planned conservative pace, the #2 Nimrod was in sixth place and third was within reach. Seahawk pressured Hamilton to send in Gonzalez, but he tapped Gonzalez's codriver, Drake Olson (at Daytona Olson had taken Nimrod from 26th to eighth during a three-hour shift), and told him to go for it. Olson began cutting low 2:40s, making Nimrod the fastest car on the track in the final hour, and got into third. But he hit an errant exhaust pipe on the backstraight and broke a radiator hose. After the repair, Nimrod finished fifth.

Hamilton's refusing Seahawk was no small thing; there was an argument, and the Nimrod crew darkly murmured things about guns and death threats. "I knew there was something shaky, something awful going on," said Olson, "but I didn't want to know what it was. This business, if you're not careful, makes you into an animal. Lying and cheating becomes a way of operating. I didn't even want to know where the money to rent the car came from; I wanted to drive racecars. When Robin talked to me about driving the Nimrod, I said, 'Yes.'"

"I don't ask a lot of questions," echoes St. James. "Where the money comes from isn't my business.

"Robin was incredibly high about the finish," she said. "Since the first four cars weren't technically prototypes he said we'd won the prototype class, and he was sure that it would solidify the team's future, that it would be all downhill from there. I was flabbergasted at his reaction."

Doc Bundy drove for Pepe Romero, who owned the pink 935 Doc had driven to 11th at the Daytona 24-Hour. Romero was a handsome and smiling 32-year-old immigrant from a wealthy Cuban family. He was reportedly in the plumbing supply business in Miami, although there was no mention of it on the car, and Doc thought Romero had an auto repair shop. He lived in a house that he'd had designed to look like Dan Tana's, the private-eye in the TV series "Vegas," and didn't like to have his picture taken.

After the Miami Grand Prix, Romero had purchased Holbert's winning March from the factory for $130,000; Holbert had wanted to build a new one with a Porsche engine anyhow. He repainted it hot pink with maroon shading, his own racing colors. He'd been impressed by Doc's driving at Daytona and had wanted a new car, so he had asked Doc to suggest one. Doc suggested the March, not unaware of the possibilities. His deal for Sebring was again $1,000 against a percentage of the purse. He also tutored Romero, although Pepe didn't intend to drive much in the race so there was a third driver on the team: Bill Whittington, whom Doc had recommended after Whittington's good job at Daytona. But after the first practice session he told Doc, "This car is a rocket. It's a winner. It's so good I'm going to blow you out of the deal." (See DD's crack about junkies.)

Whittington started the race; his deal with Romero, whatever it was, bought him that privilege. Said Doc, "Before the race he said, 'I'm gonna run a conservative pace, 2:35s,' and then he went out and just went banzai: He ran 2:25s."

Faster than that. On the third lap his 2:22.7 beat John Paul Jr.'s pole position time. By the eighth lap he led the race by about a mile; on the ninth lap the March broke an oil line and the rear end burned up. Afterward, Whittington said that Romero had told him to drive flat-out because the car wouldn't finish anyhow. If that were true, no one had told the crew. Doc never asked Romero. "Lots of things went on that weekend that I have no way of knowing about," he says.

I didn't know any of this until much later, of course. About all I knew until I called Doc the next week and got my *On Track* two weeks later, was that the ugly ochre Porsche had won, and we had finished. I only cared about the latter. Everything else was like the bomber and the cows — and where the money comes from. I'd been oblivious and indifferent to anything that wouldn't make me faster.

DD and I had a lovely drive back to Key West on Sunday, down remote Florida two-lanes in the open convertible. She said her behavior was all because of her mother, who had sometimes locked her out of the house as a small child. She said I was the only one in her life who had ever seen her good qualities. I decided that maybe all she needed was more understanding.

Looking like a frog and lurching like a bear.

Tony Neste

Tony Neste

Tex Powell liked to say that he was from "down-town Houston."

Billy Hagan — was there a power bar swinging around inside him?

Bill Eppridge

Gene Felton was an outfielder with booming homers and a .330 average.

Tony Neste

The good news was that this was a no-pressure situation.

Tony Neste

*After 12 hours,
the Hagan Camaro
squeezed out 41st.*

Chapter 12

Ken Pamatat

Heavy Metal Rules

T wo weeks before Sebring, I'd been sitting by the phone in a Best Western motel room near Chicago's O'Hare airport after an *SI* assignment. I'd been trying to convince a Los Angeles PR agency, Lapin & Associates, that I was notable enough to compete in the Pro-Celebrity race at the Toyota Grand Prix of Long Beach, a Formula 1 world championship event. The agency handled the Pro-Celeb race for Toyota, and the phone call would determine my next move. If I were accepted, I'd fly to Riverside for a day's practice; if not, I'd go back home, to the blank racing future.

The call was affirmative, just under the wire — I was the last of 16 invited entrants, Jackie Lapin had said — and I caught the next plane to L.A. That night, like too many on the road, the phone wires between my motel room and Southernmost Condo crackled. DD hung up on me twice. She'd called back to hang up the second time, and if I could tell you her parting line — it was dirty beyond any reasonable stretch of the imagination — you might go to bed laughing, as I did.

Everyone in the 10-lap race would drive a stock Toyota Celica GT. The grid would be inverted — slowest qualifier on the pole — and the Celebrities would get a 30-second head start. They were required to attend the British School of Motor Racing and spend at least one day practicing at Riverside or Laguna Seca. Under Jacques Couture's tutelage, a Celebrity had won the previous two races.

The next day about half the field was at Riverside. Dan Gurney and Parnelli Jones were the superstars, and there were three more Pros: Bruce Jenner and Gene Hackman, upgraded after having run the race four and three times as Celebrities, and Margie Smith-Haas, who had years of experience driving mostly Porsches. Margie was the 17th invitee; Toyota had needed a woman, she said.

Jenner was the defending champion and the only driver to have won the race twice, which made him king, with an asterisk because of the Celebrities' head starts. At the time his driving career was remarkable, if not substantial. Not counting Pro-Celebrity events, his first race was the 1980 Daytona 24-Hour. He'd been approached to take up driving by a Southern California sports marketing firm, which believed that deals could be made around him, and one was, for Daytona and Sebring. Jenner drove an exotic, expensive, brand-new BMW M-1 prototype. Rick Knoop, one of his codrivers, tutored him for three days, and off they went to Daytona with *People* magazine following. Jenner drove decently although not much, since the car broke early; at Sebring, the BMW broke again. By his third race, at Elkhart Lake, he'd moved up to Budweiser sponsorship. This time his ride was in an immaculate $150,000 candy-apple-red Chevy Monza prototype. By then, racing was his "consuming passion." That's what he told *Sports Illustrated* for a big, excellent story by Bob Ottum. There were photos of Jenner playing with his go-kart, his Hobie Cat, his airplane, his Jet Ski, his Jeep and his guitar. There was also a picture of him posing in his racing suit, next to his Monza. The car belonged to Chris Cord — grandson of E.L. Cord, designer of the Cord automobile — who was a Beverly Hills rich guy/fast guy. At Elkhart, the Monza broke after 13 laps. Jenner never drove the car again; Cord had reservations, and Jenner had other consuming passions.

Now, Jenner had just gotten a factory-backed ride in a new GTO Mustang for the rest of the IMSA season. I'd heard of the deal on *Motorweek Illustrated*, the solid racing news show on TBS. I'd known Ford had been planning some Mustang effort ever since Nelson Ledges, and their racing manager had known I was available. I'd visited his office in Detroit to tell him.

Jenner drove up to Riverside in a red Mustang convertible with white interior, the Boss 302 engine, and a five-speed. It had Michigan license plates, and I figured the car was part of his deal with Ford. His T-shirt said "He who has the most toys when he dies, wins."

Each Celica was equipped with a rollcage, stiffened suspension and open exhaust. As I strapped myself into one of them to begin the day's third half-hour session, Jenner got in the car ahead of me on pit row. I dallied with my helmet and gloves in order to tail him. After a warmup lap, he picked up the pace, and when his brake lights flashed before Turn 2, the 90-mph kink, I smiled inside my helmet, since I'd been taking Turn 2 with a light confidence lift. We came up on two slow cars in the esses and he slowed down. I thought he was trying to get me to pass, so I lined up behind him; but I couldn't stand it and whizzed past all three of them. Jenner followed, passing them at the end of the esses into Turn 6. My seat was warmer, now; this wasn't what I'd had in mind. For five or six laps, I watched his white Celica in my mirror, sometimes coming out of the bend onto the backstraight hard but ragged. I could see him losing a few yards each lap, and I loved it — aware, of course, that I was running a race that he might not have even been in. Jenner left in his red convertible then, probably back over Malibu Canyon Road to the beach where he lived with his wife, son and toys. I got faster in the final session.

Parnelli Jones gave me a tip. He said the Celica's four-cylinder engine worked better when it was *under*reved. Such advice seemed ironic coming from PJ, Mr. "Outtamyway" himself. But if shifting like a little old lady would make the car run faster, Parnelli would be the first to figure it out.

Jones, 49, had won the Indy 500 in 1963, and twice more as an owner — 1970 and '71, with Al Unser driving. He'd been retired from Indy car driving for 15 years, but he still raced a roaring yellow monster of a Chevy pickup truck in off-road races, and in the desert he was the same old PJ. He'd started racing in the California Jalopy Association in the '50s, and was its hot dog for five years. He figured you could recognize a good driver by the number of dents on his fenders, and his car looked like it had been beaten with a duffel full of bowling balls. Once, after a race in which a driver had gotten in his way, Jones stormed after the culprit, who was smart enough to stay buckled in his car with his helmet on. Parnelli climbed on the guy's car and stomped on his roof. "All it takes is guts, and I'm the bravest bastard in the whole damn world," he said back then.

Parnelli won the '63 Indy in an Offenhauser roadster he called Ol' Calhoun — its official name was the J.C. Agajanian Willard Battery Special — and it's now berthed in the Indianapolis Speedway Museum. Ol' Calhoun split its oil tank while Jones was leading, which left a slippery trail to deter Scotsman Jimmy Clark, who was gaining in his slick little Lotus-Ford, entered by the English Lotus factory. There was a controversial absence of the black flag for Jones. He'd been holding off a foreign threat in America's heartland, after all.

Four days after Sebring, I was in Long Beach. I'd gone without DD, who hadn't resisted. I checked onto the Queen Mary — once a famous ocean liner, now a hotel — registered for the race, and was given my personal Celebrity Itinerary. I went to my cabin, a room with rich wood, brass fittings, a big bed and a porthole over Queensway Bay. I stood there with proof of my Celebrityhood in my hands, looking around the wonderful room with the big bed, an exciting four days ahead. Why did DD make it so difficult to share these things? She would be here with me, but for the demands she'd make when she got here.

It was against my better judgement — I supposed — but I couldn't stand the waste. After about 10 minutes in the room I called her and asked her to come. I had to talk her into it. I picked her up at LAX the next evening.

At dawn on Friday morning I left her sleeping, in order to sneak an unfair advantage: a few laps on the 2.0-mile, 14-turn circuit. I drove at 15 mph with the service and maintenance vehicles until I was evicted. I was certain that this advance knowledge of the track — it had been changed from the previous year — helped me in the half-hour practice session that noon, but my lap times didn't reflect it. I was a disappointed eighth, with a time of 2:21.7.

Gurney was fastest at 2:17.8. He was a leader among the founders of the Long Beach Grand Prix — along with Phil Hill, America's first world driving champion — and this was his fifth Pro-Celebrity race, but he'd never won it. After Gurney came Jones at 2:18.1. Gene Hackman was third, way back at 2:20.6; Jenner was

.05 behind him, and Margie Smith-Haas, the final Pro, was fifth.

California has gotten more credit for Dan Gurney than it deserves. His Gary Cooperesque profile and easy-going smile make him appear to be the classic Californian, but he grew up on Long Island, the son of a bass-baritone in the New York Metropolitan Opera. Gurney's engineering talent probably came from his grandfather, inventor of the Gurney ball bearing; his essence for life may have come from his mother, who used to sit by her father in the family Model T shouting, "Faster! Faster!"

When Gurney was 17, just after WWII, his father quit the opera and moved the family to Riverside, where he'd bought the American Dream: an orange grove. On summer nights, young Dan would slip behind the wheel of his five-window Deuce Coupe, whose roof was chopped so low his crewcut scrubbed the headliner. He'd head for the city limits, where the orange groves were connected by dirt roads. He and his buddies would set up detour signs to divert standard citizens, and race 'til dawn over circuits they built through the sweet-smelling trees.

By 1957, when he was 26, Gurney had five or six sports car races under his belt. Although he was unknown, he managed to get a ride in a Ferrari for the first big race at the new Riverside circuit — no one else wanted to drive the car, its reputation for evil handling was so bad. The field boasted some of the biggest names of the day — Carroll Shelby, Paul O'Shea, Walt Hansgen, Masten Gregory — in some of the best cars: Maserati, Mercedes, Jaguar, Aston-Martin. After the race, at a roisterous victory celebration, the winner, Shelby, said of the novice he had barely beaten, "Dan Gurney is a potential world champion."

They heard about the race all the way back in Italy. Gurney was invited to the Modena circuit to test for the Ferrari endurance team, and earned a slot. The next year Enzo Ferrari, who called Dan "my big Marine," made him a Formula 1 driver — at $163 per month and half the slim prize money. Enzo believed that a driver should feel gratified simply driving a Ferrari.

Over 16 years at the wheel, Gurney became one of the greatest drivers of all time. He never won the world championship or the Indy 500, acute disappointments to him, but he was America's best road racer in the '60s, a time etched in the memories of those who were part of the culture so influenced by him.

In 1966 Gurney formed All American Racers, his racing and car-building business. The object was to win in Formula 1 with an

American car, driver and team. AAR designed and built the Eagle, a "Race Fan Special" since it was financed in part by 5,000 fans who paid $15 each to join the AAR Eagle Club. Gurney drove it to victory in the 1967 Belgian Grand Prix, beating Jackie Stewart by 63 seconds. He averaged 145.67 mph, at the time the fastest F1 race ever. It was the first grand prix victory for an American car in 46 years.

AAR experienced some lean times over the next 15 years. Gurney built a best-selling Eagle Indy car in the early '70s — in 1975 he won the 500 as an owner, with Bobby Unser driving — but follow-up models didn't win enough and AAR lost money. But now, Japan had joined with the All Americans. In addition to featuring an engaging Dan Gurney in television commercials, Toyota had contracted AAR to manage its factory IMSA team and prepare its GTU Celicas. Toyota had had enough of Mazda's dominance in the GTU class, and Gurney's latest assignment was to change that.

During that first practice session for the Pro-Celeb race, somebody either spun, hit a wall, hit another car — or any combination — nine times. Bruce Penhall spun four times. Excepting Gurney and Jones, Penhall was the most naturally talented driver in the field, although this was his first car race. He was one of Gurney's spiritual descendants; there have been a number of them, and they keep coming, these easy-going Southern Californians, blond and good-looking, with a fire under their foot. Penhall's fire was in his right wrist, however. He was the speedway motorcycle world champion, a title decided during one night of five 60-second races over a 400-meter dirt oval on alcohol-burning 500cc bikes with skinny tires and no brakes. You can't get any more sideways than that. Penhall had won the title twice; then, at 25, he retired — to a sidekick role on "CHiPS." That was six months earlier; he was a teen heart-throb and pinup already. You could find him wherever fan magazines were sold, his pretty blue eyes flirting from the pages. On the track he'd cut one ragged, blazing lap...and on the next he'd spin twice. Given two serious weeks with Jacques Couture and a few races, he'd be on Gurney's bumper. But he wanted to be a Celebrity.

His 2:21.5, recorded on the only lap he didn't spin, was sixth, then Robert Hays' 2:21.6, my 2:21.7 and the 2:21.9 of Ted Nugent, whose practice was cut two laps short when he hit a barrier and broke something in his Celica's front end.

As the train of Toyotas inched from the track to the Celebrity Compound just outside the lobby of Long Beach Arena, a guy shouted from the sidewalk, "Who's Sam Moses?"

I laughed and said, "You must be my best friend."

He walked up to the window and said, "Really, who are you?"

I said, "I'm an adventure writer."

"Oh," he said.

In qualifying later that afternoon, Hackman was astounding; he cut *3.8 seconds* off his practice time, and took the pole at 2:16.8, pushing Gurney and Jones back to second and third, with 2:17.1 and 2:17.5.

Hackman had begun racing in 1979, turned on by the driving he'd done in the spectacular chase-and-crash scene in "The French Connection." He had driven in the recent Daytona 24-Hour in one of the three redesigned and screaming AAR Toyotas that Gurney had unveiled there. Hackman drove with two Japanese factory aces. He said that his codrivers' banzai style had revved the car to death on the banking, early. I'd seen Japanese motorcycle road racers, and didn't doubt it.

He had passed me during qualifying, and his own banzai style amazed me. It seemed so young and hungry. He was loose, off line, and locking his brakes — but still fast. The spirit of Michael Zimicki. I'd seen him coming in my mirror, hanging it out in a quick, second-gear bend; after he passed, I watched him pull away like that. Later I told Gurney that Hackman seemed to defy the rules. And Mr. Classic Stylist said, "There are no rules. Lap times are all that count."

My goal for qualifying had been to gain two seconds; instead, I lost .3. It was an awful session; I never found a rhythm, never settled down and spun twice on the same lap, barely missing the wall the second time. I fell to ninth, behind Ted Nugent.

Nugent was a heavy metal rock star. This was his second Pro-Celebrity race; the year before, he'd smashed his way to fourth. He'd been racing off-road for 10 years, and currently drove a four-wheel-drive Jeep in the stadium races. (The seminal stadium event was held in the L.A. Coliseum, and the dirt course ran off the field, up into the stands and out of the park for a quick U-turn, after which the vehicles burst back into the Coliseum through the peristyle — booming pickup trucks, floating about half the distance from the top row to the end zone. The crowd went nuts.) Nugent's fame was tied to the havoc he wreaked. He cultivated his image: "Terrible Ted," "the Redneck Rocker," "the Motor City Madman." According to *Rolling Stone* — even *them* — Nugent's music was "roughly akin to pressing a stethoscope to the roaring engine of a trail bike." He'd been a professional rock 'n' roller since he got out of high school in the late '60s and had recorded 18 albums, sold 16 million records, and was currently *Playboy* magazine's readers' fifth-favorite guitarist.

Politically, Nugent was a heavy-metal conservative. He was a devoted father, to his two havoc-wreaking children. He objected to drugs and alcohol, but he had nothing against guns. He often wore camouflauge clothes and combat boots; with his wild, shoulder-length hair (bound in a ponytail when he dressed for survival) he looked like a hippie mercenary. He was good at acting crazed. He was smarter than he looked.

From the *Rolling Stone Rock Almanac* for November, 1974:

Ted Nugent has won the National Squirrel-Shooting Archery Contest by picking off a squirrel at 150 yards. Nugent also wiped out twenty-seven more of the small mammals with a handgun during the three-day event.

December, 1975: Ted Nugent, known for gun-toting hunting forays in his native Michigan, ends up looking at the wrong end of a barrel at a show in Spokane, Washington. Twenty-five-year-old David Gelfer points a .44 magnum at the Motor City musician but is wrestled to the ground by members of the audience and security guards.

March, 1978: Nugent appears at the California Jam II at Ontario Motor Speedway in California, before 250,000 fans. (I mention this only because in the 12-year history of Ontario, before the zillion-dollar track was bulldozed under, there were two profitable events: California Jams I and II.)

After qualifying, I was informed that Lee Sawyer, Toyota's motor sports manager, had made me a Pro. Until then I'd believed I would be a Celebrity, although he hadn't committed himself. But how could he justify this? I was nearly three seconds slower than Jenner, the slowest other Pro. There were three *Celebrities* faster than me.

I was stranded in mid-field, forgotten and watching from the fringes. Gurney was leaning against his car, holding the black helmet that was his trademark (as a boy, he'd fantasized about being a jousting knight in shining black armor), and was going on about how fast Hackman was. It was my once-in-a-lifetime opportunity to race with Dan Gurney and Parnelli Jones, and I was so far out of contention that I had nothing in common with them to even talk about. My grandchildren were losing, too — for the story I wouldn't be able to tell them of racing with those two legends.

It was *embarrassing*. I was as low-down and disappointed as I'd ever been at a race. Six days earlier, I'd held my own in the Hagan Camaro at Sebring; now, I was slower than Ted Nugent. It was cause for glum self-doubt.

I went to Lee Sawyer and presented my case for Celebrityhood. He said, "How do I know you're not sandbagging?"

"Believe me," I said.

In the press room, there was an air of disdain over the Pro-Celebrity race; in previous years at Long Beach, I'd carried it myself. I didn't want to believe that the crowd loved it. But it was true: When the Celebrities took the track in the stock Celicas, the grandstands stirred. Not many fans could recognize Keke (kay-kay) Rosberg, or even knew he was world champion, but the Celebrities were in the fans' homes all the time and had identities; Hackman was the best-known driver there. And there was often more action in the Pro-Celebrity race than the Formula 1 event, even though the Celicas were half as fast and the race one-fifth as long. The tires screeched a lot, and the cars ran into things. The Celica responds very well to outrageous abuse, by the way.

Technically, it was as difficult to get the most out of a box-stock Celica on city streets as it was to get the most out of the Hagan Camaro —even the wrecked one — at Sebring; it just took less nerve. The perfect lap was every bit as elusive. Driving purity could be found, in the calm center of the publicity stunt. You simply had to drive around the car's limitations and finesse it a lot — not that I'd done much finessing in qualifying. It seemed to be like ice racing: Go slow, to go fast.

That night on the Queen Mary, I had dinner with Jacques and Kathy Couture. DD stayed in the room. She'd been slow getting ready, so I'd gone to the restaurant to be punctual. After about 15 minutes she called and said she wasn't coming. She was mad that I went ahead of her, I guess. I'd left her. So what if she was running late? I could be rude to the Coutures. Who were they to me? She was the one I supposedly loved. That's how she thought. She'd never give in. Where did she get such notions?

Couture was easily the best man for the job of teaching the

Celebrities to drive. But this was not a BSMR race, so he didn't control things. He couldn't temper Hackman's WFO style, as he would have liked. And he was disappointed that the show mattered so much more than the race to Toyota. The race didn't seem to be worth the extra effort of preparing the cars equally, he said.

Aha, I thought, even before he added, "Maybe you have a slow car."

But my car *felt* as fast as the others. Hackman's was the only one that seemed any faster, and maybe that was because of how he drove it. I didn't know how to feel about the possibility of my car being weak — glad for the excuse, or sad for the inevitable. It was ironic that Couture was the one to bring it up, however, since it brought back the lesson he'd taught me at Laguna Seca: You can't let a slow car get you down.

He also said that Lee Sawyer had made me a Pro because he only wanted *bona fide* Celebrities in that division. I could understand that. It was clear that you got invited based on your ability to draw attention to the race, and there would be less media coverage if I won. I wasn't the only Unknown Celebrity, but I was the only one with a year's experience racing, or much chance of winning.

As I headed back down to the cabin, I met Dan and Evi Gurney on the wide, carpeted staircase that zigzagged elegantly between decks. (They had met in Germany in 1962, when Evi worked for the Porsche team and Dan was the factory's fair-haired driver.) There on the landing, we chatted about the day, and although it was painful to bring up my qualifying time — maybe he hadn't noticed — I revealed my frustrations. Gurney said, "It's true, a lot of this race is the luck of the draw. You just have to deal with it." Then he added, "Check your tires." He implied that that had been what rocketed Hackman in qualifying. "I know Gene is good, but he looked like Fangio out there today," he said.

My tires! Of course! Why hadn't I thought of that? I'd even made a note on the subject at my very first race, in the Rabbit at Road Atlanta: "If you're slow and don't know why, it's probably tires." It was a lesson I'd had to learn twice, now; it made me mad at myself. I'd been so wrapped up in technique that I'd forgotten about mechanics, not to mention unfair advantages.

I slept on-and-off that night; before this, I'd always slept very well before a race. But I'd never been this unconfident before. Once, in the middle of the night, I heard chairs being moved on the teak Promenade Deck overhead; at first I'd thought that the rumble was thunder, and my heart leapt. Great! Rain! An equalizer. But it was just the waning sounds of a late party — held without me, I thought in my semi-slumber.

I had a nightmare. I was in last place. The five other Pros had quickly passed me after the inverted start, and I couldn't catch any of the Celebrities up ahead.

At the track Saturday morning, first thing, I checked my tires. I was kind of relieved: They were terrible. Nearly new. The stock Bridgestones had funny flaps on the tread, like little paddles, and mine looked like a thousand tongues, taunting me. If it had been raining, I'd have been unbeatable. I checked the other cars, as inconspicuously as possible, starting with Hackman's. His paddles were worn away, along with most of the tread. Jones' and Gurney's were second and third best, with nubs. Jenner's were good, Nugent's were pretty good. Everybody's were better than mine. Jones and Gurney, of course, wouldn't be racers if they hadn't finagled the best of tires. I assumed that the big U.A. was in for Hackman because of his publicity value. Besides, he was the Toyota factory driver.

The apparent favoritism didn't bother me; all that bothered me were the flaps on my tires. I spoke to one of the mechanics about them. He volunteered to ask Brownie, the crew chief, for another set. He came back a few minutes later and said, "Brownie says there's no difference in the tires."

Give me a break. "Of course there is," I said. He spoke to Brownie again, and this time the word was, "We don't have any more."

I was trying not to get surly, now. After all, I'd asked to be invited here, and I was being treated like a Celebrity, for sure. Toyota was affording me the privilege of racing against Dan Gurney and Parnelli Jones in front of tens of thousands of people. How could I want more? But all I'd ever really wanted was to race, and all I wanted now was to race without *two* handicaps — bad tires and giving a head start to two-thirds of the field. Was that the moon?

I managed to contain most of my annoyance. The only person that I complained aloud to — other than DD — was my friend H. Allan Seymour II, the fellow who kept my motorcycle in his garage with his Hudson. I told him I felt like giving the free racing suit back. He said, "Calm down and behave; stop being so damn moody. Smile and enjoy the pageantry. Be nice to the peasants who want your autograph because they think you're a Celebrity — or else you'll never get invited back."

I said, "I don't want to be invited back. I don't belong here anyhow; it was foolish of me to think I did." And to think that Jackie Lapin had told me I'd sounded desperate over the phone!

I'd always envied and generally admired Seymour's ability to appreciate life's "pageantry" — one of his favorite words. He appreciates it so much that every time he opens his garage door by remote control, he announces, "Release the pigeons!" His claims to greatness — another favored word —are eclectic, if not profound. He was a lifeguard for 14 years. He's been quoted in *Sports Illustrated* as an expert on a number of subjects. He's stood on the roof of some gigantic stadium in Poland — bigger than the L.A. Coliseum, he says — filming 120,00 Poles as they filed in. He once bought hundreds of straw hats having tinted plastic brims, a dollar each at a Tijuana department store, and sold them mail-order, advertising them as the "Sey-mour Hat." He sold out, at $5.95. But the promotion that demonstrates his true greatness was the "Catalina Classic," a professional skateboard race through the streets of Santa Catalina Island. He actually got the one-time event — he knew there would never be a second, which is why he called it the "Classic" — covered by both *Sports Illustrated* and *Wide World of Sports*. Afterward, there was a hop in the famous Avalon Casino, which still echoes the Big Band concerts it once drew. Corky Carroll and the Corkettes played that night. Carroll was a crony of Seymour's, a classmate in the School of Pageantry: He'd been a professional surfer in the '60s, band leader in the '70s, and now he's a Lite Beer from Miller spokesman.

Seymour was the one who should have been in the Celebrity race; he's been named "World's Worst Surfer" by *Surfer* magazine four times. Yet there he is, blown up, almost tucked under a modest tube on Hawaii's North Shore at the infamous Pipeline, the world's most dangerous and perfect wave. This one is breaking off the wall of the DoNut World in Capistrano Beach. Seymour trained for weeks to tackle the Pipeline; one sit-up for each donut he ate ("tall, portly and balding," he was once described in a write-up of a surfing contest he actually entered). He caught one Pipeline tube, one time, so the photo could be taken. And displayed. He liked to spend an hour or two every morning at DoNut World. "Somebody has to do it," he says, cackling.

Somehow Seymour has spawned two beautiful children, Vibeke and Gavin. Their mother, Gertie, mostly rolls her eyes at the pursuits that amuse her husband. Her warm, grin-and-bear-it smile greets you on the family Christmas card, framed like an old-time portrait by the oval rear window of the Hudson.

Gertie told me it had taken Seymour an hour to dress for the race that morning, for all the times he changed his outfit. He settled on a Surf Line Hawaii ensemble. Khaki walking shorts, British Army style; a 100-percent pigment-dyed cotton shirt and matching vest; and a Beau Geste hat with its flap lowered to keep the sun off his neck, which was tenderly dabbed with gardenia-scented coconut oil. Since many of the other Celebrities had brought their Publicists, I introduced Seymour as mine. Right away, he learned that Lapin & Associates had been turned down by 22 women Celebrities before they signed me. That was how he billed me: 22 Starlets Turned It Down For Him! He said it was great to finally see me with a nice girl, like DD.

I do hope it didn't show, but the pampering of the Celebrities pissed me off. Is the fancy food adequate? Do you have all the credentials you need? They handed us white linen napkins to wipe the perspiration off our brows after each run. No wonder Jenner seemed confused. Even the purse: $46,000! I was shocked when I read it in the newspaper; I'd thought the race was for fun.

It was an awful attitude, and I apologize. Some wonderfully pleasant people were doing their jobs, well. And how else would, or should, it be? But it was the Gordy Oftedahls I was irked for, and the purse is what did it; Gordy Oftedahl will probably never see $46,000 for 17 cars in a 10-lap race, and he was giving his guts to racing. But the money was there for Ted Nugent. Couldn't Toyota get any Celebrities without offering big bucks? Couldn't it have been a charity event?

As that quiet tantrum over starving children in Africa was settling down, the driver's meeting was held and the grid was posted. I would start ninth, smack dab in the middle: a Celebrity.

Suddenly I was excited. I wasn't mad at anybody at all, any more. I was ready to race. Seymour got me an interview with two reporters from a Mexican newspaper, and I told them some outrageous story about who I was, who the others were and why we were all here. They didn't seem to understand much English anyhow; they certainly looked baffled. Then he posed me with Miss Orchid Cleaners and Miss Jet America, and took a picture for his slide show. "You had the hair blowing in the breeze, the white shoes...you looked *fast*," he says, with keen appreciation for a pose.

I walked over to the fence that held back the fans. It made me uneasy to be the object of their adulation, or even their curiosity. Me, the Celebrity. "Who was Sam Moses?" they wanted to know, after they got my autograph. But it was fun with the kids — the most I'd felt like smiling for some time, it seemed. I didn't care about attention from pretty girls, however — not this morning; as Robert Redford says, "Where were they when I needed them?" I found three homely girls and flirted through the fence for a few minutes. Even the insanely jealous DD didn't get crazy about that.

DD was unimpressed by Celebrity; she would go to a ritzy party and hang out in the kitchen with the help (and I loved her for it). She found Hackman's son Chris, 22. He was tall, quiet, curly-haired, good-looking and seemed lost. He'd been a fast guy at motocross, then gone to BSMR Riverside — "Super aggressive, drove by the seat of his pants, on Cloud 9," said Couture. He then talked his father out of the money to go to England and race Formula Fords without running any BSMR races first. He had two crashes and broke his leg in the second. Now, he was in limbo.

Starting next to me on the fifth row was Robert Hays, the actor who had been so funny in "Airplane" and "Airplane II." Hays had won the race in 1981, the first time he ran it. Movie critics say he has a natural flair for comedy, and it looked as if he might be an all-around natural. On the track he was quick and neat, and he moved like that — not unlike Rick Mears, it seemed. There may be similarities between acting and driving, anyhow. Struggling racedrivers are more like starving actors than minor-league athletes; beginners can sometimes be sensational, yet each craft takes a lifetime to learn; and, as in show business, success in racing is heavily affected by so many things other than skill.

Nugent and Bruce Penhall were in the row behind Hays and me. Both of them were wild, although Penhall knew right from wrong. Under the spreading silk canopy shading the Celebs during the buffet lunch, I pulled Hays aside, apologizing to his date, Marsha Mason, and said, "I trust you, but I don't trust Nugent, so if you and I get out front, let's just draft each other and it will help us both; if we start racing each other, whoever's in third will catch up faster. Then, two laps or so from the finish, the deal's off. The only problem," I added, "is that I don't know where Nugent's going to fit into this."

Moments before the start, as the cars were clustered at the end of pit row and the Celebs were milling and posing, Richard Spenard came up. He'd been my first instructor at BSMR Riverside 51 weeks earlier.

"I saw you spin in qualifying yesterday," he said. " Where did you learn that?"

"What?"

"You was trowing the car into the turn," he replied in his French-Canadian idiom. "I sure didn't teach you that."

Ice racing, I thought. There may have been similarities, but pitching the car was not one of them; had I been doing that? It was exactly the adjustment problem Penhall was having.

All of a sudden there was fresh cause for optimism. And the tires didn't seem so bad any more because now I knew the enemy, so to speak — and it comforted me to think they would get better with each lap. Then, a couple of minutes before we were told to start our engines, I leaned out my window and asked Hays if he knew how to adjust the steering wheel. He pointed to the release, and I found a comfortable driving position. Until then the wheel's cant had made me feel as if I were driving a bus, but I was too busy trying to go fast to be bothered with it. Definitely brain fade.

There were 60,000 people lining the streets of Long Beach that day. They were stacked on the roofs and balconies of the buildings, some of which were a mere sidewalk's width from the track. Banners — mostly brand names — hung over railings. The most crowded vantage point was a condo that looked like a 30-story-high stack of tamales. Beyond that was the Villa Riviera, a tall brownstone residential hotel whose gargoyles glared toward the city and harbor. The grandstands, constructed at strategic intersections, were nearly full and bobbed with color.

The start-finish line used to be on the main drag, Ocean Boulevard, past two porn theatres. One year, just before the start, I looked up and saw a shirtless Jesus freak perching from the top of a hulking gray rococo building, his long hair blowing against the blue sky as he castigated the jet-set sinners.

The new start-finish line was on the gracefully bending and slightly banked Shoreline Drive, which ran along the harbor. Palm trees grew on the median, separating the track from pit row. There was a new blue-grass Hyatt Regency inside the first turn, a second-gear right-hander. The turn led into a left, followed by a very short chute and another right, taking the course toward what's left of the Nu Pike, where, in the old days, "A sailor could get anything he wanted — from drunk to killed to an homage to Mom engraved on his biceps," wrote Robert F. Jones in *Sports*

Illustrated. The course returned to the '80s through a tunnel under a wide walkway to the front door of the Convention center. Then it hooked left and dipped right — right into a ridiculous hairpin whose apex was a stack of tires against the barrier. Bumper-car caroms were comon there. The backstraight scooted into a canyon. On the right was a wall of four-ton concrete retaining barriers laid end-to-end; a row of old, three- and four-story boxlike buildings hung on the left. When the course swung onto Shoreline Drive again, you could see the black hull and red stacks of the Queen Mary, across the water.

On the pace lap the Pros stole back half of the Celebrities' head start, and everybody jumped the flag. I headed for the middle as I arced down Shoreline Drive, passing Rick Dees, the morning deejay on KIIS, *Billboard* magazine's Radio Personality of the Year, and a singer/songwriter (his "Disco Duck" had gone platinum). Hays came up the middle too, and we nearly rubbed fenders as we passed Ted Shackleford, the object of Donna Mills' (and others') desires on "Knots Landing." We split around Alexis Arguello, the world lightweight boxing champion soon to be a revolutionary in his native Nicaragua. Arguello had suggested that next year the event be a Pro-Celebrity boxing match.

As the first corner approached, I realized that the inexperienced drivers ahead of me would probably overestimate their starting speed and brake too early. So I kept it flat, zoomed about 100 yards farther down the inside, and was second at the right-hander. I moved into the lead in the third turn, near Nu Pike, and couldn't believe it. My nightmare in reverse. As I accelerated up the backstraight I saw Hays in my mirror, moving into second as he came out of the hairpin, skimming the wall.

I might have been surprised to be there, but I felt that the lead was where I belonged. And I was sure I could stay there. I wasn't counting the fast-guy trio of Gurney, Jones and Hackman; out of sight, out of mind. It almost didn't matter; I wasn't going to psych myself into driving raggedly, as I had on the ice. On the second lap, with the hairpin behind me, I took a long glance in the mirror; Hays was about 40 yards back, with Nugent pressuring him now, and there was a row of cars — all the Celicas were white, for some dumb reason — whipping around the turn behind them.

Speeding along the backstraight and through the canyon at about 95 miles an hour, I felt terrific. I was already driving much

better than I had in qualifying. Half of it was adrenaline; my foot
was down more, all by itself. The car was pushing a lot, but...you
deal with it. Between the backstraight and Shoreline Drive there
was a double-apex horseshoe beneath a big grandstand, and I was
hitting it just right: *punching* the throttle before the second apex,
and letting the car drift into the short uphill straight toward the
Villa Riviera. All I had to do was be smooth, and I had them
covered. I had the time and the margin to get the course right, and I
knew that if I did, I'd be faster by the finish.

At the end of the third lap I made a little mistake in the turn that
swung onto Shoreline. I upshifted from second gear to fifth, and
had to bring it back down to reach third. I checked the mirror after
the bend in the straight, and Hays and Nugent were back there
bumping fenders. "Good," I thought. "Let them slow each other
down."

I braked hard and downshifted for the first turn, from 110 in fifth
to 40 in second. I turned toward the apex, and *wham!* my car was
hit so suddenly that I actually thought something had fallen from
the sky. There were no cars near me! I'd looked in the mirror just a
few seconds ago, and Hays and Nugent were way back there.

The impact knocked me around 180 degrees, and the car stalled
broadside in the turn. Ahead of me, squeezed against the tires
cushioning the wall, was Nugent, leaving the scene. And Hays was
coming at me. Wham again! T-boned in the left front fender. Hays
backed up to extract his car, then tore away. I restarted my engine,
threw it into first and tried to take off after them — no one else had
passed — but I could feel the bad news in the front end. With the left
front wheel splayed and tugging, I drove the Celica down the short
chute to the third turn, where I'd taken the lead about five minutes
earlier. I parked the car behind a barrier in front of a full
grandstand; the crowd cheered, loving it. One guy threw me a beer;
another yelled, "What happened?" and I yelled back, "The Motor
City Madman, that's what happened!" getting into the swing of
things.

Let's go to the videotape:

After I'd glanced at Hays and Nugent in the mirror, they
continued to rub each other down Shoreline Drive. Nugent steered
into Hays, and bounced him toward the wall to their left, against
the water. As I began braking for the first turn I was about 12 car
lengths ahead of Nugent, with Hays behind him on the outside. I
braked hard and Nugent shot toward the turn as if it weren't there.

Past the most fancifully optimistic braking point, he locked up all four wheels; smoke poured off his tires as he skidded down the inside, straight into my right rear quarter panel. Hays couldn't avoid me.

I watched the rest of the race from the edge of the track. Nugent's car was all bashed up, the front bumper protruding like a big underbite. Hays' body trim dangled off the right side of his car, and the right front corner was crunched. I wanted to walk onto the track and shake my fist at Nugent —I'd seen James Hunt do that at the 1976 LBGP — but I didn't think it was that funny. I walked about 100 yards down the track, behind the barrier and in front of more excited grandstands, to the short, quick sweeper behind Nu Pike. It was a straightforward turn, but tricky because it arrived in the middle of the upshift into third gear, not quite flat-out at about 60. I'd been short-shifting — upshifting early — there, lifting for a beat, then flooring it in third gear and pulling through the turn at low rpm, sliding less as a result. I watched, as Jones and Gurney took it like that; everyone else was using second gear. Small satisfactions.

Hays came back at Nugent, and they continued bumping each other even after Gurney, Jones and Hackman — spread over 20 seconds — had passed. On the last lap Nugent thumped Hays one final time, and spun him out. Nugent finished fourth, the Celebrity winner; Hays was fifth.

Margie Smith-Haas took sixth from Jenner — also on the last lap — after tapping him out of the way. Jenner had hit her in the first turn, first lap, which had started something. On the cooloff lap he was so mad he rammed her. Jenner hadn't been very popular among his fellow drivers; he seemed so stuck-up. Margie got a lot of congratulations.

Penhall finished ninth, after spinning five or six times.

I wonder what Lee Sawyer had thought for the first three laps? That I'd been double-sandbagging? Probably just, "Oh Lord, if he wins, we won't get on 'Entertainment Tonight.'"

I returned to the Celebrity Compound on the back of the wrecker, as my Celica with the pale orange stripes — and snapped tie rod — was dragged along behind, dangling from the hook. Half a lap behind me, Gurney and Nugent were taking their victory lap in the back of a Toyota pickup, draped in wreaths and trophy queens. Gurney must have been glad to win the thing, after five times. And if anyone had been sandbagging, it was him; he'd cut a *2:14.7* in the race. But it was merely due to the old tires he had fit after qualifying, he said.

I jumped off the back of the wrecker at the Compound gate. DD was there, calmer now; when it had been announced that Hays and I had crashed, she'd nearly strangled Marsha Mason, trying to shake my whereabouts out of her.

Nugent put on his camouflage hunting cap, stood on the roof of his Celica, spread-eagled his six-foot-two frame and whooped a few times. Brownie had said that before the race had even started, there was $500 worth of dents on Nugent's car from the high heels of trophy queens.

Over the 10 laps there were 26 noted incidents of bumping, spinning or crashing. The press room release begins, "The green flag fell on the 17 contestants at 12:07 p.m. and, immediately, the 60,000 people in the stands got a taste of things to come when Ted Nugent and Rick Dees collided in turn 1." Nugent got seven mentions in the release, one of them for speeding past the black flag when it was waved at him for hitting me. A reporter asked him, "What about Hays and Moses in that tangle on the fourth lap?"

"Oh, is that who they were?" he replied.

That evening, leading into the news on one of L.A.'s TV stations, the lady newscaster said, "Ted Nugent wins the Long Beach Grand Prix." I swear it.

Toyota got the publicity it wanted. Nugent may have sold them a lot of cars. He apparently had a good time, and he gave most of 60,000 people a good time — ESPN viewers, too. And maybe the attention he brought to racing will feed Gordy Oftedahl some day. But did it have to be that way? Did he have to treat the sport like that? Did Toyota have to encourage him by letting him?

A number of kind people told me that I'd looked notably smooth, for three laps, and that they'd missed watching me for the other seven.

The next day I covered the Formula 1 race for *SI*. John Watson, an Ulsterman who lives in a converted Coast Guard cottage on the southeast coast of England — and a Motown music fan — won the race in sensational style, moving up from 22nd on the grid. The biggest difference between 22nd in qualifying and first in the race had been tires; he'd gambled on a particular compound for the race.

The next morning I awoke before daybreak again. I looked out the porthole through a drizzle at the streetlights across the bay on

Shoreline Drive. DD awoke, and we somehow started arguing. I had to escape; as I left the ship in the darkness, I felt as if I were going AWOL. I walked across the damp parking lot and got into the pitch-black Z-28 I'd rented — for *SI*'s image — and cruised up the Pacific Coast Highway in the rain.

Thirty-six hours earlier, I'd been wondering if I had enough driving talent to be good; now, after three laps — seven minutes in a stupid Celebrity race in a showroom-stock car — I felt hooked, for the first time. I'd almost been dialled-in. I can feel it now; I want more. I was sure I could be good, now. It was time to give in to idiocy. Wham.

And it was time for DD to move out of Southernmost Condo. I was tired of being unable to make a move without inciting her wrath, tired of her demands, tired of being her yo-yo, tired of her upsetting my life.

As for Ted Nugent, if he wants to learn how to play rock 'n' roll, he should go back to Detroit and listen to Bob Seger.

Trackside Photos

Lovely scenery for a racetrack.

Miss Orchid Cleaners on the left.

H. Allan Seymour II, Ace Photographer

C. Mall

Not satisfied with the damage to the front and sides of his car, Nugent tackles the top.

Trackside Photos

Dan Gurney finally won the thing.

Ed Fairfield

My Publicist and his lovely family.

Chapter 13

Doc Bundy was magnificent in Pepe Romero's hot pink March.

Every Which Way But Straight

Sunday, April 3

Had a long talk on the phone with Doc today. I told him about the shift that I'd missed on Shoreline Drive on my last lap in the Pro-Celebrity race. If I hadn't missed that shift, Nugent wouldn't have been close enough to strike — or else his dive would have fallen short and ended in the wall.

"That's exactly what you want to attain from every race," Doc snapped back, " — a concrete reason for everything that happens and doesn't happen. Since you got that much out of the race, it was a good one for you. You got run into because you made a mistake, and you learned something. The crash was your fault. It's always your fault. I don't care if you're cruising down the backstraight all by yourself and the car gets struck by a lightning bolt out of the sky, it's your fault for being where the lightning wanted to land. That's the way you have to look at it, or you'll never learn, and the same thing will happen to you again and again and again. Each time you'll cry, 'But it wasn't my fault!' but you'll still be out of the race, and you'll be walking around ripe for it to happen again."

Doc lost his Trans-Am ride with Al Holbert. It wasn't his fault. They couldn't get a sponsor for the upcoming season and without one, Holbert Racing would have been spread too thin to campaign both Doc's Porsche and Al's March competitively, since their circuits were separate. So Al sold the 924 Turbo that he and Doc had spent last season developing. "Al had the opportunity to sell it, and it was what he had to do," said Doc.

"I figure it's happening for a reason," he added. "I just refuse to accept it as a setback. I look at it as a sidestep, not a setback. I really wanted to do the Trans-Am; I really thought I could *win* the Trans-Am. Then — *boom!* — the rug got yanked out. But I've programmed myself too positively to give up. I've got too many years invested in this. Something will work out; I just have to work harder. I laid back too much last winter, thinking I had a sure thing with Al.

"When I first watched guys racing and said, 'Hey, I can do that,' never in my wildest dreams did I imagine it stretching into this long. I mean, I'm eight years behind what I could be. I think if I had chosen any other personal pursuit, I would have succeeded long ago. You say to yourself for years, 'I know I can do it, give me enough practice sessions, give me a good car, I can match anybody out there.' That's what every guy coming into the sport feels. It's because you want it. You want it but you can't seem to attain it, because you never get the chance. That's what this sport does — it gives you just enough to suck you in. You have to spend so many years in it before it returns anything to you. This torture is part of it. It's evil. It's not structured in a way that you can attain it.

"To this day, all I've really accomplished is to show some talent. And that's only been in the past three years of professional racing, since I've gotten some recognition. The four or five years before that are all invisible. Buried. But in a way, I was so lucky for that. In those early years with Al, I was able to get it right mentally before I ever got in the car. It gave me such an advantage, to have it in perspective before I ever drove.

"And what I've accomplished so far doesn't guarantee diddly for the next race. Right now, I'm negotiating with anybody and everybody. I'm still trying to make the next race.

"I recognize that the future isn't what I've picked, road racing. The future is in NASCAR or Indy cars. But I've picked this avenue and I'm going to have to stay with it; it's the only place I can keep my name in the top five. My drive has not ebbed, it's just seasoned.

That's what makes me seem calm and laid back to people.

"And don't you give up either. I know I got you out there and left you hanging, and I feel kind of guilty about that, but I want to see this story. I'd like to be reassured that somewhere along the line, this existence we're living is worthwhile."

Thursday, April 7
Road Atlanta. Back where we started.

It's the Nissan-Datsun 3-Hour, and I'm with the Stratagraph team —that's what it says on the Camaro's new hood, at least. The same deal: We'll try to get you in the car on Press Day. That was today. It rained. I got three or four laps. The joke going around is that IMSA stands for "I'm soaked again."

Friday, April 8
The big news in the paddock today was that Doc got fired. He's no longer chief instructor at the Road Atlanta Driving School.

Follow this, if you can:

Bill Whittington, who had been Doc's codriver at Sebring — "Banzai Bill" — is one of three Whittington brothers who race. Based mostly in Fort Lauderdale, they finance their racing with a variety of enterprises and backers. (One of those backers was recently sentenced to 20 years; it seems his Caribbean Marketing Systems, Inc. was connected to a marijuana smuggling operation. At least he had a sense of humor.) The Whittingtons had set a record of sorts when all three of them qualified for the 1982 Indy 500. Also when six plainclothes policemen had protected them in Gasoline Alley. The survivor of an attempted rubout about 10 days earlier — he'd been snatched from the Banana Boat Lounge on the outskirts of Fort Lauderdale, shot five times and left for dead in the Everglades — had told police that his would-be hit men had announced, "The Whittingtons are next."

Anyhow. One of the Whittingtons' holdings was Road Atlanta. Don, the oldest brother, was president there. That made him Doc's boss.

After Sebring, Bill had indeed tried to blow (spelled b-u-y) Doc out of the ride in Pepe Romero's March. But Romero's crew refused to work for Bill. Pepe could see that they were trying to tell him something, so he turned Bill down, and hired Doc to drive with him at Road Atlanta.

So Don fired Doc. Told him that he was disloyal. Said he didn't want anyone working for him who would stab someone in the back for a ride, the way Doc had Bill.

So that was Doc's week: His Trans-Am ride — *boom!* — out from under him. His job: Adios. His forseeable future consists of Sunday's race in the hot pink prototype owned by a wild and mysterious Cuban, and with the words "Candy Cane" painted in purple on the front wing.

Robin Hamilton and Nimrod are here, too. Drake Olson and Lyn St. James are driving one Nimrod, and the other car is on the truck. I walked by their garage and there was a small crowd out front. It was nice to see some recognition for Nimrod. Then I noticed a short queue trickling out of the crowd. The center of attention was actually the winner of *Gallery*'s "Girl Next Door" contest. She was autographing her nude centerspread.

It rained most of the morning, washing away any chance I might have had to get in the Camaro. I guess it's fitting that the Camaro's new hood didn't pass tech. Tex had been too creative with its aerodynamics.

I've got more desire than ever to race — something, *anything*. I spent the afternoon wandering around looking for a ride, with nothing to offer but my unproven driving ability; I could hardly promise an owner that he'd get his picture in *Sports Illustrated*.

Gene Felton lives nearby, so he towed over his own two Camaros. He raced them last year in the Kelly American Challenge, a thrilling, opening-act IMSA series. A Kelly car is a lot like a GTO car only more limited by the rules, the primary one being that the car must be made in Detroit. Felton is the undisputed all-time champ of that series; he's won it four times out of six, and doubled as "Mechanic of The Year" once. Three years ago he won every race. This year he's sitting the Kelly Series out — he says it never made him any money anyhow — but since Road Atlanta is his home track, he entered here. He'll race the older V-8 Camaro; the newer, higher-tech model, a lightweight V-6, was parked next to Tex's Doolie with a sign on it: "For Sale or Rent."

Five thousand dollars was Felton's asking price for the 30-lap race. I actually considered renting it with my own money. I checked the purse breakdown: Fifth place paid $600. I *still* considered it. I tried to justify it as a "true experience" for the story. Sanity prevailed, which only depressed me.

Saturday, April 9

This morning I almost went home. I checked out of the motel and made plane reservations in case I couldn't stand it at the track any more. But leaving would have been too much like giving up, so I couldn't. And I'm glad I didn't. Doc took the pole on this driver's course. It was a big — not to mention satisfying — step for him. The March is a ground-effects car, state of the aerodynamic art, and very difficult to drive because such cars hold the road *too* well — for starters, you have to convince yourself that corners can be taken that fast. Doc's only ground-effects experience had been a handful of laps at Sebring; the fact that he picked up the technique so quickly says a lot — to car owners, in particular — about his abilities. True, Doc knows Road Atlanta like he knows his own driveway, but that's an unfair advantage, fair and square.

Another reason I'm glad I stayed today: I learned something very interesting. There's an old, wrecked Kelly car back in Tex's shop — an Oldsmobile Cutlass. Tex casually mentioned it. That's all I know about it.

Sunday, April 10

Felton had to start at the back of the 21-car grid for the Kelly race; he'd missed qualifying because his Camaro had failed tech yesterday. He tore through traffic, setting a track record on the seventh lap, and got up to third by lap 11. But then he crashed at about 120 on the most dangerous part of the course, the whoop-de-doop after the backstraight — no sweat for a Rabbit, but in a real racecar, hang onto your hat. The car ended up crammed backward against the guardrail, without too much damage. Felton stormed away, furious at the driver who had cut him off.

The winner, Tommy Riggins, was disqualified, along with the fifth-place finisher, Patty Moise, who was his teammate; Riggins Engineering had built both cars. IMSA caught them with a surprise weigh-in and engine teardown after the race. His Chevy Monte Carlo had a bigger motor than he'd declared, and her Camaro was underweight.

In the 3-hour, Doc took off at the start, chased by John Paul, Jr. in the baby blue JLP 935. Junior couldn't catch Doc, who pitted for the driver change during a yellow flag. The skin on his buttocks and thighs was burned raw from the puddle of gas he'd been sitting in; the gullwing door had been open when the tank was filled and gas had sloshed onto the fabric seat, soaking in. Doc's "fire suit" soaked it back up. Pepe Romero ran the middle shift and had a collision in Turn 12 while he was trying to pass a slower car. The crew fixed the damage and he went back out, to spin twice more. By the time Doc got the car back, they were in 22nd place. He wrapped himself with a couple of white plastic wastebasket liners — they looked like a big diaper on him — and took the car back up to seventh by the finish.

Afterward, Pepe informed Doc that he's selling the March. Add that to Doc's week.

I hope he still has faith that it's all happening for a reason.

I watched most of the race from the railing along the Stratagraph pit. Hagan and Felton were way back, after one thing and another. It had been raining off and on, so the track was slick. It seemed as if they just kept coming: down the hill, around Turn 12...and into a spin on the front straight. Like mine in the Rabbit, except faster — and they were hitting things. The worst shunt was Dennis Aase's — he'd been leading GTU in one of Dan Gurney's Toyotas. His car snapped sideways and slammed into the tires stacked against the guardrail on the outside of the turn, driver's door first. The new Celica bounced back onto the track, and stopped — facing traffic. When you're coming down that ramp of a hill toward Turn 12 you tend to get tunnel vision, and the yellow-flag station is easily overlooked, so Aase was in a doubly scary spot. Cars came shooting at the sitting-duck Toyota as he frantically unbuckled himself and tried to climb out the passenger-side window. The second-place GTU car, a yellow Mazda RX-7, slid broadside into the Toyota, scattering fiberglass but injuring neither driver — AAR had built the Toyota well. After a couple more close calls Aase escaped and ran across the track, leaping the guardrail. And probably took his first breath in a while.

Lyn St. James ate it there, too. Drake Olson had qualified Nimrod seventh, and Lyn had started the race and been running strong. The car slithered to the outside of the track and dropped a wheel over the edge, which flung it across the road where it bounced over grassy hummocks and off the inside guardrail. She sat there for a long time. A safety worker came and opened the door for her, and she climbed out dejectedly. Two men in white pants and shirts escorted her away, each with an arm, as if they were taking her to the funny farm. Earlier, Robin Hamilton had said that St. James was the only driver he'd used — including Foyt, Waltrip, Bundy and Olson — who hadn't done something stupid.

I left before the finish to catch a plane. As I was walking away from pit row up a little hill to the paddock, I saw Lyn standing on a grassy slope just behind Hamilton, watching the final laps. The sleek and spectacular new Jaguar V-12 prototype was winning; it was Hamilton's dream, coming true for someone else — someone with sponsorship. Lyn looked tired, sweaty and drizzled-on in her racing suit. Our eyes met as I walked up the hill. I shrugged; she shrugged back. Robin thought I'd shrugged at him; he shrugged, too.

Tuesday, April 12

DD has moved out. It was easier than I thought it would be, persuading her that she needed something other than me to concentrate on. I found her a decent furnished apartment in a fourplex on Von Phister Street; it's a bit rundown — the wooden floors are warped — but it's roomy at least, and the block is nice. She wouldn't let me move all of her possessions though, so they're sitting in my hall in boxes.

It's a good thing she left when she did. We were down to the last lamp.

Wednesday, April 13

I called Tex, and asked him what it would take to get him to campaign that wrecked Kelly car. Somebody named Johnny Wheeler owns the car, but apparently it's Tex's to do what he wants with. Tex said that a Kelly program would have to break even — that's all. A lot of support would have to come from Billy Hagan, one way or another; we'd be using time he pays Tex for, and Billy owns the only engines Tex has for the Oldsmobile. Since, first of all, Tex needs new sheetmetal to repair the car, he suggested I call Tom Erb, who's in charge of Oldsmobile's engineering department. General Motors doesn't officially allow Oldsmobile to race, but Engineering can get away with providing "support" to select teams.

First I called Bill Brodrick to find out more about Tom Erb — in particular, the best way to approach him. Apparently, Brodrick was the right man; he knew Erb very well. What's more, he said he'd call Erb himself, and ask if Oldsmobile would be interested in a Kelly program. Brodrick called me back this evening and said Erb liked the idea. Brodrick likes it, too. He said he'd do my PR. He'd make me a star. I'm glad he didn't say he'd make me a Celebrity.

Monday, April 18

There I was, sitting in the nearly-empty movie theater — some lightweight flick to escape my own rage over DD and her latest "bad things." And she tracked me down. She saw my truck outside, came in, and sat down behind me. She was all dressed up and tipsy. She was wearing a dress I'd bought her — one of the few she owned; an overdose of perfume, which she never wore; and high heels, which she's never learned to walk in. She put her ankles up over my shoulders. I told her to go away, and moved farther down the row. As she left I glanced over my shoulder and watched her wobble up the dark aisle. She looked like a little girl playing dress-up. It was almost adorable, and I love her, and it killed me to see her that unhappy.

Tuesday, April 19

Tom Erb and Dave Jarrard, Oldsmobile's marketing manager, called — from Tex's shop in North Carolina. They'd been in the area trying to get something small started in Grand National with Dave Marcis. I think they just wanted to feel me out, to see if I was serious. I think I convinced them.

I like the idea of driving an Oldsmobile. It's kind of a family tradition. Dad told me that when he was 15 he was a bootleg whiskey runner around Pittsburgh in a '28 Olds Coupe.

Wednesday, April 20

I called Tex; he said that now it's mostly a matter of his sitting down, projecting the expense, and adding up the support to see if the two matched. Five thousand dollars per race is about what it takes to begin to be competitive in the Kelly Series — and that's if you have some kind of basic support to start with.

The numbers look borderline for us. Johnny Wheeler — whoever he is — has supplied the car. We have two used 331 cubic-inch Chevy engines, courtesy of Billy Hagan. The crew will be at the races anyhow, so there won't be any motel bills. Goodyear will supply one set of tires per race. Union 76 will supply gas and oil. Brodrick will supply the PR. Erb will supply sheetmetal and the few Oldsmobile parts the car uses. Tex and his crew will supply the man-hours. Tex Enterprises keeps all the prize money.

I'm trying to be stingy with my optimism (Doc has warned me about laying back), but it's exciting to think about having a car of my own to sink my teeth into.

Thursday, April 21

Today's mail brought a check from Toyota for $2,000. At first I thought they'd goofed with the zeroes. I was expecting maybe $200 for my 16th-place finish out of 17 cars. I wonder how much Nugent got. I won't keep the money, of course, but I'm not sure what to do with it. I probably should offer it to the *SI* business office for all the travel expenses it has so indulgently paid.

Sunday, April 24

Reporting from Southernmost Condo on the Los Angeles Times/ Datsun Grand Prix of Endurance, a 6-hour at Riverside. I couldn't get a ride. Doc drove the Nimrod with Drake Olson, sort of; Drake started the race and the engine — "strung-out" by now, he said — blew during his shift. Lyn St. James had been scheduled to drive with them, but Hamilton had told her that she couldn't cut it as a racedriver, and he stayed on her case so she bowed out. Al Holbert set a track record in qualifying, and he and Trueman finished second in a new March-Chevy. Hagan and Felton finished sixth overall, second GTO. Tenth overall, first GTU, was one of the AAR Celicas; after just four races, Dan Gurney had delivered the victory to Toyota that no other team had been able to. Bruce Jenner and his codriver John Bauer, a former Trans-Am champion, debuted their new factory Mustang, which had bugs. Rolf Stommelen, a German driver who had won the Daytona 24-Hour four times, was killed. The rear wing on his Porsche 935 apparently twisted as the car went down the backstraight at about 185. The sudden aerodynamic change threw the car out of control, and it hit the wall in Turn 9, flipped, cartwheeled, rolled, landed on its wheels and burst into flames. It was only the second death to a driver in IMSA's 14-year history.

Tuesday, April 26

I almost spent the night in jail.

I'd gone to the movies on my bicycle. I'd stopped at DD's apartment on the way, to invite her along — I've been working a lot since she moved out, and haven't spent much time with her — but she wasn't home. While I was at the theater she went over to Southernmost Condo, and got mad because I wasn't there — too busy for her, but not too busy to go out. So she "stole" some things.

The word has to be qualified with DD. She takes things merely to express herself. She doesn't attach much importance to possessions herself — she'd give the last of whatever she has to anyone who needs it more. And she keeps her thievery creative, at least. Once, her college boyfriend was supposed to meet her at his house; after waiting 90 minutes for him, she stole his clock and left. She only steals from people she cares for, and she always gives back whatever she takes, when she's ready. "When you make up, you return it, and the bad thing is undone," she says.

But the only way you can "make up" with DD is to give in. Which reduces her creative expression to blackmail. She knows all the things that mean something to me, and she snatches them and holds them for ransom to keep me attached. And when I meet her demands, as I always do, she hates me for having had to force me. I guess it's not a new story. She's driving me away with her terror that I'll leave her. DD, the desperado without a cause.

So she took my tapes — this story's diary. Seven micro-cassettes, 14 hours of irreplaceable notes. She also took some keys off my word processor. These were the things I'd been working on; these were the things that were keeping me from her. She started to take the keys that spelled out her name, but they were in the middle of the keyboard and sticky to remove — she was in a hurry — so she just took four or five keys from the corner.

She knew this would get me to her door, and boy, did it ever. I'm lucky I didn't get arrested for speeding, in the mile from my door to hers. Except, when I got there, she wouldn't answer it.

It was nearly midnight. Her apartment was dark and her car wasn't out front, but that didn't fool me. I went around back to her bedroom window where there was a missing windowpane, reached in, unlocked the window, slid it up and started to climb in. Out of the dark room comes this flying fan; I ducked just in time, and it bounced off my shoulder. There was a shapely silhouette backed against the wall. I yelled, "I want my tapes, DD!" She screamed, the neighbors called the police, and within 60 seconds there were three cop cars out front. Their radio call had been for a "burglary in progress," and guess who the burglar was. The cops wanted to haul me off in handcuffs; I kept trying to tell them that *she* was the burglar — and I was paying the rent on the damn apartment anyhow — but it didn't get me anywhere. DD got all the sympathy; if she weren't such a good actress, she never would have been able to keep a straight face. She was standing in the dark doorway and I was on her front walk surrounded by cops. They asked her if she wanted to press charges; she shook her head, no. I was freed, went home without the tapes, and sat on the balcony all night watching an electric storm over the ocean and gnashing my teeth.

Wednesday, April 27

DD undid the bad thing — after she collected the ransom. I had to agree to talk to her whenever she calls, and go over to her house when she demands.

She's in awful shape, but I don't know what I can do for her; she's met my every effort with hostility. I'd be glad to go over and talk to her, anytime, but her idea of talking is for me to listen to her relentless attacks. I could take even *that*, but she demands that I defend myself — debate her — which ties me into furious knots. How do you defend yourself against crimes you can't even see?

She's been leaving me notes. Since her syntax is jumbled so originally, they'd be funny if they weren't so heart-rending. They contain only emotion — certainly no sense, not that I can make out anyhow. They start with nothing and impatiently go nowhere. They tell you the anguish is real, though.

She's been sitting in her apartment for days; the blinds are drawn and she's in her rocker, listening to Jackson Browne albums, smoking marijuana, not eating, and reading non-stop. Reading is her favorite — and healthiest — method of withdrawal. Two books a day is her pace; she says it keeps her from thinking, although she remembers it all. Everything from Sidney Sheldon to the biography of Albert Einstein.

She's also been drinking a lot of wine. She took four or five bottles of French wine from my rack, figuring that if I were going to turn her into a wino for a few days, I owed her the good stuff. But I took them back; they were from a case of Bordeaux that I'd brought from New York — lugged between taxis and elevators and through airports. I figured that if she were going to turn herself into a wino for a few days, she could carry her own case for 1500 miles. She made me leave a couple of supermarket jugs of Burgundy in place of the bottles I reclaimed.

That black-and-white photo of me, taken at Sebring the morning I looked ragged and desperate myself, is tacked to her bedroom wall.

Friday, April 29

I slept over at DD's last night; she seemed so frightened. I wouldn't let her lure me into anything else, though. It must be me who's crazy.

I haven't told her about my impending ride, because I know she doesn't want to hear it. She wouldn't be happy for me. So, I can't share it with her. After all this.

Seymour called today. I told him some of my troubles. "You'd think your life would be simple," he said, "but it's not. Your life is like a 10-cent watch that has just gone kaplooey, and you're grabbing at the air to catch the flying springs."

Sunday, May 1

Talladega, Alabama. I'm here at Alabama International Motor Speedway to begin a story on Darrell Waltrip, the NASCAR Winston Cup Champion. He crashed in the Winston 500 today — the second-worst crash of his 15-year career (the worst was two months ago at Daytona). This crash was an 11-car affair, triggered when Waltrip and rookie Phil Parsons rubbed fenders, high on the banking in Turn 1 at about 195. They'd been running in a pack, with everybody drafting and darting around; Parsons' left-front fender rubbed Waltrip's right-rear, and their cars ricocheted into the others. Waltrip hit the wall and was creamed from behind by Kyle Petty; Parsons' Pontiac went into a vicious flip, over and over until it landed on the roof of Ricky Rudd's Monte Carlo. Seven other cars didn't make it through. Waltrip walked away with a sore neck, and Parsons' broken shoulder was the worst of his injuries, more testimony to the strength of Grand National cars. Said Parsons, "A gust of wind must have sucked us together. It was just one of those things." Said Waltrip, "At Talladega, when one car zigs and another car zags, there's gonna be a wreck and there's gonna be a lot of cars in it."

Out in California, IMSA held the Monterey Triple Crown, a 100-miler at Laguna Seca. It's IMSA's sole sprint race for GT cars, and the rich guys stay home because of the pace — the field is thin, but fast. Holbert won, stretching his point lead for the championship. Hagan finished eighth; Tex said it was the hardest and best he's ever seen Billy drive.

And at Moroso Motorsports Park in West Palm Beach, Florida, Gene Felton won the season-opening Trans-Am in an Oftedahl Firebird. What a kick; what an odd couple. Felton and Oftedahl had put some last-minute deal together. The Firebird spent most of the weekend on jackstands; Felton took the lead on the last turn of the last lap. He ran off the track on the cooloff lap, and brought the car into Victory Circle covered with mud. It weighed-in 35 pounds too light, but the SCCA allowed the victory to stand since there wasn't an ounce of oil in the pan; the engine had burned or leaked it all. Besides, how could they have taken the win away from Gordy? He'd been such a faithful idiot. He hasn't missed a Trans-Am in five years, and that was his first win. He was so excited in Victory Circle he kissed Felton.

The ex-Bundy Porsche 924 was one of the fastest cars there.

Tuesday, May 3

Nashville, Tennessee. Had dinner tonight with Darrell Waltrip and his wife Stephanie, who's suspended a career teaching the severely retarded to work with her husband. They live down the road in Franklin (Darrell's a Tennessee native, its Outstanding Athlete in 1977, '79 and '82). He said that "Robin Hamilton came over to the States with no idea of what he was getting into. It was a Chinese fire drill at Daytona."

After dinner, we drove the 20 miles to Franklin. On the highway, Waltrip drives like a little old lady. He doesn't like to take chances. "To be honest, a lot of things scare me," he says. Adds Stephanie, "I once got him to go rollerskating, but he'd only use one skate."

Suddenly, out of the blue, Waltrip said, "It always makes me sad, when I see those guys I've been racing with for 10, 12 years. They run up and down the highway, from race to race. They're really getting old, and they never get any farther. They keep on going like that, winning enough to keep them alive, to pay for their meals and motels. They've got everything they own in that truck. That's how they live. At the end of the season they won't have made a penny, but if they can win a thousand dollars a week in purses, they won't have lost any money either. They started out pumping gas, then they began racing; they raced for 20 years, and when it's all over they'll go back to pumping gas. They never put a penny away, never *could* put a penny away. They don't have a house, don't have any property. What are they going to do? There's no retirement home for old racedrivers.

"The more things change, the more they stay the same," he added, apparently thinking of the million-dollar season he'd just had. I looked out the window toward the dark lanes across the highway, and imagined that the trucks passing in the night were old racers'.

I told him about some of my own recent experiences. He said,

"In this business, the only time people are nice to you is when they want something. That's just the way it works." He added that he was like that, too. Then he said, "You got to remember, when somebody starts giving you something, you got to wonder why. Young guys are always asking me for advice. A lot of times they say, 'It's a really good car.' One thing I always tell them: 'If it was a really good car, the owner would have a really good driver.'"

Thursday, May 5

Back home. Bill Brodrick called. "You're going racing," he said. He'd just gotten off the phone with Tex. The Kelly program is set, beginning with Charlotte in 10 days. I excused myself from the phone, and let out a whoop that probably still hurt his ears.

"One more thing..." he added.

"What's that?" I asked.

"I don't exist," he said.

Monday, May 9

I left Key West for Charlotte today. I've got an *SI* assignment and two more Kelly races after that, so I won't be back for some time.

Getting out of town wasn't easy; my problem was I didn't want the Moon. Neither did DD. I'd found a home for him, but Jolie, the girl from the ice cream stand who said she'd take him, wasn't home when I tried to deliver him last night. My plane was at 7:30 this morning, so I went back to Jolie's at about 6:30, but she still wasn't home.

I took Moon over to DD's. She had known that I would be leaving soon, but not this morning, not for weeks, and not for a race. I told her this when I handed her the Moon — or tried to. I asked her if she would keep him for a few hours until Jolie showed up, but she refused. So I left Moon and his kitty litter outside her door, and went home to grab my things.

I can always see DD's white Mustang coming; I'm used to standing on my balcony in confused ambivalence, watching her come or go. Sure enough, here came the Mustang, up the boulevard. I went out the kitchen door and looked down to the parking lot behind the building; she was standing there in her nightgown. She waved, and left Moon and the kitty litter behind.

I called a cab. I tossed in my suitcase, my driving bag, my carry-on bag, Moon and the kitty litter, and told the cabbie we had a stop to make on the way to the airport. I dropped the kitty litter on DD's doorstep again, and Moon through the missing windowpane in back. Then I ran around to the front of the house and jumped in the cab. As we sped off, DD was in the yard in her nightgown shouting that I wouldn't get away with this.

If ever I've wanted an airplane to leave on time, this was it. No such luck. I paced back and forth in the tiny PBA terminal, looking over my shoulder with each pivot. I went out the back door. Have you ever tried to hide on an airport runway? So I turned around and went back to head her off, to face the music — to gather some momentum, at least. We faced each other for a few seconds in the middle of the terminal; the small room and people in the periphery made it feel as if we were at some cocktail party, about to have cross words over our gin-tonics. DD looked terrible. She was dressed now, in baggy pants and a thin flannel shirt, but her feet were bare, she was pale and gaunt, and her beautiful bouncy hair was stringy. She glared at me as if she despised me. She said Moon was outside, and walked off.

The passengers were boarding now. I asked the agent to hold the plane for two minutes, and searched for Moon. I spotted him underneath the building. Since the night we'd found him, until this morning, his feet had never touched earth; now his claws were sunk into it. I crawled under the edge of the terminal, tugged him loose, carried him inside, got a baggage claim ticket with an elastic band, scribbled DD's name and address on it, and put it around Moon's neck. Luckily, there was a cab in front of the terminal — my recent former getaway car. I put Moon in the back seat, gave the cabbie $10, told him to take the cat back to Von Phister, drop it in the yard and cut out — fast. The last time I saw Moon, he was standing in the back seat of the cab, his paws against the window, looking pretty bewildered.

DD had known that I would somehow rescue Moon; but she was very nearly wrong. I wouldn't have missed that flight to save Moon's life.

I scrambled onto the thunderous old DC-3 as its propellers kicked over and its engines coughed blue smoke. It took off, banked over the island and headed toward Miami. The last time I saw DD, she was sick and wretched and her face was inches from mine. The vision haunts me still. But I don't know what I can do about it. All I can do is go race.

Alan J. Miller

Sometimes all you can do is shrug — just ask Lyn St. James.

Tony Neste

Hagan drove without Felton to eighth at Laguna — the best and hardest he'd ever driven, said Tex.

PART III

Chapter 14

Don Hunter

Can't Let a Slow Car
Get You Down

Tex Enterprises was a converted truck stop along route 220 in Ether, North Carolina, the heartland of stock car racing. Scores of speed shops, many of them legendary, speckled the green hills north of Charlotte. Petty Enterprises was just up the road in Level Cross, and somebody from Tex's shop was always making the 120-mile run to Junior Johnson's in Ingle Hollow.

The building was white cinderblock, about five bays, and on its face was a faded "Tex Enterprises" sign, bordered by checkered flags. Out back, in the weeds, up on cinderblocks, was a Camaro that Hagan had run at Le Mans two years earlier. Less than two summers past its usefulness...and this. At least my Cutlass was inside.

The shop was pretty cluttered and dirty, and my first thought was that lack of organization would be our downfall in the Kelly Series.

Tex Powell had been in North Carolina more than 10 years, and had built cars or parts of cars for everyone from Richard Petty on down. He was not one to over-react. He moved in long, slow strides and stroked his chin a lot. Like most Southern crew chiefs, he knew more than he felt the need to reveal; he had a way of saying, "Is *that* right?" when he already knew what he was being told. He was known for his skill with a chassis and his ability to make a car handle. Sometimes he pulled improvements out of the dark, at the last minute; that was his mystique on pit row. He liked to say that he was 44 years old and had 34 years experience building racecars. And that he was from "down-town Houston." He wore jeans and modest cowboy boots — never a cowboy hat — and carried a pearl pocketknife engraved with an armadillo. His son Mike, 21, said that Tex liked to carry a picture of himself. Both Mike and Tex's other boy, Bill, 22, called him "Tex," and around the shop you'd never know they were his sons.

Since Sebring, the six-man crew had been spread thin; days at the shop, usually seven a week, were often 12 hours long. The Sebring Camaro had had to be rebuilt, and in the middle of the job they'd had to run cross-country to Riverside and Laguna Seca to run the second Camaro, which needed overhauling when they got back. The crashed Cutlass had been a third car to prepare, since Hagan wanted to run both Camaros at Charlotte. Tex didn't think that was a good idea, but Billy was the boss.

My Oldsmobile Cutlass had been around for four years. It had been a NASCAR Late Model Sportsman car, running a lot at Hickory Speedway, and once or twice at Rockingham. Mike said that it had been driven by everyone from Benny Parsons to Terry Labonte's little brother. Then Tex modified it to fit IMSA rules, and Darrell Wheeler, a short-tracker whose dad Johnny was Tex's silent partner, drove it in three Kelly races last season. At the Daytona Finale he crashed — into the first-turn guardrail —and broke his right leg in six or eight places. Since then, the Olds had been facing the weeds out back. The car and I had rescued each other, it seemed.

The Olds was big and ugly, although its bulging fenders were shapely. The wide mouth of a rust-tinged black exhaust pipe came out from under each door. It was freshly painted a basic and versatile white, ready for a sponsor's colors. Across each rear quarter-panel in blue script was "Oldsmobile." A broad blue #44 was on the roof, flaunting the car's past as a stocker. Forty-four was the Stratagraph number; Terry Labonte drove Hagan's #44 Chevy in Grand National.

A fellow — I guess you could call him a good ol' boy — drove up in a pickup truck piled high with furniture. He was wearing a red Joy dogfood hat. He walked in the garage and said, "Got me a couple a real nice recliners for sale. Anybody interested?"

Tim Shoffner, whose specialty was sheet metal, looked up from his work on the Olds and said, "Ain't anybody here got the time to sit down."

"Aw, come on, everbody got to set down," the fellow replied.

"That's what we keep tellin' Tex," said Bill, the cut-up son. "Any time I got a chance to sit down, I go straight to bed. Got to get caught up in advance."

I'd gone to Ether because we had planned to test the car at Charlotte the next day, but it wasn't ready. That gave me some time to find sponsorship before Press Day. We'd hoped for $5,000 from some local business but had no luck, not even with help from the Charlotte Motor Speedway promotion department. "But we have a couple of things up our sleeve," the man there had said. I figured one of those things was deal money.

"Deal money" is what they call the money quietly paid by promoters to racers, to show up. For years, it was how things worked in stock car racing. The big time has changed it, but it hasn't erased it.

H.A. "Humpy" Wheeler, Jr. was president and general manager at Charlotte Motor Speedway, and one of the South's most illustrious promoters. He'd begun his career at 14 with a bicycle race. He was short, with an almost-baby face and wispy hair so light it seemed bleached. He'd had a 40-2 record as a teenage amateur boxer, and used to have a punching bag in his office in order to spare the walls — his temper tantrums were renowned, although it was hard to picture him mad. He was a formidable competitor and recurrent thorn to the France family dynasty, the International Speedway Corporation, which owned NASCAR, Daytona, Talladega, Darlington and even had a piece of IMSA. With Charlotte, Wheeler had a deep niche — geographic, to start with — and he delighted in outpromoting Daytona. It was no accident that the World 600 was longer than the Daytona 500 — nor, for that matter, that it was held on Memorial Day, the same day as the Indy 500. Charlotte Speedway was expanding grandly under Wheeler's tenure; soon there would be condos over the grandstands in Turn 1. Humpy's latest idea. They sold out, quickly.

He'd been promoting the 500-kilometer Charlotte Camel GT

heavily. Getting Southern stock car fans excited over sports cars wasn't easy, but Charlotte was the place for the seduction since it was a "stadium" circuit. A fan could sit in the grandstands and see the whole 2.25-mile track, which wound for about a mile inside the 1.5-mile oval. Our Cutlass was bound to be a crowd pleaser, since it was so blatantly a stock car among all those sporty cars. So on Wednesday, the day before Press Day, I drove down from Ether to call on Humpy Wheeler. We'd been casually introduced once or twice, but I wasn't sure if he remembered. He probably knew why I'd come to his office, though.

He said, "Hi, howya doin', whatcha drivin' this weekend," and I said, "Nothing, unless we get some money somewhere."

I told him the crew was dragging, trying to get three cars ready, and that they had run out of time. As of last night, they had stopped working on the Oldsmobile in order to finish the two Camaros. Tex just didn't have a good enough reason to push them, I said.

Humpy had been behind his big desk, leaning back in the chair and looking at the ceiling. He swivelled 90 degrees toward me and said, "You read Toffler's 'Future Shock'?"

I shook my head.

He said, "Toffler says that in the future, people will be paying to do dangerous things, to risk their lives."

He seemed to mention that only to change the subject. Then he told me about a theory he had; it went into physiology and came back about five minutes later. As I understood it, the theory was that he could take the right young, athletic guy, put him on a training program, give him a lot of track time in decent equipment, and make a good racedriver out of him. I told him to let me know when he needed a guinea pig for this project.

Then he said, "Tell you what I'm gonna do. I'll come up with 2500 dollars — but you can't tell anybody. Here's why I'm gonna do it: I've got this theory. I've helped a lot of racers over the years, and I know that somewhere out there, there's somebody who's gonna do for this sport in the next five years what Arnold Palmer did for the PGA, what Joe Namath did for the NFL, what Ali did for boxing. I got a theory that there's probably 10,000 racedrivers out there, and there's probably 500 who could cut it on the track, and out of that 500 there's only a few who are gonna have what it takes to get through all the *bull*shit. If a story ever appears that helps them get through the *bull*shit, helps bring that person out, it'll be worth it."

I ran to the pay phone and called Tex, and told him I got the team 2500 bucks.

* * *

Each race in the Kelly American Challenge had a $20,000 purse, plus manufacturers' contingency bonuses. The series sponsor was Kelly Services, the company that rents office workers, maintenance persons and other business help. The female work force was the foundation of Kelly Services, so the series was structured to encourage women drivers; the highest-placing woman in each race received a $1,000 bonus, although it was probably unconstitutional. Kelly used its racing program for client entertainment and company morale; having a sponsor with such soft commercial objectives was refreshing, and Kelly's product — people — was easy to endorse.

That afternoon, I drove from the track to Hagan's second house, in High Point, with Vicki Smith, who had run some Kelly races in previous seasons. She was 26, worked at the Fort Lauderdale Yacht Exchange, and said racing was what got her up in the morning. She said she'd bought her first car when she was 11 — a Porsche, from her stepfather. Three thousand dollars, to be paid over the next five years. But she couldn't stand the wait, and when she was 13 she sneaked the car out for a drive. It ended with the Porsche on a sidewalk and the girl running home, certain she'd be thrown in the slammer.

Vicki had driven Hagan's Camaro at the Miami Grand Prix. Tex had modified it, and she ran in the GTP race, finishing 16th. Hagan let her drive it because she'd been bold enough to ask — and because she had sponsorship from a Pontiac dealer (the Camaro was a Firebird for the race). She wanted more. Now, for Charlotte, she'd found a sponsor to pay for her seat in Hagan's number-two Camaro. It was a product called Dr. Seltzer's Hangover Helper.

She looked out at a sprawling building along the interstate as we drove north, and said, "Superbrand. That's Winn-Dixie, isn't it? Hmm." That's how she got sponsors, she said: She sees a sign somewhere, goes to the library and finds the company's headquarters, calls and asks for marketing, and says, "You ought to sponsor a girl in a racecar."

She said she wanted a Kelly ride more than anything, but was penniless. "You seem pretty casual about your Kelly deal," she added.

I replied that I didn't count my chickens before they were hatched.

"I have to," she said. "Chickens is all I've got."

We drove up Hagan's winding driveway at dusk, made darker by the thick trees crowding the road. At the top, there was an imposing old gray stone house with a tower at each end. "Holy shit, he lives in a castle," said Vicki. We had dinner in the dungeon, warm and redolent of roast beef, with about half the crew, including Hagan and his pilot who had just arrived from Louisiana in his Cessna Commanche.

To stir things up on Press Day, Humpy Wheeler had offered $5,000 to any sports car that could break Buddy Baker's stock car record of 165.6 mph around the oval. Al Holbert was there with his new March-Porsche, but he didn't think the offer was worth the risk. A March-Chevy tried, but the record held.

As I pulled the Cutlass onto the track for the first time, my right leg was trembling (rock climbers call it "sewing-machine knee"). The car felt heavy and imprecise, which is what I'd expected. You had to stand on the brakes, which were on the soft side, and turning the steering wheel was like trying to flip a wrestling opponent. But I liked the way it boomed, and how the rear end broke loose under power, which it had plenty of. After four exploratory laps, I pitted. A front tire rubbed against the fender, the engine was smoking, the seat was agonizing, the belts wouldn't cinch tight and the location of the pedals was all wrong for me, but...small stuff.

Next time out, I picked up the pace. Hagan passed me on the short infield straight, and he vanished on the oval. "Damn, he's flying," I thought, remembering what Tex had said about having never seen Billy drive better than he had at Laguna Seca, the previous race.

I took a couple more laps and was reporting to Tex on pit road, when I heard Vicki scream, "Billy!" I looked over my shoulder and saw Hagan's Camaro smashed into the wall on the front straight, grinding down the track. He was slumped over the steering wheel, and flames licked from the engine compartment. The Camaro stopped just short of the start-finish line, right in front of us; Billy sat back up, and seemed to wave that he was okay.

The safety crew's first three fire extinguishers didn't work. They pulled Hagan out and laid him on the grass between pit row and the track as another truck with a working extinguisher arrived. Hagan was alarmingly gray; he suddenly looked 51 and then some, and my fear was for his heart. His eyebrows and moustache were singed, and blood trickled down a cheek — he didn't wear a full-face helmet. He grimaced when they moved him, and said his back hurt. Tex and Vicki went to the hospital in the ambulance with him.

He'd hit the wall coming off Turn 4 at about 150 miles an hour, at a 45-degree angle. There were three big tire marks, spaced far apart; then the scuffs got closer and closer, like a skipping stone, until there was one long, lurid black streak on the white wall.

Neither Tex nor Vicki had come back by the end of the day, so I went to the hospital with Bill Powell, who carried Billy's bluejeans, shirt and snakeskin boots, one of which jangled with a couple of big rings. We caught Hagan in the hospital hall being wheeled from X-ray to his room. All they could find was a broken little finger, but he was too sore to move. There were burns on his fingertips, blisters the size of grapes — his old gloves had had holes in them. He still looked gray, and slightly sheepish, too. "Popped a tire," he mumbled, "Yeah, I sure made a mess of things," he said to Tex. He said he didn't know what had happened; he'd been trying a different line around Turn 4 and the next thing he knew, he was in the wall.

Tex talked alone with him, and came back to the waiting room with the word: Withdraw the second Camaro, stay with the Cutlass. Vicki lost her ride and I would gain the crew's undivided attention.

I also got the bucket seat from the Camaro. I don't want to admit when I first started to covet it, and I wasn't reluctant to ask for it, right there in the hospital. Tex agreed that Billy wouldn't be needing it now.

Hagan made the 11:00 news that night — the big story from Press Day. They called it a flaming head-on crash into the wall at 160 miles an hour. He'd slid along the concrete for 700 feet. From his hospital bed, Hagan said he owed his life to the fact that Tex had built the car to NASCAR chassis specifications. He said he'd been trying to turn some hot laps early, so that David Pearson wouldn't show him up too much. He'd hired Pearson, the legendary Silver Fox of stock car racing, to codrive since Gene Felton was running a Trans-Am race that weekend.

The top three Kelly cars were state-of-the-art, and brand new. Craig Carter, the driver Gordy Oftedahl had replaced me with at the Daytona 24-Hour, was the series champion. He'd built his V-6 Camaro himself, with substantial support from Chevrolet — in particular with engine development, which gave him a wide lead in V-6 technology. He'd been racing Chevies for more than a decade, and this was his first factory deal. He was sponsored by the Peerless Machine and Tool Corporation, whose motto was "Proper Preparation Produces Performance." The Peerless Camaro was metallic blue with a discreet amount of banana yellow, was always immaculate, and Carter took pride in being first in line for every session on the track.

Robert Overby's Buick Regal, sponsored by Castrol Oil, used a special 274 cubic-inch V-6 that Buick had designed for Indy. The Regal was also the lightest car in the field, skimming the 2600-pound minimum. Tom Erb, our Oldsmobile engineer, was envious. He said that Buick's engineering department had built the Regal as a design project; when they were done, they slipped it out the back door to Overby, since racing was still technically a GM no-no. Eighty to $100,000 was probably how much Buick "didn't spend" on it, he said. General Motors wasn't that liberal with Oldsmobile's racing — ironically because Oldsmobiles sold better than Buicks and needed the exposure less.

Tommy Riggins, a former dirt track driver from Jacksonville, was a chassis man like Tex; he was the reigning Kelly "Mechanic of the Year," and Riggins Engineering had built a few of the cars in the field. He used a 305 cubic-inch V-8 in his hot and loose Centurion Auto Transport Monte Carlo; the small V-8 was intended to take full advantage of the rule requiring a car to weigh 9.5 pounds per cubic inch. The object is to maximize your power-to-weight ratio, and generally, you can't get enough additional horsepower out of a big engine to compensate for the weight the rules require you to carry.

A broom handle held up the hood of my Olds, which was tall, bulky and all-white. It looked like an old refrigerator. The only engine Tex had had available was a 331, left over from the Camaro out back in the weeds. The Olds needed lead ballast to reach its required 3,145 pounds; a rusty 50-pound ingot was bolted to the floor under my thighs. Inside it was gray, with rust in the corners — like the Navy destroyer I once spent too much time on.

In the first practice session Friday, a leaking oil line sprayed the pedals and made braking and downshifting like log-rolling. And I had some strange company. After a few laps the car acquired a dusting of gummy rubber crumbs on the floor. They were flung off the tires and through the cracks around the wheel wells, and they rolled around together like a black blob in my peripheral vision. When I'd brake, the blob would slide forward; I'd turn left and it would be thrown against the passenger door; I'd accelerate and it disappeared, crouching in the back of the car. The crumbs blew around on the backstraight and tried to get under my helmet and into my eyes. After the session I scooped out as many as I could with a french-fry container, but they retreated into the cracks when the car was stopped.

Bill Brodrick showed up with Don Hunter, the photographer he'd assigned to shoot our press kit. Brodrick brought me a new driving suit, a custom-tailored blue quilted Racestar with a handful of patches: Oldsmobile twice, Bell Helmets, Kelly Services, Goodyear, Union Oil. I added a *Sports Illustrated* patch to the sleeve. Brodrick put his big hands on my shoulders, looked at me squarely, and said, "If anybody asks about all this attention from Oldsmobile, all these decals, you tell them you're just trying to get some help from Oldsmobile dealers. If they ask why you're driving an Olds, tell them because it's a good car. And if anybody asks what I'm doing here, tell them I'm a personal friend and I'm just helping out." It had to be secret, he explained, because, "Racers all want a piece of the pie, and if they find out they'll all want help."

Brodrick's rings would have blown Billy Hagan's out of the water. He had an Indy 500-winner's ring, a checkered square surrounded by small diamonds — a gift from Dan Gurney. The right pinkie featured a gold inlayed scorpion and he joked that he intended to make a coffee table out of the third ring, a giant black onyx. He was built like Gordy Oftedahl, and he often wore orange — Union 76 colors. His beard and bouffant hair were almost orange too, and he was perpetually sunburned. Someone once described him as looking like a '58 Buick.

He's the guy you see on TV, ushering the winner of every NASCAR race into Victory Circle, which Union 76 ran. It was important that television wasn't delayed, and that the right sponsors were exposed. During a 60-second interview a hand might reach into the picture three or four times, shifting hats on the winner's head. A racing PR man once told me that his worth was measured by the number of times his product's name appeared in photos and race reports.

The thing that made Brodrick a great PR man was that he was so open about the game. He appreciated a polite hustle the way my friend Allan Seymour appreciated a good pose — Brodrick and Seymour had a lot in common, in fact. (Brodrick's garage featured a Harley chopper and Blues Brothers type cop car, among other things.) He congratulated me for the Big Bluff. He said Humpy had asked him if I were for real.

During the afternoon session, it rained. The car didn't have any windshield wipers, so the crew jury-rigged some; but there was no defroster, so I couldn't finish the session. But the new seat was perfect, and it solved the problem with the slack seat belts. The pedals were right now, and we'd gotten some of the push worked out of the handling.

Chassis adjustment is a murky art, and it's as important as money and horsepower. Doc had advised me that communicating with Tex over the suspension setup would be critical — and difficult, since, basically, I wouldn't know what I was talking about. That was an inherent weakness for a team with a rookie driver. The trick would be for me to recognize what the car was doing, and describe it to Tex. Sounds simple. But even some fast guys — experienced ones — can't do it. The best drivers know what the car's doing, why, and how to change it. Junior Johnson once told me that Darrell Waltrip was a better driver than Cale Yarborough because of his chassis knowledge. He said Cale was fast and determined in a bad-handling car, toughed it out like no one he'd ever seen; but Waltrip would work on the car during a race, suggest suspension changes by radio, and improve it at every stop. On the last lap, when you need it in Grand National, he'd have more car.

On Saturday, half of the wall where Hagan had crashed was repainted; they must have run out of time or paint.

I'd been cutting low in Turn 4, making an apex at the apron. But that positioned me wrong to brake for the infield, so I'd decided to try to take the turn wider, closer to the wall, which might have been what Hagan was trying. And I knew that I needed to get through Turns 3 and 4 flat-out, since the oval was the place for me to make time. The Olds' weight was not such a disadvantage there, and its engine was certainly stout — about 530 horsepower, considerably

more than the factory V-6s. When it got rolling on the backstraight, the Olds was a bear.

After four or five laps of qualifying I'd worked it down to a
feather of the throttle in Turn 3. I pitted for Tex to check some
things, and went back out for a hot lap. As I left the infield and
climbed onto the oval, smoke poured into the car. I cruised back to
the pit, and Tex wrapped the breather with rags. Time was running
out in qualifying now. He said, "Go out and run a couple of laps,
just as hard as you can stand it," which was his way of saying
you're not going fast enough. I did, peering through the smoke to
the needle on the tach, which was climbing toward redline for the
upshift to third on the banking.

Tommy Riggins took the pole, with a track record 1:16.2, 106.3
mph. His past as an oval-track racer had helped; so had his V-8.
Second was Craig Carter in the factory Camaro, then Robert
Overby in the factory Buick. I was 14th out of 29 in the factory
Oldsmobile, with 1:22.7. At least we were in the qualifying money;
a top-15 time paid $500.

We should have been about seventh, I believed. There was a
whole lot of time to be gained, both in my driving — especially
braking — and the car. The gearing was too tall, so the engine only
reached 7,000 rpm on the backstraight, 600 below redline. Between
Hagan's crash and the rain, we'd been shorted of practice time to
find the correct ratio. One day of testing — Wednesday — would
have given us a two-day head start.

I was happy and lucky to have the Olds of course, but I wanted to
make it better, and couldn't see why it shouldn't be for the next
session — *every* next session. That evening, I took a walk through
the Kelly compound. Most of the crews were still working; there
were lists on a few cars' windshields, and I envied their drivers. My
crew had gone home. They were already overworked and under-
appreciated, of course; but between a green driver and an over-the-
hill car we were giving the competition two advantages to start
with, and we couldn't afford to give them preparation too.

I stayed a while longer in order to have a black border painted
around the blue #44 on the doors, and Don Hunter covered the front
bumper with red tape so the car wouldn't look like a refrigerator in
the photos. On the way back to the motel, I stopped at the hospital.
Vicki was there, by Hagan's side, where she'd spent most of the
day. Billy was feeling better.

Despite the fact that I was more than six seconds behind the

fastest guy, I was already beginning to like sprint racing —
scratching for every tenth of a second. I didn't miss the Camaro.
Before, I'd liked the demands of endurance racing, but sprinting
seemed my style too. And I liked being alone in my room the night
before a race again. What had seemed lonely before DD, now
seemed peaceful. It was nice to have the freedom to think about the
car. I ate at a Shoney's that evening, and scored 52 on their coin-op
pulse-rate computer.

The morning was a gorgeous Carolina spring Sunday. I drove to
the Speedway listening to classical music on the stereo of the sky-
blue T-bird rental car, and arrived at 8:08, according to the digital
clock. People were lining up for tickets already.

Warmup was scheduled for 9:35. I sat on the workbench next to
the covered car, suited up, waiting for the crew to arrive — there
went my 52 on the heartbeat scale. At 9:15 the van screeched up,
and they piled out and began scurrying — the rear springs had still
needed to be changed. But they were fast, and I only missed a
couple of laps at the beginning of the session; I missed more at the
end, when the car ran out of gas. I bettered my qualifying time by
half a second, though; the shorter rear end — a 4.11, replacing the
3.78 — made a big difference.

In the race, the engine began misfiring on the first lap. Two cars
zoomed by, down the backstraight. "My luck," I thought. I hoped it
was a fouled spark plug and would clear up, but it didn't. Another
car passed on the second lap.

The misfire began at about 7,000 rpm and hurt the most on the
backstraight, where the Olds had lost at least 10 miles an hour.
That made it easy to get through Turns 3 and 4 flat-out, though —
still faster than the cars around me, which was a pleasant surprise.
And I'd lose less when I could find a draft down the backstraight.

The spring day had turned steamy, and the floorboard scorched
my feet. The car smelled like burning oil, rubber and asbestos. The
black crumb blob was with me, and growing. The engine was
smoking again, each time the car left the infield and tilted up on
the banking, and now around Turn 4. The water and oil temperatures were at the maximum Tex said I could run — 220 water,
270 oil. Since the car was misfiring anyhow, I considered that
abusing it might not be worth the gain; but I'd come too far not to
race as hard as I could, heat and smoke be damned. And I could see
that attrition was high; after only eight or 10 laps, a handful of cars
were flagging or already out.

On the 11th of 33 laps, I took what I thought was a quick peek at the infield scoreboard to see what lap it was. When I looked back at the track, I was on top of the next turn; I tried to trail brake to get through it — braking late, into the turn — but discovered that the Olds didn't like that technique. The resulting spin cost only 10 seconds — a Mercury Zephyr got by — but it made me mad; the next lap would be my quickest of the day.

Mine wasn't the only car with mechanical problems, so I'd been moving up. When I could draft a car down the backstraight, I'd try to pass it somewhere between Turn 4 and the apex of the first infield turn. And I'd also passed a couple of cars on the infield. By the 18th lap I was eighth, chasing the Zephyr to regain that muffed position.

Then I stuffed the Olds into the guardrail at the top of the banking.

The turn that led from the infield onto the oval was tricky. It was level but the oval banked 24 degrees, and the ideal line took you into the face of the banking. That would smash the suspension — at the least. So you had to tighten the exit and climb the bank at an angle, although you'd still feel the jerk. Tightening the turn invited the car's rear end around, however; so you had to thread a needle. And it was the circuit's most important turn, since it led onto the longest straight; any turn lasts until the next, because that's how long your exit speed affects momentum.

Because of the misfire, the only way I could hold off the cars behind me — a big red Dodge Mirada and an older-model blue Camaro — was to get a running start onto the oval; if I didn't, they'd storm up to my mirror on the backstraight and I'd want Turn 3 to hurry up and come before they caught me. So each lap I'd been trying to squeeze a little more out of the turn —punching the throttle a couple of feet sooner, trying to use every inch of the road. On the 18th lap I guess I punched it too soon. Or maybe I missed the line by a foot or so. I probably wasn't giving the turn enough respect, because until then I'd threaded the needle every time.

When it started to slide I corrected, but my front wheels got crossed with my rears on the dip where the apron meets the banking. When that happens — someone would say later — the wall at the top becomes a giant magnet.

The car twitched and took off wickedly, 90 degrees across the track, climbing toward the 40-inch-high solid Armco barrier (it's concrete, now). This was the kind of action the Charlotte fans were accustomed to. I forgot to tell Humpy that I was a promoter's dream, too.

Heading straight for the railing like that, I thought the Olds and I were going to burst through and sail down into the parking lot — I saw Lee Petty do that at Daytona in 1961, my first stock car race. I mentally prepared myself for the ride. Then I realized that such a flight was unlikely, but I remembered something I'd heard that morning. Someone had said that Darrell Wheeler broke his leg because his foot was jammed on the brake when the car hit the rail. So just before I hit, I lifted both feet. Funny how much can go through your mind in a second.

The barrier went clank and *sproing*, and the car bounced back, pivoting on its rear wheels toward traffic; the red Mirada went by my nose as the Olds pointed down the bank. The blue Camaro came off the turn and headed straight toward my door, and I thought, "There goes the program," but the Olds rolled forward and the Camaro steered clear, behind me.

I coasted onto the grass by the apron, and let the car cool down. There didn't seem to be that much damage, and at first I wanted to get back in the race; but after another look, I realized I was dreaming. I climbed back in and started to drive around the oval on the apron, but the engine overheated on the backstraight so I coasted to another stop, beneath Turn 4. Tommy Riggins walked by. With a few laps remaining, I fired it up and chugged to the pit, where Tex was waiting. He leaned down into the window, bent those long bowlegs, and said with a small smile, "Had a little light crash, huh?"

I changed clothes and told Tex about the misfire, which he had heard each lap when the Olds boomed down the front straight. I said, "I don't know, Tex; we could have won some money if I'd been a little smarter, if I'd recognized the attrition and just conserved what I had. Maybe I shouldn't have charged so hard. Maybe I should have been more careful, backed off and not pushed it to the point of spinning out."

He looked at me and shook his head firmly. He had a way of looking you straight in the eye. He said, "Nope. You did the right thing. Don't even think about the money. You don't want to just run around and try to finish in the money. If you stroke it just to finish, no one knows you're here. You've got to go for it; that's what we're here for. Anything else ain't racin'.

"Don't worry about it. You done good. Don't worry about the

damage. I've been thinking about lowering the nose anyhow. I did some looking around at the other cars, and their noses are all down to the ground. This is the perfect opportunity to lower it a bit."

Riggins and Overby blew engines, and Carter blew a tire — each while leading. Clay Young, a Georgia boy in a red Firebird, won. "Maybe they were trying to run each other into the ground," he said in Victory Circle. The $1,000 bonus for the first female went to Patty Moise (mo-eece'), Riggins' teammate, who finished third. The Zephyr got fifth.

The 500-kilometer GT race was won by Al Holbert and Jim Trueman in the debut of the March-Porsche — it had been uncrated at the track, having arrived Wednesday night at the Atlanta airport straight from the factory in England. The race was a see-saw thriller between the March and the sleek white-and-green Group 44 Jaguar prototype, which finished third after using four noses through spins and collisions. And Bobby Archer got second in the Champion Spark Plug RS race in his new Renault Alliance.

It had been a great day for American road racing — a small milestone even. Sixty-two thousand Southerners went to a sports car race and screamed for more. It was the largest crowd in IMSA history. ("I wanted to be there so bad," Doc would say later, a sad drop in his voice.) Stadium racing looked like the future, and Charlotte had put on quite a display of it. Another promotional triumph for Humpy Wheeler — and I hope we gave him his money's worth. I also hope he did something about the track's sorry safety crew.

I knew I'd been in a real race. A real stock car, going around a real oval, on a real hot day. I loved it when the smoke poured in.

The trouble was wanting another chance to do it right. How was I ever going to wait two weeks?

Tex Enterprises in Ether, N.C., the heartland of stock car racing.

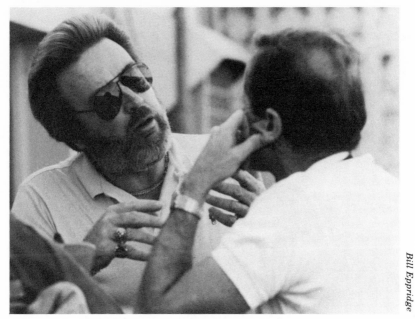

Bill Brodrick could appreciate a polite hustle.

Bill Eppridge

Tex didn't think it was a good idea to enter both Camaros, but Billy was the boss.

Jim Ellis

The boss ended up in the wall and on fire.

The Kelly Series' four fastest guys:

Stan Clinton

Craig Carter,
the series champion....

Bill Eppridge

Tommy Riggins,
the former dirt-tracker....

Stan Clinton

Robert Overby, whose
Buick came out the back door....

Stan Clinton

Clay Young, a Georgia
boy in a hot red Firebird.

Riggins' Monte Carlo and Overby's Buick, two and three, not necessarily in that order.

The V-6 Peerless Camaro was state of the art in the Kelly American Challenge.

Mark Yeager

The old refrigerator had a lift.

The Olds joined the boss in the wall.

Chapter 15

Peter Gloede

Chickens Is All He's Got

T wo days later, I was in Spain. An ocean couldn't separate me from my regret over having missed the eye of the needle, however. Eight or 10 times a day the pit of my stomach felt hollow, and hungry.

The latest round in the greatest battle in the history of motorcycle road racing was about to be held, at the Jarama circuit near Madrid. King Kenny Roberts versus Fast Freddie Spencer for the 500cc world championship. Two Americans. No one else was even close. You had to go back to Hailwood to find someone who could ride with either one of them.

Of all the racers I've known, Kenny Roberts is the most

intelligent about racing, sensitive to the track, wise about risk, and brave. When I first saw him, one Friday night at Ascot in 1971, he was a swaggering 5'6" 133-pound bowlegged 19-year-old who rode the dirt tracks as if he knew where he was headed. Over the years I watched him from the San Jose Mile to the Peoria TT, where he hung half-off a bucking 750 Yamaha and blew away a gang of factory Harleys, and at the Daytona 200 when he lapped the field, zinging around the banking at 190 in the high groove. He won all there was to win in the U.S. and claimed the world championship on his first try. The Europeans couldn't believe it. I watched him in the rain at Spa-Francorchamps in Belgium that year — *totally awesome* — and later on a treacherously ripply street circuit in Finland, again in the rain. I was there at Silverstone in England the next year when he clinched his second title. He wore a foam back support that day, as he had the entire season after crushing two vertebrae against a guardrail in a winter testing crash in Japan that had nearly killed him. That same year he'd instigated and led an international riders' rebellion that eventually resulted in safer tracks and a tripling of prize money — his proudest achievement, he says. The Europeans were believers, by now; the "cocky Yank" had won them, too. They could see the lion's heart inside that rowdy, cowboy-sized body.

Now he was a swaggering 133-pound bowlegged 30-year-old, with three world championships after five seasons. He was being paid nearly a million dollars a year by the Yamaha factory, and was a superstar in Europe and Japan but, regrettably, a mere filler in American sports pages. He wanted to regain his crown — the Suzukis had been the rockets for two years — and retire.

And along came Fast Freddie Spencer, whose factory Honda was the rocket now. He was from Shreveport, Louisiana, 21 years old, and had 15 years experience racing motorcycles. He was long-legged, quiet, uncontroversial, so modest he seemed unbelievable, and so smooth he seemed unspectacular — so much unlike Roberts that it confused the poor Europeans.

La Guardia, the Spanish militia, patrolled the Jarama circuit on race day with machine guns. The atmosphere was no less festive for that; people enjoyed their *paella* and wine and seemed not to notice. I guess they're used to it.

Spencer beat Roberts by a wheel, after a race-long dogfight. That was about how the world championship would finish. Between them, they won every grand prix that year. Six each.

Back in New York, another story had broken. Steve Potter reported in *AutoWeek* that John Paul, Sr. was wanted by the FBI for attempted murder and kidnapping. The victim was a Federal Grand Jury witness who had been scheduled to testify in an investigation that had led to the indictment of five alleged drug racketeers and conspirators. He said that Paul, who was to have been number six, had approached him on a small Florida boat landing at midnight as he returned from fishing. He said Paul ordered him at gunpoint into the trunk of Paul's Mercedes, and when he ran, Paul shot at him five times, hitting him in the chest, abdomen and leg. The old pirate was believed to be on his boat in the Bahamas, or the North Atlantic.

* * *

Lime Rock was the richest and longest race in the Kelly American Challenge: two one-hour heats, two drivers, and twice the purse — $40,000. Vicki Smith would be my codriver; her sex gave us a shot at the $2,000 bonus for the highest-placing coed team, and she had sponsorship. Her Dr. Seltzer's Hangover Helper — an elixir of pills in a packet, and a ploy to sell T-shirts — had a credit with Hagan from Charlotte.

On Press Day, the Olds was in Ether. The teardown after Charlotte had revealed both a broken valve — the cause of the misfire — and a bearing problem, so our second engine was being installed. I drove up to Lime Rock from the Time-Life Building in a rental car. It had a misfire. The only reason I went was for the track time: six or eight laps in a ragged rental car during a press session — I was the driver, taking reporters for rides. Craig Carter was there, getting the Peerless Camaro dialled-in.

The Olds arrived with a few minutes remaining in the first practice session Friday. I spotted it coming through the paddock, on the trailer. Suited up, and carrying the hopeless notion that we might get out for one or two laps, I ran over and asked Tex if it was ready to go, as he passed.

Billy had called that Tuesday; he had planned to sit Lime Rock out because of his Charlotte bruises, but at the last minute decided to enter, which upset the shop's schedule. And there were tire problems on the tow from Ether.

In the second session, the car was willful and evil; it darted with all its might. Tex said he'd forgotten to finish adjusting the front end after lowering the nose. We got permission to practice with the

GT cars; after three or four laps, the engine began faltering at 7,000 rpm. I pitted, and Tex sent Gene Felton out for a second evaluation. The engine blew to bits.

There was another engine in the trailer, but it was a 366 for the Camaro. If we used it, we'd have to fill the Olds with lead. We'd also need Hagan's permission, but after he practiced that morning, he'd flown to Charlotte for the World 600 Children's Charity Ball, a Humpy Wheeler promotion. Even if we reached Hagan and he consented, the mechanics would have to get up at daybreak to change engines — in the mud — since the Kelly race was at 12:30 Saturday. But the biggest problem was that the engine was illegal.

I wanted to go for it. That's what we're here for, I told Tex; *anything else ain't racin'*. He said he wasn't inclined to cheat when we wouldn't be competitive anyhow, carrying all that lead. But we'd call Billy and see what he said.

The Olds was on the trailer, getting rained on. The Dr. Seltzer's logo was on the hood, which was now black. It was the face of Dr. Seltzer himself, a mad scientist with haywire frizzy hair and a demented look in his eye.

The Stratagraph team stayed at the Wake Robin Inn, a big old restored house on a hill, heavy on quaintness. From the phone in the hall, I called Charlotte Motor Speedway and left a message for Hagan, and Vicki left one at his house in High Point. I told the front desk that I was expecting an important call, and went to bed. When Billy called, the night attendant told him I'd left instructions not to be disturbed. I awoke at 5 a.m. and lay in my canopied bed hoping to hear the mechanics on the creaky stairs, leaving in the dark to go lie in the mud and install the engine. Still dreaming.

I went to the track at 7:00 to try to find a Kelly ride. Robert Overby was entered in both heats, in his own Buick and Linda Sharp's Pontiac Grand Am, and I hoped to make a deal for his ride with Sharp.

The morning was crisp and dewy, sunlit yellow. I took a walk through the paddock. The Peerless Camaro was getting the inside of its windshield cleaned. Carter was standing next to it, talking to someone; he noticed a speck on the metallic-blue fender, and wiped it with his jacket sleeve.

I wanted to drive more than ever — it was always more than ever. I offered Linda Sharp my Goodyears, all of the codriver's cut of the winnings and her name in *Sports Illustrated* if I could drive with her; she said she'd ask Overby. I suited up; if he said yes, there would be time for two or three laps. But she never asked him. She said he was too busy, and then it was too late.

I changed again and took another walk. Bruce Jenner was being interviewed behind the rope that staked off an area around his team's chrome-wheeled semi-rig transporter. His new Mustang GTO car was under the canopy with him, and mechanics in white uniforms were attending to it.

The Nimrod was there, but Robin Hamilton wasn't. He'd vanished overnight, back to England. The crew didn't know why, but feared that the bank had called.

Steve Pope, who had shown me the way around West Bend the previous summer, was walking the other direction. He'd driven for Gordy Oftedahl at Sebring. He said Gordy doesn't tell a driver anything and blames him for everything.

Rick Knoop, driving the Racing Beat Mazda again, said the driver is perpetually frustrated because he cares the most. Emotionally, he has the most at stake. No one meets his standards, because it's his baby even if it's not his car. He said that Peter Gregg never really wanted to manage his own team, but he was the only person who could do it to his satisfaction.

Lyn St. James said all you can do is stick it out, and you will if you want it enough. She said she spent three years in the Kelly Series with an uncompetitive team.

"Wait until you win one," said Bruce MacInnes, chief instructor at the Skip Barber school. "It'll all be worth it." I doubted it, I said. It probably just makes you forget.

There was one bright spot, however: Doc Bundy. He was driving the Holbert March-Porsche. Holbert's regular codriver, Jim Trueman, was at Indy — he owned Bobby Rahal's car — so Doc was filling in. Not bad ... a ride in the car of his dreams, with his mentor. He had a paying ride in the Kelly race, too. I saw him over by the Holbert Racing transporter, bopping around with a Walkman. The sound track from "Flashdance," he said.

Vicki Smith was suited up. She'd gotten a ride, somehow.

When the track announcer called the Kelly cars to the grid, I wanted to punch a tree. Instead, I bought a gross knackwurst with sauerkraut, and threw it in the trash as if it were a punch. Cheaper in the long run.

I watched the first heat from a distance. On the pace lap, Vicki worked her way up. The Peerless Camaro won, driven by Carl Shafer, my codriver at the Daytona 24-Hour, now sporting a full gray beard. Doc finished third in a Camaro that sounded as if the rear end was dragging.

I couldn't watch the second heat, and left to check out of the inn and go ... somewhere. As I walked past the desk, the attendant said there was a phone call for me. It was DD. I have no idea how she tracked me down, let alone what cosmic influence led her to call at that moment.

It had been three weeks. She was much better, now. She'd been befriended by the lady who rescues wayward girls in Key West; DD's aura had attracted her. And she was living in an air-conditioned two-bedroom condo with a pool, rent-free; her room-mate, a friend of her sister, was a college girl whose parents owned the unit. She had gotten a job that entailed being nice to tourists in Old Town, and she was doubtless stunning at it. She'd found a new best girlfriend, Rhonda, 19, a six-foot redhead, married to a sailor at the Naval Air Base — "saucier even than me," said DD. Moon was happy with Jolie; he'd adjusted to the outdoors already. He ate the neighbor's chicken. Things were looking up, she said.

Tex returned from the track as I hung up the phone. Craig Carter had won the second heat, as Peerless Racing took home $10,000 and change. We watched the pre-Indy 500 show on TV, went to dinner, and my momentum to leave was lost.

When Vicki bragged about cheating on the pace lap at dinner, I told her it was cheap. She would later tell Hagan, "Sam yelled at me for passing 13 cars on the pace lap at Lime Rock. He doesn't approve of that," and Billy would look at me over an Oil-Can-Harry grin and say, "You know what they say ... 'Those who play by the rules, lose.'"

The 3-hour GT race was not until Monday, Memorial Day. My only hope for a ride was the Hagan Camaro; Billy had been sore and slow in practice, so there was a chance he might need relief during his shift. But even then, Felton would go back in. Still, I stayed, on the slim chance I'd get lucky.

Hanging around on that rainy Sunday was desperately boring; I was too glum to make the IMSA annual picnic. Allan Seymour would have told me to stop being so damn moody and enjoy the pageantry. But the only thing I wanted to do was drive.

The Coca-Cola 500 finished in the rain, and was won by the Group 44 Jaguar. Holbert and Bundy were fourth, after turbo problems — Doc had glanced in the mirror and saw a small fire behind his head. Hagan and Felton finished 18th, trailing blue smoke most of the way; the motor had come from the crashed Camaro, and Tex suspected that the rods had been bent from the impact with the Charlotte wall. Bruce Jenner drove a terrific race. The rain had waited for him to finish his shift.

* * *

Terry Pupp, the redheaded mechanic, and Keith Sawyer, 5'11" and 230 pounds — burly Keith — had left Lime Rock Saturday morning, to take the Olds back to Ether. (We had our own truck now, a one-ton, six-passenger, faded black Ford donated by the invisible Johnny Wheeler.) They had to locate, purchase (on credit) and install a new engine, and have the car in Detroit on Wednesday. That was the day the old refrigerator was scheduled to be transformed into the Miller Time Special.

I'd gone back to Miller with a slimmed-down proposal: $12,000 for the Kelly race at the Detroit Grand Prix, with an option on the seven remaining races at $6,000 each. The price seemed fair since Detroit was the showcase race, and especially now, since Hagan's $16,000 engine from Lime Rock was totalled. After considering it for a couple of weeks, Miller went for the one-shot deal for Detroit. The contract included a clause that provided for our release for "moral turpitude."

The Detroit Grand Prix was borne on the heels of booming Long Beach (after Las Vegas, before Miami), and its main event was also a Formula 1 race. IMSA's contribution to the show was a pair of support races: Kelly Series and Champion Spark Plug Challenge for cars such as Bobby and Tommy Archer's Renaults. The Kelly race would be inestimably important to its participants, since it would virtually be past the office windows of the factory bigwigs.

A Miller art director was to design the layout and lettering and apply the decals to the Olds. We were to meet him at 1 p.m. at an Oldsmobile dealership just outside the city. Terry and Keith had left Ether late Tuesday night, and I flew to Detroit Wednesday morning, arriving at the dealership at 1:00. The Olds arrived at 3:00, the art director showed up at 4:00, we called a painter at 5:30, and then I had to leave. I was due at a meeting of the Leadership Detroit Alumni Association to say a few words about the Kelly American Challenge. I said it would be the weekend's best race. American sedans roaring through the streets of Motor City: History was being made. It was a shame that the newspapers were hyping the foreigners and slighting the local iron. The irony that the grand prix was a showcase for foreign cars was not lost on the area's unemployed.

I'd spent the day dealing with logistics and promotion, half of it on the phone, the other half waiting or rushing. Especially waiting. The job was getting complicated; now the racedriver needed to be a producer. Twice as much had to be done, with no more hours to do it. It was scary to think about the encroachment into the time the rookie needed for the driving. And the cast was growing; a failure would disappoint more people now.

The team was booked at the Leland House, an old residence hotel on the edge of downtown, about 10 blocks from the circuit. My room was a spacious low-rent apartment on the eighth floor, looking across the street to a parking lot. It was after midnight when Keith and Terry parked the big black truck in the alley behind the lot.

Adrenaline woke me Thursday morning at 4:12 — had to get an early start, thinking about the day. The schedule included lunch with the program's principals, with a Miller VP the guest of honor. I picked up Tex at the airport, and we went to the fancy downtown restaurant.

Bruce Jenner was at a nearby table with some Ford people — guest of honor there, I suppose. The Ford PR man came over and took away the Miller VP to go meet Jenner, leaving an empty chair at the head of the table next to me. I hated it. But the Miller PR man said he loved it, because our table was where the action was. I wasn't sure what that meant, but it sounded good.

The VP explained to me how sponsor identification worked. I wondered who the hell he thought I was. He said that in training for his job, he was put through mock interviews with reporters of three types: easy, average and hard. His objective was to sub-liminally slip "Miller Time" into their minds, so it would follow in their copy. He gave an example of how he might do this, and it was about as subliminal as a booger falling out of his nose. I think he was trying to tell me to wear my "Miller Time" hat a lot.

Over at the circuit, Renault was offering rides to the press; Bobby Archer was one of the chauffeurs, and we'd made a date for a semi-hot lap at 3:00. But neither of us got that unfair advantage because the circuit wasn't complete yet. Next, I sped to a suburb on the north fringe of the town for the unveiling of my Miller Time Special in the parking lot of a restaurant, at an early cocktail party co-hosted by a Miller distributor. From the beltway I spotted a 30-foot-high inflated rubber beer bottle, and knew that must be the place.

Keith and Terry had been working on the Olds since seven that morning. Keith had put in one of his fresh buttery transmissions, since the tranny takes a beating on street circuits. And he said the new engine would make my pecker stand up; it was a 358 that had been run on Texas short tracks, and put out nearly 580 horsepower. The Olds was parked on a patch of grass, next to the big beer bottle. It looked really good. Its nose grazed the ground, and it was polished and detailed as never before. It was a cutlass, now. The blue numbers were painted red, the blue wheels gold, and the split grille black. Its refrigerator white was splashed with Miller red and gold; covering the hood was a big red Miller label, over the words "Miller Time" in bold black. It sure beat Dr. Seltzer's frizzed-out face. The Olds looked like Bobby Allison's Grand National car, with Terry Labonte's number.

The party's co-host had a 427 Corvette that he wanted me to take for a spin and evaluate. For almost an hour I begged off; I'd see him coming and slide toward Tex, who was trying to mingle, as was our duty. Keith and Terry were sitting in the corner over their Millers, bleary-eyed from lack of sleep. I wanted to talk to them about the car, but kept getting dragged away to be a hero to a grownup with a cocktail. I escaped to the parking lot for a breather — nearer my racecar — but the Miller PR man came and said he owned me now, so I went back in. Someone offered me a beer, and I said, "No thanks — got to drive tomorrow." The VP glanced over, as if I hadn't gotten his subliminal message at lunch.

I couldn't walk backward any longer, and didn't want to be rude to the co-host, so we got in his red 'vette and drove off.

The thing was a slug, and it pinged; my pickup truck had better acceleration. He kept urging me to open it up, and I kept saying you really can't tell much about a car by driving it around the block. He wanted me to speed around corners, and I could see children's tricycles in yards. He needed to have the car complimented so desperately it was sad. So I said, "The steering is real tight; my Cutlass has more play in the steering wheel than this." Tex was in the parking lot as we drove up. The co-host jumped out of the car and said to him, "Sam says my Corvette handles better than your racecar."

After about three hours, we got away. As Tex and I drove off, we were laughing in astonishment. "I didn't know it was going to be like this," I said. But Tex had been there before. "It just goes to show you, nothing is free," he replied. "They'll squeeze everything they can out of you. Pretty soon that PR cat will have you carryin' around a bottle of beer, even if you don't drink it."

That night I took a dramamine to sleep better. At daybreak I rose and went to the track. As I'd hoped, a barrier was down, and I stole six or seven laps before being chased off — enough to get some basic lines worked out.

The circuit wandered like a stroll around downtown, near the waterfront. It encircled the tunnel to Canada and the Renaissance Center, which rose like a blue-glass Oz. It was 2.5 miles long, and had 17 manhole covers scattered along the way. Thirteen of its 16 turns were right angles or tighter, eight of them at intersections. It was shaped by the usual barriers, guardrails and tires, and surrounded by tall mesh fences that reminded me of the anti-crime screen that had protected the downtown dry cleaner who had sewn one big and seven little "Miller Times" on my driving suit.

The backstraight had three legs, each about one-third of a mile long. The first and fastest leg crossed the Chrysler Freeway, and led to a left on Beaubien Boulevard, followed by a right on Larned; next, you sped along between three long blocks of skyscrapers before a left on Woodward and a right on Jefferson; then sprint toward a 110-degree left in the face of Cobo Hall.

But the final quarter of the circuit was the killer. There was another left away from Cobo Hall — off-camber, and boasting a railroad track on the apex. It dropped to a sharp right, which led through an underpass and into another 110, against the water. Most of the short straight that followed was inside a slippery tunnel under a wing of Oz. Almost finally, there was Ford Corner, an impossible right-left leading onto the front straight along the Detroit River. Just before the start-finish line there was an artificial chicane. A barge inched up the river in the gray dawn, as I finished my inspection laps.

The Formula 1 cars were garaged in Cobo Hall. The IMSA cars were garaged on the street, down the road along the river. The lucky ones were sheltered by the auditorium overhang; the nose of the Olds was pressed against the ticket window of Joe Louis Arena. We had a piece of roof there.

It began raining shortly before the day's only practice session. On the third lap my windshield wipers stopped; on the sixth, the brakes went limp. But it was better than no practice at all, so I stayed out, searching for blurry lines and pumping the brake pedal, concentrating so hard I was oblivious to puddles I could have avoided, not to mention the manhole covers — forgot it was raining again, so to speak. The few laps at dawn certainly paid off.

The problem with the brakes was that the fluid boiled, which filled the lines with air, which left the pedal flat. With the giant 358 cubic-inch engine, we'd had to add 250 more pounds of lead to reach the required 3,400 pounds — the class maximum. It was not the hot setup for any street circuit, let alone one with 13 sharp turns. I'd watched the F1 cars drop from brake exhaustion the year before, and had warned Tex that brakepower would be the fast ticket. The front discs on Robert Overby's 2600-pound Buick were water-cooled; the discs on the beefy Olds didn't even have air ducts.

The rest of the day I tried to organize and shepherd people, and planned promotion with Rick Burton, the Miller PR man — he had fought for our proposal and wanted to make something of the program. I got back to the Leland House at 10:30 p.m. and walked into the misty street to a diner on the corner. Except for random bites, it was the first I'd eaten all day. When I left, I wearily walked into the ladies' room, thinking it was the door to the street.

Tex said there wasn't much he could do about the brakes: I'd have to deal with them. He didn't believe that air ducts were effective. And he might have thought I was simply using the brakes too hard. So qualifying would be a race against the clock in more than the standard manner: I'd have to get my hot lap before the fluid boiled. It was a scorching day, on top of it. I charged from pit row, was squirrelly and knew it, and forced a couple of passes because I didn't have time to follow. The brake pedal was an eggshell, and I was standing on it at 130 miles an hour.

And the Olds was suddenly a *monster*. It felt like a car whose power steering had conked out. Tex had quickened the steering but that had also stiffened it, while the slack in the wheel remained. And there wasn't much leverage, since the steering wheel was small — a 13-incher, my choice. If the Olds had been a wrestling opponent before, we were now in the gorilla division. It took all my strength to twist the car around some of the turns. At Ford Corner, I couldn't work the steering wheel fast enough between the right and the left; my hands got tangled, yanking a glove half off. Another time through there, I felt the ice-racing technique at work: As the car burst between the turns the steering wheel spun through my fingers. My flying elbows were the session's most entertaining attraction there, a corner worker would say later. An IMSA official would tell Tex that Overby and I were about the only drivers taking the correct line through there, and I could scarcely believe it. That evening, puzzling bruises would appear on the inside of my forearms. All I could figure was that the opposing elbows must have been whacking them.

When the brakes started to boil I backed off from squirrelly, but kept driving hard, as I'd planned. Qualifying would be my dress rehearsal. I knew I'd need practice driving without brakes. The downshifts — 15 per lap — would have to be quick and brutal, and a missed one could bring big trouble. And I wanted to see how much strength the 45-minute race would require.

The brakes were used the hardest — needed the most — at the end of the first backstraight, which wound pleasantly past a small park. The car had to be dragged down from 130 to 30 for the hard left onto Beaubien. There was a short escape road, which ended with a concrete barrier cushioned by tires.

That turn was where the brake pedal first reached the floor with an alarming clank. But it responded after a few desperate pumps, so I kept going and it got no worse. Six or seven pumps would slow the car down for Beaubien: Two clanks; two more pumps to get enough pressure to heel-and-toe; bang a downshift to third; two more pumps; slam it into second; and stand on the pedal, hoping it wouldn't reach bottom again. The escape road was a mere pocket, but I didn't fear for my safety because I was beyond worrying about it. Besides, the 1.7-ton Miller Time Special was a very secure car.

And was the engine ever *stout*. The car breathed fire out of the turns, even with the too-tall 4.11 gear. Its thundering exhaust echoed off the buildings. Tex said the Olds was coming out of the chicane as fast and as close to the rail as any.

The session lasted 26 minutes, and the checkered flag fell not a moment too soon. I was breathless, drenched, and my shoulders were limp. We were 16th out of 32, at 2:23.5 — .087 seconds over the $500 cutoff. It had been my fourth lap. After the brakes went, the times had grown to 2:31s. Tex said the Olds was the only car to stay out in the heat, and I wondered if I'd been driving around alone at the end.

Overby took the pole in the factory Buick at 2:13.3, a 65.9 mph average; the boxy lightweight Regal was the most nimble car on the track. Craig Carter was second at 2:14.5, then Tommy Riggins, 2:14.8. One guy backed his new car into the wall around the first turn; it was the ex-Peerless Camaro, now a steel-blue accordion.

The driver was an upstate New York fireman named Scott Flatt, who had introduced himself as "Flash Flatt, the Zoomin' Human." Another driver, in a taxicab yellow Cutlass, lost control coming out of the chicane and executed two complete donuts down the front straight. He sped toward the first turn having barely broken stride, to rousing cheers from the main grandstand.

Thirty-first, at 2:52.9, was Vicki Smith. Her car had arrived that morning. It was the ex-Felton V-8 Camaro which had taken the Kelly championship two seasons earlier. She said she was paying Felton $5,000 for the race, to be applied toward the purchase; he would prepare the car and send it with a crew. The clutch slipped; the crew was a kid fresh from high-school graduation who brought his mother and father to help. They'd been a day late because Felton's truck had broken an axle just outside Atlanta, and they'd had to go back and rent one.

I saw it coming from my apartment window that morning, when Vicki's purple, white and gold #98 appeared in the parking lot on a trailer towed by a U-Haul truck. Tex had seen it coming, too; he'd feared and dreaded it for some time. Hagan was involved in the deal, which may have explained how Vicki had gone from "penniless" to car owner in three weeks, and she'd had some understanding with Billy that she would get two mechanics from Tex Enterprises. After qualifying she called him, and then told Tex that Billy said the crew should lend a hand. Suddenly they were dealt a second car, which needed about two days work. Tex didn't see how he could turn her down — it's part of the code to lend a hand, and he didn't want to buck Billy. I tried to get him to see that he was handing away an opportunity for Tex Enterprises. We maneuvered our paddock space away from Vicki, but she followed.

Soon, all four of my mechanics — Yogi Barker and Tim Shoffner had driven from Ether in the van — were under Vicki's car, getting their Miller uniforms filthy. The Miller Time Special was up on jackstands, unattended, with greasy palmprints on the fenders. Rick Burton was standing beside me, watching. We agreed that for $12,000 Miller deserved a better effort.

I walked Vicki across the street from our cars, to the sidewalk against the river. I wanted to throw her in. But I put my arm around her five-foot-three-level shoulder, and, as sweetly as possible, told her that if she screwed up my deal with Miller, I'd punch out her rotten little heart.

Bobby Archer walked past the Olds — he'd qualified third for the

RS race — carrying a burned brake pad from his Alliance. He reached in the Olds' window and flipped the steering wheel, and his eyes got huge. "How can you drive this?" he asked, referring to the play in the wheel. He found a worn-out slot that surrounded a bolt in the steering shaft. Keith growled at him for kibitzing. I showed the slot to Tex, and he apologized for missing it, and a thicker bolt reduced the play in the steering by about half.

Archer had some ideas on how to drive without brakes. The gist was to drive sideways whenever possible; *now*, it was like ice racing. In reviewing the course, we came up with six turns where the brakes might be avoided altogether. The necessary hoggish lines wouldn't be the fast ones, but they might lead to survival. This only-hope approach sounded good to me, and to Tex too, so we prepared the car for a brakeless sideways sprint through the streets.

Tex readjusted the steering to reduce the effort needed to turn. He softened the front suspension and stiffened the rear, so the car would be loose because the front would bite and the rear would slide. He directed the brake bias toward the rear wheels, which would swing the tail under braking and take some heat off the fronts. We used a 4.56 gear in the rear end to drag the car down under deceleration. The changes were extreme, and it was a shot in the dark since there would be no warmup before the race.

Also, I asked Tex to disconnect the brake lights — which was illegal — to hide our weakness from the competition. One more thing: I told him to take the lead out. We left two bars in, for the benefit of the technical inspector's roving eye.

The race wouldn't start until 4:45 p.m., so I stayed out late Saturday night. Frustration was chinking my shield of self-discipline; after qualifying, I'd actually drunk a beer — Miller Time! It tasted great, and I had another. Rick Burton had invited me to dinner at a restaurant in Greektown, and, after all, he owned me. There were eight in the party, and the evening was fun. There was Greek wine, and we toasted to bigger brakes. I sipped mineral water.

I took another dramamine and went to bed at two, and woke up at eight feeling guilty for having gone out. I puttered around the apartment, did my daily stretching and calisthenics routine, and fooled around with my driving gear — I knew I was a racer when my bag started smelling comfortable instead of making me apprehensive. The taxi driver who took me to the track said that he once had a cab that was hot enough to run in the Kelly race. "That baby be backfirin' alla time," he said. He reckoned he could drive around out there, too.

I got out at a barricaded corner and walked across crowded and sunny Hart Plaza, courtyard of Oz. It was a festival, with ethnic food and silly balloons for sale. The river was full of boats, clustered along the front straight and bobbing; the paddock was full of kids, straight from some hole in the fence and mostly black. One asked me why there were no black racedrivers. Another told me to give him my new Miller Racing jacket. "Why should I?" I asked. "Because you're rich," he said.

Bobby and Tommy Archer finished one-two in the RS race, upsetting the factory Dodge Charger of Joe Varde, a popular and scrappy 5'4" Vietnam vet who liked to show his war wounds. It was the best day of the Archers' careers, and the first win for the new factory Alliance; Renault was ecstatic. I watched the Formula 1 race from the roof of a building over Ford Corner, and the drivers barely had to flick their steering wheels to get through the right-left. Piece of cake, an F1 car.

The Kelly race closed the show. The Formula 1 cars had been our opening act. My plan was to drive as if it were a 45-minute endurance race, the extroverted brakeless style notwithstanding. I'd conserve my brakes so conscientiously that, near the end, I would move up when the lesser-disciplined drivers burned theirs out.

Gridded 16th, the Olds was smack dab in the thick of the Detroit iron, which was raring to begin the futile attempt to squeeze through the streets and stage a thunderstorm between the buildings. Keith cinched me in; only he was strong enough to get the waist belt tight enough for me. On the pace lap I checked out the crowd of 72,000 and glanced up at the RenCen, reflecting gold in the late sun. The artificial chicane before the starting line was so narrow that two sedans couldn't get through side-by-side, not even at 20 miles an hour, so the start was slow and ragged. I was in first gear, and when the flag dropped I stomped on the gas pedal. The tires spun, as the big motor blasted the car off.

There was a tangle ahead of me in the first turn, which was like a wide short-track turn; I think one of the cars was facing backward as I passed. I stayed wide, looking for space; a red Camaro burst from a tangent, and we dragged down the short straight toward the next turn. There, two cars were crashing. I steered clear of the wreckage and glanced in my mirror; a dark blue Camaro was speared by a white one and mashed against the concrete barrier. "Good. Two less to worry about," I thought. At the end of the first lap I was 11th, and I don't think I passed a car on my own.

The pace car came out on the second lap, with the handsome black grille of a red Monte Carlo SS in my mirror. It took two laps to tow the wrecked cars and clean the puddle in the second turn, while my precious engine overheated in the parade. But I was glad for the opportunity to spare the brakes; the shorter this race, the better. For two laps after the restart the Olds felt great; Tex had pulled another one out of the dark. I could throw it into the turns with relative ease, and between the 4.56 and the weight loss it pounced out of them. It was frustrating to look ahead — I could see to fifth on the backstraight — and think that I could be there with decent brakes.

They started to boil on the sixth lap, and the Monte Carlo in my mirror moved up to my bumper. It was driven by Bob Penrod, owner of successful saloons around Fort Lauderdale, an ex-Marine who was sometimes called "Bluto." I gained five or six car lengths on the first backstraight, but expected him to outbrake me into Beaubien since I was slowing so early. I think he missed his opportunity. But without my brake lights, he might not have recognized how vulnerable I was. As we came out of the tunnel and into Ford Corner, he rammed me — but he'd been rammed by the same red Dodge Mirada that had tailed me at Charlotte. And I'd started the chain reaction by slowing so early, which had sandwiched Penrod. I still wouldn't be pressured into using my brakes, but I reminded myself not to give him an opportunity to take me out.

Our lap times were identical to the hundredth on that lap; with my strong drive out of the chicane, he was the same four or five car lengths behind as we went down the front straight. I could hold him off through the 70-mph first turn, which I had almost dialled — a stab of the brakes and forceful downshift into third — but by the fourth turn he was on my bumper again. It was a ripply off-camber left-hand bend just past the Christ Church ("Spiritual Pit Stop available here daily," said the sign), and it was followed by a very short spurt to a tighter left leading onto the backstraight. I'd been trying to get through the entire section without touching the brakes. I'd cruise up in third gear, then come in from the wide side, near the church.

I wish my memory weren't so short. Penrod stuffed it inside me, and I reflexively shut the gate. His right front wheel hit my door and spun me half around. For a moment we were a T, plowing toward the barrier outside the turn; with a slight twist of my head, I could have looked him straight in the eye. We drifted apart and hit the tires separately, the Olds with a relatively soft thud at the rear. I restarted the engine and tried to pull away, but could feel a dragging left front wheel. The tie rod.

Before I made a move, I told myself to be steely and stoic, and pretend this hadn't happened.

I climbed out and walked away, without glancing toward Penrod's wreck. I didn't even look up at the grandstands. Grim and sweaty, I strode toward the pits through a maze of barriers and fences. The only thought I allowed myself, watching the cars go by, was how much I wanted to be out there.

Tex was standing along pit wall watching the front straight, as if for me. It was the first time I'd seen him dejected, and it wasn't a pretty sight. "Penrod got into me," I said with a shrug, over the roar of the cars speeding by.

"Did you talk to him?" Tex asked.

"No, I couldn't see the point," I said. "I would say he ran into me, and he would say I cut him off."

Tex nodded.

It might have been as hard for everybody to stand there and watch the rest of the race, as it was for me. Tex, the mechanics, Tom Erb, Rick Burton ... everybody. But the paddock was on the other side of the course, so we were imprisoned with our disappointment. I'd done my best but felt responsible for their long faces. The final opportunity had been mine.

Robert Overby — he looks like the Pillsbury Dough Boy, and is about as resilient — led every lap. I hope the Buick bigwigs were dancing in their suites; this one race should have justified the tab of the Regal design project. Not coincidentally, the roadgoing Buick V-6 Turbo Grand National is an exceptional car. I might buy one if I were rich.

Clay Young took second in his bright red Firebird and Riggins was third. Carter faded to sixth with his brakes. Vicki Smith finished 16th, stuck in third gear.

I felt so rotten that it took will power to move enough to change my clothes. I told Tex that I knew Penrod had wanted to pass, but that I couldn't bring myself to let him — not by lifting my foot, anyhow. "This is the kind of trouble you get into when you try to run conservatively," I said. Tex nodded, again.

The driver of the Mirada, Paul Gentilozzi, had been a witness from about six feet. "Was it my fault?" I asked. "Yes," he said. "I'd been trying to pass Penrod, and I told myself, 'If these guys don't hit each other in five laps, I'm going by.' When I saw Penrod go under you, I knew you two were going to hit." I figured if he knew it, Penrod should have.

Then he said, "I don't know how you drive that thing. It's the most evil-handling car I've ever seen. I could see Penrod's front wheels with yours as you went around the turns, and yours were cranked about 10 degrees more than his in order to get your car to do the same thing."

I told Tex that Gentilozzi believed the crash was my fault, so maybe I should apologize to Penrod. He didn't say anything but looked at me with horror. Then he drawled, "Well, the way I see it, with a car like his Monte Carlo, anyone who's not runnin' up front is kinda jukey anyhow."

The Monte Carlo came up pit road on the hook, with a smashed front end. I approached Bluto with my hand extended, and he shook it with a small smile and said, "I thought you saw me, buddy." Our versions were the same, except from different vantage points. He said I drove my door into his wheel.

The unwritten rule is that it's the passer's responsibility to avoid a crash. But I knew the accident was my fault. As Doc says, it's always your fault.

I took the crew to dinner that evening, not wanting them to start the all-night drive to Ether on an empty stomach as well as a sour one. I tried to ply Keith with hamburgers, as if he were as easy as Wimpy. Tex wasn't there; he had slipped away after the race and flown back.

After dinner I hit the town with Bill Eppridge, the *SI* photographer on the scene — he's the one who called Penrod "Bluto." We went to Greektown, across the circuit from the RenCen. I wanted to get drunk, but had no taste for it. I wondered where all the alleged groupies were. We went to the Greek restaurant where we'd been the night before; I wanted to taste the wine. We sat down with three girls and offered to share a bottle and leave, but they told us to leave first. I might have explained that I was a lonely racedriver who had given it his valiant all that afternoon, and merely longed for a laugh or two to forget...and that my companion was a decorated photojournalist...but I couldn't bring myself to. When DD and I had met, she'd thought I was a shrimper.

Eppridge went back to the Leland House and I stayed in Greektown, with nothing to do but lean on a lamppost and wait for another opportunity, when she walked up.

She was foxy and friendly-looking, and with a couple. There was a flower vendor on the corner, and the guy bought a flower for his date but wouldn't buy one for her. I could tell she had spirit by the way she told him what a jerk he was. I was standing five feet away. I watched them walk down the sidewalk. She looked back over her shoulder and smiled.

I sprung into action, after a few minutes. I bought a rose and took off down the sidewalk to the corner. Greektown seemed to end there; every direction was darker. I carried the rose back to the Leland House and went to bed not because I wanted to, but because there was nothing else left.

At 5:30 the next morning I was wide awake, thinking about how to get the Olds ready for Mid-Ohio.

Bill Eppridge

Tex had been there before.

Bill Eppridge

Tex said the Olds was coming out of the chicane as strong as any.

Mark Yeager

Riggins in the rainy practice.

Bill Eppridge

The trick is to accurately describe the handling to the crew chief.

Bill Eppridge

Tex and Keith Sawyer hear some last-minute fat chances.

Bill Eppridge

*At least
Bob Penrod was an
easy-going Bluto.*

Mark Yeager

Penrod pushed the Olds until it took him out.

The only escape was to pretend it hadn't happened.

Another snapped tierod.

Bill Eppridge

*That's my car
Vicki Smith is leaning on.*

Mark Yeager

For its first win, Overby guided the Buick past the office windows of the factory bigwigs.

Chapter 16

Bill Eppridge

Saved by the Kid

During the month that I'd been gone, DD had often driven past Southernmost Condo, looking up from the boulevard at night to see if the lights were on, although she knew they wouldn't be. I didn't call her when I got back. I longed to see her, but didn't want to push our luck. She was doing fine, I was doing fine too; one plus one clearly equalled two — or zero, as the case may have been. The evidence was substantial that we were better off without each other.

I'd been in town about three days when she called from the pay phone across the street one night. I could see her as we talked, standing on the sidewalk in the headlight beams of her Mustang, but she couldn't see me, behind the screen in the window of the dark bedroom. It was a familiar little game of ours; we had these conversations often.

She promised to be nice, and came up. We had a soft talk on the balcony, watching a soundless electrical storm over the horizon. Golden slivers of lightning split the clear black sky. Gigantic sparks. Attraction between charged opposites. I wondered what it would be like to be in a rowboat out there in the middle of it.

We agreed on almost everything this night. We loved each other, we wanted to be with each other. But we didn't know how. She said that she'd had nuclear-bomb nightmares since childhood, and now her worst fear was that when the cloud came over the horizon we wouldn't be together when it hit. "Sometimes I feel like a stranger in a strange land," she said, "and you're the only one on my planet." Flattery got DD everywhere.

We spread out some cushions and slept there that night, as the gigantic sparks silently broke over us.

* * *

From the gun, the Kelly program had gone downhill. The proposal at Miller was still alive, thanks to Rick Burton, but it was in jeopardy. Since neither Tex nor I was satisfied that Miller had gotten its money's worth at Detroit, and since it would be better for us if they had a second look, we wore the Miller colors to Mid-Ohio at no charge.

The night before Press Day, I called Tex from a motel in Mansfield, Ohio. The car was on its way, he said, but he wouldn't be coming. He was busy building a new Camaro. He didn't say so, but I knew he was also distressed with Hagan. At three races in a row now, Hagan had yanked the rug on Tex Enterprises — Charlotte with two cars, Lime Rock with his last-minute entry, and Detroit with Vicki. Tex's absence seemed to be his protest. The Olds was caught in the middle. Tex said his son Mike would be there to fill in. His other son, Bill, had quit over continued disorganization.

When I got to the track early the next morning, Mike was under the hood of the Olds, which was positioned in a choice grassy paddock spot. He and Keith had arrived at 2 a.m. and slept in the truck outside the track.

The 2.4-mile Mid-Ohio Sports Car Course had a reputation as the most difficult in the country. It was often bewildering to new drivers; it took me nearly an entire session to get my bearings. There didn't seem to be much rhyme or reason to the layout. Most of the turns felt as if they were intended to interrupt any flow. I wanted to locate the designer and tell him he was either a dolt or a rat. *On Track* reported that the Brazilian Enrique Mansilla, driving Mid-Ohio for the first time, was asked why he pitted so many times during practice. "This is a tricky track and I have to stop to let my brains catch up," he replied.

The first turn was a constant-radius third-gear bend, but after that it got confusing. The road ran into an aimless chicane consisting of a right and two lefts, the second of which tightened, narrowed and popped into the Keyhole, an off-camber right-hand loop leading into the backstaight, which was long enough for the Olds to stretch its legs, at least. Some tricky rolling esses followed the backstraight, and the indirect return to the starting line had about three twists too many for me. The final turn was a tight Caroussel, which had a hitch in the middle and a drop at its decreasing-radius exit. This time, the tradition-bandits had gone too far in applying the name "Caroussel" from the Nurburgring.

Meandering chicanes, loopy keyholes, tricky esses and distorted caroussels. The Olds was not the car for such foolery.

In the second session, the engine fluttered at the end of the backstraight and the oil temperature climbed to 270. Mike checked the plugs, and came up from the engine compartment looking like a doctor about to announce gangrene. He was afraid the engine was about to blow. He almost changed it on the spot, but pulled the valve covers and was reassured when things looked okay. He changed the plugs instead, I took it easy in the final session, and the engine ran better.

After practice, Tommy Riggins offered to lend a hand. He and Tex were friends; Tex might even have asked him to keep an eye on us.

We were standing over the exposed engine of the Olds. He asked, "How much weight you guys carryin' — 2900 pounds?" That would have been our weight had the engine been a 305.

"I wish," I said. "Thirty-four hundred. This is a 358." At that moment, we were carrying about 3200 pounds.

He looked at me funny, and I wondered if he were shocked that we'd use a huge 358, or shocked that I'd admit it if we did. "Damn, that's got to be a handful," he said.

"I followed you some in practice at Charlotte," he continued, "and the front wheel was lifting 18 inches." He went straight into chassis setups, and I helplessly faded out. He was using geometry-words that sounded neat but never registered. How to fine-tune a front end, in an infinite number of ways. Nothing seemed constant; everything was relative. The perfect setup was as elusive as the perfect lap. I envied him his understanding of chassis; it was an important advantage and an opportunity that I was missing. He was hard evidence that I would never be a complete driver. I might as well quit because anything else ain't racin'.

I tuned back into Riggins when he looked into the wheel wells of the Olds and said, "I can see why it doesn't handle." But he caught himself; it was Tex's car, not his, and he wasn't inclined to present his opinion unless it was requested. I should have, but I didn't pursue the subject; the information probably would have been Greek to me anyhow. And what could I have done with it?

The Olds had been leaning in the turns, half of which seemed to break away. In the second-gear right-hander at the end of the backstraight, the right side of the car rose as if on a swell. Riggins talked to Mike about it for awhile, and when he left, Mike said, "I know that everything he was tellin' me was jack-up straight; but damn, this is a little bit tricky. I'm used to just turnin' left all the time. That car's doin' everything but speakin' English to us."

Mike raised the Panhard bar, which lowers the center of roll, and reset the carburetor floats in chase of the flutter. And he had Terry hook up a water-cooling system for the brakes; water would squirt on the front discs when the pedal was pressed. The reservoir was a plastic five-gallon can strapped to the rollcage beside me, like a midget passenger.

I showed Mike the slack in the steering wheel. "No problem," he said. "I can get that out."

Mike Powell was 21 years old and had nine years experience building racecars. At 12, he "wanted to get started on something," so he bought a '54 Ford pickup from a local widow — "an old lady in a farmyard" — and a 427 Ford engine from Tex, and built his first set of wheels. Now he drove a '68 Corvette that he had rebuilt from a wreck. He was a junior partner in Tex Enterprises — Johnny Wheeler, Tex, and Mike — and his own racecar was the sharpest thing back in the shop. It was a black-and-red Oldsmobile Starfire, which he ran in NASCAR's Darlington Dash Series for four-cylinder cars. He was his own crew chief in that program, and he emphasized his independence by calling Tex's IMSA crew "the sporty-car boys."

The name "Mike" somehow seemed too grown-up for him; I found myself calling him "Mikey." He was the kind of kid a mother would (and did) adore. He was lanky like his father, but smaller and looser, and was fair-haired, fresh-faced and hard-working. He said "m'am" and "sir." And he carried a little notebook in his hip pocket to scribble reminders, which made me delirious with joy. As Tex liked to say he was from "down-town Houston," Mike liked to add, "where it's 90 degrees before the sun come up."

Outside of his own team, Mike had never had a major crew-chief assignment. Fortunately, mostly for me, the Camaro wasn't his responsibility at Mid-Ohio; Yogi, Tim and Terry were on it. Yogi was in charge, there (I think they called him Yogi because he talked like Yogi the Bear). Joining Mike and Keith on the Olds was Jeffrey Almond, a cousin of the Almond Brothers, engine builders. Jeffrey had just finished his junior year of high school, and had been hired by Tex for the summer.

We were making progress; the Olds fluttered and leaned less in the morning session on Friday. But it pushed; and when the oil temperature rose to 260 I pitted, with a clocking of 1:47.7. After the engine cooled, Mike sent Felton out, to tap his experience. I didn't like losing the practice time, but if it would make us faster on Sunday, I was all for it.

Felton held the Mid-Ohio Kelly record in the now-Smith Camaro, at 1:36.6, 89.5 mph. His first lap in the Olds was 1:43, and in five more he got down to 1:40.8. He pitted and reported to Mike, and when he went back out I burned. All he wanted to do was lower the lap time, I thought, and I was afraid he was going to. I was glad when the checkered flag fell on his first attempt.

Our evaluations of the car's handling basically jibed, but his seemed considerably understated. He said it pushed some, but seemed neutral where it mattered. The brakes were soft, but it was nothing you couldn't handle. Mike asked him what the oil temperature had been, and he said, "Oh, about 220." I'd checked the gauge when he'd returned, and it had read 260. I'd seen Mike check it too, so apparently he was testing Felton's credibility — not bad, for a virgin crew chief. Later, I told Mike that I hadn't minded Felton going out, but we didn't learn enough for it to have been worth six hard laps on the car, so no more. He nodded.

Back in the paddock, Irv Hoerr, a fast guy in a neat white V-8 Camaro, came over and told me I'd gotten in his way during the session. Since it was only practice, it surprised me that he would complain; besides, I'd given him an opportunity to pass in traffic on the backstraight, which he conceded he hadn't taken. So his protest didn't bother me; it mostly just gave me the impression that he was a crybaby. I mentioned it to Mike, whose scoff indicated he was bothered even less. I was liking the kid more and more.

By now, I'd followed Robert Overby around enough turns to see how his Buick turned on a dime — not to mention how it dove about a mile deeper into the turns. Craig Carter's Peerless Camaro seemed sucked to the road. Riggins' Monte Carlo looked as if it had a hinge in its tail, but that was how he liked it, at least. With such contrasting styles, it must have been exciting to watch the three of them dice.

I didn't know what to think of the Olds' handling, because I didn't know how much to expect of it. I couldn't believe that I was simply driving it wrong; that would be accepting that the car was right. From discussions with Doc (he was driving the Holbert March-Chevy, sitting in for Al, who was off winning Le Mans in a factory Porsche), I was reassured that I was innocent of the things that make a car push — the wrong line, too much throttle at the wrong time. And he reminded me that I'd set a record for short braking at his school at Road Atlanta.

It would be the rare rookie who could sort out a chassis, but it would be the rare crew chief who could do it himself, since the driver is the only person who can feel it. So I accepted responsibility for the handling; if it wasn't right it was my fault, and I'd have to live with it. I was certainly seeing some of what Doc had wanted me to see. "Ninety percent of racing success is the car and preparation," he said. "There are probably 10 drivers who could win any given race if they had the winning car. The driving is the easy part."

Felton had proved at least one thing: The car could be driven 6.9 seconds faster per lap than I was driving it. Motivated by that icy reality, in the afternoon session I clocked 1:48.6, 46.2, 45.3, 44.7, 44.3, and 1:43.9 before the oil got hot and the brakes went limp — the plastic water line had melted from the heat generated by the discs. And I could see where four more seconds could be pared — two in the car and two in me. My grasp of the circuit's geometry had the slack, now. And the handling was no better. The problem was that when you tune a chassis at 1:48, it's not always right at 1:44. "Every tire is cryin' a different tune," said Mike.

I believed that a 1:42 in qualifying might make the top 10, and it seemed within reach. On Saturday morning Mike raised the Panhard bar to the top rung, stiffened the rear springs some more, and replaced the fuel pump. But it still leaned, pushed and fluttered; and now it was loose, too. The tail slipped going into the turns, without the power; the nose plowed coming out of them, when I got on the gas. In the slow corners it did the opposite. Trail braking, supposedly the technique for heavy sedans, was treacherous. And there was no way I could get the Olds around the Caroussel without the right front wheel pawing like a merry-go-round pony. That made the car push even more, since half as much rubber was on the road to steer. Each lap was a new futile attempt to get down to the apex there.

And there was a thudding chatter when I braked and downshifted at the end of the backstraight — the rear wheels were hopping. Water from the brake tank sloshed around and bounced out the vent, showering the black blob and me. But that stopped when the water-cooling line melted again, and the brakes faded away.

And suddenly it was difficult to concentrate. The physical effort was distracting, like trying to wrestle and listen to music at the same time. My body was never still; it was either tugging on the steering wheel or throwing a shift while pouncing on the brakes and/or stomping on the clutch. It was hardly serene, the way I thought it was supposed to be — and could be, in a Formula Ford. Maybe in the Peerless Camaro, too.

It was a fast field; most of the competition had raced at Mid-Ohio before. Nothing less than a 1:40.6 made the top 10. Craig Carter broke Felton's lap record with 1:36.3. I was 21st out of 24; the time of 1:44.9 was crushing — a second slower than my practice time. I hadn't expected it, despite the troubles. Even Vicki Smith was faster. Her Camaro had been back to Felton's shop and was better prepared this time, and Yogi was helping when he could.

Patty Moise was driving a brand new Monte Carlo, a twin to teammate Riggins' car. She was 24, had curly hair, freckles, big eyes and cheeks, looked great in tight jeans, and sometimes got chased by the other drivers. She was the Kelly Series' "Most Improved Driver" from the previous season, and was sponsored by the 15 Famous Amos Restaurants in Jacksonville, which her parents owned. Her father, a former driver, managed the team. She'd been on my bumper for three laps during qualifying.

She came over and asked, "How's it handling?"

"What did it look like to you?" I replied.

"Dreadful," she said. "It looked like you almost had to park it to get around the turns." She was either giving me the benefit of the doubt or approaching her subject diplomatically.

"Maybe it's me," I said with a shrug. "Maybe I don't have to slow down that much."

"You slowed me down, too," she said. "I didn't think you saw me."

I'd seen her all right, weaving impatiently on my bumper. But I'd figured if she could pass me, she would — I certainly felt easy enough to pass. Her car was as fast as mine, although the Olds could jump her by a couple of car lengths out of the Keyhole. She finally outbraked me at the end of the backstraight, as I'd known she would.

I confess to lightly manipulating her. She seemed eager to point out how fast she was, so I let her, and she continued by telling me exactly where I was slow. It helped a lot to know where I was losing time. She got her message — "Stay out of my way" — across quite well, but I didn't think it would be a problem in the future.

Altogether, I'd done about 25 laps. Bobby Archer said he'd raced at Mid-Ohio seven times before he got the rhythm. He said he'd been watching me, and I was getting it. He told me I worried too much.

He was right. But I'd *slowed down.* I didn't have time for setbacks. Was it a setback in skill? When it started raining, I went back to the motel to worry about these things. But soon I was sorry I'd left the track — imprisoned in my room with my disappointment. I drank four beers, and kept going outside and checking the parking lot for the big black truck with "Johnny Wheeler Enterprises" on the airfoil.

At about 9:00 the crew returned. Mike couldn't get out of the front seat. His head was on the sill of the open window, and he slurred sing-songy, "I'm so sorry, I screwed up, a fella works hard, he tries to do a good job, I came here and tried to be so responsible, and I got carried away. Had five or six beers and now I'm drunk."

Yogi, only slightly less drunk himself, his gold tooth flashing inside a helpless grin, took the blame. He'd taken Mike to some shindig at the track and encouraged him. Now he helped him off to bed. Billy Hagan and I were left standing in the parking lot, and we agreed that the kid was a winner.

That night I finished last in my dreams, again. This time it was a motorcycle race.

At 7 a.m. sharp, Mike was at my door, just as sharp. "I apologize for last night," he said. "It's not my style. I made myself look bad. It won't happen again."

Cheating in the race was more a matter of practicality than morality. The risk of getting caught outweighed the unweighable gain this time: blowing the deal with Miller vs. a jump from maybe 12th to maybe 10th. Besides, it was raining again — I'd gotten a helpless grin of my own when I'd looked outside. A wet track would absorb some of the weight, and help neutralize the bad handling — draw the others nearer the Olds' level, at least. So we carried all the lead, and weighed the full 3400 pounds.

The Olds was on the 11th of 12 rows. On the pace lap, three turns before the start, a bright lemon Camaro moved from the last row to the ninth, which outraged me; such blatant cheating was shocking this time, since I was a victim.

Accelerating down the backstraight on the first lap, I passed two cars and gained on the bunch just ahead. The Olds clearly had horsepower on the back half of the field, or else I was less daunted by the drizzle than they were. On the second lap I passed two more cars, including the cheating Camaro, but gained six positions. The two Camaros that had tangled in Detroit were on the grass in separate turns, Patty Moise had pitted (later to christen her new Monte Carlo tail-first against a guardrail), and a fellow Cutlass dropped out.

Vicki Smith was the second car that I passed. She was hanging onto two other cars as they swept into the chicane. I followed them through the right-hander, and when they bottlenecked I ran up on them. I ducked around Vicki in the second left, squeezing outside of her and dropping a wheel off the track; we nudged, and the Olds carried away her tire marks on its left rear fender.

The Olds was sliding to the edge of the track a lot, which made some of the turns tight-ropish — there was a quick, blind left-hander that was especially heart-fluttering — and some of the second-gear turns were better taken in third; otherwise, the rain was no problem. But on the fourth lap, I skated off the track around the small sweeper that shovelled the cars at the start-finish line. Stones scattered as I raced along beside the front straight, edging back. Two cars passed — those two Camaros from Detroit, Bruce Nesbitt and Allan Chastain, regrouped already. I re-entered behind Chastain, an M.D. from Tennessee, and he went into the first turn too hot; he drifted wide, spun into the slick grass, and crashed after I passed. Nesbitt was already on his way through the field, leaving me by 100 yards a lap.

On the fifth lap my wipers stopped dead in their tracks. I'm afraid I'd been expecting it; they had faltered during the warmup. It wasn't Mike's fault; he didn't know that they had failed at Detroit. Riggins had told me he used wipers designed for bread trucks, available at your local auto parts store; now, at two races in a row, Tex's investment would bring him little return because of the same junk part.

The drizzle tapered to a mist for a few laps, as a brown film built up on my windshield, worsening when I approached another car. I couldn't pinpoint the apexes, but I could make out the white line at the inside edge of the track and tried to follow that, avoiding the "alligator teeth" — tiny speed bumps on the curb. With the track that slick, an untimely jounce could throw the car out of control.

Unfortunately, my clearest view was in the mirror, and there was #98. It had taken Vicki a few laps to catch up, but she didn't seem to be able to get any closer than about five car lengths. She lingered back there, her head riding low in the cockpit on her short frame; she looked like the child car thief she once had been. Her little head proclaimed that it was some silly girl I couldn't shake. I tried in vain not to look and hoped my crew was aware that the Olds was impaired.

She pulled closer, disappeared after a half-loop spin in the Keyhole, and six or seven laps later re-appeared in my mirror. Carter and Riggins, running one-two, arrived behind us, and Carter passed us both at the end of the backstraight. Vicki pulled out as if to outbrake me, and blocked Riggins. He had to follow her through the esses, while Carter escaped. I watched in the mirror, and knew there would be hell to pay. I made it easy for Riggins to get by me.

By the 20th of 31 laps I was 10th and Smith 11th. The drizzle had returned as rain, and my windshield was coated with brown slime. I couldn't see the white line anymore, and was driving down the middle of the road to avoid the edges, peering out the window in the blind left-hander, which was now a heart-thumper.

At least the engine hadn't been fluttering. The cool air probably helped, and the backstraight rpm's were lower because of the wet track. But then a solid misfire struck, at low rpm this time. I recognized the futility of pushing things and decided to merely hang on. The difference between 10th and whatever wasn't worth the risk of a spin. Survive and try to salvage the sponsorship deal on moral-victory grounds. I waved Vicki by, and other cars trickled past. The irony struck me: I wasn't trying to go as fast as I could now, I was trying to raise money. The object of the game had changed, and it stunk.

At the finish, I almost hit the flagman. They should warn people that he comes down out of his box and stands on the track to wave the checkered flag.

Carter, Riggins, Young and Overby. Smith finished 10th, first woman — give the girl an extra grand (she's gonna need it). Riggins said he was one turn away from tapping her into the bushes. I was 15th, and won $100 for Tex Enterprises, the first bacon I'd brought home.

"We'll gain on it; it just takes time," said my 21-year-old crew chief, the voice of experience and maturity.

I left before the end of the Lumbermens 6-Hour, won by Jim Trueman (he owned the track),Bobby Rahal, and the "otherwise unemployed" Doc Bundy, as the next *On Track* would say. It was Doc's first Camel GT win. Much of the race had been run in the steady rain. The Jaguar had crashed in traffic, head-on into a guardrail. The Nimrod — minus Robin Hamilton —also crashed. Nimrod Racing, Robin's dream, was dead.

Hagan and Felton took third overall, first GTO — and they nearly finished second. Felton had done two hero shifts when the conditions were at their worst. He was fast, consistent and brave, on a treacherous track. I doubt if even Doc would have suggested that the driving was the easy part this time.

* * *

I no longer simply wanted to race, what I wanted now was to succeed in the Kelly Series. Whether this was a welcome step away from idiocy —motivated by the challenge, not the sensation — or channeling deeper into it, I don't know. Professionally, such streamlined desire was a step in the right direction at least. And I do know that the only reason I entered the Longest Day of Nelson Ledges was to become a better driver, not to have fun. It was a good thing.

It's a long story. I was offered a ride in a new Renault Fuego Turbo which wasn't delivered on time, so the team — Yorkshire Motorsports out of Kenosha, Wisconsin — retrieved its five-year-old Mazda RX-3 from the weeds. Too bad the shock absorbers hadn't been buried back there. One of my codrivers had a light crash in the warmup, twisting the car's chassis just in time for the start. As the car was being frantically straightened, I stood on the grid waiting for it — 49 vehicles and 50 drivers. At least I had the white shoes. The car tugged on the pace lap, and fell on its face with a continuing carburetion problem when the flag dropped. "Shitbox" is the racing term for such vehicles.

The Mazda surged all day, but ran better as the air cooled, and except for another light crash, the night went okay. My second shift, a double one, began just before daybreak; a lovely orange sun rose over the backstraight.

In order to keep the engine from surging in the 90-mph Caroussel, you had to take it nearly flat, which meant flirting with the two big potholes, which were still there from last year. They'd been patched, but had thrown out their tarmac overnight. The second hole was about two feet square and God knows how deep, and located just outside the apex. There were a couple of ways to avoid it, but not if your foot was on the floor. I didn't really care about the time that would have been lost by being reasonable and lifting there. I merely refused to allow that shitbox to misfire on me.

I pitted for gas and went back out. The car was running relatively great; I was cutting 1:30s — almost as fast as my qualifying time, which had been fastest on the team and second in class. I clipped the Caroussel's pothole with the left rear tire, the car lurched sideways on its soggy shocks, slid into the dewy grass, grazed a stack of tires and tipped over on its roof. Hanging upside down was odd; I felt like an astronaut. I was too disgusted to get very excited.

Three hours later the Mazda was back at it, with chicken wire where the windshield used to be, a mashed roof, and weaving all over the track. The crowd — many young beer-drinkers on a summer solstice outing — had taken to the Mazda; to them, it was the ugly underdog that could, or something. We finished last, 353 laps behind the winners' factory Camaro Z-28 — the same car my Boss Mustang had been dicing with the previous year. It was a moral victory for my teammates, and Yorkshire Motorsports raised $2,800 for the Cystic Fibrosis Foundation. A few of the spectators that crowded around the car at the finish asked for a piece of it.

But I missed the pageantry. It wasn't a moral victory for me. All I'd seen was an uncompetitive car. And that the endurance pace was no longer comforting. Now it was frustrating.

I was better off than the old pirate, however. That Monday, John Paul, Sr. had his own longest day. He spent it in jail, after surrendering in St. Augustine. He said he hadn't known that he'd been wanted for the past month, but declined to say where he'd been. He appeared for his arraignment in handcuffs and leg irons, pleaded not guilty, and after 10 more days in jail was released on $500,000 bail.

Patty Moise visited the victory podium a lot, as first woman.

Bill Eppridge

Mark Yeager

She christened her new Monte Carlo against a guardrail.

Vicki's little head lingered in my mirror, and I hoped my crew could see that the Olds was impaired.

Craig Carter was making the superiority of the Peerless Camaro clear.

Chapter 17

Schulman Photography

Pedal to the Metal

J uly in Key West sizzled as always, and the heat lightning was a nightly show. When I wasn't transcribing tapes, I was usually under water — swimming a mile a day in the pool, snorkeling for lobster across the street. From the sea, Key West looks as if it's sinking.

I didn't know whether I was crazy for sleeping with DD, or for not. The reality that we were doomed as lovers was a fragile stone wall, like DD herself. It collapsed on my head when I tested it. But she was more tenacious than I, and more accustomed to such crashes. She said that our love wasn't a bad thing, like stealing; the difference was that you couldn't undo love. "You can't take it back," she said. "You can try and you can try and you can try, but you can't take it back. It's like trying to un-know something. It was there before we even met. You're the closest kind of love I could ever have to like loving a child."

So we slept alone, separated by a steamy 2 a.m. bicycle ride, which I was tempted to make so many times. And I did, on the nights when we were like the heat lightning. Do I need to say those nights were unforgettable?

We "dated" — DD thought it was romantic when the cavepersons picked bugs off each other and ate them, in "Quest for Fire." And we fought — we had a great one which started when she told me she had a terminal disease and I wouldn't believe her. She ripped my Marshall Teague T-shirt half-off (Marshall Teague was a factory Hudson driver in the early '50s, and Seymour — who else? — had given me the shirt) and knocked me half-out with a dictionary at her house, then tried to foil my getaway by chasing my pickup in her Mustang and cutting me off. It was just like her to take on a truck. I tapped her quarter panel, to let her know how foolish she was.

There were nights when I slunk around my apartment in the dark, so she wouldn't know I was home. Afraid of a 115-pound girl. But when DD was determined to "talk" there was no stopping her, and there was always trouble. It wasn't only me. She had a fight with her girlfriend Rhonda, who almost strangled her in the Pier House parking lot.

My snorkeling partner Jeffrey (he'd sailed the Atlantic solo) said that I should look at DD as if I'd simply messed up badly — hit the wall — and get on with the next race.

There were two of them coming up, on IMSA's second swing West: Sears Point in Northern California, and Portland, Oregon. But the team was still hanging on a decision from Miller. Committees. Miller had had the proposal since May, and it was dropping by $6,000 per race. "You haven't been a racedriver until you've grovelled in the mud for a sponsor," Rick Burton had said.

Two days before the car should have left for Sears Point, Tex called. Distress tends to show in his voice, more than his face. "We got a problem," he said. I was prepared for him to announce that we wouldn't be going West, but he said, "Billy wants to discontinue the program. He's decided it's just not in his best interest any more." It was a bad summer for the oil business. I asked if Vicki would be going West, and Tex said she would.

Maybe I shouldn't have been surprised. Our effort had foundered from the start. In four races, we'd crashed twice and blown two of Hagan's engines. The reason I had respected him in the first place was that he treated me like any other racer; now I was losing my ride for poor results. But he didn't own the Olds, and the program was self-supporting in tires, gas, oil and sheet metal. We weren't through yet, Tex said.

July 24. Sears Point. While trying to take the lead in the big slow bend by the main grandstand, Overby punted Riggins off the track and went off himself. Three laps later they were together again, and Overby tried the same pass in the same place. Riggins let him by on the inside, then dove down and speared the Buick's passenger door as they came out of the turn. Corner workers commented on Riggins' perfect execution, and reported that smoke had poured off his tires as Overby was being pushed to the wall. Riggins said their bumpers had locked.

The finish was Carter, Young, Riggins. There were only 11 cars in the field because most of the V-8 Camaro teams were on strike; they wanted bigger carburetors. Vicki finished 11th, a lap behind, with mechanical problems.

Holbert and Trueman won the Ford California Camel GT. All the Ford bigwigs were there — they'd flown from Detroit in the company jet. But they had no car to cheer for. Bruce Jenner had stuffed the factory Mustang into a bank on Press Day, wiping it out.

July 31. Portland. Carter, Riggins and Patty Moise, who beat Young in another fender fight; cheers from the female fans. Eight cars finished. Vicki was sixth, two laps down, with mechanical problems.

Holbert won the G.I. Joe's Gran Prix 3-Hour driving solo on a staggeringly hot day, and clinched the Camel GT championship. He stayed in his 125-degree cockpit for 152 laps, with his life depending on his strength, coordination, reactions and concentration. Afterward, he calmly defied anyone to suggest that racedrivers weren't athletes. People sometimes think that, because it's the car that does the running, and because racers aren't very good at ballgames. Doc had been suited up in the pits to relieve Al. "Simply another redundancy," *On Track* would say.

Rick Burton called with the bad news from Miller. The rejection was official. The race at Elkhart Lake — Road America, my favorite circuit —was in 10 days. Without sponsorship, our chances of making it seemed nonexistent. I talked myself into not caring.

It was a relief. I wasn't an idiot. I loved going fast no less, but that wasn't "racedriving" any more than mountain climbing was lunch on the summit. It wasn't worth it, because of all the *bull*shit. Then Tex called.

He wasn't ready to throw in the towel. He'd talked to Tom Erb, who wasn't ready either. Erb offered Tex Enterprises a development job worth $3,000. Our factory support was there when we needed it most. And I was moved by Tex's faith in me.

I thanked Tex by firing him. I knew I'd been hoarding the $2,000 payoff from the Pro-Celebrity race for something, and now I'd found it. I hired Mike to be my crew chief, at $500 per race. Tex was spread too thin. All three of us thought it was a good idea. And Mike could use the money on his Darlington Dash program.

Rick Burton hadn't given up, either; he was trying to get us $2,000 from a Wisconsin Miller distributor. But even that small deal faced corporate bureaucracy. And he said the distributor might want us to display the car somewhere. I hoped that didn't mean a party.

It was a new me on Press Day at Elkhart. I wore my favorite Hawaiian shirt — Seymour would have approved — and cracked jokes like a stand-up comic. I smuggled some charcoal-grilled steaks out of the press lunch for my crew: Mike, Keith and ever-willing Jeffrey — with Terry, Tim and Yogi lending a hand when we needed one. My plan was to abstain from worrying about anything but the moment on the track, and barely even that. Since I wasn't an idiot, I was unburdened by the desire to drive, which freed me to enjoy the pageantry of the act. Zen driving, I guess, although I hardly looked at it that way. To me, it was just letting the Olds rip.

Also, I was enormously relieved to discover that I had a story; the tapes had revealed what I'd been too single-minded to see. There was no telling how much pressure the journalist's hat had added; overall it was an advantage, but it brought a few chicanes, not the least of which were a deadline and a satisfactory ending.

Our 358 cubic-inch engine had been touched-up since Mid-Ohio, where the problem was a broken rocker-arm stud — improper assembly, said Mike. Keith said that it was stouter than ever. "I'm gonna tell you whut," he said. "Shake the ground, when you crank that sucker up." He was right; it boomed and cracked. The Olds was the beefiest and best-sounding Kelly car out there. I was biased, of course.

But on its first lap, it went *blddppp* all the way around the track. We changed the distributor during the session. In the next session it did the same thing; we changed the battery, which didn't help either. Then Keith found two spark plug wires that he had crossed, and the engine exploded to life for the remaining laps. "It's pretty embarrassing," admitted Mike, "but I'm just as guilty a dog as him. Basic rule of trouble-shooting is check the simplest things first, which we didn't do."

In the final session the motor fluttered and the rear wheels chattered. Mike suspected that the flutter was caused by a low fuel level, and, as far as I still knew, the chatter — back again from Mid-Ohio — was because my braking was crude.

Another day lost. But it didn't bother the new me; emotion wouldn't get the practice time back. And it kept my string alive: Since I'd turned "pro" at the Daytona Finale nine months earlier, I hadn't had the opportunity to drive one lap — in practice, qualifying or a race — without something significantly wrong with the car. *Any* car (except maybe Old Reliable).

When I'd raced the Barber Formula Fords at Elkhart Lake, only two of the circuit's 4.0 miles were used, so now there was more pretty scenery. Mario Andretti believes Road America is the best circuit in the country, and I would second that. Besides having beautifully maintained grounds, the track itself was fast, smooth and straightforward. It was by no means easy, but there were no tricks; the car was not required to do pirouettes or change direction in the middle of a turn. Plain old hardball, which was the Olds' best game.

There were three straights, all of them in the 165-mph neighborhood. The Olds loved that part; the problem was getting slowed down for the turns at the end of those straights. Turn 1 was a broad right-hander after the front straight, about half a mile past the start-finish line; you barrelled into it at about 90 — there was a great view of the cars ahead of you — and came out at 100. Turn 5 was a merciless 40-mph left, arriving at the bottom of a long hill called Moraine Sweep. The hill was gentle to the foot, but storming down it flat-out in a stock car, you could feel the momentum in your bones. Turn 12 was called Canada Corner, and its entrance was as slow as Turn 5, but the exit was faster. It followed the back-straight, which wound through woodsy Kettle Bottoms. Potentially, the backstraight was the fastest of the three straights; if you hung it out in the wavy Caroussel and took the kink perfectly, you might touch 170 just before you had to brake to 40 for Canada Corner, deep in the trees.

At the end of the day, I called Rick Burton. The distributor wasn't interested, but Burton said that Tex had agreed to keep the Miller colors on the car anyhow. I called Tex, who said it was Tom Erb's idea. Erb probably thought it would appear more professional, and he was right, corporation-to-corporation. But I was no idiot; it wasn't a distinction to me to drive a billboard for free. I'd actually been looking forward to stripping off the decals and driving the old refrigerator again. However, I didn't mind sponsoring Miller for this race.

The distributor had offered 10 cases of beer, however, and Burton would send some "Miller Time" shirts for the crew. I politely accepted the shirts knowing I'd tell the crew not to wear them. The beer, we would gladly drink.

I sat down and cheerfully cut the eight "Miller Times" off my driving suit.

The crew's motel was 45 miles away. I hadn't reserved a room, partly because I hadn't expected to be there, and partly because I wanted to unburden myself of that, too — it makes me feel free to not know where my next bed is coming from. Accommodations are a problem at Elkhart because it's country, but a nearby college rented its summer-vacant dormitory rooms, and I was asleep before my crew had gotten to their motel. A poster of Tanya Roberts over the bunk kept me warm.

Our first practice was at 9:15 a.m., and at 9:05 — I wasn't suited up, this time — the truck arrived, tailing Tex's Doolie. My crew had gotten hooked up with Tex for breakfast, and I could tell that Mike regretted it too. But they got the car ready in five minutes; they were getting pretty good at it.

The hop at the rear wheels was worse than ever. I tried to control it by modulating the brake pedal at the brink of chatter, but I wasn't always successful, and once the hopping started it didn't even help to release the brakes altogether. A couple of times I found myself sitting there with both feet raised, as if the janitor's broom were sweeping by, while the car shuddered toward a 40-mph turn at about 100. I could have braked early and gently, of course, but that ain't racin'. The problem only lasted for the first few laps, however. When the water-injection valve got plugged and the brakes boiled, I coudn't have made the wheels hop if I'd tried. For the rest of the session, I cruised and enjoyed the ride.

The inconsistent brakes had made it difficult to tell if the gearing was right. "Right" is when you hit redline in top gear at the end of the fastest straight. But I hadn't been looking at the tach because I couldn't afford to miss my braking point by so much as a foot. Steve Pope thought that was funny. He was there still scouting, hoping and looking for rides.

When the lap times from the session were posted, I was surprised to see myself eighth. In the afternoon session the track slowed down because the heat made it greasy — it was 98 degrees in Milwaukee, the hottest August 19 in history here. I lost 1.5 seconds, but gained a spot to seventh fastest.

But the flutter had returned. Evidence suggested fuel starvation, since it only happened when the gas level dropped. And because it occurred at the same spot every lap — just after the kink, through Kettle Bottoms — it seemed to have something to do with centrifugal force, the gas rolling like a wave in the tank. Or maybe like my constant floorboard companion, the black blob.

The car's weaknesses forced things out of me. My footwork in particular was rapidly improving. I got more delicate with the brake pedal, and could keep the rear wheels on the ground if I exaggerated the throttle blip when I downshifted (which helped match the rotating speed of the gearbox shaft to the engine's crankshaft, smoothing the transition at the rear wheels when the clutch was released). But a big blip required a big pivot in my right ankle, which rubbed a big raw spot onto my calf, where it touched the edge of the square hump over the transmission. Delicately modulating the brakes wasn't using them fully, and the big blips slowed shifting, so dealing with the problem cost time; but it was smoother, faster and easier on the car than wheel hop.

In the ripply Caroussel — Elkhart's only unsmooth turn — the Olds' tail twitched at 90 miles an hour, but I kind of liked that. The car pushed in some of the turns — once right off the track in Turn 5, the greasiest. And it was loose in some others, but at least the two conditions never occurred in the same corner. That was because the turns were all constant-radius, although I didn't realize it was that simple at the time. And — to borrow a phrase from Felton — the handling seemed neutral where it mattered. I had no complaints for Mike, and we wouldn't make a single suspension change.

My attitude remained unaffected by the ongoing mechanical problems. By the end of the day I was still smiling, forgetting the past, not dwelling on the future, and focussing on the fun. And our beer arrived! Miller Time! A Miller High Life delivery truck transferred its payload to the big black Johnny Wheeler Enterprises Special — more stuff for Fibber McGee's closet. Mechanics love a driver who has a beer sponsorship.

That evening, I crashed something new: a private Ford barbecue. The Ford bigwigs were out in force again, since this race debuted the new Ford prototype, the highest-tech racecar in history. The affair was held at Schwartz Hotel, a rustic old resort on Elkhart Lake itself. Since I couldn't get through the front door without an invitation, I swam over from the public beach on the proles' side of the lake. Steve Pope started out with me, but got cold feet. I waded out of the water in the hazy dusk hoping I looked like a sea creature, walked up to Ford's racing manager, and drippingly announced my arrival.

I was welcomed with a chuckle, and served a great steak. Then a belly dancer put a cup of beer on my head and her breasts around my nose while she undulated, and I proved my power of concentration by staying dry. I wouldn't undulate with her, however; I wasn't that much of a new me. I didn't even get bored when a PR man at the table babbled on about how wonderful Bruce Jenner was, although I did start to get chilly. When it was time to leave I waded back into the lake and swam off into the blackness toward the lights across the water.

I liked the atmosphere back at the dorm, too: Bellying up to the sink in the morning, brushing my teeth next to Elliott Forbes Robinson — generally known simply as EFR — who had edged Doc for the Trans-Am championship the previous year, and who also liked Hawaiian shirts.

Qualifying and the race were both on Saturday. As I drove through Road America's gates, I had a small premonition that things would go well. I set it aside, acutely aware that racing can bite you in the back real fast. Even Bruce Jenner knows that.

Billy Cook, the Kelly Series' flamboyant technical inspector whose roots — like the Olds' — were in Southern stock car racing, had reminded us that there was a rule requiring the hood to bear lettering indicating engine displacement. So I'd bought some black mailbox numbers: 3's, 0's, and 5's. Now the hood displayed "305 cu. in." And Mike had done his part in the strategem: Back in the shop, he'd fabricated a hollow black tube that looked like a bazooka, which was bolted to the floor at the base of the passenger door and marked "140#." It even fooled me. Our real lead was in the truck. The Olds weighed 3100 pounds, which was 300 less than required with the 358 engine. I had no problem justifying it. We would have been legal had we been able to afford it.

For qualifying, we borrowed a pair of stiffer rear shock absorbers from Paul Gentilozzi. They completely cured the chatter. I was as glad that the problem hadn't been me as I was that it had been solved. And Mike had switched the fuel line from the tank's right side to the left, which almost erased the flutter. For the first two laps of qualifying I seated new brake pads and scuffed new tires. I took a third lap to seat myself and went for it on the fourth. It must have been a good one, because I remember no untoward thrills. I kept flying into the fifth, but the oil flag was waving in Canada Corner and I backed off thinking there was trouble there, which ruined the lap. But the flag was out all over the course, to inform the drivers that the road was greasy. Thanks. Then the brakes went away — the right line melted and the left valve got plugged. I pitted to cool them, and tried to go back out for a final blazing lap, but the starter was dead. My three crewmen pushed, but pit row was uphill so they didn't get very far. They then pushed it backward — embarrassing — and I caught the Olds in reverse. I drove off intending to banzai, but the checkered flag fell.

But I'd broken my record, although "spell" might be a better word. I'd gotten one hot lap with everything working on the car.

Steve Pope had been spotting for me, in Turns 1 and 5. He said my right front wheel never touched the ground in Turn 1, drifting through at 95; yet the Olds hadn't even felt as if it were pushing there. And he said four cars looked good in Turn 5: Carter, Riggins, Overby and me. Yogi and Hagan had also been watching there, on a broad grassy slope that was a popular vantage point, and they said I was going in as deep as anyone. I'd thought I was braking too early.

No one watched me in the kink — the private challenge — but I knew I was taking it well. Back off at 120, then punch it at the turning point and remember Doc's driving secret: Let the car do what it wants. The Olds wanted to rip. "If you don't scare yourself half silly then you ain't doin' it right," Felton had said of the kink, and I knew what he meant.

In the paddock after qualifying, a guy walked up, looked at the Olds, then at me, and asked, "You drive that thing?"

I nodded.

He said, "You get right with it," and walked on. The simplicity of the compliment somehow made it special, and the fact that my style was conspicuous was gratifying.

I hadn't expected my position from practice to hold up, since some fast guys had had problems. My time of 2:30.1 was 10th out of 31. Carter was on the pole with a record 2:24.6, 99.6 mph, with Overby and Riggins next. Vicki was 23rd, at 2:40.1. Her Camaro had been repainted and looked terrific: a rich red and black where the purple and gold had been. Around her name on the door was pin striping, reminiscent of chicken scratching.

The heat wave was lingering; some drivers said they had never seen Road America slicker. But the temperature was fine by me, a day like any other in Key West. About an hour before the start I lay down in the shady grass under the truck, and dozed off long enough to have a dream about hardboiled eggs — a step in the right direction, I suppose.

Just before the start, Tex came over — our paddock space was about 100 yards from the Camaro's, which created an independence I liked. He said, "I thought you might like to know that IMSA has misplaced the gauge they use to measure engine displacement, so they can't tear anybody down." He was right, I did.

On the grid, my butterflies flapped more than usual — subliminally afraid my premonition would be wrong. My grid position was especially potentially hazardous. On my right was Patty Moise, who was clean and safe, but behind us were Bluto Bob Penrod and Charles Pelz, a laid-back fast-guy Texan who drove a battered bronze-and-yellow Buick Skylark sideways. Behind them were Dr. Chastain and Flash Flatt, the Zoomin' Human. Among us, the toll of sheetmetal recently had been heavy.

I'm too impatient to enjoy the pageantry of pace laps; all I want to do is get the show on the road. You're supposed to swerve the car around to warm up the tires but I hated the chore; it interrupted the calm I would have liked, the poise before the start. Cars snake individually, out of sync, and in my worst fears I imagined crashing into someone who was swerving right while I was swerving left — it wouldn't be hard to do, and I suspect other drivers have that hidden fear too. But the neat thing about the pace lap is that you can check out the crowd. As the field wobbled down Moraine Sweep and into Turn 5, I looked up at the grassy slope on the right, which was coated with fans and patched with the colored canopies of sponsors' hospitality tents.

The dropping of the flag was a cue for my motor to misfire. In front of me was a jet black Cutlass that had been especially quick at Detroit, and it ran off. Moise's hot Monte Carlo outdragged the sputtering Olds, and Pelz, a silver fox, got a strong start and passed on the right. At the end of the first lap I was 11th.

On the second lap the motor cleared up; that had never happened before. Near the bottom of Moraine Sweep there was a bunch of cars ahead, lined up single-file and beginning to brake for Turn 5. It seemed too soon to back off, so I shot down the inside at 165, with no particular plan for how to get back in line and in position for the turn; I couldn't see the head of the line anyhow. I only knew that if I waited for my turn, I'd be missing an opportunity.

From here on, everything I report is reconstructed, including the incidents involving myself. What went into the tape recorder was all wrong; my recollections were vague, their chronology confused, and some of them missing altogether.

Immediately ahead of me was Clay Young, who had dropped from sixth, then Charles Pelz, Dick Danielson, driving a Camaro that Patty Moise had half-seriously suggested was a 454 because of its straightaway speed, and Moise. After I'd pulled out and saw in my peripheral vision how tight the line was, I realized that I was committed to passing the whole thing. I zoomed by Young as I stomped on the brakes, rubbed Pelz as I downshifted into third, banked off Danielson and knocked his fender flares skyward over both Pelz's and Young's roofs, then dropped it into second and bumped Moise from behind, just before the turning point. I dove straight for the apex as if everything were under control, which it seemed to be. I'd slowed exactly the right amount to get through the turn, no problem. The spectators on the hill were howling in appreciation. At the end of lap two I was eighth, chasing Moise.

When I saw her brake lights flash before Turn 7, I knew I'd soon have her. The turn was a quick sweep right that headed into a stretch called Hurry Downs, and I loved it. Just a rhythmic light lift of the throttle and an abrupt but easy twist of the steering wheel, and if you started six inches from the left edge of the road and hit the turning point perfectly, the right front wheel would nip the rounded curb at the apex — hell, mine might have lifted over it. I can feel it now; I want more. I passed Patty on the next lap going into Turn 6, and got my breathing room in 7 again.

On the fifth lap the black Cutlass, driven by Roy Stamey — he gets right with it — was off the road in Canada Corner, and I was sixth.

But my brakes were fading already, and when they started to fade, they always faded fast. Stamey repassed me into Turn 1, but then he pushed off the outside of slimy Turn 5, and I followed him into the dirt. It was the magnet phenomenon: If you watch the guy in front of you, you go where he goes. That's one reason you race the road, not the other cars. I knew I'd suckered myself off the track, and it was exasperating; I hadn't even been going too fast for the turn. Pelz and Young passed, and I got back on the track ahead of Moise. Danielson had already blown his hot engine.

The five of us — Pelz, Stamey, Young, me, Moise — sped along Hurry Downs toward Turn 8, a second-gear left-hander before the Caroussel. Young, whose Firebird's brakes were also failing, bumped Stamey and knocked him off the end of the turn, sliding into the grass himself about 100 feet farther on. It was a golden opportunity dropped in my lap. But Stamey's front wheels were on the track and pointed across my path, and I backed off and cut my wheels to avoid the spot where I was afraid he might go. I should have punched it. That wrong move threw the Olds around in a tight 180, and I couldn't believe I'd blown it. Moise weaved through the three of us, hot on Pelz's heels. I jammed it into first gear, cut a screeching U-turn and peeled off toward the Caroussel, trying to beat Young and Stamey from the scene. They were both pulling back onto the track, with Young on the pole because he'd spun the farthest. They each blasted out of the dirt, and Young must have been behind a mound because his red Firebird flew about three feet in the air streaming clumps of red dirt, and landed in the middle of the track — "Dukes of Hazzard" sign the boy up. I almost laughed out loud. Into the Caroussel we were nose-to-tail again, but Stamey was now in the middle. Lap times would reveal — amazingly — that the entire incident had taken just five seconds.

Since I wasn't using the brakes for the kink, their absence was no loss there. But Young slowed down way before it, which surprised me. Stamey slowed with him, and my foot stabbed the brake pedal, which responded with a clank. I creamed the trunk of the black Cutlass — it was a factory Oldsmobile, too — at about 110 miles an hour, with my foot on the floor of the empty brake pedal.

Between the kink and the start-finish line, Moise passed Pelz and Stamey passed Young. After six laps I was 10th again, back where I started, and the five of us were still together.

On the seventh lap, in Turn 5 again, Pelz knocked Moise into the marbles; she got her picture in *National Speed Sport News*, sideways on the track with Pelz, Stamey, Young and me in there as extras, passing through. Stamey had to brake to miss her and was passed by Young. We got as far as Canada Corner without further incident, but there, Young pushed off the outside; Stamey was smart enough not to follow, but that big magnet behind the grille of the Olds drew me off the track with Young. I ended up perpendicular to the road, the Olds' front wheels on the track in the line out of the turn. Bob Penrod skimmed by, nearly hitting me, followed by a Mustang. Moise had spun yet again, and never came; her brakes were also boiling, and she had chosen to back off. I beat Young back onto the track. He would retire three laps and two more spins later, out of power. His list of mechanical woes had doubtless been long.

After seven laps, I was still 10th.

Worried that my radiator had been pierced by Stamey's bumper, my eyes had been bouncing like a dribbled basketball between the track and the gauges. But the temperatures were steady: water at 220 and oil at 270. That might be alarming to some racers — it was redline — but I was used to it by now.

I was really getting into it now, and had no intention of allowing anybody new to stay ahead of me. I repassed the Mustang using horsepower and a draft down the front straight, which goes through a deep dip before the finish line. Penrod was about 100 yards ahead, and beyond him was Stamey, whose Cutlass was smoking — he'd been getting the black flag, but was probably mad and ignoring it. As Stamey went into Turn 1 on the ninth lap, his car began wobbling as if it were on the pace lap; Penrod scooted by as pieces flew off the Cutlass, scattering jetsam for me to dodge. His right rear tire had shredded; either Young or I had bent his fender into it. The next time around, his car was parked beside the track and he was standing beside it. My peek was brief, as was my wondering if he were giving me the evil eye.

I came off the final turn of the 10th lap on Penrod's tail, rode his bumper past the pits thinking that it probably looked good to my crew, and pulled out to pass just before the braking point for Turn 1, knowing that the move might be futile because he should have been able to outbrake me.

Since Detroit, I'd been considering attempting to pump the brake for the first couple of times with my left foot, in order to keep my right foot on the gas pedal for another second. But then I'd have to shuffle the left foot to the clutch as half of the right foot went to the brake, and the other half blipped the throttle during the downshift. I hadn't experimented with it because I'd been afraid I'd get my feet in a needless tangle. But now, with Penrod so near, this seemed to be the time to try my shuffle, if I were really daring. Then again, that sort of move was either the kind of thing you'd only try in a pressure situation, or the kind of thing you should never try for the first time in a pressure situation. In any event, I didn't try it. Instead, I slammed a cruel downshift into third — thank heaven for Keith's stout tranny — braked as hard as was necessary but as lightly as was possible, and Penrod didn't come back at me. I was back up to seventh at the end of the lap.

On the next lap the fourth-place Irv Hoerr dropped out, and Pelz was creeping around Canada Corner on a flat tire. Suddenly I was fifth, with four laps remaining.

But Penrod hadn't gone away. The Olds was lighter than it had ever been, but the engine had lost something since Detroit. Bluto's Monte Carlo was a match for the Olds this time; who knows what was under his hood. He tailed me through the trees at Kettle Bottoms — the Olds still fluttered there, but lightly — and as Canada Corner approached I thought, "How am I ever going to get this thing stopped and still keep him back there?" All I could do was pump clank-clank and downshift like crazy. He mashed his front bumper against my rear, and accelerated as we went through the turn. I don't know if he was trying to push me off or if I'd merely gotten in the way of his momentum, but I lifted my foot off the gas and let him push; I was afraid that if I gave myself any momentum of my own, I'd be bulldozed into the woods.

As we accelerated up the slight hill they call Thunder Valley, he pulled out and got beside me entering the quick blind left-hander where Jerry Titus, a writer/racer who had quit writing for racing, had been killed in 1970. We went into the turn abreast, but I had the inside line; Bluto was on the scary side. I made sure that I went in deeper and hogged most — but not all — of the track coming out. He backed off, and the position was mine. Maybe he hadn't trusted me, or maybe he thought he could pass somewhere else. As we left the turn behind, I glanced in my mirror and watched him kick up a cloud of dust at the edge of the track. He would get ragged two or three more times as he chased the Olds, which pulled away.

Pit signals never mattered very much to me; I was always so far behind that WFO was the only strategy worth employing. But I'd asked Mike to hold up a board indicating the last lap, and when I saw "SAM LAST LAP" I had about 75 yards on Penrod. I told myself not to do anything stupid. At the bottom of Moraine Sweep sat Jerry Thompson's Camaro, which I figured must have been ahead of me; he was a fast guy with 22 years experience. I took the checkered flag knowing the finish had been good, but with only a rough idea of my position.

On the cooloff lap, I did something stupid — spun out in Turn 3. I'd been trying to reset the tach, because the telltale had somehow gotten to 8600 — probably during a big blip — and I didn't want Mike to know. I was reaching across the instrument panel to put my finger in the little hole over the button, wasn't watching where I was going, got into the marbles and ran off the track.

I pulled up to our pit, and Tex leaned in the passenger window; he looked flushed with excitement, and wore a Texas-sized grin. "You had these boys jumpin' up and down," he said. I think I shouted something back about it being the most fun I'd ever had in my life. I drove back to the paddock feeling exhilarated and exonerated — heroic, even — although *On Track* would say the bunch of us were like a parade of Keystone Kops.

At that moment, the most satisfying thing about the race was that I'd justified Tex's faith in me. He had stretched to get us there, and I was glad I'd delivered. Our take was $1300.

And 10 cases of beer. I grabbed a cold one out of the cooler, chugged about three-fourths of it, crushed the gold can in my hand, and threw it spinning and raining across the paddock. Miller Time. "Damn sure gave them their 10 goddamn cases worth," I spit out, mostly to myself. I think the Miller rejection had inspired me more than I realized.

Felton came over, grinning, and said, "This ain't a dirt track, boy." He shook my hand and said I'd done a good job. He and Hagan had been watching from the hillside by Turn 5 on the second lap. "You were running down the inside with too much steam, so you banked off them to get around the turn. That's the way to do it. You showed me something there." He said I never would have made it if there hadn't been some cars to hit. I hadn't thought it was that close, myself.

He looked at the smashed grille and said, "How did that

happen?" I told him, adding, "Maybe I ought to go over and say something to Stamey."

"Do you know Stamey?" he asked. I said I didn't — all I knew was that he was pretty big — and Felton said, "I think maybe you ought to wait a while, if you're going to go over there." He jerked his head toward burly Keith and added, "And I think you ought to keep your boys around you for a while."

The left half of the grille was gone, mashed and jagged around the edges. The left front fender, where it had once been so nicely flared by Tim, was wrinkled and pressed against the edge of the tire, which had red and white paint streaks on it. The right front fender was also crumpled; that must have been from Pelz and Danielson. There was another dent and more tire marks over the right rear fender. The right side of the rear bumper was bashed; that was from Penrod. And smack in the center of the driver's door, over the big red #44, was a black semi-circle. That was an interesting mystery. I had no recollection of anyone's tire rubbing there, inches from my elbow.

By all rights I should have had two flat tires, since both front fenders were grazing them. And I was lucky that the oil cooler, mounted behind the left headlight frame, wasn't punctured; crunched metal pressed sharply against it, but the core had been spared. Actually the new hole had probably helped cool the engine.

The consistency of my lap times impressed even me. The fastest lap was the fourth, at 2:32.9; the last four were 2:36, 35.2, 35.8, and 35.2. The shortage of brakes had only slowed me by about three seconds a lap.

Billy Cook came up paddock road, handing out result sheets. There had been so much confusion that we weren't certain where we had finished, until we read it on the official scorecard: Carter, Riggins, Overby, Moses. It gave me goosebumps. I was the sole survivor of what must have been the wildest Kelly race for sixth place ever. I was the lucky one; no one had run into me.

The Peerless Camaro had run away with the race; it was Carter's fourth consecutive win, and clinched his defense of the KellyChampionship.

Billy Cook came back a few minutes later, and I thought, "Uh-oh," as I watched him stride purposefully toward the Olds. "Is it good news or bad news?" I asked, holding my breath but trying not to show it. "Well, neither," he said, in his thick backwoods Georgia accent and throaty-squeaky voice. "I've just gotta check and make

sure of one thing, got to confirm this: Your engine *is* a 305, isn't it?"
I immediately thought of IMSA's missing gauge, and spied Mike
out of the corner of my eye; he looked as if he suddenly needed to
check a plug or something, but loitered to eavesdrop. The lie came
through my teeth without hesitation. "Yep," I said. Then I com-
pounded it.

"I gotta admit we were tempted to use a bigger motor, but we
figured it wasn't worth the risk because we couldn't afford to have
you catch us," I said. "It would have been too embarrassing with
Miller involved, and all."

He said, "Okay, that's all I needed to hear. But if I tear you down
at Pocono, am I gonna find a 305?"

"Yep," I lied again.

It's how the game is played. He was getting me to commit to the
deception. It was also a word to the wise: If you're gonna start
runnin' up front, be prepared to be torn down.

But he'd caught my conscience off guard. I'd had no choice but to
lie, of course, but it was a consequence I hadn't considered. I didn't
like it. Cheating is one thing; but they're not supposed to ask you
straight-up if you're doing it.

We loaded the Olds on the trailer, and got it out of there fast. The
boys headed back to Ether and I sped off on another post-race dash
to the airport, headed home via Milwaukee and Memphis. I
considered staying for the Budweiser 500 on Sunday (the Ford
prototype would win its debut in a downpour, and never win
again), but I knew that my only reason for staying would be to
savor the glory and hear the compliments, and I decided that my
ego would be healthier if I didn't pander to it; besides, it was only
fourth place, and inherited. And how would I feel if there were no
compliments? But I should have stayed. After a year of failures
and frustration, I might have treated myself to a few strokes. All I
had in Key West were the lobsters.

I made a dumb wrong turn on the interstate and had to drive 15
extra miles, which was enough to have missed the plane. But I'd
also misread the departure time on the ticket, by 15 minutes. I
made the flight with five minutes to spare. If there's ever been a
day on which I could do no wrong, that was it.

Bill Eppridge

For the trip West,
Vicki slipped under
Hagan's wing.

Peter Gloede

Moise, Moses, Danielson, Pelz and Young thunder down Moraine Sweep.

Mark Yeager

Clay Young winds
his sleek Firebird
through Woodsy
Kettle Bottoms.

Mark Yeager

Charles Pelz, a laid-back fast-guy Texan who drove his battered Buick Skylark sideways.

How dare they say we looked like Keystone Kops.

R.T. Patterson

The Olds' finest hour.

Peter Gloede

Chapter 18

Greg Patton

Bandits, But Still Bugaboos

S ummer vacation was ending, so DD had had to move out of her condo to make way for the college girl whose parents owned it. She'd gotten a new home and a new job in one stroke: She became manager of a small clothing store on Duval Street, and moved into a lovely old Conch house on William Street owned by the same woman who owned the clothing store, and who wasn't in town very much since she owned a fancier store in Tampa and managed that one herself.

A black daytime maid came with the house, and DD and Julia became fast friends with a shared irreverence. Julia called her owner "Miz Liz," as in Liz Taylor; DD liked to say that Miz Liz treated them both like niggers, and Julia got a kick out of that.

DD's first act as manager was to hire her girlfriend Rhonda. Rhonda hung out at the house too, and they were some trio: Julia who looked like Aunt Jemima, Rhonda the six-foot redhead, and DD the Classic Underachiever of Dubious Sanity. Whenever Miz Liz was in town she was woefully out-horsepowered in her own house by her sassy staff. "Yez, Miz Liz," went their sniggering chorus to their employer's commands. It was just like old times, when young DD had spied over the wall on Tennessee Williams with her giggling girlfriends. They even recruited Miz Liz's 14-year-old son, which added a bit of bass to the chorus.

The house on William Street was rich in character (there was a small jungle out back), knee-keep in legend (supposedly Jimmy Buffett had once roomed there), high in real estate value (it was nicely restored, and if you want to drop a quick quarter mil, pick up a quaint little restored Conch house in Key West's Old Town), and sometimes other-worldly — it was lightly haunted. Footfalls, clinking dishes and vague music in the walls were the extent of it. Julia always split when it started up — she said she didn't cotton to no spooks — but DD liked the company since she spent most nights alone there. She'd press her ear to the wall to see if the spooks liked Jackson Browne, too. But when she got that close, there was static.

DD's upstairs bedroom faced William Street, whch gave her a window on weird Key West life. Across the street was another restored Conch house, which was a fat farm during the day. Rich fat ladies began arriving at 7 a.m., and went straight into a stretching and gabbing routine on the porch, which usually woke DD up even though she slept with earplugs. She said they'd stand there lifting one leg like flamingoes, whooping and cooing to each other about how much weight they'd lost since yesterday. One morning she yelled down, "You might not be as fat, but you're still loud and obnoxious!" and slammed her window shut.

She had another light crash in her Mustang. She was turning onto Duval Street when a bicyclist popped into the crosswalk. DD slammed on her brakes and stopped in time, but the woman on the bike started yelling at her. When she said, "You can't do that!" DD said, "Yes I can, I have the car," and drove on, accidently knocking the bike, and the girl, over. That evening, the sheriff showed up at DD's parents' house up the Keys, looking for her. DD was frantic when she called me. "Please don't let them put me in that locked-up place," she pleaded. I hid her in Southernmost Condo that night, aiding and abetting the fugitive, and if anyone had come for her I would have fought them to the death. She saw her father's lawyer in the morning, and the police didn't do anything because they knew the victim, who made a living suing people. The tap had been so light that the bike didn't have a scratch, and the girl had probably laid down beside it in quick calculation. DD's sparks; they have a way of drawing these loonies. Yes, I know.

The incident became a joke between us, which I used against her. Whenever DD would say to me, "You can't do that!" I'd smile and reply, "Yes I can, I have the car."

* * *

Over Labor Day weekend, I travelled to Quebec for a story on Willy T. Ribbs, America's only black fast guy, who was racing in a Trans-Am through the streets of Trois-Rivieres. Ribbs (formerly plain old "Bill," but he'd changed his name to be more promotable) had won three Trans-Ams and was second in points. He'd been racing for seven years, but most of that time he was a plumber. His idol — and pal — was Muhammad Ali, and he was sometimes as cocky as Cassius Clay; he worked out at Joe Louis Memorial Gym in Santa Monica under Ali's former trainer, Bundini Brown. "Hey, I skip rope for a reason," he said, the reason being to quicken his footwork. His car owner admitted that he'd hired Ribbs because he thought a black driver might get him a sponsor — and it did, in Budweiser. He admitted he was pleasantly surprised to discover Ribbs could drive like that.

The Pocono Kelly race was the next weekend, and again, I didn't think we'd be going; the breakthrough at Elkhart — to borrow Doc's assessment of such accomplishments — had guaranteed us diddly for the next race. But then, in my office in New York that Tuesday, I got a call from Bill Brodrick. As of yesterday, I was a Skoal Bandit.

The Southern 500 at Darlington had been run the previous day, Labor Day. Before the start of the race, on pit row, Brodrick had approached Louis Bantle, president of U.S. Tobacco, and told him our sob story. I don't know if it had been news to Bantle or not; six weeks earlier, Steve Goldberg, my quasi-agent, had sent Bantle a sponsorship proposal (in the letter he called Miller "a notorious purveyor of promotional one-night stands"). But we'd gotten no reply, and had no idea whether or not Bantle had even read it, since he gets a jillion proposals a week from racers, who all want a piece of the pie, as Brodrick says. Brodrick told Bantle that all we needed was $10,000 to finish the season — two more races. Bantle replied, "Why not? I can authorize that." Just like that. In the end, it's who you know.

Brodrick's call to me was his second that morning; he'd already told Tex to get the car painted right away. Mike scratched his Darlington Dash race for that weekend, and by Wednesday evening the Skoal Bandit Oldsmobile was on its way to Pocono. "You sure got these boys pumped up around here," Tex said, the compliment a tiny treasure.

Wednesday afternoon at the track, I caught the final hours of the Bertil Roos School of Motor Racing. Roos was a wild-eyed unorthodox Swede, an active driver respected for his speed and car control; he'd just clinched the Can-Am Series' under-two-liter championship. I drove a teaching-aid contraption that he'd invented and named the "Slide Car." It was a Saab fitted with a rear axle that allowed the rear wheels to turn, so the car felt as if it were sliding — on air — in every bend. Weird.

Thursday morning, as I was leaving the motel for Press Day, I met Mike and Keith in the parking lot (Jeffrey had returned to high school). The Olds was on the trailer, and it looked sensational! It was obviously born for Banditry. Cutlass lines deserve more than refrigerator white, even with splashes of red and gold. Darker now, the Olds looked lower, smoother and shapelier. It was rich loden green, with wide cutouts of white on the hood and trunk, surrounded by a thin gold border. The gold wheels gleamed in the morning sun. And there was a new face on the hood, a shifty-eyed character like a stagecoach robber, wearing a red mask that spelled out "Bandit" and a green cowboy hat whose band said "Skoal." The Olds looked like Harry Gant's Grand National car (even better)...with Terry Labonte's number.

Keith said, "You been practicin'?"

"What do you mean?" I asked.

"Dippin'," he said, and stuck an index finger under his lip. Drinking Miller beer had been easy; but now we had to dip snuff — or chew, or suck, or whatever it is you do with "oral tobacco," as the Skoal PR men called it. Actually, I had been practicing; the previous day a Swedish instructor at the Roos school, Uve Falck, had been dippin', and I'd tried some. He preferred the potent Swedish stuff, not the mild wintergreen Bandits, which are pouched like tiny tea bags to increase their palatability and marketability. ("Skoal" comes from the Danish salutation *"skaal."* "Bandit" comes from the movie "Smokey and the Bandit;" its director, Hal Needham, named his Grand National car "The Bandit." U.S. Tobacco, which sponsored the car, attached the name to their new product. Strange, but true.)

As I tucked the pinch of Uve's oral tobacco between my lip and gum, I reminded myself not to swallow, believing that as long as I didn't I wouldn't get sick; but right away I started turning green like my car. Uve and Bertil Roos rolled their eyes at each other and said in unison, "You better spit it out." They explained something, in my inexperience at dippin', I'd never known: It's not ingesting the stuff that makes you sick, it's the absorption of nicotine through gum tissue.

U.S. Tobacco had delivered a box of Bandits to Tex Enterprises from its North Carolina branch, so everyone around the shop had been trying them — except for Mike, who was kind of fresh for oral tobacco. Yogi said they made his gums numb. Keith said they tasted like a damn burlap bag. Tex, who had once worked for Harry Gant, kind of liked them. He said that when Gant got his Skoal sponsorship, "he had to stuff that stuff down inside his mouth and couldn't stand it at first, but he got used to it." Uve Falck said Swedish girls loved their men to use it; you'll have to use your imagination to figure out why.

For Press Day, three Skoal PR people drove the Bandit Van over from U.S. Tobacco headquarters in Greenwich, Connecticut. Steve Goldberg's letter had found its way to their department. It included my bio, which listed a couple of past *SI* adventures, in particular a three-man climbing expedition to the top of a 16,000-foot equatorial glacier. "Erstwhile cannibals" had led us to the base of the hidden peak through a deep jungle, which we'd been chased into by Indonesian soldiers after having escaped from their detention one morning before daybreak. We'd been off limits, the area politically sensitive after natives had destroyed a government helicopter with sticks and stones. President Bantle, through a press release, said that I reflected a true bandit style. And in that same release, I allegedly replied, "U.S. Tobacco and

Skoal Bandits have contributed so much exposure and support to auto racing that I'm pleased to be part of such a prestigious team." Now I know why I've never quoted a driver from his sponsor's press release. But I guess I was being treated like any other driver, and most driver/spokesmen prefer their PR people to do their speaking for them.

The UST photographer was also there, to shoot the new press kit, with orders not to snap his shutter unless I was wearing my Bandit hat.

Since the *SI* story had ballooned into vagueness by now anyhow, Bantle told me that UST intended to get its money's worth solely through promotion of the two-race program, which is how the company proceeded. U.S. Tobacco and Skoal Bandits have contributed a lot of exposure and support to auto racing, and I was pleased to be part of such a prestigious team.

And it was great fun being a Bandit. I even considered growing a moustache to better fit the image, except the last time I had one, people asked me for Geraldo Rivera's autograph. The Bandit theme captured kids' imagination, especially little girls'. Signing autographs and doing PR with six-to-twelve-year-olds seemed as if it would be a great way to make a living. As long as they didn't take up dippin'. Which, unfortunately, was the general idea. I tried to ignore that thought.

I've saved the best for last. I ran into a friend at Press Day: the new factory Jaguar driver, Harry Doc Henry Bundy. Doc had been negotiating with Group 44 since Mid-Ohio, but had kept it to himself; he doesn't like to count his chickens. His number was 44 now, too. He'd already moved to Virginia, where the shop was located and the car — including most of its V-12 engine — was built. We didn't have much time to talk; he was in demand for interviews, which he loves to give.

The 2.5-mile Pocono International Raceway oval is actually a rounded triangle, two turns and 1.6 miles of which were included in the road circuit. The infield portion had only five corners, two of which were first-gear hairpins. The Olds had not been created to be pitched around at 25 miles an hour like that. It was like asking a hunting dog to do tricks.

You left the infield via Devil's Hairpin and accelerated clockwise through Turn 2 and up the backstraight, to nearly 160 mph by the time you had to back off for Turn 1 of the oval. It was banked at a relatively shallow 16 degrees, and there was no way it could be taken flat. A lot of drivers stabbed their brakes for it, either for security or — as with Robert Overby — to get their front end to sink and bite. Then they'd get back on the gas, hard. I tried to be less drastic with the Olds: Roll off the throttle, roll it back on. But whatever your technique in Turn 1, you were either bold or left behind. And since it was taken in the reverse direction, the driver's door was against the wall, which I'd given no thought until Keith mentioned it. On Press Day the Olds was as quick as any around the oval, according to Uve's stopwatch. And Tommy Riggins' radar gun caught it at 156 on the front straight, which was tops among the cars he'd shot. But it was apparent that the infield — those two damn hairpins — would undo the effects of our horsepower.

At the end of the day, Clay Young cornered me in the drivers' locker room. I hadn't known him beyond an introduction and an occasional nod, but had liked his style ever since Mid-Ohio, where I watched him hop on an untethered Harley Sportster, fire it up, pop the clutch in the grass, get sideways, bounce off our truck and disappear over the paddock hill.

"What happened to you at Elkhart?" he asked.

"Ran out of brakes," I replied.

"You know, Patty's kind of peeved," he said. "You hit her twice and you hit me twice."

"*What?*" I said. I didn't really doubt it, but neither did I recall it.

"You don't *remember?*" he asked.

I shook my head.

"Was you even *there?*"

Apparently, it was Patty's Monte Carlo that had put that mysterious rubber stamp on my door. Clay said that I'd stuffed it inside her once, and it was her right rear tire that had rubbed. He also told me about Dick Danielson's flying fender flares; it was the first I'd learned of my launching them. He said he had ducked when he'd seen them coming, but fortunately they sailed over his roof. And he said that I'd hit him from behind when he, Stamey and I had spun together.

I asked him why he had slowed down in the kink, which had triggered my smacking Stamey. He said it was because he was losing his brakes and wanted to test them. It didn't make much sense to me — testing your brakes in a turn that doesn't require them when two guys are pressed to your tail. But I didn't tell him that.

"Let me ask you this," I said. "Did I do anything to you that cost you time?"

"No, not really," he replied, and I was relieved to hear it. "But it was close, and close calls make me nervous."

I said, "Well, if I didn't hinder your race, the way I see it, it was just rubbing fenders, and rubbing fenders doesn't count." By this time, both of us were suppressing smiles.

"Okay," he said, eyeing me carefully. "But you know I'm in it with Riggins and Overby for second place in the series, and for these last two races I'm gonna do whatever I have to, to protect my points. Anyone gets near me, I won't give them a chance to fuck me up." He added that he'd built a crash bar into his Firebird behind the nose, to be used on people who got in his way. I didn't think he was serious; but who knows?

Our smiles were apparent to each other now, even when he added, "If you do that to me again, I'll run you off into the weeds. Understand what I'm sayin'? Payback's a bitch."

I left the locker room wondering how it could be that so much of the bashing at Elkhart was blank to me. The explanation could only have been Doc's famous Cavern of Concentration. I'm satisfied that I wasn't in the clouds when I was behind the wheel; I must have been aware of somebody's — especially Patty's — rear tire rubbing against my door. But I've got a theory: There's no room for storage in the cavern. The moment each incident had ended, I'd swept it under some rug in my brain because it no longer mattered. What matters is the next inch, not the last one. I've always had a close-calls-don't-count attitude; my heart rarely keeps thumping after I see that I'm still in one piece.

Mike had mentioned that Patty had grumbled to him after the race at Elkhart. She had pointed at a red streak on the Olds and said, "That paint is mine." Mike was amused by it. "The way I see it," he told me, "if they don't like you beatin' on their cars they can slow down and pull over on the inside and let you by."

Later, Clay told Mike that things between us were "okey-doke." And instead of nodding when we passed in the paddock, we began needling each other, which was more friendly and more fun.

The Olds felt pretty good in the morning practice session Friday, and I was ninth fastest at 1:41.6. Bob Penrod and I ran a few laps together, feeling each other's horsepower. To see if the Olds could do it, I tried to pass him on the backstraight without using his draft, and got nowhere; in fact, out there in the wind on my own, I lost ground. Our engines were even-steven, which we noted to each other afterward.

In the afternoon the car pushed worse than ever, despite Mike's softening the front springs to give the front wheels more bite. The push made the hairpins doubly murderous. When I'd throw the Olds into the turn, it wanted to go straight. At such slow speeds, trail braking — turning with your foot on the brake — helped, but not enough. And apparently I hadn't been helping much either. A friend of Tex's had watched from the paddock hairpin, and said that he could have closed his eyes and known it was me because I stayed on the gas a full second longer than anyone else — which was no compliment, since that approach demanded more from the handling. Al Holbert watched there too, and said the push was "horrendous." He should have seen it in Devil's Hairpin. Accelerating out of that one, I had to back off to keep from thumping the wall, which ruined the drive up the backstraight. Uve clocked some Kelly cars through the turn and said that Patty Moise was smoothest and second-fastest after Robert Overby. He suggested that I be more gentle. In his Swedish idiom, he said, "You trouble is you is too hot."

Despite the push — and the engine flutter, which had returned — since we'd improved the gearing and I was taking Turn 1 faster, the afternoon's best time of 1:42.7 was unexpected. It was puzzling as well as disappointing, a combination that equals frustrating. The track had gotten greasier as the day got hotter, and I wondered if that had caused it. "How greasy was it?" I asked Overby, who had followed me for a lap. He said it was certainly slick, but not enough to slow him down, and his 1:35.9 proved it. He also said the Olds looked awful. "If you point it and set it, it will track steady, which is a characteristic of stock cars," he said. "But it's not flexible at all; if you have to make an adjustment in a turn, it just won't do it. In one turn it was loose going in and pushed coming out." It was his opinion that the steering or suspension geometry, in the front end or rear end or both, was all wrong for road racing. "You're doing all a driver can do," he added. "You can't make a car do what it just won't do."

When I took off my driving suit, there were those big pink bruises on the insides of my forearms again. Still, my only guess was that the opposing elbows were whacking them when I pitched the steering wheel. Mike said that what I needed was a bigger one.

His Olds Starfire had a huge wheel which he hovered over, in the stock car style.

Doc had seemed less upbeat than usual. Wasn't the Group 44 Jaguar a dream ride, his big career break? The Jag was the most glamorous car on the track, and maybe in the world. He explained that he was merely nervous, that it was just the pressure — unconvincingly. I invited him to dinner and he hesitated; a little bit more of the story came out, then. He would have to ask permission. The hardest thing about the deal, he said, was the rules he suddenly had to follow; the driving was the easy part. The owner of Group 44 and Doc's codriver, Bob Tullius, was notorious for his tight ship — and he had a long string of successes to show for his methods. Doc had to report for work at 7:30 every morning, wearing a uniform. This was Doc Bundy, who a *Car and Driver* writer once said, "goes with the breeze, and likes to follow his imagination." Apparently his imagination didn't always wake up that early. Doc was being paid a salary, with zero percent of the prize money. Driving was the fringe benefit. The dream ride was not necessarily a dream job.

On Saturday morning, Mike said he'd discovered that the left front tire had been worn out in Friday afternoon's session. You can't always recognize a worn slick by looking at it; you have to poke a small gauge in a tiny pit in the rubber. That worn tire would have caused the push — and the slow lap time. Worse, it rendered my feedback on the handling from that session meaningless. Now Mike wasn't sure what to do for qualifying; he said he might "fool some with the camber and toe."

I tried to shrug it off, since shrugging had worked so well at Elkhart. But this mistake was far-reaching. Because of that bum tire: I'd flailed the car futilely; we'd put miles on the equipment that it could ill afford; we'd blown 25% of our available practice time; we were presently confused; and the driver's confidence had been lightly shaken (again), although that was the least of the problems since it's easier to adjust an attitude than a suspension. In short, we'd wasted time and money. My faith in Mike wasn't broken, but it was evidence that we were still a long way from being ready to run up front.

Johnny Wheeler showed up! The phantom car owner appears. I'd almost forgotten he existed. Tex had told him about our adventures at Road America, which had apparently gotten him excited about the program; our Bandit-hood likely had something to do with it too. He drove his motor home up from High Point, where he owned a large construction equipment business. He was a big guy of about 50, with a moustache and sideburns that hung below his ears and then spread. He wore bluejeans, cowboy boots and a straw cowboy hat with a feather, and was a contender for Bill Brodrick's heavyweight jewelry crown. There was a big gold ring on his left hand, and his left pinky bore one with 10 or 15 diamonds in it; on his right hand was another enormous diamond ring. And around his neck there was a gold chain dangling a gold cowboy boot with a diamond spur. He complemented it with a toothpick dangling from his lips.

His motor home was about 10 feet longer than any other in the paddock; it had to be, for all the family and friends Johnny brought, including his fiancee. It was a Royal Queen, but when I tried to describe it to Mike when it was his turn to get fed, I forgot the "Royal," and "African Queen" came out. Its Southern hospitality hummed as steadily as its generator, and the door was open to almost whoever was hungry. Any old race fan could drop by and visit, especially if he brought a compliment on the Skoal Bandit Oldsmobile.

By the second lap of qualifying, I knew the car was good. Just like his old man: Mike had pulled one out of the dark. The Olds didn't even push. It had new tires, of course. And weight-wise, we were legal again: 3400 pounds. The lead ingots — six 50-pounders — were all on the right side, in order to distribute weight to the inside around Turn 1.

The timing lights were located about 50 yards past the start-finish line, which was just past the braking point for the bumpy first turn, entered at about 60. Their position offered a clear opportunity to beat the system, especially since the escape road was the continuation of the oval. If you didn't bother to take the first turn, you could shave a few tenths off your lap time, maybe more. That would sacrifice the next lap, but you were only shooting for one hot lap anyhow.

I got a clean lap and played it straight, for security. On the first lap that felt fast, I shot through the lights and past the first turn, dodging the pylons across the oval. I cruised back to the pits to cool the brakes before trying again. Riggins' Monte Carlo was pitted behind us, and Mike told me to wait for him so I could use his draft when I went back out. But his teammate Moise was behind him, apparently also waiting, so I would have to follow the duo. I pulled out behind them and the three of us took a lap to get our tires warm and sticky. As we got a running start around the oval, Riggins parted the wind for Patty and I snuck in before the draft slammed shut. Then we went for it; I stayed with them through the infield, and was in great shape as we rounded Devil's Hairpin. But then —damnit — the engine began fluttering, through a bend on the backstraight that was actually the oval's Turn 2, but was barely recognizable because you were only going about 90 when you hit it. The misfire must have been caused by centrifugal force again, or maybe simple gravity since the bend was slightly banked. I lost the Monte Carlo twins' draft, and was 50 yards back by the end of the lap —about three-fourths of a second. There was no reason to believe that the next lap would be better, so I ignored the first turn again. Patty braked, and I zoomed up so fast that I had to swerve to miss her as she peeled off for the turn.

I pitted again and went back out for a last-ditch banzai lap. As I braked for an infield turn the Olds was ambushed by its chattering rear wheels, so I let it hop straight off the track. Later, Terry found a cracked trailing arm in the rear suspension. As the car was up on jackstands and he was welding it, Tommy Riggins walked by. He looked at the suspension design and asked Mike, "Do you have a problem with wheel hop?"

It was a tight field. Overby was on the pole with a record 1:35.4, 105.6 mph. Then came Carter, 1:35.5; Riggins, 1:35.98; and Jerry Thompson at 1:36.03, after an overnight rebuild of his V-8 Camaro's nose. He had crashed in practice — right in front of me — braking for the paddock hairpin, as the car lurched face-first into the guardrail before the turn. The V-8 Camaros and Firebirds were faster than they'd ever been; the big carburetors that they had been crying for had been approved by IMSA.

We were 12th at 1:40.6, which was the time for one of the laps that I'd considered a throwaway. Keith had gotten me at 1:38 flat on the lap that I'd tailed Riggins and Moise, but IMSA had disallowed it, along with the other lap in which I'd skipped the turn. They were wise to the trick. I'd been afraid that they might be, but I could hardly have asked in advance. I considered arguing the point since there was no written rule that said you couldn't spin out on the lap after your qualifying lap, but I knew we wouldn't win. Riggins said he'd tried the same thing two years earlier, and they hadn't allowed his time either. He'd seen me fly away in his mirror, and figured that's what I was up to.

Moise was seventh at 1:37.8, so we would have been eighth had I not tried to squeeze the system. But I wasn't sorry, and we knew that we were faster than the numbers revealed. Enjoying their carburetors, V-8 Camaros filled three of the four spots between Patty and me; Penrod's Monte Carlo was ninth.

I should have been quicker — upstairs. Because I'd expected the Olds to push, I hadn't punched the throttle soon enough in the turns — at least I didn't think so. Inexperience. If things were the way they're supposed to be, the driver shouldn't have to adjust so much in each session; but things are never the way they're supposed to be in racing. Now I sound like Doc.

Race morning was gorgeous. On my way to the track, a big orange sun rose over the Pocono Mountains in my mirror. All season — when it wasn't raining — it had seemed that the tropical sun had stowed away in my suitcase; Saturday had been the hottest day in Philadelphia since 1966 (although I barely noticed it). This morning was especially gorgeous because we were the first Kelly team to arrive at the track, which meant we beat even the Peerless Camaro boys. That might have been because I drove the crew there, but no matter.

Four PR people from U.S. Tobacco showed up, as did Bill Brodrick, Steve Goldberg and my parents. And there was the Wheeler tribe in the African Queen. The attention spawned big butterflies again, but I was able to lock them out of the cavern. Were the stands full, half-full, or empty? Don't know; never thought to look this time.

Overby won, leading from flag-to-flag, chased by Jerry Thompson. Riggins was third, Young fifth, Moise sixth. Carter's transmission broke. We were 10th. At the halfway point I'd been 1.5 seconds behind Moise and gaining. Then both bugaboos struck, one lap apart: boiling brakes, fluttering motor.

On the pace lap, Lanny Drevitch, who drove the lemon Camaro that had moved up two rows on the pace lap at Mid-Ohio, did it again, from his 14th grid position. He qualifies poorly, then tries to steal what he's evidently not a good enough driver to earn. But this time he got caught and was black-flagged on the second lap.

The first 11 and last 15 of the 27 laps were relatively uneventful. I passed three of the V-8 Camaros on the short infield stright on lap three; two were in the dirt on opposite sides of the track, and the third was facing traffic in the middle of the dust cloud that I sped into. That put me ninth, about 100 yards behind Penrod, and in five more laps I'd whittled the distance to nothing. I stayed behind him for a couple more laps, letting him think about my presence while I thought about when to make my move; there seemed to be no rush since we were gaining on Moise, another 100 yards ahead. My main concern was that my engine would overheat from a lack of fresh air, following him so closely. I had little doubt about where I'd make the move: into Turn 1, where he was using his brakes. On the lap that I decided to try it, I braked early into Devil's Hairpin and took it carefully, which allowed him to pull out a few yards but enabled me to punch the throttle without creating a push, and provided room for a drive up the backstraight timed to pass him at the end.

As I drafted him, a funny thing happened. We were speeding along at about 150, with three or four feet between his rear bumper and my front, and I felt a drop of sweat trickle down the side of my nose and land on my lip. It lingered and tickled, so I casually poked a gloved finger up inside my Bell M-1, and scratched. I realized how relaxed that was; then I realized how relaxed it was to realize how relaxed that was. I remember that so clearly, but still haven't the foggiest of half the stuff that happened at Elkhart. I guess the explanation is that there wasn't very much going on, while I was on Bluto's bumper at 150 miles an hour.

I had a lift-off reference point for Turn 1, but could go deeper if I used the brakes. The smooth and fast way through a turn is not necessarily the best way when you want to pass someone — which is one of a handful of reasons why qualifying times are faster than race times. The reference point came and went and both our feet stayed mashed, at more than 160 now. I whipped out of his draft and we approached the bend side-by-side, again. Also again, I was on the inside and confident. When I was sure I had him I got on my brakes — they'd been working fine so far. And then I stayed on them, a tad longer than I needed to, which kept him out of the fast groove. His two choices were to slow down with me or try to speed past in the high groove, up there with his shoulder against the wall. I knew he wouldn't do that; I wouldn't have, if I'd been him. A good stock car driver would have, and a good stock driver wouldn't have done what I had. But this wasn't a stock car race; it was only 27 laps, and there was nobody behind us to involve.

I led him across the start-finish line on that 12th lap, and set my sights on Patty. Then, on the infield, the brakes started to go limp. Penrod repassed as we braked for the first infield turn on the 14th lap. I stayed with him for another couple of laps thinking I might have a chance to repass; but the fuel pressure was dropping, and the flutter appeared as the car leaned through the quick banked bend on the backstraight. It started at 7,000 rpm in third, but as the race progressed the misfire crept downward; at the end, it was a rotten sputter all the way around the oval. But the Olds had handled better than ever. And Keith's transmission had taken the abuse — 54 unreasonable downshifts into first gear — without a crunch.

Back in our garage, with the bulge of a Bandit under his lip, Tex said, "You know, in the beginning, we had a car that was better than the driver; now we've got a driver that's better than the car." It's as complimentary as he gets, and it's plenty.

Pocono had been an important race; we'd wanted to impress our new sponsor and prove that Elkhart had been no fluke. This was a new kind of disappointment — maybe easier to take, but the bottom line was unchanged. The record book shows that we finished 10th, period; no buts. Afterward, my father said, "They were just too fast for you, huh?" and I bristled. "They weren't too fast for me," I snapped. "My car was misfiring." Mom and Dad had watched from the roof of the African Queen. Dad spent half the race bragging about me, and Mom had to remind him that he had three other kids. It was only the second time she'd seen me race — anything. Johnny's fiancee had asked her, "Aren't you scared?" and Mom paused and thought — she always pauses and thinks before she answers even what seem to be simple questions, and then her answer reveals that the question hadn't been so simple because of all she'd been considering. My mother the English teacher replied, "Yeah, but *good* scared."

Bundy and Tullius won the Pocono 500 by three laps. The IMSA telephone hotline described it as a "tingling" race, with six lead changes between the Jaguar and the Holbert March-Porsche, which finished ninth after fuel-injection problems. Hagan and Felton were third overall, first GTO — their fourth win of the year. Tex was doing a terrific job with the car he was able to give his full attention to.

On Track called Doc's season "a rollercoaster of disappointment and accomplishment," and said that he was "effervescently happy" about his Group 44 debut. So it was, and so he was.

Bill Eppridge

*Johnny Wheeler,
phantom car owner,
appears.*

Bill Eppridge

Burly Keith built buttery transmissions.

The Olds might have made a better hurdler than sprinter.

A crash bar behind the nose of Clay's Firebird?

Stan Clinton

Doc was older and wiser now, but no less effervescent. On the right is Bob Tullius of Group 44, whose tight ship left a wake of success.

Stan Clinton

Doc's V-12 Jaguar was the most exotic prototype.

Chapter 19

David Darby

There But for Fortune....

Fortunately (I think) this September didn't change my life, but it did bring me the nicest birthday I've ever had.

It was another day in which I could do no wrong — in DD's eyes, which made it unique. That was her basic present. She also showered me with material gifts, the biggest of which was a huge painting of two sliced watermelons, sitting on the weathered gray porch of an old house on an empty white beach. At first, I wasn't sure about the painting; the watermelons were awfully dominant, and so...red. It wasn't really my style. But the more I looked at it, the more I liked it; I began to see DD in it. The watermelons were also very happy; they seemed to be what she wanted to be, all the time: carefree, with no pressures or commitments. Nothing to do but hang out on the porch.

It was the only day I could recall that our emotions hadn't zapped us at least once, and the painting soon represented that single untainted time. Sometimes as I walked across my living room I'd stop, sit down on the couch against the far wall, and just look at the watermelons. They made me feel warm; they made me smile; they made me think of DD at her best.

If only the rest of the month had been like that. We had a fight at her house early one morning, and when I tried to leave she ran outside in her nightgown and sat in the bed of my truck; she wouldn't get out until we talked. So I stood on the sidewalk ranting and revealing things to half of William Street that I hadn't even wanted to reveal to DD — no big secrets, nothing worth hiding, nothing even worth discussing, but magnified by the context. The fat ladies were probably lined up on their porch — ringside seats for weird Key West life — wearing satisfied smiles of revenge.

Another time, she stole my truck and I couldn't get it back for a week. My friend Jeffrey said he saw it on Simonton Street, being driven by a Cuban fellow with about 10 of his chubby children falling out of the back. DD knew she couldn't hide it from me on the small island, so she must have loaned it to a needy neighbor. She never has admitted what she did with it.

Then there was the day she saved the store where she worked. The incident is a more significant measure of her character. DD at her best, more truly.

Miz Liz was not very responsible with her debts, and a creditor had gotten a judgement against the store for some $600. (In managing the place, DD had risen to the task brilliantly; she'd never even had a checking account, and now she was required to be a bookkeeper and to juggle bills with her hands tied. All the while, her naturalness, smile and honesty made her a charming salesperson.) One afternoon a county sheriff's van pulled up, and a bull-like deputy stomped in and announced that she was there to clean the place out. DD went for the phone, and the deputy actually went for her gun. DD said, "This can't be legal," and the deputy said, "I'm the law," adding that if she felt like it, she could take the air conditioner out of the wall. She was a freelancer, called upon for such special assignments!

DD made the call anyhow, but couldn't reach Miz Liz, who was perpetually out to lunch. I know how terrified DD was; the situation was tailor-made for her over-reactions. But she stood her ground and said, "You may be the law on the street, but you're in my store, and I'm the law in here," not believing that she was actually talking like that to a bully with a badge and a gun. DD held off the deputy for 45 minutes, as Rhonda moved around between racks of clothes and sniped at the "law." She called all over town and solicited support and contributions from everyone she could think of; Julia carried over DD's shoebox savings. They came up with the $600, and the deputy told DD that she was $50 short because the meter had been running on the county's van. All this time, the creditor himself — a Miami rich guy who had been burned by Miz Liz before — had been standing on the sidewalk. DD handed him the money, looked him in the eye, and told him that if that wasn't enough he wasn't human. He called off the dog — er, deputy — who wouldn't leave until he agreed to pay for the van's time out of the sum.

* * *

Steve Towle, a former Miami Dolphin linebacker (he said he single-handedly kept them out of the Super Bowl, since his nine years were their nine between bowls) was in charge of "Celebrity Presentations" at U.S. Tobacco. That included the promotional activities of UST's eight sponsored drivers. But recently Towle had been pushing them more toward PT — physical training —than PR. He also supervised UST's Sports Medicine program, whose generous grants had contributed to the training of hundreds of amateur athletes. Towle had sent his three Winston Cup drivers — "Handsome" Harry Gant, Benny Parsons and Benny's rookie brother Phil ("Skoal Brother") — through the program's physical, psychological and motor-behavior tests. I became an interested volunteer.

My first stop was the Department of Zoological and Biomedical Sciences at Ohio University, where hundreds of Olympic-class swimmers, skiers, marathoners and the Cincinnati Reds had been tested for flexibility, strength, endurance and aerobic capacity. Overall, the swimmers blew them out of the water. It would be unscientific and unfair to present the other drivers' results as representative, if for no other reasons than their average age was 37 and there were only three of them. Let's say that their scores would be ammunition for those who contend that racedrivers aren't athletes, and leave it at that. (But it would have been interesting to see motocross riders' scores.) I was working out 10 or more hours a week — as I'd been from the start, all to go faster —

and compared more favorably to the other athletes. According to the readout from the leg-strength machine, my thighs are identical to Pete Rose's (which Dave Parker calls "vanilla milkshakes," presumably because they're white and they churn).

Next came the Arizona State Sport Psychology Laboratory for motor-behavior, visual and psychological tests. The racers' revenge.

Phil Parsons' reactions were out of sight. In the simplest test — a light flashed and you pressed a button — he scored .147 seconds. Benny had .162, I had .166 and Gant .180. The quickest player among those tested on the Chicago Blitz football team: .220.

One visual test flashed automobiles on a screen for five milliseconds, after which you had to describe the cars and their positions. Twelve out of 20 was considered "very good." Harry and I got 16, Benny and Phil 15.

In the hearing test, Gant heard mostly ringing in his left ear, the one against the car's open window, which isn't unusual for older stock car drivers. My hearing was best; at races, I wear earplugs religiously.

The psychological tests were more entertaining than deep. Harry never mailed back the forms. Benny was very extroverted; he's the best racedriver/commentator going, and one of the most natural athlete/commentators around. Phil was so confident it was disgusting. A selected sampling:

Talking to Self During Race (on a scale of 1 to 10): Sam 8, Benny 7, Phil 3.

Cursing Self: Sam 8, Benny 8, Phil 2.

Praising Self: Sam 8 (at least I'm balanced), Benny 6, Phil 5.

Confidence: Phil 10, Benny 8, Sam 7.

Self-Doubt: Sam 6, Benny 3, Phil 2. (But a qualification: The questions referred to skill rather than potential.)

Anxiety Before Race: Benny 10 (!), Sam 4, Phil 2.

Concentration on Task at Hand: Sam 10, Benny 5, Phil 5. Evidently I crawl to the bottom of the Cavern.

After that appetizer, I flew to California to interview a San Jose State psychologist named Dr. Keith Johnsgard. He'd spent seven years researching racedrivers, querying and evaluating more than 700 of them, from amateurs to the likes of Parnelli Jones and Stirling Moss. He'd also tested a wide variety of other athletes, and had published many of his findings. "Racedrivers' scores on aggression make those on professional football players seem almost docile," Johnsgard reported in *Car and Driver.* "Psychologically, the pro racedriver is the toughest of all athletes."

Another provocative finding: "Few racedrivers are neurotic, but most have mildly psychopathic personalities. Quite unconforming, they avoid close interpersonal ties and have a remarkable absence of guilt."

He told me, "The strongest trait of the racedriver is an almost incredible need to achieve, as well as a strong need to see things through to completion. But of all the ways racedrivers differ, they're simply smarter."

I visited him mostly to face my own music. I'd taken his tests by mail, and the results were back from the computer. My profile was roughly consistent with the other 700, but there were two areas where I was in the 99 percentile: "Abstract Thinking," a gift I would never trade in but could have sometimes done without; and "Self-Sufficiency," which might explain why it had scared me so much when DD said the only thing that could make her happy was having someone who needed her.

I was in the 89 percentile in "Creativity" and "Tough Poise." He said that I appeared to dip toward depression because of an apparent perfectionism. I didn't bring up my problem with the moon.

There were 15 or 20 adjectives on the evaluation. I'm not sure if they were his or the computer's. The juiciest and most relevant few were: "cool, skeptical, precise, rigid, temperamentally independent," and sometimes, "critical, obstructive, or hard." The description I liked was, "His refusal to be bound by rules causes him to have less somatic upset from stress." It reminded me of one Navy quarterly report that had called me "pugnacious, bellicose, and sometimes bordering on downright insubordinate." I must have mellowed since then.

When he said that the results indicated that I tended to be a loner, I thought of the astrologer, Mary Orser, who had dazzled me with her portrait of DD. I'd also given Mary my own time and place of birth, without attaching a name. My chart was almost as unusual as DD's — in the opposite direction, a different corner of the universe. I was something called a "Singleton Moon," and, on top of it, born under a full moon — a one-in-6,750 shot, give or take a few. There was my moon on the chart, out there in the celestial sphere on the edge of the coffee table, all by its self-sufficient self.

Mary had added, "This person looks for excitement and needs to go fast, or else gets all cramped up."

I don't know what any of it proves, or means. All I know is that by the time I arrived at Laguna Seca for Media Challenge IV at the British School of Motor Racing's annual Formula Ford Festival, I was beat. In four days I'd been in New York, Columbus, Phoenix, Los Angeles, San Jose and now Monterey. I'd been probed, wired, exercised, tested and queried until my muscles were sore and my head was floating like those little planets on the table.

Had it not been my only chance to drive between Pocono and the Daytona Finale, a period of 11 weeks, I might have declined the invitation to the Media Challenge. Because I'd felt so safe in the Olds — you might say I was spoiled — I'd been thinking about the exposure in a Formula Ford. It was the most thought to danger in racing that I'd yet given. My reservations put me in good company. Many stock car drivers — Darrell Waltrip and Richard Petty most notable among them — won't set foot in a car without fenders. You could tell them it was a limo to heaven, and they'd...agree with you. Waltrip refers to what he calls the "crush factor:" The more metal you have around you, the longer it will take to get crushed. "I'd love to drive at Indy," he says, "but I'd have to be on Quaaludes to do it. I don't want to drive anything where I'm 10% of the total weight." In a Formula Ford it's closer to 20%.

But there was more to this new concern than that. Since Mid-Ohio, three drivers that I knew had been racked up: Herm Johnson, Kathy Rude and Michael Jordan. They were all still in the hospital.

Johnson, the unemployed Indy car driver who had run me down in vain on the ice, was the most recent victim. He'd suffered what the hospital called a "serious concussion," which sounded like a sizeable understatement, since he'd been unconscious for five days. He'd hit the wall while testing a Super Vee, a car that's one step below an Indy car, at the tricky dog-legged Phoenix oval. He'd been running on old tires. No money. It had been the first day of his comeback after his sponsor's pullout the previous year.

When Kathy Rude was 16, she told her high school counselor that she wanted to be a professional racedriver; her 20th birthday present had been a course at a driving school. She'd been the top woman in the 1980 Kelly Series, and this season she'd been driving the Brumos Porsche 924, a GTU car. Brumos Racing was Peter Gregg's legacy. Rude's codriver and car owner was Deborah Gregg, Peter's widow — she and Peter had been married about three months before he killed himself. He'd left her his car dealerships, and she'd recently taken up driving. The moral to the story is: Everyone wants to drive.

Rude, now 26, the shyest of women, had been attracting attention for her solid drives. At Charlotte she'd set a GTU lap record. And at Nelson Ledges she finished third, driving a Brumos Porsche 944 with Steve Potter, who also covered the race for *On Track*. The final line of his story was a quote from his teammate: "'God, I love racing,' Kathy said."

Since July, she'd been IMSA's biggest story.

She was driving a Porsche 935 in the endurance race at Brainerd, Minnesota — her first-ever GTP ride. She ran into the back of a car that was limping into the pits; she was going more than 100, the other car barely moving. The crash was brutal and fiery. Another sizeable understatement.

Along with the rest of the racers in the country, I'd been following her progress, mostly through Chris Economaki's "Editor's Notebook" column in *National Speed Sport News*.

July 27: "...the list of injuries is monumental. She has been immobolized since the crash and is in a respirator. Two major operations have been performed and there are more to come. The poor thing has been on morphine (to keep her from moving) and doctors now hope to defuse several broken vertebrae in her neck. This surgery will ultimately limit the movement of her head and...."

August 10: "Doctors say Kathy will be hospitalized at least a year more."

August 31: "Good news from St. Paul, in that Kathy Rude has surprised doctors with her progress. The life of the game Seattle lass was hanging by a thread....but now the medicos say she should enjoy a full recovery. However it will take some time."

Then the reports started appearing about her hospital bills. The IMSA insurance coverage of $44,000 was exhausted in two weeks. Estimates of her eventual financial responsibility started at $250,000.

That's two down. Then there was Michael Jordan.

Jordan was a fellow writer/racer, contributing editor at *Car and Driver*. DD had met him at the Riverside Media Challenge the previous year, and had liked him; it was a relief for her to talk to someone so easy-going. He could scarcely believe how lucky he was. I remember him simply shaking his head when he considered that he travelled around the world driving exotic cars and got paid for it.

Michael was paralyzed now. He had crashed a BSMR Formula Ford at Laguna Seca. The car had slammed backward into a bank and the engine was pushed into the back of his seat, cracking two cervical vertabrae and traumatizing the ganglia in the area. That was a month ago; he was still on his back with tongs attached to his head, unable to move from the armpits down.

DD and I had recently discussed the danger. It was beyond her comprehension why anyone would take such risks. When she was in college, she was involved in seven car crashes in two years, four of them totals; only once had she been driving, and that time she'd been hit from behind. "Each time, I thought my life was coming to an end," she said. Those crashes were seven reasons why my racing was so hard on her. She admitted that she had sometimes wished that I would crash and break my ankle — hurt myself just enough to have to quit.

She asked me if racing were more fun because it was dangerous. I replied that I didn't believe that there was a single professional driver who, given the choice between being able to die at racing or not, would choose being able to die. She said, "Well, it's a good thing you can get killed at it, because if you couldn't, every rich turkey in the world would be out there. At least the danger sorts the serious ones out."

She's had her jaw broken, her neck broken and re-broken...I don't even know what all else. So she goes through life trying to avoid dangerous situations. Some people might think I do the opposite; yet the only injury I've ever had is a broken collarbone, which occurred in a desert motorcycle race when I was riding over my head and flew over the handlebars. Some people would say that my good health only proves my good fortune. I would say that I've avoided the right dangerous situations.

The idea of scuba diving terrifies Kenny Roberts; as for riding 180 miles an hour in the rain at Spa, he says, "No problem." Racing an almost-brakeless stock car through downtown Detroit doesn't scare me; but I think riding a bicycle in Manhattan, which conservative people do every day, is asking to be killed. It's the opposite kind of risk-taking as motor racing: Your life is in the hands of every maniac that comes up behind you. To my mind, those odds are insane.

Doc says, "As much control as you can have in life, you have in that car. Nothing can hurt you in there, except your own mistakes." Kenny Roberts says, "You have to believe that you're invincible, at the same time reminding yourself that you're not." Kathy Rude made a mistake, and it hurt her; maybe she momentarily forgot Roberts' contradiction. You have to believe that you're too smart to make a mistake like Kathy's; but you have to know that you're not.

Niki Lauda and I believe that the Hemingwayesque notion that you're more alive when you're close to death is not what it's all about; look what that fool did. But you are more alive when you're close to perfection in a flat-out kink.

The risks that are taken in racing are weighed in advance and calculated in a split second. The satisfaction that comes from taking them successfully — getting the most out of yourself — is worth it, to some of us. But if there were no price to pay, it would be more "fun." And every rich turkey in the world would be out there.

DD and I had that conversation the day I returned from Wales after an *SI* assignment — the International Six Days Enduro, a cross-country motorcycling event. The day had begun 21 hours earlier for me, which was how long it had taken to get from my hotel in Llandrindod Wells to Key West. I'd left before daybreak and driven to London's Heathrow Airport in a black BMW 316 five-speed, probably the best rental car I've ever driven. The first half of the four-hour drive was over narrow, twisting, wet, fog-patched roads on the left side. I was racing to the airport, because I wasn't sure how long it would take. The BMW was sliding, but I kept my foot in it to challenge myself — it was also good practice. Then it struck me that what I was doing was more dangerous than any racedriving I'd ever done, and I backed off. It kept me alive, but left a hole in my spirit. In hanging it out, I'd gone too far; in backing off, I'd not gone far enough. That hole could have been filled if I'd been more skillful.

The final flight to Key West was an hour late. DD had been especially extremely nervous waiting for me. She said she'd had an awful feeling that I'd been in danger.

Fragility wasn't the only quality of Formula Fords that I'd been considering before the Media Challenge. I knew that I'd also have to readjust to their quick handling; if I turned a Formula Ford the way I had to turn the Olds, it would do about seven loops. And I'd have to remember how to get the most out of four little cylinders. With V-8 power you acquire bad habits, since it's easy to bury your mistakes with your foot. From a purely technical standpoint, drivers of low-powered cars are generally better at execution, because they have to be. I bet if Bobby Archer had the opportunity to move up, he'd smoke.

For the first practice lap at Laguna Seca, I felt exposed; after that, it was just like old times. Basic fatalism at work: There was nothing I could do about it, so why worry? And right off the bat, things that had been difficult were easy; what had seemed fast, now seemed slow. By the end of the session I was as quick as I'd been on the day I'd won my first race.

On the third lap after lunch I spun in Turn 4, an interesting and deceiving bend that climbs from its apex and hides its last hundredths of seconds. You crest a light grade at about 110, punch the brakes as you pass under a bridge, clip a rounded curb at the apex, then shoot up a steep hill and hear the tires go *rattaratta* over the ribs at the outside edge of the track. The geometry of the turn is simple; it's the two hills that complicate things. The grade going in disguises the turn's radius, while the climb coming out repeatedly fools you with its inertia.

The spin occurred on my way to the apex, so suddenly that one instant I was fine — or thought so — and the next instant I was backward. It amounted to a 90-mph pivot; things never happen that quickly in a 3400-pound car. I looked up to see another car heading straight at me, but he had enough time to avoid me.

Sometimes you feel free during a spin. I did during this one, at least. Maybe it was because there hadn't been time to get nervous; maybe it was because there was nothing at stake since it was only practice. Or maybe it was because I've never been injured and don't know what I have to fear. As the car whipped around, it was almost fun.

The engine didn't stall. I've developed an instinctive reaction to throw my foot on the clutch during a spin in order to keep going — preparing for the next inch. I shoved it into first gear and drove on. After the session I told Jacques Couture about it, and he winced. That was the worst place on the track to spin, he said, and told me to be more careful. I'd expected him to scold me for charging so soon after lunch, which is something he rails against. I don't know why I even told him.

In the final session for the Media Challenge I clicked off six or seven quick consistent laps, the best of which was 1:20.4. The three points leaders from the BSMR Series at Quebec's Mont Tremblant circuit — two young French-Canadians and a young German — had gotten into the 1.18s, although they had no rev limit while we writer/racers were restricted to 5500 rpm. When they went back out, I climbed the fence and walked to the edge of the guardrail inside Turn 2, a downhill left-hand kink taken at about 110. I listened to their engines to see if they were going through flat-out, and they were. I'd been using a confidence lift there. It didn't bother me that they were better in the turn, because they were the best in their series and had been racing Formula Fords all summer. But now I knew the standard.

On Saturday, I had a slow car and responded by never using fourth gear; the engine was so weak I barely overrevved in third. I'd thought that I was being clever, since it felt faster like that. But the hurried approach was unthinking; the car would have run better if I had upshifted. My times were high 1:21s, and it almost amounted to a wasted day.

But it was a special day for the Jim Russell British School of Motor Racing. There was a small ceremony to announce a new car and series: Formula Russell. Couture had commissioned the construction of 21 lovely open-wheeled Hayashi-Mazdas, and the first one had just arrived from Japan. It was undraped as if it were a statue. It might turn out to be a milestone.

Formula Russell would be a pro series sanctioned by BSMR and run at major events, where there were crowds and sponsors. It would cost a small fraction of Super Vee, currently the next open-wheeled pro step, and the Hayashi-Mazdas were nearly as fast. An entrant could either rent or buy one, and use his own mechanics or BSMR's; but no modifications were permitted, and technical inspections would be rigid. It was the school premise: Talent, not money, should prevail. The ideal had just taken a giant step. As far as I was concerned, it was the best thing to happen to racing since the last time Couture introduced a series. He was on the threshold of what he'd set out to accomplish, 17 years earlier.

On Sunday morning I qualified at 1:19.1, which put me on the front row even after a one-second penalty for overrevving. I'd actually deserved a two-second penalty, but had cheated. The tachometer on my car had been calibrated and found to register 100 rpm low, so there was a piece of tape on its face to remind both the driver and the mechanic who checked the telltale that redline on this particular car was 5400. My telltale had read 5600, which was actually 5700 — 200 over redline, and the penalty was one second per hundred. But I'd torn off the tape so the mechanic wouldn't know.

Steve Nickless, then the editor of *On Track* and frequent BSMR entrant — he'd run in the Festival with the fast guys the previous year — was on the pole with 1:19.0. Third was Jeff Zwart, a superb photographer of cars and racing; fourth Tony Swan, editor of *Motor Trend;* and fifth was my former codriver, Steve Potter.

Nickless and I took off at the start, and I followed him for 2½ laps until he lost control in Turn 4; I passed while he was fishtailing in the dirt. That gave me a good lead over Potter, and after four laps he was 60 or 70 yards back.

I decided to dispense with the confidence lift in Turn 2. It was time to take it flat. I'm not sure why I felt so; from a strategic standpoint, it was an unnecessary risk. I think I just wanted to meet the standard. Turn 2 is where Michael Jordan had crashed. He'd been trying to take it flat.

I'd been twitchy through there all weekend, and it should have concerned me more. I was much too cavalier about it. The car would twitch to the left and I'd correct; once or twice it had twitched to the right after the correction, but I'd gotten it straightened out — no problem. I'm fairly certain (now) that I was lightly squirrelly because of my season in the looser-handling Olds.

The track was greasy that day, another hot one, and the sun was glaring on the apex. When I lost control, the slide carried me out of the turn and down the track backward — spectacularly, said Potter. I locked the brakes, which is what you're supposed to do. So far, Jordan and I had done exactly the same things. But then, he attempted to pull out of his spin; I let the car do what it wanted. Doc's basic rule of racing. Jordan drifted off the track to the outside, toward the bank. I drifted inside, onto the open grass.

The entire field passed, and I reported to the pits as required by the rules, mad at myself for blowing what should have been an easy win. Couture told me to park it. Maybe I hadn't been scared, but he probably was.

There had been a light collision back in the pack on the first lap, which meant that in four laps, four drivers had screwed up. Then there was another spin. Couture had enough. He climbed to the starter's box and stopped the race with the checkered flag, after eight of ten scheduled laps. Potter had been passed on the last lap by Ed Wheeler, who ran SCCA National Formula Ford races and edited an SCCA newsletter.

I caught a redeye flight from San Francisco to Miami that night, knowing that I'd been asking for it. And wondering why. I might have thought about the danger too much, or maybe I hadn't thought about it enough. But the mistake was technical, not psychological. Over-steering. It was also mental; in the heat of the moment, I forgot that my car didn't have fenders. I'm glad that the mistake didn't hurt me.

David Darby

A 90-mph pivot that was almost fun.

David Darby

Couture called off the race when things got too hot.

David Darby

More than a festival, an important step.

Chapter 20

Bob Costanza

Going out with a Bang

The two weeks between the day I got back from Laguna and the day I left for Daytona were difficult for DD and me. I had thought — hoped — that we were becoming pals, but she suddenly seemed as moody and mercurial as ever. The discouraging thing was that racing had little to do with it any more. Even she acknowledged that. "Now that you've relaxed about the racing you're a lot easier to be with," she said. "You were so impatient before. Anything set you off, any teeny thing. You took that stupid racing so seriously. You never smiled; you wouldn't do this, you wouldn't do that. Everything was for your racedriving. I'm so glad you got out of that phase.

"You were wild then," she added. "I thought you were a nut. So did everybody else."

And she actually took some responsibility for our earlier troubles. "If I'd been smarter, I could have handled it better," she said.

She might have been speaking for us both, of course. We reacted on our emotions with each other — that's the way we were too much alike. The fact that those emotions were so different was what doomed us. We couldn't balance or temper each other: She took me too seriously, I took her too literally. We never learned how to ignore or laugh off the things we said and did. But I suppose that's all obvious, now.

She admitted something else. "I cracked under the pressure," she said. "You didn't."

Unfortunately, looking more calmly at the past didn't help the present. For me, mostly, the effects of the months of arguments were cumulative. The daze from the most recent one rolled into the rage of the next, and my spirit was captive. "You can't exist just to exist," she once complained. "You live in the future." Which she couldn't see coming. And for someone with a photographic memory, she sure knew how to forget.

But then I kept forgetting, too, how little control she had over it. It always gets back to the sparks, and the planets. When her electricity got turned on, it wasn't her hand on the switch.

We weren't exactly distant when we were together during those two weeks — that's one thing we've never been — but things just weren't...working. Or fun. We couldn't get through a meal or a movie and enjoy it. We were at the Pier House one night, and she went to the ladies' room and didn't come back. Her house was dark when I went there, and there was no answer when I phoned. I worried until she called at 6 a.m. She demanded that I take her rocking chair to her, immediately. Until then, she'd insisted that I leave it in my living room.

But what we'd been trying was futile — not to mention a frustrating paradox. We weren't sleeping together, which is where we showed our love the most, because if we slept together that meant we loved each other, and if we loved each other, then DD expected me to show it the same way she did. Desperation continued to separate us.

We made love once. Before we went into the bedroom, we agreed that it wouldn't change anything. It didn't mean that we were going to try again. It did change things, of course. It reminded us that there was no one who could touch us like the other.

We had tried just about all there was to try. We'd made the most complicated compromises and ridiculous deals, none of which worked. What she still wanted was for me to be someone I wasn't, and vice versa, I guess. She wanted us to be like two watermelons: nothing to do but hang out on the porch. It sounds like such a simple desire.

Two days before I left for Daytona, she came over to Southernmost Condo and declared that I had never loved her, which meant that I'd accepted the watermelon painting under false pretenses. So she took it back. I wouldn't let her have the frame. It had been made by an old local craftsman named Pie, and we'd gone to see him together. I left the big weathered-wood frame hanging on the white wall. As the watermelons had reminded me of our one untainted day together, the frame now reminded me that the day had been an illusion, like the relationship itself. DD could undo good things, too. And the dangling frame was a symbol of how I felt: empty. It was the last thing that I looked at, before I left for Daytona.

Doc's words followed me out the door. "The car is my relief," he says. "It's only when I get out of the car that problems start coming back."

* * *

All the good news was in Ether. Mike had spent the all-night drive from Pocono thinking about the Olds. "I'm just getting the hang of this road racing, and I'm beginning to get a bunch of ideas," he had said. "As soon as we got back to the shop I made a long list of stuff we gotta do, areas we can improve the car. We'll have a better car for you at Daytona."

An engine compression test had revealed one weak cylinder, which explained our lost horsepower. I'd been telling Mike and Keith that the motor wasn't as strong as they believed, and they had been skeptical. It's always hard for a driver to convince his mechanic that the car isn't a killer. (I'd dreamed that the men in white coats were hauling me away, and I was crying, "It's not me who's crazy, it's the Olds!")

Mike had gotten a set of aluminum heads for the motor, as well as a new intake manifold. In an attempt to eliminate the flutter, he'd had the carburetor rebuilt. And he'd made major changes to the brake system: There were dual master cylinders now, a new pedal that provided more mechanical advantage, and — finally — air ducts for the front discs.

We were psyched for Daytona: a freshened engine, new brakes, a course made for the car — nearly four miles long and only five turns — and a driver on the run. I was optimistic for a strong finish and hopeful for an outstanding one. Visions of Tommy Riggins' bumper danced in my head.

I'd wrangled us an invitation to Press Day on Tuesday, which was officially exclusively for GTP cars. That morning in my motel room, I realized how much I'd changed. In the beginning, I had consciously looked away from newspapers so that I wouldn't be distracted by the real world. And I never ate until after I drove, in order to stay hungry on the track. But now I was puttering around the room, unafraid of cluttering my concentration by the silly psychologist on Phil Donohue. My former severe single-mindedness wasn't necessary any more. Doc had said that it would go away.

Johnny Wheeler had gotten married that Saturday, and Mike was talking about the reception as we sat on pit wall waiting for the course to open. Johnny's son Darrell, who had crashed the Olds at the Daytona Finale the previous year, had pulled a big bag of bolts from his tuxedo pocket. They'd recently been in his leg. "There must have been three pounds of them," said Mike. "There was more than we've got in our bolt box in the truck. You should have seen them! There was a couple of wood screws as big as a pencil!"

Time to buckle up, now.

The brakes were markedly firmer, but the Olds felt slow; the prototypes streaked by. It also still fluttered, up on Turn 2 of the banking. And it was loose, which I hoped was because of the film of sand that accumulates on the infield between races.

When I returned with the bad news, Mike offered some of his own. The Olds was loose because the rear tires were worn out, and we didn't have any better ones. He hadn't realized that the Goodyear truck wouldn't arrive until Friday.

The handling got worse in the next session. There was little sense to sliding around, so we quit to save our remaining rubber for the next day. My best time was a forgettable 2:05.

Wednesday was the annual seminar conducted by the Road Racing Drivers Club. After the morning lectures, the class of about 20 broke into groups under instructors. I made a beeline for Bobby Rahal, the bright Ford prototype driver and Indy car fast guy.

Most of Daytona's blowouts occur on the banking in Turns 3 and 4, where the tires heat up. Often a tire will be cut on the infield and then blow on the banking. Rahal said he releases his grip on the steering wheel as he goes down the backstraight; that way, he might be able to feel a leaking tire.

It was certainly a useful tip, but I hardly wanted to remind myself of the tire situation every lap. Road racing tires lack the innerliners of stock car tires; what's more, racing tires are thin in order to dissipate heat. When they're worn there's not much rubber to absorb things, such as small seashells, which are alleged slashers at Daytona. I took a walk on the front straight, and there seemed to be a million evil little pieces of junk: coins, pebbles, bits of wire, old nuts and bolts, all lying in wait for my tenuous tires.

The afternoon schedule included five brief observed sessions followed by an open half-hour. From inside the Olds, every reflection on the track looked like one of Darrell Wheeler's wood screws, and I found myself steering around gum wrappers. In the second session the Olds began pushing; this time it was worn-out front tires. By the third session the handling was hopeless; in the Horseshoe I was backed way off the gas and the steering wheel was at full lock — it was against its stop! The car still wouldn't turn into the apex. "Poor Sam," Rahal supposedly said, watching and shaking his head.

So we parked it again.

But we needed to test some changes that Mike had made to the fuel system, and the test had to be flat-out to lure the flutter. So during the half-hour at the end of the day, we mounted the two best tires up front and I pretended they were new. Damn the tires, full speed ahead. It had to be done; it would have been wrong to balk. For two laps, I took the oval head-on and flat-out (releasing my grip on the steering wheel down the backstraight). The engine ran clean, but it still had no power. And the handling was so bad it was funny. The time was 2:06.

At least I'd learned by now that you can't over-react to such troubles: Can't let a slow car get you down. Take the problems as they come, and keep on plugging. Racing crews are naturals at being stoic, by necessity; they also know how quickly things can change. So nobody on the team was dispirited. We may not have gotten much track time so far, but we'd identified our problems, and most of our competition was still on its way to the track. So was the Goodyear truck. And we had another engine.

Since this was the end of at least three roads — for the car, the season and me — it seemed appropriate to go out with a bang. Wednesday evening, I asked Tex what it would take to run the Olds in the 3-hour GT race, which followed the Kelly race. I suggested that a good showing might help him — us — get Skoal sponsorship for next year. I had to suggest some justification, since we'd have to run against the prototypes for prize money, in a special class called GTX. Tex scratched his long jaw, and replied that it would take two sets of tires — and a motor rebuild, which was another $4,000 or $5,000.

On Thanksgiving morning I called Garnis Hagen, our man at U.S. Tobacco; he was out raking leaves before his turkey dinner. I told him our plan and pitched it on the exposure angle. The race would be televised by TBS, and the Skoal Bandit Oldsmobile would probably be the only stock car in the field. It would stick out, and be cheered for. Instant sentimental favorite. It was not a bad promotional idea, or deal.

"Okay," he said; "I won't even bother Lou with this. Just try to keep it at $5,000." I could scarcely believe it. I guess it's what happens when a corporation is run by individuals rather than committees.

The marketing game was becoming clearer to me, and I was beginning to enjoy it. I was even dippin'; it's true — we all were. Dippin' was part of the deal. And it was fun — numb gums and all — although I always abandoned my limp Bandit when it turned me woozy, and never dipped until after I'd driven. (Bandit Time!)

But the best thing about being a Bandit was signing autographs for kids. I was in my element with them. It had seemed as if every conversation I had with an adult was about some damn deal or another, so kids were a great relief to talk to. And they were less impressed by the racedriver than grownups; baloney still went over their heads. A lot of guys like being a racedriver because it makes it easier to meet girls; I liked being one because it made it easier to meet kids.

Doc missed his traditional Thanksgiving dinner at Valle's, and I missed joining him. Group 44 hadn't entered the Finale, in order to get a jump on next season. So Doc spent Thanksgiving working in the shop with the crew, to meet the February deadline. "I thought the Jaguar deal would be the step to greatness," he would say, "But it was only another small step, with new hassles to learn."

There was only one practice session Friday. We mounted fresh rubber and the Olds handled well, but it fluttered again. And Craig Carter passed me on the backstraight as if the Olds were towing a yacht. He was 100 yards behind when we left the infield, and 100 yards ahead at the start-finish line. The Peerless boys really had the Camaro dialled-in. He clocked 1:56.9 that session, .1 second off Felton's lap record. Next was Clay Young, way back at 2:00.1. We were 2:03.1, ninth fastest, but the others were just getting started.

At least the Olds looked good. The African Queen — a Love Boat this week, since it was Johnny Wheeler's honeymoon — was parked inside the first turn, and Johnny said the Skoal Bandit was strong through the infield, and looked like a Grand National car up on the banking, with its big green #44 on the roof.

Kathy Rude showed up. "Game lass," indeed; she was supposed to be in the hospital for months longer. She was bundled in braces and casts, and was being chauffeured around in a golf cart and getting kissed a lot. She'd gained weight, and the soft skin under her neck, normally fine and milky — her complexion is one of her best features — was chafed raw by the neck brace. She said there were a few more operations scheduled. But she was smiling, and she cracked jokes about getting her crutches fitted with rearview mirrors, and talked about racing again. She said she would be driving on the street before the leg brace came off.

We needed a codriver for the 3-hour, and Kathy said that Drake Olson was looking for a ride, as he had been at every race since Nimrod went poof. Drake and Kathy were close; he'd spent weeks with her at the hospital in St. Paul.

Drake was 28, talented, full of aspirations and broke. What else is new. Pursuing rides was a full-time endeavor for him. "I've given it all I've got for years, and it's taken everything out of me," he said. "I'm exhausted, drained and depressed — but I'm *pissed*. I've committed so much to it that I'm not going to quit now...although I might have to make a career out of bumming rides."

He'd driven two Indy car road races that season. "Never again," he said "— at least not like that. I was with second-rate — no, third-rate —operations, and it was life-threatening. To drive a bad car in an IMSA race is one thing, but to drive one in an Indy car race is insane."

We couldn't have done any better than Drake, and Tex agreed. Most owners would have expected the codriver to pay. Tex never considered it, since the Olds wouldn't be competitive. "The way I see it, the man's kind of doing us a favor," he said.

Two PR men from U.S. Tobacco came to Daytona, and their main mission was to get free samples of Bandits distributed. But they were having trouble getting permission from the Speedway, since the IMSA series was sponsored by R.J. Reynolds. It appeared as if R.J. Reynolds was threatened by two pretty young girls handing out smokeless tobacco. I tried to help unwrangle the politics, and some sort of compromise was worked out. The girls had to work under cover, or pass the Bandits over a fence or something.

When I got back to the car — we were set up just outside the Camaro garage — Larry Penn, a top wrench from Harry Gant's team whom Tex had borrowed for Daytona, was ducked under the raised trunk, groping in the gas tank for the flutter. I half expected him to pull out a dead mouse. At the other end of the car, Mike and Keith were yanking out the engine. Mike had talked to Tex about the reworked motor's inexplicable lack of power, and Tex had said, "You gotta do what you gotta do to run with them."

The second engine had replaced one which Billy Hagan had reclaimed when he dropped us. It was a borrowed and slightly-used 358, a short track motor built by the shop at DiGard, the team that had just won the NASCAR Winston Cup for Bobby Allison. A short track motor has dynamite acceleration but peaks early. Since Daytona was no short track I'd have to run the bejesus out of it on the oval, but it was bound to be better than what was under the hood.

The PR boys had booked me on a radio show that night, and the host Bill Bowser asked how it felt to be competitive. I think I startled him by saying we weren't. "We were ninth fastest today," I said. "I don't really consider that competitive. To me, competitive means running up front." He replied that he'd asked other Kelly teams, and they said I was. It was nice to hear, but I stuck to my standards.

The crew started working on the Olds before daybreak on Saturday and continued all morning, while I tried to stay busy. I tripped over another team's industrial vacuum cleaner, and it made my day — almost made my season. Out out, damn blob! I dove in the window of the Olds and ruthlessly sucked out every rubber crumb, then greedily searched for more. A rusty can opener turned up, under the seat; also a soggy Bandit. For the rest of the weekend I was a compulsive housecleaner and chronic borrower. If I had discovered that vacuum cleaner earlier in the season, I could have been a contender.

As Terry was bolting on the wheels, he noticed a crack in the right front brake disc. He ran off and found a spare in Tex's trailer, but it was rusty and had to be sanded. About 30 seconds before the session began, the car was finished.

The new motor was a short tracker, all right. It had a ton of torque, and blasted off the turns. It flattened in the middle of the backstretch but still reached 7600 rpm, about 180 miles an hour. And the flutter was gone — for good. The Olds had gotten new plug wires with the different engine, and Larry had modified the pickup valve in the gas tank that morning. We didn't know or care which of those changes did it.

That afternoon, GT qualifying came first. The plan was for me to cut one decent lap right away, then let Drake get some track time. On my third lap the clutch began slipping on the backstraight. I pitted, Terry squirted it with a hose, Drake drove off and we never had any more clutch trouble. Instead, we had rear end trouble; on his third lap, it blew. "Clackety-clackety-bang-bang," is how Drake describes the sound of shattering steel teeth. Our qualifying time of 2:05 was 51st out of 68.

The first thing Drake had noticed about the Olds was that he couldn't see over the fenders — he's 5'6". He said the power had scared him at first, and that it would take a few laps to build up the courage to take the banking flat-out. Last, he said he couldn't believe how hard it was to steer; he'd been under the impression the Olds had power steering. Power steering! "You should have driven it at Detroit," I said.

During qualifying, a cheer had gone up from Tex's sporty-car boys. It had been announced that Felton had gotten fast GTO time: 1:50.8, 124.8 mph, 12th overall. But they had just missed the track record they'd been after. Since a chicane was planned for the backstraight the next year a record would mean immortality, so Tex had fit the Camaro with what Felton called "Land Speed Record Hubcaps" — aluminum wheel covers to improve aero-dynamics. But they blocked airflow to the discs, and Felton knew he'd have exactly three laps before the brakes boiled. He got his hot lap, and on the fourth lap the brakes vanished in the Horseshoe. He'd been in the middle of a 540-degree spin as the announcement was being made.

Redline on the Olds' new engine was 7500 rpm; my reaching 7600 on the backstraight that morning meant that we'd been under-geared with the 3.68 rear end that had burst. We had a 3.53 and 3.64 to replace it, and I voted for the taller 3.53 in order to bring the revs down. "With the 3.64, on a good lap in the draft I might see 7800 rpm," I told Tex. Since it was more than a mile from the middle of the backstraight to the shutoff point for the first turn, the engine would be screaming over its theoretical limit for more than 20 seconds. That was winding it as if it had no top at all. Tex and Mike voted for the 3.64; there was no denying it would be faster. "During qualifying, if you have a bad lap and there's nothing to gain, then give the engine a break," Tex said. "Otherwise, just run 'er flat out." Their choice didn't surprise me.

The transmission began crunching in third gear during qualifying, and there was a shudder under braking, but neither problem cost time. I did, though; I got so wrapped up that I dismissed the draft. None came my way, and I didn't look for one. Brain fade. A bunch of smarter drivers got hooked up together, and I was beaten by four cars that shouldn't have out-qualified the Olds. I ended up with 2:00.4, 11th fastest. Robert Overby got the pole with a record 1:56, 119.2 mph. The 30-car field was as quick and competitive as any Kelly field in history.

After qualifying, Oldsmobile hosted the First Annual Sam Moses Retirement Party. The title was my idea; I wished that it would be recognized for being as hopeful as it was facetious. The party went on around the Olds while my crew worked; it was 90 minutes they didn't have to spare. I tried to take them all food, and those that accepted worked with their meatball sandwich in one hand and a wrench in the other.

I'd spent virtually all of my time away from the track alone. I wanted to savor and memorize the final race, even if I didn't want it to be so. That afternoon I'd actually met a groupie — finally, after two years. My loins didn't think it had been very bright of me to pass up the opportunity, but if I hadn't, I wouldn't have gotten my laundry — the Bandit suit — done that evening. I'm glad there weren't any questions about such priorities on those psychological tests I'd taken. Oh well. The hole left by DD's absence in my bed would have only been made bigger.

Meanwhile, Bill Brodrick and Bill Eppridge, my *SI* cohort from Detroit, were having dinner at the best restaurant in town, with a lively group that included a French champagne heir. The way I heard it, they lopped off the top of a bottle of Moet with a saber, right there on the table.

As I was falling asleep, I dreamed my motor blew on the backstraight. It was barely a dream; it was more like a two-second intrusion into my fading consciousness. I awoke with a start, my left foot jerking toward the clutch pedal under the sheet.

I'd gone to bed early because I knew that adrenaline would be a pre-dawn alarm. I moved as slowly as I could bear to that morning, and 8:00 was as long as I could put off my arrival at the track. The sun was already bright and warm as I popped into it, through the tunnel under Turn 4. The huge bowl of the Speedway seems to gather the sun uniquely. Once, covering the Daytona 500, I went to the track before daybreak to beat traffic. At sunrise, the infield glowed hazy amber through the dewy air and rising smoke from the campers. Other times I've seen the sun drop sharp and pink into the marshy woods behind Turn 2.

It was quiet except for the seagulls, cawing and bickering over garbage. Both of the Tex Enterprises cars were covered, and the truck's rear passenger door was wide open, apparently left that way all night. I hung around, hoping the crew would show up, and thought: "I bet Al Holbert's and Craig Carter's crews are here."

They arrived at about 8:30, and Mike informed me that we still didn't have enough tires. He'd only gotten six on Friday when we'd needed 12; he thought that I was going to get the rest. We had used four in practice and qualifying, and now Goodyear had run out of our size.

Starting a race at Daytona with two worn tires is not the way to win.

At 9:14 the car was ready for the 9:15 warmup. Mike had installed new brake pads, and the brakes were fantastic! I couldn't believe it! I thought, "Well ho-lee shit; what does this prove? They could have been this good all along." I might have even said it aloud to myself. I treated the brake pedal as if it were crystal, taking no chance of glazing the pads by overusing them before they were bedded. And I cooled it around the oval, for general principle.

My mechanical knowledge might have been shallow, but my common sense never was — nor was my sensitivity to the car. After one glance at the map of the Detroit circuit, I'd said to Tex, "Do all you can to make the brakes as good as possible." He had said they were. I never believed it, but how could I challenge it? All I had on my side was instinct. And how could I avoid self-doubt? What a stigma: It appeared that the brakes kept boiling because the driver was trying too hard to slow down.

Bobby Rahal had said, emphatically, "A driver can't accept a car that's not right," adding that he'd done so for years and it had hurt his career. But A.J. Foyt says you're not a real racedriver unless you can drive a disaster into Victory Circle. They're both right. My problem was that I had neither the authority for the former nor the skill for the latter.

And my perfectionist urges and critical tendencies had to be tempered by the realization that we would have had better equipment had I raised more sponsorship money. Also, I was grateful simply for the ride. And rookies shouldn't complain or demand because they haven't earned the right yet. I believe that. It's the stock car way, and it's a good attitude for overall growth and character. Unfortunately, it's not always the best approach for immediate success. Either you want to win, or you don't. Many of the things that could have improved our car were not expensive. Forethought is free. "It just takes time," Mike had said. Too much time, for me.

The Kelly warmup ended at 9:30, and the GT warmup was to begin at 9:45. Those 15 minutes were the season's most exasperating, infuriating, frustrating, you name it. Either I was the innocent victim, or it was all my fault. I wish I could figure these things out; my abstract thinking fails me. My mistake was not being mercenary. I should have insisted that we skip the GT warmup — Drake's — and save the car for the Kelly race.

The Olds was in the pits, and Mike told me to take it back to our garage. Traffic in the garage area was like Times Square without stoplights. The engine stalled in the gridlock. When I tried to restart it, nothing happened; the starter was dead again. It had first failed at Detroit, and again at Elkhart. At Pocono, we'd frequently had to push the car to start it.

If racecars had horns, 67 of them would have been honking at me. The GT session was minutes from beginning, the crew was back at the garage waiting, there had been no sign of Drake all morning. This was not good for my nerves. I felt helpless and angry. Did they want me to carry the car on my back? If I'd been cool — and smart — I would have simply walked away and left it.

Jeffrey appeared out of the heaving sea of racecars, and I sent ⸳him back for Mike. It would have taken forever to push the Olds back to the garage against the tide, so we shoved it to the edge of the Union 76 station, jacked it up, mounted the two new tires so Drake could scrub them in, and Mike might have changed starters; at this point, it didn't seem to matter. Drake showed up, and took the Olds away.

I couldn't stand watching him — absolutely could not *stand* it. I'd known I would be uneasy, but hadn't suspected anything like this. Seeing him on the track filled me with terror that the car didn't have enough laps left in it. The Kelly race meant everything to me; why had I been so stupid as to jeopardize it? That was my race motor out there, already stressed half to death because of the gearing. But I worried more about the tires; with each lap, I could feel the rubber peeling away as if it were my skin. How could I have forgotten to tell Drake to conserve them? I know how: rushed and upset.

I paced, hopped, gritted my teeth, talked to myself without caring who noticed, and wanted to bite the chainlink fence behind the pits. I glared over Jeffrey's shoulder at the stopwatch, and counted the seconds until Drake appeared each lap. 2:03! That's too fast! My tires will burn away! He must be turning 7600 rpm! And the new brakes that I'd just bedded so tenderly; he must be using them hard. How can we slow him down? I had to fight the urge to run across pit road to the edge of the track and wave him in; the only thing that stopped me was the fear that I'd look foolish and probably be chased and tackled by an official. I was so conspicuously distressed that Tex and Billy were chuckling. "Now you know how I feel most of the time," Tex said. I doubt it.

Drake did five laps. Ten minutes. It was, without question and by far, the most nervous and uncomfortable I'd been since I'd started driving.

It had been a wholly unsatisfactory morning. We had dangled weeks of effort over a dark precipice. Doc had called it long ago: "Rush jobs have a way of ending up like that," he said. And it had started when the crew arrived late.

The engine and brakes may have been fairly fresh, but the rest of the Olds was on its last legs, and those legs would have to carry it faster than it had ever gone. To put it another way, I knew I'd be driving a used car around a big bend at 180 miles an hour. But it was my final shot; I would have done it with my eyes closed if I'd had to.

As I was about to climb in the car for the race, someone delivered a good luck note from a friend. I read and appreciated it, then crinkled it up and threw it in an oil-drum garbage can. I imagine things in my pockets to intrude into my concentration — especially notes, which are too much like unfinished business. But as I turned away, superstition and guilt tugged me back. If something were to go wrong in the race, I would look back and think: That's what I got for treating a friend so shabbily. Good wishes do not belong in garbage cans. So I reached down into the oozing oil cans, Pepsi cups, half-eaten hot dogs and other yukky stuff, retrieved the note, uncrumpled it and put it in my pocket.

I believed I should have qualified sixth, so that was where I planned to move right up to. Charles Pelz was beside me on the grid, and I was certain he'd move up too; the previous year he'd finished second to Riggins by half a car length. Patty Moise was in front of me, with a qualifying time .2 quicker. She had a new car, sort of. Riggins and Moise had been added to the factory Buick deal, and would get V-6 Regals next year; for Daytona, Buick had wrapped the two Monte Carlos in Regal attire.

At the flag, Pelz got a jump that I envied the instant I saw him coming. I got stuck behind Moise; I couldn't squeeze under her without running in the grass, and only briefly considered going to her right, since attempting to pass on the outside of the first turn in the thick of traffic would have been unproductive, at best. And she was probably stuck behind someone, too.

Moise was smooth, good and didn't back down, but she wasn't as aggressive as the fast guys. Nor was she as good as she thought she was. Her cockiness seemed to come by rote; I think if the hunger had been there, it would have shown more. I suspected she was seduced into thinking she was hot because she stood on the victory podium after her fifth and sixth-place finishes. She seemed to forget why she was there. It's a hazard for good women drivers intent on being equal; when they deny that their sex gives them advantages, they slow down. Some of them think that admitting it would be like saying it's easier for them. It's not; for starters, mechanics won't listen to them. But sometimes — in the midst of male chauvinism that must seem oppressive — it is.

Patty probably thought that I was frequently out of control. I thought she protested too much. It's the trouble with girls.

There was a crash in the first turn behind me. Allan Chastain's version was that I ran him off the track; he said he was ahead of me, and I squeezed him. We never touched. Maybe you can picture it, because I couldn't. "Are you sure it was me?" I asked. "Well, I thought we were going to hit," he said. He might have seen me in his peripheral vision and swerved into a trap on the outside of the turn, an off-camber dip that can suck a wheel over the edge. He hit the guardrail on the outside, bounced back onto the track, and was creamed by the Firebird of Buzz Cason, a Nashville songwriter and nice guy. I saw none of it, since I was on my way to the Horseshoe.

As the pack sped through the kink into the fourth infield turn, a distorted second-gear right-hander that nobody likes, I was so close to Moise that I couldn't see anything but her trunk. Somebody ahead of her slowed down more than he needed to. It must have been one or more of those guys who had qualified well but didn't race that well. It caught me by surprise; it shouldn't have, but traffic was so *slow* into the turn. I had to lock the brakes to avoid mashing Moise's shiny new sheetmetal, and in that split second thought, "Oh Jesus, I don't want to hit Patty, she's such a crybaby." But it would have been my fault if I had.

We'd been hugging the inside, and the Olds whipped across the track. There was no one close enough to hit me from behind, which was luckier than I deserved. As I fought for control in the grass outside of the turn, the corner of my eye caught a short train of cars passing, to my dismay. Back on track, I was 15th. So much for charging right up to sixth.

But in the next 3,500 feet — the length of the backstraight — I discovered how stout the motor was. Sailing along in the draft, it was no problem repassing three cars; one of them was Lyn St. James, whose Capri was sputtering with crossed plug wires. I could feel the suction of the advancing barrage of cars ahead of me, and near the end of the backstraight I glanced at the tach: 7800 rpm. Oh, boy. But it was too late to worry about it; what was I going to do, *back off*? Besides, Tex had freed me. His words were, "The motor has all the best pieces. There's no reason it shouldn't be able to stand it." That had been good enough for me. In fact, I loved hearing it, even if I didn't believe it.

The yellow lights on the banking wall were flashing because of the first-turn crash, where Chastain's Camaro was mingling with a tow truck. The pace car came out, and I counted myself 12th in line. It pulled off as the field left the infield on the third lap, and the leaders broke away as the cars ahead of me lagged. I booted it, and chased onto the banking.

In the next 1½ laps I moved up to sixth, confidently and methodically. The backstraight was the only place where I passed. I would use the engine's potent acceleration to get a drive onto the oval, tuck in a draft just long enough to get a boost, then shoot by. The other cars were sitting ducks for the killer Olds. I came up behind a white Camaro drafting a red one, and as I pulled out the white one whipped into my path. But I'd been prepared for it; I dropped down on the apron — cringing, since it carried invisible tire-cutting debris — and for a moment the three of us flew along abreast. The white Camaro stayed in my draft, but he must have been lifting for Turn 3; just before we peeled off, he vanished from my mirror as if we were two skydivers and only he had yanked the ripcord.

The Bandit felt great. It was loose, but I didn't mind; it drifted nicely through the infield, and the handling responded to the throttle without fighting back. I was taking the banking with my foot mashed and wishing the throttle went even farther. Self-confidence made driving a lot different — much more fun, mostly — than the year before, when my foot was perpetually ready to flinch in the Oftedahl Firebird.

On the fourth lap I looked up between Turns 3 and 4 — you have to raise your chin to see ahead because of the 31-degree angle of the bank — and there was the red trunk of Patty's Buick, blurred by speed and vibration. She was in fifth and I was catching her. I realized how costly my first-lap blunder had been; I should have been way ahead of her. "You're next, Patty," I thought.

But Patty wasn't next. Accelerating away from the first infield turn, the motor blew. My dream come true. It felt as if someone had punched a hole in the block, which is about what had happened. A connecting rod had snapped and started an explosion that came out the lower left side, spraying oil and scattering chunks of metal onto the track. Thud, *daaah*, silence. I flipped my foot onto the clutch and swung the car off the track into the grass. The tow truck pulled up and the driver asked if I was all right. "What time is it?" I replied. Before the car had stopped rolling, I'd thought: Can we change engines in time for the GT race? The next inch.

I climbed out and looked across the track, where Johnny Wheeler was watching with some others on the roof of the African Queen. I shrugged and threw up my hands in a gesture of "Ka-boom!" Overby, Carter, Young and Pelz went by. Riggins was out with transmission troubles. Moise was way back, and her deck was smashed; she'd spun into a guardrail. I realized I would have followed Pelz, and felt a dull stab somewhere inside of me.

On Track's version of my race: "...Moses's farewell appearance ("maybe") came to an early end on lap five: Going into the first turn, someone "centerpunched" him in the driver's door and sent him plowing off the course." Such a fantasy was rare for *On Track*, but the accuracy of the things I'd read about myself during the year was abysmal. I'm afraid I came to understand why drivers often don't respect reporters.

I watched from the center of the track with the seagulls, which were pecking away oblivious to the thrilling race around them. Up on the banking, Young appeared to have the steam under his long hood. Once, he went way up in the high groove between 3 and 4 as Richard Petty does; his stylish red Firebird swooped past Carter's metallic blue Camaro and alongside Overby's boxy white Buick.

On the ninth lap a car hit the wall coming onto the front straight, bringing out the pace car again. It pulled off as they left the infield on the 11th lap, which reduced the race to a 2½-lap dash.

Pelz dropped back as if an anchor had fallen from his trunk; his old Buick Skylark was stuck in second gear at the most heartbreaking time. Then, in the infield's goofy fourth turn, Young looped the Firebird in a big puff of blue tire smoke. Trying too hard, no doubt; Clay's spirit shows. On the final lap Overby led Carter onto the banking by a few car lengths, and it was all over; the Buick V-6 had about 50 more horses than the Chevy. Both drivers merely mashed their throttles, steered and waited. The bigwigs from Buick and Chevy were watching from suites over the main grandstand, and the Buick boys were doubtless enjoying the drubbing of their big brother division.

The Castrol Buick led the Peerless Camaro all the way around, and took the win by .11 seconds. Young tailed in third. Moise finished 10th, first female, and climbed up on the podium with them. With her $1,000 bonus, she took home as much as Young.

Said Overby, "I'm glad I don't always have to work that hard to win." Replied Carter, "It's better than working that hard to lose."

Since Overby had managed to get the faster engine under his hood, he was the better "driver," this day. There's no knocking it. And the driving was the easy part.

"Ifs" are cheap, but I can't help it. Given the yellow flag which bunched the field at the end, and Pelz's and Young's untimely troubles, if the Olds' motor hadn't blown, we might have been on the victory podium at Daytona, in third place. But so would have some other teams, if they hadn't had their own problems. And we weren't, so we didn't deserve to be.

Bill Eppridge

*Mike Powell
did what you gotta
do to run with 'em.*

Mark Yeager

Robert Overby proved there's no beating horsepower at the big D.

Chapter 21

Bill Eppridge

Some Hole, Huh?

A s soon as Overby took the checkered flag I got hooked up to
the tow truck, and when the last car passed we moved out.
Back at the garage, Mike lifted the hood and Larry looked in and
said, "Yep, you blew the side off the motor. Big Time."

I was by no means sure that the team would want to do the same
thing that I did. There was little — if any — practical motivation to
race. We had about 90 minutes to change engines, which wasn't
enough; our spare motor was a reject; our tire situation was
comical; our expectation of prize money was nil. The sensible thing
would have been for the Bandits to call it a day.

We were still gawking and saying things like, "Yep, Big Time
blowup," and, "Some hole, huh?" when Mike began unbolting the
engine. He'd had the tools ready and waiting. The choices had been
simple: race it or park it. For Mike, that was no choice.

He turned 22 today; he'd forgotten it was his birthday. His "mama," Tex's wife Cathy, mentioned it.

The kid's got such a bright future. All season, he'd run his Darlington Dash team up front. He could be a NASCAR Grand National star in a few years, if he gets the help. The driving will be the easy part. And somebody's going to be missing a good crew chief. If I controlled the sponsorship budget of some company — say, U.S. Tobacco — I'd sign him up today, and support and guide him along the way. He'll bring back every penny.

The crew went to work. About three guys dove under the hood and three more crawled under the car to disconnect the driveshaft and drop the tranny: Mike and Keith and Terry and Larry and big Jerry, a recruit from Mike's team, and also Jeffrey, who was on Thanksgiving vacation, Johnny Wheeler's son-in-law Ben, and maybe one or two others. Terry, sometimes moody, sometimes inspired to frenetic spurts of energy, was moving as if it were a pit stop. Tex, calmest of the bunch as ever, was directing things. Wrenches twisted and clanked, and bodies were soon as hot and greasy as the parts they were tugging. Hips and legs hung out of the engine compartment, and torsoes shuffled on pavement soaked with the oil that dribbled from the grapefruit-sized hole in the motor. An occasional exclamation or curse rolled out from under the car.

They pulled the motor and swung it aside on the hoist, then lowered it onto the pavement where it continued to bleed oil, which formed a puddle around some cigarette butts. It looked like a mortally-wounded animal. Big game.

This was a mechanic's moment, his own opportunity to meet his potential. I was the beneficiary. But they wouldn't have bothered if they hadn't believed that the driver was worth it. Standing there watching them work, in the middle of the heat and noise and commotion, I got choked up and had to turn away; I was thankful that sunglasses hid my glistening eyes. I'm not sure that I could have explained how their actions — faith — made me feel. I forgave them for screeching up to the track at the last minute so many times; I forgot that the back of the truck was so cluttered that you had to leap backward when you opened the door; empty clanking brake pedals were unimportant. I realized that this was why I liked my crew so much. It was because of their style, their spirit, their class...the idiots. I once heard Tom Sneva say after a victory, "I'm just proud of the car and everybody in it." I couldn't have said it better.

We heard the roar that meant the race had started, and the pack of 68-minus-one cars sped around the oval. I climbed to the top of the truck and watched Bobby Rahal's high-tech factory Ford prototype sprint off in the lead. The Ford crew hadn't expected the undeveloped car to finish, so maybe the plan was to lead Daytona by as much as possible for as long as possible; if the lead couldn't last, the TV impression might. Ford has a better idea. It's what I would have ordered, had I been Ford's racing director. Go for the show.

As I strapped myself into the Olds one more time, Mike said, "I'm really sorry, Sam, that we didn't get it ready for the start of the race." I replied, "Don't worry, it doesn't matter," and it didn't. I tore away from the garage, spinning the tires because it seemed the thing to do, and because I wanted to.

There was a vibration on the backstraight and the oil pressure was dipping, so I pitted after one lap. Tex said to go back out, keep your eye on the gauges, and do what you can. Since we were already 18 laps behind, the best strategy seemed simply to finish. Seems obvious, doesn't it? But it also seemed a shame to settle for that. What did we just go through all that for — to stroke it? I felt as if it would be cheating the crew not to run hard. But considering everything, including that we'd entered the race mostly to improve our chances with Skoal for the next year, a finish was probably the best thing that could happen. Besides, pushing a car with an unknown vibration when you're out of contention might be the mistake to kill you.

So I shifted at 7,000 rpm and held it there on the backstraight, which also kept the vibration to a minimum. That was loafing; ironically, the Olds was faster than it had been in the Kelly race because the engine was now allowed a bigger carburetor.

Turning 2:09s, I was running with some GTU cars and the assorted wounded. The pace allowed me time to daydream. I realized how much I'd come to enjoy sprints — scratching for every inch — and felt a little bit superior, since the drivers passing me were cruising, by Kelly Series standards. I thought about Tex, and how it would be obvious to him what I was doing. Watching one of his cars merely chug around was probably difficult for him, and I hoped I wasn't disappointing him too much.

Since we hadn't bothered with a signal pit at the first turn, the plan had been for me to watch the tower scoreboard and pit for gas after 20 laps. The easy pace left enough fuel for a longer shift and I would have taken it, but the caution lights flashed on the lap that I was expected — big chunks of yellow fiberglass were scattered along the front straight — so I went in. I killed the motor and jumped out, and as Terry dumped in the gas I cinched Drake's belts and shouted a brief report. "There's a big vibration on the backstraight! I think it might be the motor! But it's not getting any worse! I never went over 7,000 — keep it there and you'll be able to do 25 laps! It should run forever at that pace!" But I was wearing my helmet. Drake later told me he had heard "vibration!" and "mffmffmff."

On his second lap, he turned 2:03. My first thought was that unless we somehow slowed him down, he'd run out of gas on the track, and it would be horrible not to finish because of such a thing. Mike worried aloud about something else. "If he keeps running at this pace we'll flat run out of tires," he said. With all there had been to do, no one had scouted around the garages and bought any used ones, so all that remained in the pit were four hopelessly worn tires, which Terry was examining and shaking his head over. Jeffrey went to the edge of the track and waved his arms at Drake, but the non-results were predictable as the Skoal Bandit flew by at 170 miles an hour. It certainly did stick out, and looked great.

Kathy Rude was in our pit, supporting Drake. She was sitting in a lawn chair and seemed awfully sad. I wondered what she was thinking about. Could anyone imagine? The past six months of her life? The next six? The rest of it? I walked over and gently pushed up one corner of her mouth, and she offered a game but wan smile. I hope she was merely bored.

Drake continued to cut 2:03s and we continued to worry, until it became unnecessary. We heard the track announcer say, "The Skoal Bandit has pulled off the track in a big cloud of smoke." Another connecting rod had broken. Drake's hole was in the other side of the engine, slightly smaller than mine — about the size of a tennis ball. Nobody on the crew seemed terribly disappointed; we all were, of course, but what could you do? *That's racing.* There wasn't that much lost. Mostly just money — maybe $20,000 in the last three hours. Mike said, "Well, we about blowed everything we had up." Terry turned to Tex and said, "If you don't mind, I'm going to go to the bathroom. I've been waiting a long time for this."

Drake said the engine had gone "boom-clanketa-clanketa" and the car had filled with steam and smoke. Since he hadn't heard me say I was shifting at 7,000 rpm, all he knew was that the telltale read 7800, where it had remained from the Kelly race. He'd been shifting at 7500. But who can say the extra revs caused it to blow? We all appreciated the job Drake had done.

Rahal's factory Ford prototype broke after leading for 53 laps, and Holbert and Trueman won the Eastern Airlines Finale. After rear axle trouble, the Hagan Camaro finished 14th overall, third GTO. The race's most impressive finish was Robert Overby's; he'd driven his Regal solo, and blew the engine in a spectacular burst of white smoke as he crossed the finish line in 10th place. Long live Detroit iron.

Nimrod finished eighth, without Robin Hamilton, the dream sold and left behind in America.

I invited Tex and the crew down to Key West for a few days R&R. He looked at me dumbfounded. "Never have done such a thing," he said. So all I could do was dole out the remaining $500 Celebrity money, which is the kind of thanks a mechanic doesn't get enough of, among others.

Long after the last engine had been silenced, the Olds was towed to the garage for the second time that day. It made me melancholy, watching it come. I'd never drive it again. I'd grown truly fond of it.

Mike, Terry, Jeffrey and a few passersby pushed it up on the trailer, and the big black Johnny Wheeler Enterprises truck headed back to Ether. The Olds rode tall in the trailer in all its Bandit glory, and didn't seem broken at all. The sky was full and pink, and I felt as if I were watching the final scene of some epic movie.

The IMSA banquet at the Daytona Plaza Hotel that night wrapped it up. Holbert got a check for $60,000 and a giant gold-plated camel trophy that would have been more at home on a sheik's roof than someone's mantel. It's how sponsor identification works. R.J. Reynolds signed the check, which gave them the privilege of making the trophy in their image.

Craig Carter, rigid with stage fright, got $12,000 from the Kelly Services point fund. Robert Overby edged Clay Young for second by one point, with Tommy Riggins fourth. Patty Moise was seventh and received a $5,000 bonus. Vicki Smith was tied for 23rd and got $2,000 for third woman.

But Brian Redman stole the show. Redman was the 1981 Camel GT champion, retired from driving. He, Deborah Gregg and Bob Snodgrass, who managed Brumos Porsche-Audi, had established the Kathy Rude Fund. More than raising money for Kathy's hospital bills, the Fund would be a pool for future catastrophes.

And better than that, Redman — who had a fiery crash of his own burned into his memory — had pursued IMSA to its insurance agent. Together with the SCCA, IMSA had secured a revolutionary major medical policy for its members, providing up to $500,000 coverage for accidents.

A couple of weeks before Daytona, Tex had been told by an IMSA official that they were impressed with my improvement. I had resisted thinking about it, but it seemed a hint that I might be named the Kelly Series' "Most Improved Driver." Clay Young was. It was a surprise since Clay had been in the series six years and was fifth in the all-time points standings, and the award usually goes to a less experienced driver. Clay regarded the honor as a slightly dubious distinction, but appreciated it just the same. I was disappointed, but might have voted for him myself. He knew how to go for it.

At that moment, I mostly wanted the award for the opportunity to go to the podium and say what was on my mind. I wanted to publicly congratulate Craig Carter for his professional program and peerless preparation. I wanted to thank Billy Hagan for opening the door for me, and Tex Powell for standing by me. I wanted to tell everyone what a good crew chief Mike was, and how hard the crew had worked all season.

All I carried out of the ballroom was hollowness, and the hope that it would be temporary. But it had a new twist. I knew what I would be missing, now. Behind me was nearly two years of the excitement that I supposedly look for, but the moon was still ahead of me. Literally; it was over the ocean behind the Plaza, where I'd walked. I wished DD were there to share it as we had the sunset at Riverside, which seemed like only days ago. The vow we'd made to never forget that moment was one thing that couldn't be undone.

I knew I was at the end of this story — and more, since an ending was what kept me going. I considered walking off down the beach, for the melodrama of it. But all I really wanted to do was go home.

It seemed as if it would be a waste to walk away from racing, since it had taken 20 months to get good enough for it to be fun. But what could I do? Twenty months guaranteed me diddly for the next race. And — echoing Doc one more time — all I had accomplished was to show some promise.

Maybe I was an idiot, but I was in good company. Yes, I wanted to continue racing. I can feel it now, and I want more.

* * *

Bill Eppridge

There are worse ways to go.

Epilogue

The following year:

The Caroussel at Road Atlanta was the scene of the biggest crash in SCCA history. During the National Championship Runoffs, a rain squall swept 18 cars over the edge and down the slope into the woods, where they piled into each other and started a small forest fire.

IMSA set records in entries, attendance, purses and quality of competiton.

Paul Hacker successfully defended his Rabbit/Bilstein Cup championship.

Eddie Wirth won five Ascot main events and set a new track record.

Gordy Oftedahl ran fewer races.

John Paul, Sr. jumped bail and was a fugitive for 13 months. He was arrested by Swiss police in a Geneva bank where he had an account under an alias, and was indicted on Federal charges of leading a marijuana smuggling ring. In addition, an underground marijuana plantation was discovered on his farm in north Georgia.

Robin Hamilton lost his house and business in England over Nimrod Racing debts. He went to work for BMW in Saudi Arabia.

The Archer brothers dominated the Champion Spark Plug Challenge, sweeping eight races. Tommy took the crown.

Al Holbert finished fourth in the Indy 500 and second in the Camel GT Series.

Tommy Riggins won the Kelly American Challenge.

Michael Jordan sat up in February, stood up in March, walked in May, and by October was road testing for *Car and & Driver* again.

Keith Sawyer was hired by Junior Johnson.

Billy Hagan won the NASCAR Winston Cup as a car owner. He pulled out of the IMSA series in September under orders from his banker.

Gene Felton came within one victory of becoming the winning-est driver in IMSA history. In October he crashed at 140 miles an hour at Riverside, breaking a cervical vertebra, shoulder and six ribs, as well as rupturing a disc and crushing his larnyx. He was partially paralyzed and spent nine weeks in traction and a body cast. Four months later he was racing again.

Tex Powell built a new GTO Corvette, which never ran because of Hagan's pullout. He also built a new Oldsmobile, which Felton drove in most of the Kelly races. His best finish was a second place.

Mike Powell took six pole positions in nine Darlington Dash races, and won the two that his low-budget engines survived.

Doc Bundy, codriving with the unretired Brian Redman, won the Miami Grand Prix, the richest sports car race in history. He received none of the $60,000 prize money, as per his contract with Group 44. At the end of the year he accepted an offer from the Ford factory to drive and develop their latest prototype. It was the most prestigious ride in sports car racing.

U.S. Tobacco rejected my proposal to run the Kelly Series in the new Tex Enterprises Oldsmobile. I moved back to the woods and wrote this book.

DD moved back to Jacksonville and resumed her occupational therapy career, working with crazy people. Doctors found a chemical imbalance in her brain, and now pills control her electricity, apparently altering the path of the planets as well.

We continued to love each other.

* * *

Contributing Sponsors
(In order of appearance)

Jim Russell British School of Motor Racing
Road Atlanta Driving School
Volkswagen of America
Hacker Express
Bell Helmets
Ford Motor Co.
Skip Barber Racing School
Goodyear Tire and Rubber Co.
Oftedahl Racing
Archer Import Motors
Buck Baker School of Stock Car Driving
Tex Powell Enterprises
Stratagraph, Inc.
Toyota Motor Co.
Johnny Wheeler Enterprises
Unocal Co.
Oldsmobile Division, General Motors
Kelly Services
Charlotte Motor Speedway
Miller Brewing Co.
Yorkshire Motor Sports
Bertil Roos Racing School
U.S. Tobacco Co.